HUMAN DEVELOPMENT AND ECONOMIC DEVELOPMENT

HUMAN DEVELOPMENT AND ECONOMIC DEVELOPMENT

Edited by
RUDDAR DATT

DEEP & DEEP PUBLICATIONS PVT. LTD.
F-159, Rajouri Garden, New Delhi-110027

ISBN 81-7629-379-2

Typeset by S.S. COMPOSERS,
3190, Mohindra Park, Shakur Basti, Delhi-110034.

Printed in India at ELEGANT PRINTERS,
A-38/2, Maya Puri, Phase-I, New Delhi-110064.

Published by DEEP & DEEP PUBLICATIONS PVT. LTD.,
F-159, Rajouri Garden, New Delhi-110027.
Phones : 25435369, 25440916

Contents

Foreword xi

Preface xiii

List of Contributors xv

Editor's Introduction
Ruddar Datt:
Human Development: India in World Context xix

PART A

HUMAN DEVELOPMENT: CONCEPTUAL ISSUES

1. *N. Nettimi and N.H. Fidzani*
Human Capabilities Approach to the Development of Developing Countries 3

2. *Ashir Mehta*
Human Development and Economic Growth: The Experience of India, 1980-96 12

3. *R.Y. Mahore*
Human Resources and Economic Development 26

4. *N.M.P. Verma*
Human Development: Concepts and International Standards 42

5. *P. Jegadish Gandhi*
Human Development—Conceptual Issues and Realities 57

6. *R.S. Mishra*
Concept of Human Development with Special Reference to India 71

7. *M.S. Subramanian*
Determinants of Human Development 82

8. *S. Narapa Reddy, A. Rajasekhar and P. Kodandarami Reddy*
A.K. Sen's Contribution to Human Development 89

9. *Arabinda Ghosh*
Development Planning and Grass-root Level Democracy in India: Need for a Development Index 95

10. *P. Duriasamy*
Returns to Investment in Human Capital: Indian Evidence 101

11. *G. Karunakaran Pillai*
Human Development and Poverty: Some Policy Issues 112

12. *Kasturi Bai Dhanasekaran*
Human Development through Poverty Alleviation 123

13. *Arindam K. Sen and Mausumi Manna*
Human Capital Development: Towards a New Approach in Research and Intervention 134

14. *Swagata Das Bhowmick*
"Well-being" of People—A Journey from Per Capita Gross National Product to Human Development Index 148

15. *R. Annapoorani*
Concept and Estimation of Human Development Index 159

16. *Keya Sengupta*
Economic Growth and its Impact on Human Development in the Indian Economy 167

17. *Kaushal K. Srivastava and Tanuja Srivastava*
Role of Investment in Human Capital Development: An Empirical Study on Developing Society 186

PART B

INTER-STATE COMPARISONS AND MEASUREMENT OF HUMAN DEVELOPMENT

18. *Debabrata Mandal*
Inter-state Comparison of Human Development in India—An Alternative Measure 197

19. *Biswajit Guha*
Human Development in India—A Study of Interstate Disparity 211

20. *Inderjeet Singh and Reena Singh*
A Modified Measure of Human Development 230

21. *S.S. Dhillon and Jasmeet Kaur*
Measuring Human Resource Development 241

22. *Krishna Mazumdar*
Measuring Human Well-being of the Countries: Achievement and Improvement Indices 254

23. *Bishwa Nath Singh and S.M. Humair Ahmad*
Human Development: Achievements in the Indian Economy 289

24. *Nisar Ahmad Khan*
Human Development in India: A Study of Inter-State Variation 301

PART C

POVERTY ALLEVIATION, EDUCATION AND HUMAN DEVELOPMENT

25. *Hem Chandra Lal Das*
Human Development and Poverty:
The Context of India 321

26. *Naseem A. Zaidi*
Poverty Alleviation Programme in India—
A Critical Assessment 338

27. *Asok Basu*
Primary Education, Human Development and
India's Disadvantaged Groups 347

28. *K.N. Bhatt*
Human Development Profile: A Study of
Primary Educational Standards in Uttar Pradesh 359

PART D

HUMAN DEVELOPMENT: CASE STUDIES

29. *M.A. Razzaque*
Human Development and Deprivation in
South Asia 377

30. *R. Pushpavathi*
Human Development in SAARC Countries 383

31. *C.B. Padamanabhan and Kanakasabai Nagarajan*
Measures of Human Development and Related
Concepts: A Case Study of Tamil Nadu 398

32. *Basabi Bhattacharya*
The Concept of Human Development and
its Implications—Understanding in Terms of the
System Approach: A Case Study of West Bengal
Economy 410

33. *Anju Kohli and Sadhna Kothari*
Human Resource Development and Human Development Index in Western India 429

34. *K.S. Sivaprakash*
Human Resource Development and Management in Small Scale Industry—Coimbatore District: A Case Study 439

Index 450

Foreword

The Indian Economic Association is a premiere body having on its rolls the largest number of economists in any professional association. Over the years, the Association has extended its membership to economists working in colleges and universities in all parts of India and even abroad. Every year, numerous scholars respond to the invitation from the Association to contribute papers on selected themes for discussion at each Annual Conference of India Economic Association.

Since the number of papers received is large, the conference volume can usually accommodate not more than half a dozen papers in full on any given theme. The rest of the papers are included in the "Abstract" form. Thus many well researched papers fail to find a place in the volume. In view of this, the Association, under the leadership of its former presidents Dr. G.S. Monga and Dr. A.K. Sinha initiated a scheme to bring out separate books on different themes, containing most of the papers contributed by the members along with an editorial by the respective editor(s). This would help in accommodating more papers and creating a larger audience.

As President (1998) of the Association, it gives me great pleasure to write a Foreword for the book entitled *Human Development and Economic Development* edited by Prof. Ruddar Datt. The book contains a substantial collection of articles submitted for one of the conference themes.

In view of the fact that the theme continues to generate great interest, the Association has decided to bring out this volume containing the expressions and experiences of the concerned authors.

Ever since the publication of the First Human Development Report, the subject of human development has drawn the attention of many economists and social scientists, especially those from developing countries where human development suffered great neglect for a long period of time. After the arrival of the Report, many Indian economists started working on it and produced commendable materials. It is now being realised that income, literacy and life expectancy only are not adequate decisive factors in understanding the concept of human development which demands the inclusion of such factors as evolvement and fulfilment in life. It may also be useful to include in the human development index such ingredients as ability of the people to grasp the contents of their environment involving an inner social maturity. In recent year, the dynamics of human development has been undergoing transformation involving internalisation along with externalisation. It is being realised that human development in a socialistic or globalised regime would not be complete without freedom and inward growth.

In the well defined sections of the book the editor has exhaustively covered the material on development, growth and social well-being along with social comparative studies and guidelines. The book ably and aptly brings out the main issues of the theme and provides ample food for thought for scholars in various fields as well as for philosophers, politicians and others.

Bareilly

G.S. MONGA
President (1998), IEA

Preface

The Indian Economic Association (IEA) in its 80th year of academic activities, decided to publish theme-wise edited volumes out of papers contributed to IEA Annual Conference during 1994-2000. As a result of sustained efforts, the IEA could publish in 1999 as many as five such volumes arising out of IEA Conference/ Seminar Papers of 1999 itself. In 2000, altogether twelve volumes were published based on the themes of previous years' Conferences including those related to the 2000 conference. As many as eight volumes arising out of 1994-2000 Conference themes are yet to the published. Of these, we are happy to present this volume on *Human Development and Economic Development* in 2001. This volume contains altogether 34 articles. The major contribution of these articles are available in a summarised form from the Introduction which follows. We sincerely hope that our readers will find the contents of this volume both light and fruit bearing.

We are thankful to Dr. G.S. Monga, IEA President (1998) for his Foreword to this volume. Dr. Monga was the President of the IEA 81st (2nd Amrit Jubilee) Conference at Bangalore where one of the technical sessions was devoted to the theme of the present title. We also thank Prof. Ruddar Datt for his hard work as Editor of this volume and the Introduction. We thank all the contributors of this volume without whose co-operation this volume could not be published. Last but not the least, we thank Shri G.S. Bhatia of Deep & Deep Publications Pvt. Ltd. for the co-operation and help to publish this and other volumes (altogether 18 so far) in this series in record time and elegant manner. We also apologize to our members for any of the lapses that may remain in these volumes for reasons beyond our control.

Kolkata

PROF. RAJ KUMAR SEN
Managing Editor
for the Series (1994-2000) and
Former Secretary & Treasurer, IEA

List of Contributors

1. **Prof. N. Nettimi and N.H. Fidzani**, University of Botswana, Botswana.
2. **Ashir Mehta**, Department of Economics, Faculty of Arts, Maharaja Sayajirao University, Vadodra-390 002, Gujarat (India).
3. **R.Y. Mahore**, Reader, Department of Economics, Nagpur University Campus, Nagpur-440 010.
4. **N.M.P. Verma**, Babasaheb Bhimrao Ambedkar University Lucknow (UP).
5. **P. Jegadish Gandhi**, Professor of Economics, Vellore and Hony. Director, Vellore Institute of Development Studies.
6. **R.S. Mishra**, Assistant Director, Ministry of Commerce, N-563, Sector 9, R.K. Puram, New Delhi-110 022.
7. **M.S. Subramanian**, Professor, School of Economics, Madurai Kamraj University, Madurai-625 021 (Tamil Nadu).
8. **S. Narapa Reddy**, Tirupati.

   A. Rajasekhar, Hindu College, Guntur (Andhra Pradesh).

   P. Kodandarani Reddy, Hindu College, Guntur (Andhra Pradesh).
9. **Arabinda Ghosh**, Calcutta.
10. **Prof. P. Duriaswamy**, University of Madras, Chennai.
11. **Prof. G. Kurunakaran Pillai**, Department of Economics, University of Kerala, Trivandrum-695 581 (India).

12. **Kasturi Bai Dhanasekaran**, "Sundeep", 12-4/25, Moovendar Nagar, Vishwanathanpuram, Madurai-625 014 (Tamil Nadu).

13. **Arindam K. Sen and Mausumi Manna**, Field Research Operation Network, 19/B, Chakraberia Road (N), Calcutta-700 020.

14. **Sm. Swagata Das Bhowmick**, Department of Economics, Hiralal Mazumdar Memorial College for Women, Dakshineswar, Calcutta-700 035.

15. **R. Annapoorani**, Reader in Economics, Department of Economics, Avinashilingam Institute for Home Science and Higher Studies for Women (Deemed University), Coimbatore-641 043 (Tamil Nadu).

16. **Keya Sengupta**, Reader, Department of Economics, Assam University, P.O. Dargakona Silichar, Assam.

17. **Kaushal K. Srivastava and Tanuja Srivastava**, 214/6, Saraswati Kunj, University of Roorkee, Roorkee-247 677.

18. **Debarata Mandal**, Asstt. Professor, Department of Economics, Barasat Government College, North 24 Paragana (West Bengal).

19. **Dr. Biswajit Guha**, Reader, Department of Economics, Netaji Nagar Day College, 7/68, Netaji Nagar, Calcutta-700 092.

20. **Inderjeet Singh**, Reader, Department of Economics, Punjabi University, Patiala-147 002.

    Reena Singh, Lecturer, Department of Economics, M.M.H. College, Ghaziabad (U.P.).

21. **S.S. Dhillon and Jasmeet Kaur**, Punjab School of Economics, Guru Nanak Dev University, Amritsar (Punjab) 143 005.

22. **Krishna Mazumdar**, Indian Statistical Institute, Calcutta.

23. **Bishwa Nath Singh**, University Professor, Department of Economics, Magadah University, Bodh Gaya (Bihar).

S.M. Humair Ahmad, Professor and Head, Department of Economics, Mirza Ghalib College, Gaya.

24. **Nisar Ahmad Khan**, Reader, Department of Economics, Aligarh Muslim University, Aligarh-202 022 (UP).

25. **Prof. M.A. Razzaque**, Department of Statistics, University of Rajshahi, Bangladesh.

26. **(Mrs) R. Pushpavati**, Reader and Head, P.G. Department of Economics, Vivek Vardhini College, Jambagh, Hyderabad-500 265 (Andhra Pradesh).

27. **C.B. Padamanabhan**, UNESCO Expert, No. 7, Manickavachakar Street, East Tambram, Chennai-600 059.

Kanakasabai Nagarajan, Lecturer in Economics, Vivekananda College, Mylapore, Chennai.

28. **Basabi Bhattacharya**, 63/114-B, Prince Anwar Shah Road, Flat 5B, Rhine View, Calcutta-700 045.

29. **Anju Kohli**, Associate Professor, Department of Economics (CSSH), M.L. Sukhadia University, Udaipur (Rajasthan).

Sadhna Kothari, Associate Professor, Department of Geography (CSSH), M.L. Sukhadia University, Udaipur (Rajasthan).

30. **K.S. Sivaprakash**, Research Scholar, Department of Economics, Bharathiar University, Coimbatore-641 046.

31. **Hem Chandra Lal Das**, University Professor, P.G. Department of Economics, M.S. College, Motihari-845 401 (Bihar).

32. **Prof. Naseem A. Zaidi**, Department of Economics, Aligarh Muslim University, Aligarh-202 002 (UP).

33. **Asok Basu**, Chandra Lok, 10, Garia Station Road, Calcutta-700 084.

34. **K.N. Bhatt**, G.B. Pant Social Science Institute, Allahabad (UP).

Human Development—India in World Context

RUDDAR DATT

THE CONCEPT AND MEASURES OF HUMAN DEVELOPMENT

Elucidating the concept of human development, UNDP *Human Development Report (1997)* describes it as "the process of widening people's choices and the level of well-being they achieve are at the core of the notion of human development. Such theories are neither finite nor static. But regardless of the level of development, the three essential choices for people are to lead a long and healthy life, to acquire knowledge and to have access to the resources needed for a decent standard of living. Human development does not end there, however. Other choices highly valued by many people, range from political, economic and social freedom to opportunities for being creative and productive and enjoying self-respect and guaranteed human rights".[1]

Elucidating further, HDR (1997) states: "Income clearly is only one option that people would like to have, though an important one. But it is not the sum total of their lives. Income is also a means, with human development the end".[2]

Ever since the publication of the *Human Development Report 1990* under the guidance of Mahbul-ul-Haq, efforts have been made to devise and further refine measures of human development. Three measures have been developed. They are Human Development Index (HDI), Gender-related Development Index (GDI) and Human Poverty Index (HPI).

Human Development Index (HDI)

HDI measures the average achievement in three basic dimensions of human development:

- A long and healthy life as measured by life expectancy at birth.
- Knowledge as measured by the adult literacy rate (with two-third weight) and the combined primary, secondary and tertiary gross enrolment ratio (with one-third weight)
- A decent standard of living as measured by GDP per capita (PPP US$).

Before calculating HDI, an index for each of the three dimensions is created. For this purpose, maximum and minimum values are chosen for each indicator.

TABLE 1

Maxmimum and Minimum Values for Calculating HDI

Indicator	*Maximum Value*	*Minimum Value*
Life expectancy at birth	85	25
Adult literacy rate	100	0
Gross enrolment ratio	100	0
GDP per capita (PPP US$)	40,000	100

Performance in each dimension is expressed as a value between 0 and 1 by applying the following formula:

$$\text{Dimension Index} = \frac{\text{Actual value} - \text{minimum value}}{\text{Maximum value} - \text{minimum value}}$$

The HDI is calculated as a simple average of the dimension indices.

In Table 2, we present Human Development Index for 1999 for selected countries as reported in HDR 2001. Countries have been grouped under three categories: (i) Countries in the HDI range 0.8 and above are in the High Human Development group;

(ii) Countries in the HDI range 0.5 to 0.8 are in the range of Medium Human Development group, and (iii) Countries in the HDI range less than 0.5 are in the Low Human Development group.

The data has been collected for 162 countries. Among them 48 countries were in the High Human Development range, 78 countries were in Medium Human Development range and 36 countries were in Low Human Development range. India which was at No. 138 in HDI in 1994 has improved its position to No. 115 in 1999 (Refer Table 2).

In Table 3, we present the HDI trends for selected countries. A close perusal of the data for the last over two decades (1975 to 1999) reveals that all countries are making efforts in varying degrees to improve their human development indices. Among the high performers during 1980-99 can be considered as Iran, China, South Korea, Egypt and India, and to a certain extent Pakistan and Bangladesh. If the trend is maintained, several medium HDI countries will enter the high HDI group and several low HDI countries will join the medium HDI range. This is a welcome development. India has improved its HDI index from 0.433 in 1980 to 0.571 in 1999. It is still a long way to go, before India would enter the high HDI group.

Gender-related Development Index (GDI)

While HDI measures average achievement, the GDI adjusts the average achievement to reflect the inequalities between men and women. The three components used for the purpose are: (i) female life expectancy, (ii) female adult literacy and gross enrolment ratio, and (iii) female per capita income.

If gender inequality is not penalised, the value of GDI and HDI would be the same, but if gender inequality exists, the value of GDI would be lower than that of HDI. The greater the difference between HDI and GDI, the greater is the gender inequality. Table 4 provides data both for HDI and GDI for selected countries. It may be noted that near gender equality exists in Norway, Canada, United States, United Kingdom, Japan, Mexico, Russian Federation, Malaysia, Venezuela, Philippines, Sri Lanka, China, Vietnam and Indonesia. Countries which indicate higher gender inequality are Saudi Arabia, Pakistan, Iran, India, Egypt and Nigeria.

TABLE 2

Human Development Index (1999) for Selected Countries

HDI Rank	Country	Life Expectancy at Birth (years)	Adult literacy (%age 15 and above)	Combined Primary, Secondary and Tertiary enrolment ratio (%)	GDP per capita (PPP US$)	Life Expectancy Index	Education Index	GDP Index	Human Development Index
						P_1	P_2	P_3	$P=p_1+p_2+p_3/3$
High Human Development (HDI 0.8 and above)									
1.	Norway	78.4	99.0	97	28,433	0.89	0.98	0.94	0.939
3.	Canada	78.7	99.0	97	26,251	0.89	0.98	0.93	0.936
6.	United States	76.8	99.0	95	31,872	0.86	0.98	0.96	0.934
9.	Japan	80.8	99.0	82	24,898	0.93	0.93	0.92	0.928
14.	United Kingdom	77.5	99.0	106	22,093	0.87	0.99	0.90	0.923
27.	South Korea	74.7	97.6	90	15,712	0.83	0.95	0.84	0.875
Medium Human Development (HDI 0.5 to 0.8)									
51.	Mexico	72.4	91.1	71	8,297	0.79	0.84	0.74	0.790
55.	Russian Federation	66.1	99.5	78	7,473	0.69	0.92	0.72	0.775
56.	Malaysia	72.2	87.0	66	8,209	0.79	0.80	0.74	0.774
61.	Venezuela	72.7	92.3	65	5,495	0.79	0.83	0.67	0.765
68.	Saudi Arabia	71.3	76.1	61	10,815	0.77	0.71	0.78	0.754

69. Brazil	67.5	84.9	80	7,037	0.71	0.83	0.71	0.750
70. Philippines	69.0	95.1	82	3,805	0.73	0.91	0.61	0.749
81. Sri Lanka	71.9	91.4	70	3,279	0.78	0.84	0.58	0.735
87. China	70.2	83.5	73	3,617	0.75	0.80	0.60	0.718
90. Iran	68.5	75.7	73	5,531	0.73	0.75	0.67	0.714
101. Vietnam	67.8	93.1	67	1,860	0.71	0.84	0.49	0.682
102. Indonesia	65.8	86.3	65	2,857	0.68	0.79	0.56	0.677
105. Egypt	66.9	54.6	76	3,420	0.70	0.62	0.59	0.635
115. India	62.9	56.5	56	2,248	0.63	0.56	0.52	0.571
Low Human Development (HDI less than 0.5)								
127. Pakistan	59.6	45.0	40	1,834	0.58	0.43	0.49	0.498
132. Bangladesh	58.9	40.8	37	1,483	0.57	0.39	0.45	0.470
136. Nigeria	51.5	62.6	45	853	0.44	0.57	0.36	0.455
161. Niger	44.8	15.3	16	753	0.33	0.15	0.34	0.274
162. Sierra Leone	38.3	32.0	27	448	0.22	0.30	0.25	0.258

Note: HDI ranks are indicated as given in the *Human Development Report, 2001.*

Source: UNDP, *Human Development Report, 2001.*

TABLE 3

Human Development Index Trends for Selected Countries

HDI Rank	Country	1975	1980	1985	1990	1995	1999	Change in HDI	
								1980-90	1990-99
High Human Development									
1.	Norway	0.856	0.875	0.887	0.899	0.924	0.939	+0.024	+0.040
3.	Canada	0.867	0.882	0.904	0.925	0.930	0.936	+0.043	+0.011
6.	United States	0.861	0.882	0.896	0.912	0.923	0.934	+0.030	+0.022
9.	Japan	0.851	0.876	0.891	0.907	0.920	0.928	+0.031	+0.021
14.	United Kingdom	0.839	0.846	0.856	0.876	0.914	0.923	+0.030	+0.047
27.	South Korea	0.687	0.729	0.771	0.814	0.851	0.875	+0.085	+0.061
Medium Human Development									
51.	Mexico	0.688	0.732	0.750	0.759	0.772	0.790	+0.027	+0.031
55.	Russian Federation	...	0.809	0.826	0.823	0.778	0.775	+0.014	-0.048
56.	Malaysia	0.614	0.657	0.691	0.720	0.758	0.774	+0.063	+0.054
61.	Venezuela	0.715	0.730	0.737	0.756	0.764	0.765	+0.026	+0.009
68.	Saudi Arabia	0.587	0.647	0.669	0.706	0.736	0.754	+0.059	+0.048
69.	Brazil	0.641	0.676	0.690	0.710	0.734	0.750	+0.034	+0.040
70.	Philippines	0.649	0.683	0.687	0.716	0.733	0.749	+0.033	+0.033
81.	Sri Lanka	0.614	0.648	0.674	0.695	0.717	0.735	+0.047	+0.040
87.	China	0.522	0.553	0.590	0.624	0.679	0.718	+0.071	+0.094
90.	Iran	0.556	0.563	0.607	0.645	0.688	0.714	+0.082	+0.069

101. Vietnam	—	—	0.581	0.604	0.647	0.682	—	+0.078
102. Indonesia	0.467	0.529	0.581	0.622	0.662	0.677	+0.093	+0.055
105. Egypt	0.433	0.481	0.531	0.573	0.603	0.635	+0.092	+0.062
115. India	0.406	0.433	0.472	0.510	0.544	0.571	+0.077	+0.061
Low Human Development								
127. Pakistan	0.343	0.370	0.403	0.441	0.476	0.498	+0.071	+0.057
132. Bangladesh	0.332	0.350	0.383	0.414	0.443	0.470	+0.064	+0.056
136. Nigeria	0.326	0.386	0.402	0.423	0.447	0.455	+0.037	+0.032
161. Niger	0.234	0.253	0.244	0.254	0.260	0.274	+0.001	+0.020

Source: Compiled and computed from UNDP, *Human Development Report,* 2001.

However, there is a greater awareness in the world about gender inequality and efforts are being made to reduce gender inequality by promoting the education of females and giving them a better status in the family. Some countries have lagged behind due to cultural biases against the females. However, in them also, women movements are promoting the cause of bringing about gender equality.

Human Poverty Index (HPI)

Human Development Report, 1997 introduced the concept of Human Poverty Index which concentrates on deprivation in three essential elements of human life already reflected in HDI—longevity, knowledge and a decent living standard.

The first deprivation is vulnerability to death at a relatively early age and is represented in the HPI by the percentage of people expected to die before age 40.

The second deprivation is related to knowledge and is measured by the percentage of adults who are illiterate.

The third deprivation relates to a decent standard of living, in particular, overall provisioning. This is represented by a composite of three variables—the percentage of people with access to (a) health services, (b) to safe water, and (c) the percentage of malnourished children under five.

It would be relevant to understand why income does not figure in Human Poverty Index (HPI). According to the HDR (1997), the logic underlying the construction of economic provisioning is that the GNP included in the HPI is actually a combination of private and public facilities, since public services are paid out of aggregate national income.

One of the problems in assessing the prevalence of income poverty is that the use of the same poverty line in different countries can be very misleading because of the variation in "necessary" commodities. Depending upon the prevailing pattern of consumption—clothing, accommodation and such tools of communication and interaction as radios and telephones—many provisions are taken to be essential for social participation in one community without being treated as such in other communities. As a result, the minimum income needed to escape social estrangement can be quite different between communities.

For this purpose, the HPI decided to use the prevalence of

TABLE 4

Comparison of Human Development Indices (1999) of Selected Countries

	Human Development Index (HDI)	*Gender-related Development Index (GDI)*	*Human Poverty Index (HPI)*	*Income Poverty line US$ 1 a day 1995 PPP 1983-99*
High Human Development				
1. Norway	0.939	0.937	7.5	4*
3. Canada	0.936	0.934	12.1	7*
6. United States	0.934	0.932	15.8	14*
9. Japan	0.928	0.921	11.2	...
14. United Kingdom	0.923	0.920	15.1	16*
27. South Korea	0.875	0.868	...	<2.0
Medium Human Development				
51. Mexico	0.790	0.782	7.9	12.4
55. Russian Federation	0.775	0.774	...	...
56. Malaysia	0.774	0.768	10.9	...
61. Venezuela	0.765	0.759	8.6	18.7
68. Saudi Arabia	0.754	0.719	17.0	..
69. Brazil	0.750	0.743	12.9	9.0
70. Philippines	0.749	0.746	14.7	..
81. Sri Lanka	0.735	0.732	18.0	6.6
87. China	0.718	0.715	15.0	18.5
90. Iran	0.714	0.696	17.3	..
101. Vietnam	0.682	0.680	29.0	..
102. Indonesia	0.677	0.671	11.3	7.7
105. Egypt	0.635	0.620	31.7	3.1
115. India	0.571	0.553	34.3	44.2
Low Human Development				
127. Pakistan	0.498	0.466	39.2	31.0
132. Bangladesh	0.470	0.459	43.3	29.1
136. Nigeria	0.455	0.443	36.1	70.2
161. Niger	0.274	0.260	63.6	61.4

* for 1994-95 using $ 11 a day (1994 PPP US $).

Note: Countries have been arranged in the descending order on the basis of HDI.

Source: Compiled from UNDP, *Human Development Report,* 2001.

malnutrition of children which is relatively easier to measure and for which data are more readily available, along with access to health services and safe water. Combining these three variables, it was thought, would provide an adequate and broad picture about human poverty.

For selected OECD countries, a different human poverty index has been used. This includes four variables:

(i) Probability at birth not surviving to age 60.
(ii) Percentage of adults lacking functional literacy.
(iii) Percentage of people living below the poverty line US $ 11 a day (1994 PPP).
(iv) Long-term unemployment rate (12 months or more) or the determinant of social exclusion.

HPI is a the average of these four variables. A close perusal of Human Poverty Index for developing countries reveals the existence of high value of HPI in Niger (63.6%), Bangladesh (43.3%), Pakistan (39.2). Even India which has a medium HDI has a very high HPI (34.3%) and Egypt with a high HPI of 31.7%.

In Table 4, HPI and Income poverty index (measured by percentage of population below US $ 1 a day (1993 PPP) have been juxtaposed. It may be noted that in the case of Nigeria, 70.2 per cent of the population suffers from income poverty, but HPI index is 36.1%. However, in the case of Bangladesh, the situation is totally reversed—HPI 43.3, but income-poor population is 29.1 per cent. In the case of India, proportion of population below international income poverty line is 44.2%, but Human Poverty Index is 34.3. Human Poverty Index is thus a more comprehensive measures which takes into account differences in degress of deprivation measured by three variables listed above, while the income poverty line, though important, is based on only one variable.

Reviewing the progress of the world in achieving the goals of human development, the UNDP *Human Development Report (2001)* mentions: "At the United Nations Millennium Summit, world leaders agreed on a set of quantifiable and monitorable goals for development and poverty eradication to achieve by 2015. Progress the world has made over the past 30 years shows that these

HDI, HPI-1, HPI-2 and GDI—Same Components, Different Measurement

Index	*Longevity*	*Knowledge*	*Decent Standard of Living*	*Participation or exclusion*
HDI	Life expectancy at birth	1. Adult literacy rate 2. Combined enrolment ratio	GDP per capita (PPP US $)	...
HPI-1	Probability at birth of not surviving to age 40	Adult illiteracy rate	Deprivation in economic provisioning, measured by 1. Percentage of people not using improved water sources 2. Percentage of children under five who are underweight	....
HPI-2	Probability at birth of not surviving to age 60	Percentage of adults lacking functional literacy skills	Percentage of people below the income poverty line (50% of median disposable income)	Long-term unemployment rate (12 months or more)
GDI	Female and male life expectancy at birth	1. Female and male adult literacy rates 2. Female and male combined primary, secondary and tertiary enrolment ratios	Estimated female and male earned income, reflecting women's and men's command over resources	...

Source: UNDP, *Human Development Report*, 2001.

United Nations Millennium Declaration for 2015

- ❑ To halve the proportion of the world's people living on less than $ 1 a day
- ❑ To halve the proportion of world's people suffering from hunger
- ❑ To halve the proportion of world's people without access to safe drinking water
- ❑ To achieve universal completion of primary schooling
- ❑ To achieve gender equality in access to education
- ❑ To reduce maternal mortality ratios by three-quarters
- ❑ To reduce under-five mortality rates by two-thirds
- ❑ To halt and begin to reverse the spread of HIV/AIDS, malaria and other major diseases

goals are attainable. But many developing countries will not achieve them without much faster progress. While 66 countries are on track to reduce under five mortality rates by two-thirds, 93 countries with 62% of the world's people are lagging far behind or slipping. Similarly, while 50 countries are on track to achieve the safe water goal, 83 countries with 70% of the world's people are not. More than 40% of the world's people are living in countries on track to halve income poverty by 2015. Yet they are in just 11 countries that include China and India (with 38% of the world's people), and 70 countries are far behind or slipping. Without China and India, only 9 countries with 5% of the world's people are on track to halve income poverty."[3]

TECHNOLOGY ACHIEVEMENT INDEX (TAI)

Human Development Report, 2001 has devised a new measure which has been responsible for differences in levels of economic development as well as human development among different countries. This is referred to as Technology Achievement Index (TAI) in HDR 2001. Justifying the new index, HDR 2001 states: "Throughout history, technology has been a powerful tool for human development and poverty reduction . . . In fact, the 20th century's unprecedented gains in advancing human development and eradicating poverty came largely from technological breakthroughs—The rapid gains of the 20th century were propelled by medical technology—antibiotics and vaccines—while progress in the 19th century depended on slower social and economic changes such as better sanitation and diets . . . Moreover, technology supported advances in health, nutrition, crop yields and employment are usually not just one-time gains. They typically have a multiplier effect—creating a virtuous cycle, increasing people's knowledge, health and productivity, and raising incomes and building capacity for future innovation—all feeding back into human development".

"Information and communication technology can provide rapid, low cost access to information about almost all areas of human activity . . . the Internet is breaking barriers of geography, making markets more efficient, creating opportunities for income generation and enabling increased local participation . . . Revenues from India's information technology industry jumped from $ 150 million in 1990 to $4 billion in 1999."[4]

For new crop varieties, transgenics offers the hope of crops with higher yields, pest and drought-resistant properties and superior nutritional characteristics—especially for farmers in ecological zones left behind by the green revolution.

To assess the technological achievement of different countries, the *Human Development Report,* 2001 devised the Technology Achievement Index, which aims to capture how well a country is creating and diffusing technology and building a human skill base-reflecting capacity to participate in the technological innovations of the network age. The composite index measures achievements, not potential, effort or inputs. In is not a measure of which country is leading in global technology development, but focuses on how well the country as a whole is participating in creating and using technology. For instance, United States has progressed very far in making inventions and may have far more internet hosts in total, but it does not rank as No.1 in TAI since in Finland the internet is more widely diffused and more being done to develop a technological skill base throughout the population.

TAI uses four dimensions and eight indicators to develop a composite index. They are as under:

Components and Indicators of Technology Achievement Index (TAI)

Dimension	*Indicator*
1. Creation of technology	a. Patents granted per capita
	b. Receipts of royalty and license fees from abroad per capita
2. Diffusion of recent innovations	c. Internet hosts per capita
	d. High and medium technology exports share of all exports
3. Diffusion of old innovations	e. Telephones per capita (mainline and cellular combined)
	f. Electricity consumption per capita
4. Human skills	g. Mean years of schooling
	h. Gross enrolment ratio at tertiary level in science, mathematics and engineering

Creation of Technology

To capture the level of a country in the creation of technology, two indicators are used: First is the number of patents granted per capita. This is intended to reflect the level of invention activities. Second is the receipts of royalties and license fees per capita received from abroad. This indicates the use of the inventions which have become commercially successful and thus have market value.

Diffusion of Recent Innovations

All countries must adopt innovations to benefit from the opportunities of the network age. This is measured by internet hosts per capita as an indicator of the extent of participation in new technology. Along with this, the share of high and medium technology exports in total exports of the country also indicates the degree of diffusion of recent innovations.

Diffusion of Old Innovations

Two indicators are used to measure the diffusion of old innovations—Telephones and electricity consumption. Both of them are especially important to use newer technologies as well as to access them. They are important at the earlier stages of technological advance, but become a routine affair at the most advanced stages. Thus while it is important for India to focus on diffusing electricity and telephones to the remotest corners of the country so that all people can participate in the technological revolution, United States, Japan and Sweden have passed that stage. Still these indicators will give an idea of the distance to be covered by the developing countries like India compared to highly developed countries.

Human Skills

Development of skills is essential for use of technology as well as to its adaptation to local needs. Two indicators have been used to reflect human skills needed to create and absorb innovations. They are: mean years of schooling and gross enrolment ratio of students enrolled in science, mathematics and engineering. The Human Development Report, 2001 clarifies that though it would be desirable to include indicators of vocational training, these data are not available.

Data Sources and Limitations

HDR 2001 has claimed that the data used to construct TAI has been taken from international series that are most widely used in analysis of technology trends. However, besides the conceptual problems, the data of some countries are serious under-estimates because innovations are sought to be reflected only through recorded patents and royalty received. But since important technological innovations such as those occurring in the informal sector and in indigenous knowledge systems have not been recorded, to that extent, the Technology Achievement Index underestimates the value for several underdeveloped countries.

Similarly, to measure diffusion of technology only by internet hosts also understates TAI in many underdeveloped countries, because there are other informal ways of transmission of information and technology.

HDR 2001, therefore, concludes: "The TAI is constructed using indicators, not direct measures, of a country's achievements in four dimensions. It provides *a rough summary*—not a comprehensive measure—of a society's technological achievements".[5] (Emphasis added).

TAI Values and Rankings

Due to non-availability of data for several countries, the TAI estimates have been prepared for only 72 countries in HDR 2001. In several underdeveloped countries, data about patents or royalties received was either missing or very unsatisfactory and hence they could not be covered in TAI.

The results of TAI show wide variations—the value of TAI ranging from 0.744 for Finland at the top to 0.066 for Mozambique at the bottom. These countries on the basis of TAI values have been grouped under four categories: leaders, potential leaders, dynamic adopters and marginalised (Refer Table 5).

Leader (TAI above 0.5)

This group includes Finland at the top accompanied by United States, Sweden and Japan. Countries in this group are at the cutting edge of technological innovation. Next is South Korea which has also advanced rapidly in technology. In these countries, technological innovation is self-sustaining and these countries have achieved high levels in technology creation, diffusion and human skills.

Potential Leaders (TAI 0.35-0.49)

Most of these countries have invested in high levels of human development and have diffused old technologies. They have very little to their credit in the form of innovations. Malaysia, Mexico, Spain, Italy, Poland, Romania, etc. are in this group. These countries compare favourably with the top in terms of skill development.

Dynamic Adopters (TAI 0.20 to 0.34)

These countries are rapidly adopting new technologies and are developing higher levels of human skills. Included in this group are Brazil, China, India, Indonesia, South Africa and Tunisia among many others. Although the process of technological diffusion has started, it is still slow in many countries, but is likely to gather momentum in the near future.

Marginalised (TAI below 0.20)

Technology diffusion and skill development have a long way to go in these countries. Large parts of their population have not

TABLE 5

Technology Achievement Index (TAI) for Selected Countries

TAI Rank	Country	Technology Achievement Index (TAI) Value	Technology Creation		Diffusion of recent innovations		Diffusion of old innovations		Human Skills	
			Patents granted to residents (per million people) 1998	Receipts of royalties and licence fees (US $ per 1000 people) 1999	Internet hosts (per 1,000 people) 2000	High and medium technology exports (as % of total export of goods) 1999	Telephones (main line and cellular, per 1,000 people) 1999	Electricity consumption (KWH per capita) 1998	Mean years of schooling (age 15 and above) 2000	Gross tertiary science enrolment ratio (%) 1995-97
1	2	3	4	5	6	7	8	9	10	11
Leaders (TAI above 0.5)										
1	Einland	0.744	187	125.6	200.2	50.7	1,023	14,129	10.0	27.4
2.	United States	0.733	289	130.0	179.0	66.2	993	11,832	12.0	13.9
4.	Japan	0.698	994	64.6	49.0	80.8	1,007	7,322	9.5	10.0
5.	South Korea	0.666	779	9.8	4.8	66.7	93.8	4,497	10.8	23.2
7.	United Kingdom	0.606	82	134.0	57.4	61.9	1,037	5,327	9.4	14.9
8.	Canada	0.589	31	38.6	108.0	48.7	881	15,071	11.6	14.2

(Contd.)

TABLE 5 *(Contd.)*

1 2	*3*	*4*	*5*	*6*	*7*	*8*	*9*	*10*	*11*
Potential Leaders (TAI between 0.35 to 0.49)									
30. Malaysia	0.396	-	0.0	2.4	67.4	340	2,554	6.8	3.3
32. Mexico	0.389	1	0.4	9.2	66.3	192	15,13	7.2	5.0
Dynamic Adopted (TAI between 0.20 to 0.34)									
43. Brazil	0.311	2	0.8	7.2	32.9	238	1,793	4.9	3.4
44. Philippines	0.300	-	0.1	0.4	32.8	77	451	8.2	5.2
45. China	0.299	1	0.1	0.1	39.0	120	74.6	6.4	3.2
50. Iran	0.260	1	0.0	-	2.0	133	1,343	5.3	6.5
57 Egypt	0.236	-	0.7	0.1	8.8	77	861	5.5	2.9
60. Indonesia	0.211	-	-	0.2	17.9	40	320	5.0	3.1
62, Sri Lanka	0.203	-	-	0.2	5.2	49	244	6.9	1.4
63. India	0.201	1	-	0.1	16.6	28	384	5.1	1.7
Marginalised (TAI below 0.20)									
64. Nicaragua	0.185	-	-	0.4	3.6	39	281	4.6	3.8
65. Pakistan	0.167	-	-	0.1	7.9	24	337	3.9	1.4
72. Mozambique	0.066	-	-	-	12.2	5	54	1.1	0.2

Note: The ranks of the countries are as indicated in *HDR Report*, 2001.

Source: UNDP, *Human Development Report, 2001.*

benefited from the diffusion of old technology. Nicaragua, Pakistan, Mozambique, Kenya, Tanzania and some other countries fall in this category.

Human Development Report, 2001 after making an analysis of the ranking of the countries concludes: "These rankings do not shadow income rankings and show considerable dynamism in several countries with rising technological achievement—for example, Korea ranks above United Kingdom, Canada and other established industrial economies. Ireland ranks above Austria and France. Large developing countries—Brazil, China, India—do less well than one might expect because this is not a ranking of "technological might" of a country".[6]

Although technological developments are important for human development, yet TAI only measures technological achievements and indicates the disparities in levels of achievements. The real issue is: how can societies harness technological achievements in the task of human development so that ultimately they lead to reduction in inequality and poverty?

HUMAN DEVELOPMENT INDEX FOR VARIOUS STATES IN INDIA

Many of India's states can be compared with medium-size countries. It would, therefore, be appropriate to construct human development index (HDI) for various states so as to understand the differences in HDI among them. The UNFPA published a report on human development in India in a book entitled "*India: Towards Population and Development Goals*" in 1997. Mahbub-ul-Haq, the main architect of UNDP Human Development Report in his book *Human Development in South Asia, 1997* also carried out a study of human development in the various states of India. The UNFPA in its study used three dimensions of Human Development: (i) The index of life expectancy, (ii) the index of per capita income, i.e. per capita state domestic product, and (iii) the index of education based on literacy rate and school enrolment ratio. Mahbub-ul-Haq also considered similar three dimensions of human development with a minor difference that he used only literacy rate in his index of education in the study while neglecting the indicator of school enrolment ratio.

Dr. Biswajeet Guha has questioned both these studies by

asserting that they neglected many important aspects of human development. He made an attempt to overcome this inadequacy by including three additional dimensions of human development, such as, the quality of life, poverty eradication and urbanisation. Thus, on the basis of six dimensions, Dr. Guha constructed four indices of human development. All these indices pertained to the period 1988-94. Dr. Guha used the UNDP, Human Development Report methodology for the purpose.

DIAGRAM 1

Human Development Indices

Dimensions				
(i) Life Expectancy (ii) Per capita state domestic product (iii) Literacy rate and gross enrolment ratio	HDI_1	HDI_2	HDI_3	HDI_4
(iv) Quality of life				
(v) Population above the Poverty line				
(vi) Urbanisation				

The index of quality of life was constructed based on the five indicators : (i) access to safe drinking water, (ii) electricity connection, (iii) enjoyment of two square meals a day throughout the year, (iv) residence in pucca houses, and (v) availability of beds in public hospitals to total population.

The index of poverty eradication has been prepared with respect to the eradication of poverty in the total population of the state. The index has been developed on the basis of proportion of population above the poverty line as outlined by the Expert Group of the Planning Commission.

The index of urbanisation for each state has been prepared on the basis of statewise data derived from the census of 1991. In diagram 1, we have indicated the different dimensions of human development used by Dr. Biswajit Guha in his study as HDI_1, HDI_2, HDI_3, and HDI_4.

In Table 6, we present the results of the three studies, viz., UNFPA, Mahbub-ul-Haq and Guha in developing HDI mainly based on UNDP, Human Development Report methodology.

HDI data on the basis of these studies with minor variations reveals Kerala, Maharashtra, Punjab, Tamil Nadu and Haryana—

five states at the top. By ignoring school enrolment ratio, Haq's study provides different ranks to the states, but UNFPA study ranks the states more or less in the same order. At the bottom are five states, viz., Madhya Pradesh, Orissa, Rajasthan, Uttar Pradesh and Bihar showing poor HDI values. In the middle range of HDI are five states, viz., Gujarat, Karnataka, West Bengal, Andhra Pradesh and Assam.

The range of HDI values in UNFPA study varies from 62.8 for the top most Kerala to 34.0 for Bihar. In Haq's study, the variation is from 59.7 in case of Kerala to 34.1 for Madhya Pradesh and in Guha's study from 74.3 in the case of Kerala to 41.1 in the case of Uttar Pradesh.

Biswajit Guha, however, has developed four indices of HDI as HDI_1, HDI_2, HDI_3, and HDI_4. HDI_1 is based on UNDP methodology as given in HDR, but he has enlarged the scope of human development index by including three more dimensions: quality of life, poverty eradication and urbanisation. The results of Guha's study are summarised in Table 7. The most comprehensive index of human development in Guha's study is HDI_4. Comparing the results of HDI_1 and HDI_4 reveals several sharp variations in these values. One unique feature, however, is that the top rank in all the four indices is with Kerala. But the bottom rank and other ranks for different states have shown divergences. For instance, as against rank No. 2 for Maharashtra in HDI_1, inclusion of poverty eradication and urbanisation dimensions shifts its rank to position No. 5.

However, opposite is the case with Andhra Pradesh whose rank stood at No. 9 in HDI_1 but improved to No. 6 in HDI_4. In case of Orissa it ranked at No. 11 in HDI_1 but shifted to the bottom most rank No. 15 in HDI_4.

There is no double that Dr. Guha in his study has enlarged the number of dimensions and has included some additional and very meaningful dimensions such as poverty eradication, extent of urbanisation, but still there is scope for including some more relevant dimensions which have a bearing on human development. Dr. Guha rightly mentions: "the non-availability of some important official statistical data, say, on sanitation, per capita availability of food, clothing, footwear, etc. of all the states separately could not represent the true picture of the quality of life of rural and urban population as well as that of the entire population of each state in the present study. On account of similar non-availability of official statistical data of all the states, it was not possible to consider the factors, like statewise growth of employment opportunities, progress of land reform etc . . . so, there are always some conceptual and practical limitations involved in this type of analysis. However, in spite of all these limitations, it can be stated that even if some factors are excluded from the analysis of human development, these will have some impact upon the per capita state domestic product. So per capita income will still act as an important index of development".[7] Similar views have also been expressed in Human Development Reports regarding the inclusion of dimensions and indicators of human development. According to *Human Development Report, 2001*, "the HDI is a summary, not a comprehensive measure of human development."[8] But, these indices do provide "an approximate picture", if not a complete and true picture. It is better to have an approximate picture than not to have any picture at all. Various countries, India being no exception, are continuously making efforts to improve and enlarge the scope of available statistical information, but this should not prevent researchers to develop indices of human development.

PROGRESS OF HUMAN DEVELOPMENT IN INDIA

The basic purpose of planning in India is to widen people's choices and improve the well-being of the people. In this context, human development was the key issue so that people could lead a long and healthy life, they could acquire knowledge so as to have better vertical mobility in life and last, but not the least, to achieve a decent standard of living of all. It would be, therefore, appropriate to examine the progress of human development in India.

India has been categorised by the *Human Development Report, 2001* as a medium human development country. The Human Development Index has risen gradually from 0.406 in 1975 to 0.510 in 1990 and stands at 0.571 in 1999. In fact, it can take quite long for India to cross the mark of 0.8 in HDI to join the rank of high HDI countries.

A major impediment to progress in human development is the very fast growth of population experienced in India. India's

TABLE 6

Major State-wise Alternative Studies of Human Development in India (HDI)

Rank	*State*	*Value of HDI as studied by*		
		UNFPA	*Haq*	*Guha (1988-94)*
1.	Kerala	62.79(1)	59.7(1)	74.33(1)
2.	Maharashtra	55.49(2)	51.3(3)	59.24(2)
3.	Punjab	54.86(3)	51.6(2)	57.36(4)
4.	Tamil Nadu	51.11(4)	43.2(8)	57.53(3)
5.	Haryana	50.56(5)	47.4(4)	53.75(5)
6.	Gujarat	47.82 (6)	45.8(5)	52.48(6)
7.	Karnataka	46.83(7)	44.2(7)	52.24(7)
8.	West Bengal	45.37(8)	45.2(6)	51.33(8)
9.	Andhra Pradesh	41.28(9)	39.3(9)	46.82(9)
10.	Assam	39.48(10)	37.4(10)	44.25(10)
11.	Madhya Pradesh	36.71(11)	34.1(15)	41.56(14)
12.	Orissa	37.25(12)	36.8(11)	43.18(11)
13.	Rajasthan	37.11(13)	35.03(13)	42.56(12)
14.	Uttar Pradesh	35.51(14)	34.3(14)	41.06(15)
15.	Bihar	34.05(15)	35.04(12)	42.14(13)

Notes: 1. States have been arranged on the basis of UNFPA study in the descending order of HDI.

2. Figures in brackets indicate respective state-wise ranks.

Sources: 1. UNFPA, *India: Towards Population and Development Goals*, OUP, 1997.

2. Mahbub-ul-Haq, *Human Development in South Asia*, OUP, 1997.

3. Biswajit Guha, Human Development in India—Study of Inter-state Disparity, Indian Economic Association, *Conference Volume* (1998).

population increased from 620.7 million in 1975 to 1,016 million in 2000 giving a growth rate of 2.0 per cent per annum during the period (1975-2000) which is fairly high. It is expected that the growth rate of population during 2000-2015 will come down to 1.3 per cent. This would provide a welcome relief to push forward the process of human development.

Urbanisation is considered to be a factor which promotes human development. The share of urban population which was

TABLE 7

Major State-wise Alternative Studies of Human Development in India

State	HDI_1	HDI_2	HDI_3	HDI_4
1. Kerala	74.33(1)	73.14(1)	74.47(1)	73.54(1)
2. Maharashtra	59.24(2)	59.67(3)	61.27(5)	60.02(5)
3. Punjab	57.36(4)	62.16(2)	70.29(2)	69.26(2)
4. Tamil Nadu	57.53(3)	57.99(4)	59.07(6)	57.99(7)
5. Haryana	53.75(5)	55.78(5)	65.78(3)	65.11(3)
6. Gujarat	52.48(6)	55.24(6)	63.30(4)	62.47(4)
7. Karnataka	52.24(7)	53.52(7)	55.79(9)	54.64(9)
8. West Bengal	51.33(8)	52.07(8)	56.84(8)	55.84(8)
9. Andhra Pradesh	46.82(9)	48.85(9)	58.51(7)	58.07(6)
10. Assam	44.25(10)	43.95(11)	54.71(10)	54.49(10)
11. Madhya Pradesh	41.56(14)	43.45(12)	46.74(12)	45.81(12)
12. Orissa	43.18(11)	42.92(14)	43.50(15)	42.77(15)
13. Rajasthan	42.56(12)	45.43(10)	54.08(11)	53.64(11)
14. Uttar Pradesh	41.06(15)	42.72(15)	45.91(13)	45.08(13)
15. Bihar	42.14(13)	43.24(13)	45.12(14)	44.61(14)

Note: States have been arranged on the basis of UNFPA study in the decending order of HDI.

Source: Biswajit Guha, *op. cit.*, Table 6.

21.3 per cent in 1975 has reached a level of 28.1 per cent in 1999, but by 2015, urban population would reach the level of 35.7 per cent. In absolute terms, urban population was 278 million in 1999 and would reach a level of 442 million in 2015. The would certainly help to enlarge human development because it has been observed that urban areas are better looked after in terms of education and health facilities.

Another healthy feature of likely demographic transition is the proportion of children or population under age 15, whose proportion stood at 33.9 per cent in 1999 but is likely to decline to 26.9 per cent by 2015. In absolute terms, population under age 15 was 336.5 in 1999 million and would get reduced to 331 million in 2015. This will imply decreasing population pressures from below in future which would also help in releasing resources to improve human development.

It would be quite useful to consider factors related with the education of the population that are likely to promote human development. The most important factor is adult literacy rate which was 56.5% in 1999. This implies an adult illiteracy rate of 43.5 per cent. In absolute terms, 285 million adults were illiterate in 1999. The share of India in the world's illiterate population is 33.3 per cent. According to the Human Development Report, 2001, a total of 854 million persons were illiterate in the world in 1999 and nearly one-third of these were accounted for in India. As compared with the total world population, the share of India in world population is only 16.6 per cent. In other words, in the total world population, India's share is one-sixth, but among the world's illiterates, her share is one-third. This only underlines the need for strengthening literacy rate still further to reduce adult illiteracy in India. Although evidence of substantial increase in literacy during the decades of the nineties has become evident, still India has a long way to go. Compared to China which has improved its literacy rate to 83.5 per cent in 1999, India lags behind considerably in this very important area of human development.

Another important indicators is the combined Gross (Primary, Secondary and Tertiary) Enrolment Ratio which was only 56.0 per cent in India. China had a gross enrolment ratio of 73 per cent in 1999. India is lagging behind and has to catch up, not only with reference to developed countries, but also with reference to some developing countries like China.

Public expenditure on education as a percent of GNP is considered as an indicator of state policy towards promoting education. This proportion has remained unchanged between 1985-87 to 1995-97 at 3.2% of GNP. According to the Report of the Education Commission (1964-65), this expenditure should have been raised to 6% of GNP. Although it is more than three decades now, but the target set by the Education Commission has yet to be realised.

The proportion of education expenditure devoted to pre-primary and primary education has marginally increased from 35% in 1985-86 to 39.5% in 1995-97. This is a welcome change and consequently the expenditure devoted to tertiary education has marginally declined from 15.3% to 13.7% in total education expenditure at all levels. There is a strong need to enrich state-run schools at the primary level so as to bring about a decline in drop-out rates. Since the children belonging to upper middle class and affluent sections are now going to the so-called public schools, it should be possible for the state to improve facilities both in terms of human and national resources deployed in state-run primary schools.

The Information Technology revolution has necessitated an increase in the proportion of tertiary students in science, math and engineering to be stepped up. Their proportion was only 25% during 1994-97 in India. As against this, their proportion in China was 53%. This proportion was about 49 per cent in Russian Federation. India has to bring about a shift to meet the changing demands of the new economy.

So far as youth literacy rate is concerned, it is 71.8% in 1999, but ironically in a majority of medium human development countries, youth literacy rate is above 90 per cent. India has, therefore, to improve its literacy rate among the youth, i.e. population in the age group (15-24).

Health Indicators

Life expectancy at birth has shown a continuous improvement from 50.3 years during 1970-75 to 62.3 years during 1995-2000. However, the probability at birth not surviving to age 40 is 16.7% in 1999. India has to improve health facilities as well as nutrition levels so that it can reduce the probability at birth not surviving to age 40 at the level of China (7.9%) which is half that of India. Several medium human development countries have much better survival rates. A few worth mentioning are Philippines, Thailand, Malaysia and Sri Lanka.

In this context, it would be relevant that 53% of the children under five were underweight during 1995-2000. In absolute terms, 178 million children under five were under weight. The country should support a programme of improving nutrition in poor families to reduce this massive number of underweight children.

Population not using improved water sources was 12% in 1999. This is a very healthy development, but in absolute terms 119 million persons are unable to make use of improved water sources and thus become victims of all kinds of water-borne diseases. Similarly, improved sanitation facilities were not available to 69% of the population. In absolute terms, 665 million persons were living under insanitary conditions. India's record in the sphere of sanitation is, to say the least, tragic. Even in medium human development countries, population using adequate sanitation facilities ranged from 70 per cent to 99 per cent, but the proportion in India was palpably low at 31 per cent in 1999. India has a long way to go in this area of access to health services.

It is really distressing that 65% of the Indian population did not have access to essential drugs in 1999. This implies that 645 million persons were without effective medical cover. This reduces the survival rate in India.

The proportion of under-nourished people in India in 1999 was 21%. This implies that 208.5 million people were under-nourished. This under-nourishment is primarily due to the existence of poverty. There is a need to strengthen poverty eradication strategies to reduce under-nourishment.

The survival rate has considerably improved in India. In 1970, infant mortality rate per 1,000 live births was 127, it has been brought down to 70 in 1999. Similarly, under-five infant mortality rate has been reduced from 202 per 1,000 live births to 98 in 1999. These are healthy developments. Likewise, maternal mortality rate per 1,00,000 live births has been brought down to 410 during 1980-99. Control of diseases and improvement in hospital facilities have contributed to improvements in survival rate.

Gender-Related Development Indicators

Life expectancy at birth of females in 1999 was 63.3 years, but for males, it was 62.4 years. Comparing with medium human development countries, Indian achievement, though good, is still much lower in relation to Mexico, Venezuela, Russian Federation, Thailand, Philippines, Sri Lanka, Iran, Vietnam, to name a few among them.

Although gap between life expectancy of females and males is very small, but in other gender-related development indicators, this gap is very wide. For instance, adult literacy of females was barely 44.5 per cent as against 67.8 per cent of males in 1999. Similarly, combined Gross Enrolment ratio of females was 49 per cent as against 62.0 per cent for males in 1999. Likewise, Estimated Earned Income of females was $ 1,195 as compared with that of males to be \$ 3,236 in 1999. This implies that female income was just 37 per cent of male income. Obviously, either females suffered from gender discrimination in wage income or they did not have regular employment and a big proportion was employed as casual labourers or a large proportion of females worked part time. There may be many more factors, but it cannot be denied that females suffered gender bias both in education and employment.

Economic Indicators

GDP per capita of India was \$ 2,248 in 1999 (PPP US \$). The average annual growth rate of GDP during 1980-90 was 5.8 per cent and during 1990-98, it slightly improved to 6.1 per cent. This growth rate can be considered as quite good for a medium human development country.

However, the measures of inequality of consumption revealed that the share of the poorest 10% in total consumption in 1997 was just 3.5 per cent and that of the richest 10% was 33.5 per cent. Thus, the ratio of consumption between the richest 10% to the poorest 10% was 9.5. Similarly, the poorest 20 per cent shared only 8.1 per cent in total consumption, but the richest 20 per cent shared 46.1 per cent. Thus, the ratio of consumption of the richest 20% to the poorest 20% was 5.7. Compared with medium human development countries, India shows moderate inequality. A very large number of countries in this group show much higher inequality of income or consumption. However, there is a need to improve the condition of the poorest 10 per cent or 20 per cent of the population so that India is able to reduce inequality still further and compare herself favourably with high human development countries.

Data on priority in public expenditure on education reveals that it was 3.2% of GNP in 1985-87 and has remained stagnant at that very level in 1995-97. But public expenditure on health was distressingly low at 0.9% of GDP in 1990. There is, therefore, an urgent need to improve the proportion of public expenditure both on education and health so as to foster human development. This, however, should not mislead us to conclude that India is spending more on military expenditure or has to use a big proportion of GDP in total debt service. Data available on both the indicators reveals that military expenditure accounted for 2.9 per cent of

GDP in 1990, but it has shown a decline to 2.4 per cent of GDP in 1999. Similarly, total debt service payments were of the order of 2.6 per cent of GDP in 1990 and they also shared a decline to 2.3 per cent in 1999. Obviously, India is neither using a big proportion of its public spending on military expenditure nor on debt service payment. We have, therefore, to search for some other areas like general administration and subsidies which may be appropriating a big proportion of public expenditure.

Lastly, we may consider fuel consumption as a proximate measure for industrialisation or modernisation of our economy. Data reveal that traditional fuel consumption in total energy use declined from 31.5% in 1980 to 20.7% in 1997. This was natural and is in accordance with the process of development. However, commercial energy use measured in terms of kg. of oil equivalent improved from 424 kgs. in 1990 to 497 kgs. in 1997—indicating a growth rate of 1.9% per annum. It may be noted that per capita electricity consumption marginally improved from 130 KWH in 1980 to 134 KWH in 1998. This only underlines the fact that sources of energy other than electric energy, such as coal and oil, have contributed more to energy use. Energy is a basic constraint on development. India has become more dependent on non-renewable sources of energy like coal and oil and less on renewable sources like hydro power. It would be more desirable to tap hydro resources more effectively.

To sum up, the fact sheet on human development has many plus points. Population growth rate has begun to decline and would be 1.3 per cent per annum during 1999-2015. This will release quite a good proportion of resources being currently used for supporting a higher growth rate of population. Growth of urbanisation will strengthen the sinews of human development since urban areas are better looked after in terms of education and health. The proportion of child population in total population has already indicated a decline and the trend is likely to be strengthened.

Although India has shown a better record in improving its literacy rate and gross enrolment ratio, yet it lags behind considerably, even with reference to medium human development countries, not to speak of catching up with high human development countries. Public expenditure on education has stagnated at 3.2 per cent of GDP during the last 25 years and India has not made any progress in reaching the goal of 6 per cent of GNP set by the Education Commission (1964-65). The proportion of tertiary students in science, math and engineering has been around 25 which is rather low. Similarly, youth literacy at about 72 per cent is much lower than the achievement of a majority of medium human development countries around 90 per cent and above.

Health indicators reveal a continuous improvement in life expectancy, infant mortality rate and maternal mortality rate, though our achievement is not commensurate with the levels attained in several of the medium development countries. But our record about the proportion of underweight children around 53% is very dismal. Equally distressing is the fact that 69% of our population lived under insanitary conditions and 65 per cent of the population did not have access to life saving drugs.

Gender-related development indicators revealed the gap between male and female in adult literacy, gross enrolment ratio and earned income was too wide and indicated the existence of a strong gender bias.

The growth rate of the Indian economy has remained about 6 per cent during the last two decades and can be considered as satisfactory. Similarly, India showed moderate inequality of income/consumption, although there is further scope for reducing inequality by poverty eradication programmes targeted to the poorest 20 per cent of the population.

Public expenditure on health has been pitiably low at less than 1 per cent of GDP. Military expenditure as a percentage of GDP indicated a decline during the nineties.

In nut shell, it may be stated that human development index of India has improved from 0.406 in 1975 to 0.571 in 1999, but India still has miles to go before she can enter the group of high human development countries. But our process of development has to accelerate the pace of human development so that India can feel proud to be a member of high human development countries.

Notes and References

1. UNDP, *Human Development Report, 1997*, pp. 13-14.
2. *Ibid.*, p. 14.
3. UNDP, *Human Development Report, 2001*, p. 1.

4. *Ibid.*, p. 13.
5. *Ibid.*, p. 46.
6. *Ibid.*, p. 47.
7. Guha, Biswajeet, Human Development in India—A Study of Interstate Disparity, *Indian Economic Association Conference Volume,* 1998, p.125.
8. UNDP, *Human Development Report, 2001,* p. 14.

References

UNDP, *Human Development Report, 1997.*

UNDP, *Human Development Report, 2000.*

UNDP, *Human Development Report, 2001.*

World Bank, *Human Development Report, 2000/2001.*

World Bank, *World Development Report, 2002.*

Dreze, Jean and Sen, Amartya (1995), *Indian: Economic Development and Social Opportunity*, Oxford University Press, Delhi.

Indian Economic Association, IEA Amrit Jubliee (81st), *Conference Volume, 1998.*

UNFPA, (1997), *India: Towards Population and Development Goals*, OUP.

Mahbul-ul-Haq (1997), *Human Development in South Asia,* OUP.

APPENDIX

FACT-SHEET ON HUMAN DEVELOPMENT OF INDIA

Demographic Indicators

Total population	1975	2,000	2015
(In millions)	620.7	1,016	1,230.5
Annual Population Growth Rate	1990-2000	1999-2015	
Percent per annum	2.0	1.3	
Urban Population	1975	1999	2015
Percentage of total	21.3	28.1	35.9
(In millions)	132.2	278.9	441.7
Population under age 15	1999	2015	
Percent of total	33.9	26.9	
(In millions)	336.5	331.0	
Adult Population Age 15 & Above	1999	2015	
(In millions)	656.2	899.5	
Total fertility per woman	1970-75	1995-2000	
(In millions)	5.4	3.3	

Education Indicators

Adult Literacy Rate	1999	
% (age 15 and above)	56.5%	
Adult Illiteracy Rate	1999	
% (age 15 and above)	43.5%	
(In millions)	285.4	
Combined Gross ((Primary, Secondary and Teritiary Enrolment Ratio	1999	
	56.0%	
Public Expenditure on Education	1985-87	1995-97
As % of GNP	3.2	3.2
As % of total government expenditure	8.5	11.6

Public education expenditure by level of education (as % of all levels)

Pre-primary		*Secondary*		*Tertiary*	
1985-86	*1995-97*	*1985-86*	*1995-97*	*1985-86*	*1995-97*
35.0	39.5	25.3	26.5	15.3	13.7

Youth literacy	1999
% (age 15-24)	71.8
Tertiary students in science, maths and engineering as % of all tertiary students	1994-97
	25

HEALTH INDICATORS	1999	1970-75	1995-2000
Life expectancy at birth (years)	62.5	50.3	62.3
Probability at birth not surviving to age 40	**1995-2000**		
	16.7		
Population not using improved water resources	**1999**		
% of total population	12%		
(In millions)	119		
Underweight children	**1995-2000**		
Under five (%)	53%		
(In millions)	178.3		
Population not using improved	**1999**		
Sanitation facilities	89%		
(In millions)	665		
Population without access to essential drugs	65%		
(In millions)	645		
Undernourished people	21%		
(In millions)	208.5		
Physicians per 1,00,000 people (1995-2000)	48		
Infant mortality Rate	**1970**	**1999**	
(per 1000 live births)	127	70	
Under five Mortality Rate	**1970**	**1999**	
(per 1,000 live births)	202	98	
Maternal Mortality Rate	**1980-99**		
(per 10,000 live births)	410		

GENDER RELATED DEVELOPMENT INDICATORS

	1999	
	Female	*Male*
Life expectancy		
At birth (years)	63.3	62.4
Adult Literacy Rate (age 15 & above)	44.5	67.8
Combined Primary, Secondary and Tertiary Gross Enrolment ratio	49.0	62.0
Estimated earned income		
(PPP US $)	1,195	3,236

ECONOMIC INDICATORS	1999
GDP per capita (PPP US $)	2,248

		1980-90	1990-1998	
Average Annual growth of GDP(%)		5.8	6.1	
Average Annual Change		1990-98	1998-99	
In consumer price index		9.5	4.7	
Share in Income or consumption (1997) (%)				
	Poorest 10%	Poorest 20%	Richest 20%	Richest 10%
	3.5	8.1	46.1	33.5
Inequality Measures				
	Richest 10% to poorest 10%	Richest 20% to poorest 20%		Gini Index
	9.5	5.7		37.8
Priorities in Public spending				
		As per cent of GDP		
Public Expenditure on education*		1985-87	1995-97	
		3.2	3.2	
Public Expenditure on Health		1990	1998	
		0.9	-	
Military Expenditure		1990	1999	
		2.9	2.4	
Total Debt service		2.6	2.3	
Traditional Fuel consumption		1980	1997	
(as % of total energy use)		31.5	20.7	
Electricity consumption per capita		1980	1998	
(kilowatt hours)		130	134	
Commercial Energy Use		1990	1997	**Average annual rate of growth** 1990-97
Per capita (Kg. of oil equivalent		424	497	1.9

* Data extracted from UNDP, *Human Development Report, 2001* and *World Development Report* 2000/2001.

PART A

HUMAN DEVELOPMENT: CONCEPTUAL ISSUES

1

Human Capabilities Approach to the Development of Developing Countries

N. NETTIMI AND N.H. FIDZANI

Human resources are as important as material resources in the process of economic development although it is very difficult to strike the correct balance between the two. It is realised that human resources are a critical factor in developing countries since their basic problems such as poverty, unemployment, malnutrition and undernourishment are due to underutilisation of manpower and lack of adequate development of human resources. If there is proper development of human resources by raising human capabilities at the grass-root level, balanced absorption of human resources among major economic activities can be achieved. This paper attempts to analyse the immediate need for the enhancement and utilisation of human capabilities in developing countries.

Human resources are perhaps the most strategic and crucial determinant of growth, yet its development has not received the required attention. Even though some of the countries may possess abundant physical resources, they are not making rapid economic and social advancement since they have not developed the requisite human capabilities in terms of education, skills and attitudes to mobilise and use their resources effectively. Similarly, some of the states within a country are lagging behind in their development as the available natural resources are not exploited fully, while a few other states with far less natural endowment have achieved remarkable progress. The difference is primarily due to the human factor, the knowledge, skills, attitudes and the initiative of the people. Human resource development would involve upgrading these qualities of the people. Clearly, any country which is unable to develop the skills and knowledge of its people and to utilise them effectively in the national economy will not be able to develop anything else.

SIGNIFICANCE OF HUMAN RESOURCES

The term 'Human Resources' has multiple meanings. Human resources can be thought of as the total knowledge, skills, creative abilities, talents and aptitudes of the work force as well as the values, attitudes and beliefs of the people in general. Human resources according to F.H. Harbison, "are the energies, skills, talent and knowledge of people which are, or which potentially can or should be, applied to the production of goods or the rendering of useful services."[1] Adam Smith included the acquired and useful abilities of human beings in his analysis of capital. Any expenditure incurred by an individual in acquiring these abilities is capital in him. Alfred Marshall considered the investment in human beings as "the most valuable of all capital."[2] A country that cannot develop the skill and knowledge of its people and put them to effective use, will not be able to prosper.[3] Arther Lewis observed, "there are great differences in development between countries which seems to have roughly equal resources, so that it is necessary to enquire into the differences in human behaviour."[4] It is often felt that, though the exploitation of natural resources, availability of physical and financial resources and international aid play prominent role in the growth of modern economies, none of these factors is more significant than efficient and committed manpower.[5]

In fact, the human resources are solely responsible for transforming traditional economies into modern and industrial economies. The difference in the level of economic development of the country is largely a reflection of the differences in the quality of their human resources. The key element in this proposition is that of the values, attitudes, general orientation of the people.[6] The socio-economic transformation in the economies is possible with the development of human resources which in turn leads to sustained economic development.[7] Simon Kuznets established the relationship between economic development and change in the structure of labour force and skills. He pointed out that the process of economic development is with full of positive changes in the nature of skills and knowledge of people.[8] As the production process becomes more complex in the course of time, technical specialisation increases. This technical change is also reflected in the technical skills of the labour force. The nature of economic production is also influenced by the level of development of human resources through visible changes in the structure and the pattern of consumption.[9] McClelland in his empirical study felt that high educational attainment accelerates economic growth since education enhances human resource and it has potential to produce what is needed for the country. Attainment of higher levels of education is the necessary and sufficient condition for alleviation of poverty and further economic progress. Proper and efficient utilisation of knowledge and skills could help to improve economic and social standards of the people.[10] Human resources development should become important in developing countries since it has potential to produce according to the needs of people.[11]

The significance of human capabilities was further analysed by Schultz as "capable people are the key to the abundance of a modern economy. They are the major source of economic growth. Economic growth is neither interesting nor rewarding if we neglect improvement in skills and knowledge of people."[12] For Paul Streeten, "better education, nutrition and health are beneficial in reducing fertility and raising labour productivity, enhancing people's adaptability and capacity for change and creating suitable social and political environment for stable government. Basic education, for example, improves the impact of health services and better health enables children to benefit from education. The effects of investment in sanitation facilities on health status depends on educational levels and these in turn will promote human capabilities to yield a return to the society no less than the return from physical capital.[13]

The qualitative aspect of human capabilities is much more important as it encompasses attributes such as initiative, enterprise, capacity for sustained work, interests and attitudes towards work which have direct correlation with output and productivity. Viewed in this manner, human resource development combines in it the process of promotion of human capabilities with learning experience to the people for professional growth. The qualitative aspects of human capabilities in developing countries leave much to be desired as there has been rapid quantitative addition to the population on the one hand, and widespread poverty, illiteracy, unemployment and underemployment, low standard of living and low per capita productivity on the other.[14]

HUMAN CAPABILITIES APPROACH

Hitherto, economic planners and policy-makers in almost all developing countries were concerned with the physical production of goods and supplying the most essential services and neglected the development of human capabilities. Human development by promoting human capabilities is an important commitment of economic planning as there has been growing awareness of the close inter-relationship between population, human capabilities and development planning. The process of economic development can be seen as a process of expanding the capabilities.[15] Further, creating the right categories of human capabilities at the right places would help to achieve optimum utilisation of resources in the economy.[16] Evidently, in recent years, there has been growing concern in developing countries for long-run improvements in the basic capabilities of people as reflected in the life expectancy, nutritional levels and school enrolment although these trends have been constantly interrupted by their serious economic problems. Inspite of these problems, the ultimate goal of these countries should enhance human capabilities by restructuring their human resource development programmes in order to achieve higher levels of economic development.

The enhancement of human capabilities often requires changing technologies, institutions and social values so that the creativity within human beings can be generated. This in turn, results in economic growth. But growth in national output is not the same as growth in people's capabilities. Of course, the size of the production and human capabilities are inter-linked as increase in the output would generally help to increase the standard of living of people and thereby the capacity to develop a sound body and mind. Taking a long view, there is no doubt that human capabilities will increase life expectancy at birth.

The macro indicators suggest that there has been increase in human capabilities and cumulative knowledge in developing countries in recent years. The stock of knowledge in almost all countries in the world has increased rapidly and also widely disseminated. Primary education has proved important in the quality of education. School enrolments have expanded rapidly. The position of girl children has improved even though less favourable treatment in educating young girls continues to be a problem in developing countries.

The development of human capabilities should become a continuous process since it is an approach to socio-economic development. This approach regards human beings simultaneously as both the means and the ends of social and economic policy. Promotion of human capabilities requires a strategy which can organise the population to make them participate in the country's development. People's participation in development will smoothen the process of human development. Participation in representative community-based organisations can help to identify local priorities, determine which needs are essential and crucial, and the content of development programmes so that they reflect local requirements, aspirations of people clearly. In democratic set-up, education and access to the information on latest developments will help the people to be aware of the issues facing the country and can participate in socio-economic and political process very effectively.

Keeping in view the importance of human resources, development of human capabilities has to be viewed as the obligation of the governments in developing countries. It has to be regarded as a right to which all people are entitled. This right includes the access to the basic education, health and subsistence. There is greater need for raising human development expenditure to enhance the mental capabilities of the people through education and training, health and sanitation programmes. The manpower planning has to be designed suitably for efficient deployment and full utilisation of knowledge and skills of the people. The major task of the government policy should be to transform the existing institutional structure and to give new directions to the human development.

HUMAN CAPABILITIES DEVELOPMENT PROGRAMMES

Keeping in view the rapid growth of population in developing countries, expenditure on improving human capabilities needs to be raised significantly as it has potential to yield a return to society no less than the return from physical capital formation. When all costs and benefits are taken into account, the social rates of return from human development expenditure turn out to be no less than the average rates on fixed capital investments in the economy.[17]

Programmes relating to the development of human capacities have to be successfully implemented in developing countries since the ability of these programmes to increase the production of the economy and the welfare of the people depends on the size of expenditure on education, training and skills formation, health services, water supply and sanitation, food security and nutritional levels of the people. The programme of mid-day meals in schools intended to improve the nutrition levels of school children, often leads to reduced school dropout rates and hence to an increase in the quality of the education system. Similarly, reduced infant mortality rates, combined with greater education for women and greater non-farm employment for women in semi-urban and urban areas, are associated with lower fertility rates and a lower rate of increase of the population. Women, indeed, play a key role in human development not only because they account for half or more of the total population but also because they have major responsibility in most of the economies for ensuring adequate nutrition for the family, caring for the sick and educating the very young before they enter the formal education system.

The programmes of the development of women need to be intensified in developing countries as women have much less access to education and employment and their levels of health and nutrition are often inferior to those of men. The improvement of human capabilities requires, in particular, that the capabilities of women be improved. The attitudes towards women and rigid social and religious customs which prevent the participation of women in all spheres in some of the developing countries must undergo change. It is the responsibility of the governments to prepare and implement the programmes for women development.

Generation of employment opportunities becomes the part of the utilisation of human capabilities which are accumulated in the process of human development in the countries, employment requires and is dependent upon skills present in the manpower. But employment also generates skills in the process of learning by doing and conversely lack of employment leads to wastage of human capabilities and skills. So unemployment results in not only loss of current output but also future output due to unutilisation of human capabilities and skills. The relevant employment generation programmes to be drawn and implemented to absorb manpower with skills and knowledge in different fields of the economy.

More feasible programmes must be chalked out in developing countries as the quality of education is frequently unsatisfactory with rapid expansion of education. More years of schooling in these countries may be due to lack of early environmental stimulation of children and the inadequacy of their health and nutrition. Improving educational quality may be possible by involving teachers, parents and communities and inculcating enthusiasm for educational improvement through an integrated programme. Reliable solutions to most of the health and nutrition problems that afflict millions of people in the developing countries have to be identified. Immediate attention to be paid on increasing expenditure on health care, improved water supply, sanitation and health education, reduction of malnutrition and hunger. These expenditures are justified not only by their positive effects on human capabilities but also by their effects on productivity.

As human capabilities may be hidden and untapped in developing countries due to lack of organisational initiative, they can be utilised properly through greater participation of people at the lower levels. The obstacles may arise from inequalities in political and economic power, wealth and income between different classes of people. Where there are discriminatory practices based on caste, religion, race, gender, etc. and limited facilitates of education and health exist, the participation of individuals in the nation-building and promotion of human capabilities will be difficult to achieve. Perhaps the governments of developing countries must create the atmosphere for the promotion of human capabilities and their utilisation so as to ensure better standard of living and welfare of the people.

Some of the above issues are more amenable to the policy of promotion of human capabilities if the governments in developing countries are sincere in preparing and implementing suitable human development programmes. The benefits of these programmes must be distributed equally for economic and social reasons as any expenditure on promotion of human capabilities has potential to reduce social rigidities, increase social mobility and thereby ameliorate poverty. There is thus a need for change in the structure and composition of human development programmes to ensure fair distribution of their benefits among different sections of the society since most of the benefits of these programmes are reaped disproportionately by the well-to-do people.

The socio-economic structures, institutions and organisations in most of the present developing countries hampering full development of human resources in developing countries have to be transformed. The heavy burden of population can be mitigated and channelled towards economic development only by appropriate education, training and inculcation of proper values and attitudes. The scale of economic change and the speed with which it has to be brought about in developing countries makes it imperative that maximum development and utilisation of human capabilities in all spheres is needed. Widespread poverty, slow rate of economic growth and social backwardness are perhaps a reflection of the deficiencies in human capabilities in these countries.

Certainly, development of human capabilities paves the way for rapid economic development although some of the economically advanced countries are showing signs of social tensions, alienation of workers and distance between man and man and ecological imbalance. But human resource development must be undertaken with all seriousness in all developing countries for the betterment of the individual in the society. The strategy for the development of human resources has to be drawn taking care of all these as quality of the people depends on their strategy and productivity.

Notes and References

1. Harbison, F.H. (1973), *Human Resources as the Wealth of Nations*, Oxford University Press, London.
2. Harbison, F.H. and Myers, C.A. (1964), *Education, Manpower and Economic Growth*, McGraw Hill, New York.
3. Harbison, F.H., *op. cit.*
4. Lewis, A.W. (1965), *The Theory Economic Growth*, George Allen and Unwin, London.
5. Megginson, L.C. (1977), *Personnel and Human Resource Administration*, Richard D. Irwin Inc., Homewood, Illinois.
6. Ginzberg, E. (1980), 'Men and Work' (ed.) Dale S. Each, *Managing People at Work*, McMillan Publishing Company, New York.
7. Levitan, S.A., Mangum, G.L. and Marshall, R. (1972), *Human Resources and Labour Markets*, Harper & Row Publishers, New York.
8. Kuznets, Simon (1967), 'Quantitative Aspects of Economic Growth of Nations', *Economic Development and Cultural Change*, University of Chicago, Jan.-March 1965.
9. Rostow, W.W. (1962), *The Process of Economic Growth*, Oxford University Press, London.
10. McClelland, D.C. (1966), 'Does Education Accelerate Economic·Growth', *Economic Development and Cultural Change*, University of Chicago, April-June 1966.
11. Harbison, F.H. and Myers, C.A., *op. cit.*
12. Schultz, T.W. (1968), *Economic Growth and Agriculture*, Tata McGraw Hill Publishing Company, Bombay.
13. Paul Streeten and others (1981), *First Things First : Meeting Basic Human Needs in the Developing Countries*, Oxford University Press, New York.
14. Kohli, U. and Gautham, V. (1988), *Human Resource Development and Planning Process in India*, Vikas Publishing Company, New Delhi.
15. UNO (1988), *The CDP Report: Human Resource Development*, United Nations Publication, New York.
16. Kohli, U. and Gautham, V., *op. cit.*
17. UNO, *op. cit.*

2

Human Development and Economic Growth: The Experience of India, 1980-96

Ashir Mehta

Ever since the emergence of classical economics and for many years thereafter, economic growth remained a major economic objective of policy-makers and political leaders alike. The basis for such unwavering faith in growth stemmed from the view that the best course to enhance people's standard of living was to provide them with larger and larger quantity of goods and services and that the benefits of such opulence would eventually trickle down to the poorest.

But of late, such misplaced optimism and assumptions have begun to be questioned and criticism of the pursuit of material growth, only in terms of quantity, has become stronger. The development experience of a number of low-income countries mainly in the Sub-Saharan Africa, Latin America, South Asia, Eastern Europe and the CIS, have led economists and policy-makers to search for answers to one critical question. What kind of economic growth? Is growth a meaningful objective? Or is it the overall development of human society? If it is human development, then growth must not be judged by the plentiful production of goods, but rather by how it enriches people's lives and should be the basic purpose of economic growth. It has become pertinent to inquire into the costs and benefits of human development, who benefits and who pays.

The real purpose of economic growth is ignored when policies are merely 'pro-growth'. At the same time, criticisms of the nature of growth and doubting its service to human development does not imply being 'anti-growth'. *The central issue is not quantity but the quality of growth which is equally important.* Human development, thus, becomes the end and economic growth, the means. What is imperative is to place growth in its right perspective and to measure it on a human scale. In terms of quality, 'good' economic growth is growth that promotes human development in all its dimensions—empowerment, cooperation, equity, sustainability and security.

The present paper seeks to explore the association between economic growth and human development particularly with reference to India. Three broad sections are designed. Section I outlines the two-way relationship between economic growth and human development and develops the theoretical basis for subsequent analysis. Section II, the central theme of the paper, tests the strength of the links from growth to human development and from human development to growth for India taking major indicators of growth and human development. The final section concludes with related policy perspectives.

1. THE HUMAN DEVELOPMENT—ECONOMIC GROWTH NEXUS

Countries having similar levels of income and growth can vary quite significantly when it comes to rates of advance in human development. In almost all countries, over the past three decades, inspite of economic upheavals, key indicators of human development—health, education, life expectancy, child mortality, poverty and deprivation—have registered progress. In fact, developing countries have made significant progress in human development than in income.

Nevertheless, in some regions, mentioned in the beginning,

human progress has been slow. The various Human Development Reports (HDR) of the UNDP since 1990 continue to underline the fact that rankings by the human development index (HDI) do not always match income rankings. Countries may either fare high on human development and low on income, or low on the former and high on the latter. These indications refute the implicit assumption that an economy that is growing rapidly will automatically sweep away poverty and deprivation. Such complacency is now shaken.

The record of economic growth and human development over the past 30 years shows that though short-term progress in human development is possible, it is unsustainable without further growth. At the same time, growth would be unsustainable without further advances in human development. It is highly unlikely that a country will manage to follow a course of lopsided development for a long time where economic growth is not matched by advanced in human development or *vice-versa.* Over the longer term, may be a decade, any lopsided development either shifts to rapid rise in both, incomes and human development or falls to slow improvements in both. As the HDR 1996 concludes— ". . . "more economic growth, not less, will generally be needed, as the world enters the 21st century. But more attention must go to the structure and quality of that growth—to ensure that it is diverted to supporting human development, reducing poverty, protecting the environment and ensuring sustainability" (UNDP, 1996). Conversely, a determined effort to expand human capabilities through improved education, health and nutrition will serve to transform the prospects for economic growth particularly in the low-income, low-human development countries. The focus for policy-makers now must lie in strengthening the links between growth and human development. Indeed, fast-growing economies have the potential for strengthening these links.

The new growth theories attribute rise in per capita incomes to the 'endogenous' factor of the behaviour of people responsible for accumulation of factors of production and knowledge. The departure of these endogenous growth theories from the conventional 'neo-classical' theories is the fact that the latter assumed capital and labour productivity to increase from an 'exogenous' factor, technological progress. But the unanswered question of how to accelerate technological progress resulted in the emergence of the new growth theories that brought into analysis the human-capital dimension.

The human capabilities that are the central focus of human development, however, are much broader than purely the productive abilities and human capital that are central to the new growth theories and differ from the concept of human resource development. The basic difference is between the means and the ends. While human resource development considers human beings merely as a means of generating greater output of goods and services, human development, by contrast, identifies people as ends—their well-being as being the ultimate and sole purpose of development. While human resource development judges the value of social investments in health and education mainly by their economic rate of return—private or social—human development, by contrast, treats them valuable in their own right, whether they increase productivity or not.

Two fundamental questions emerge from the human development—economic growth nexus: Is an automatic link between the two implied by their close association? Do the benefits of economic growth trickle down automatically to the poorest and the most vulnerable sections of the society?

Evidence from a number of developing countries, particularly those of East Asia, as also from the rich advanced nations, suggests that in the long-run economic growth and human developmental generally move together and tend to be mutually reinforcing. However, it is highly unlikely that economic growth invariably and automatically translates into human development in the absence of certain critical factors. In the final analysis, countries differ in their "human development efficiency"—their ability to translate income into human development.

From Growth to Human Development

The strength of the links between income growth and advances in human development is crucially dependent on—

Equity

Greater the equality in the distribution of resources, greater the likelihood of income growth being reflected in improvement in the well-being of individuals.

Priority Social Spending

Channelising a higher proportion of public revenue into priority social expenditures—health, education, welfare, housing and universal provision of other basic social services—will most definitely enable governments to influence the state of human development to a great extent.

Increasing Opportunities

Expanding opportunities for earning income will finally translate economic growth into human development improvements which requires employment-generating growth patterns.

From Human Development to Growth

The strength of the reverse links from human development to growth depends on two critical factors, one, on accumulation of human capital through investments in education and skill formation, health and nutrition and research and development. Two, on accessible opportunities for people to contribute to economic development through social, political and economic participation.

While education and skill formation enhance the quality of workers and equip them for the 'absorption' of modern, technology-intensive production processes, better health and nutrition improves longevity and enables them to sustain higher productivity for longer periods of time. Their income-earning life-span increases. At the same time, research and development, combined with an educated manpower, helps timely innovation, adoption, adaptation and absorption of new ideas and knowledge which ultimately serves to increase the quality of output and income.

2. THE EXPERIENCE OF INDIA

India, with its history of misguided economic policies, discouraging attitude towards foreign technology and inward orientation, presents an interesting case study in testing the association between human development and economic growth. For almost four and a half decades since independence, India's growth rate has averaged at around 3.5 to 4 percent per annum—popularised as the 'Hindu Rate of Growth' which does not seem so low when compared to other developing low-income countries of Sub-Saharan Africa. After its shift to liberalisation and structural adjustment in 1991, the growth rate touched almost 7 percent in 1994-95 and was around 5.5 percent per annum on an average for the period 1991-97.

Inspite of a turnaround in economic growth, India's record of human development remains pathetically low. Though its HDI rank of 135 and GDP rank of 141 (UNDP, 1996: 29), betrays a better human development than economic growth, the actual state of affairs in the economy leaves much to be desired. Basic social amenities like potable water, improved health and medical facilities, nutrition, universal primary education, better sanitation, housing, provision of basic infrastructure and poverty reduction continue to remain on the policy agenda without any extensive and committed implementation. At the same time, the educated personnel and many high-level research institutes that India boasts of, have failed to contribute as they should have to rapid productivity growth.

Against this pessimistic scenario, an attempt is made here to examine the strength of the two-way links between human development and economic growth for India. An Ordinary Least Squares technique of multiple regression analysis is carried out using time-series data from 1980 to 1996.

The first part of the analysis involves examining the impact of economic growth, social expenditure and income distribution on the levels of and changes in two human development indicators—life expectancy at birth and child mortality. Four equations are employed specifying the links from growth to human development:

Levels of Human Development

$$\log LE = a + g1 \log RYP + e1SE + i1\ Yd + u1 \qquad ...(1)$$
$$\log CMR = b + g2 \log RYP + e2SE + i2\ Yd + u2 \qquad ...(2)$$

Change (Rate of Advance) in Human Development

$$PRLES = c + g3Y + e3SE + i3Yd + u3 \qquad ...(3)$$

and $$PRLES = d + m \log CMR + g4Y + e4SE + i4Yd + u4 \qquad ...(4)$$

where,

LE = Life Expectancy at birth in years.

PRLES = Percentage reduction in life expectancy shortfall—the difference between a maximum life expectancy of 85 years for advanced countries and that of India for each year.

CMR = Child Mortality Rate—number of infant deaths per thousand.

PRCMR = Percentage reduction in child mortality.

RYP = Real GDP per capita in Rupees.

Y = Rate of growth of real GDP per capita.

SE = Social expenditure expressed as percentage of GDP invested in health and education.

Yd = Income distribution expressed as income share of the poorest 40% of the population.

The second part of the analysis involves examining reverse links by observing the impact of life expectancy, gross domestic investment and income distribution on growth. The equation specifies these reverse links from human development to economic growth:

$$Y = e + p \log RYP + f \log LE + dI + kYd + u5 \qquad ...(5)$$

where,

r = Gross domestic investment as percentage of GDP and all other variables as defined earlier.

The analysis uses one-year lags of the original variables in order to remove any bias of correlation between the two time periods in the equations which may have a clear two-way flow of influence. The results of the regression analysis are presented in Tables 1 and 2.

Equations 1 and 2 regress the log of life expectancy and the log of child mortality respectively on the log of real GDP per capita, social expenditure and income distribution. As observed in Table 1, none of these indicators of growth have had any significant impact on the levels of human development as defined by life expectancy in years and child mortality per thousand

TABLE 1

Links from Economic Growth to Human Development, India: 1980-96

Equation	Dependent Variable	Constant	log RYP	Y	SE	Yd	log CMR	R^2	F
1.	log LE	-8.90	1.79	—	-0.73	0.01	—	0.29	2.03
			(0.47)		(0.85)	(0.58)			
2.	log CMR	3.04	0.28	—	-0.71	0.01	—	0.47	4.50**
			(0.07)		(0.81)	(0.52)			
3.	PRLES	5.04	—	0.03	-1.28	-0.02	—	0.15	0.87
				(0.14)	(1.50)	(0.34)			
4.	PRCMR	-158.36	—	-0.06	6.22	0.13	33.3	0.35	1.90
				(0.22)	(2.05)*		(2.62)**		

Note: Refer end of Table 2.

TABLE 2

Links from Human Development to Economic Growth, India: 1980-96

Equation	*Dependent Variable*	*Constant*	*log RYP*	*log LE*	*I*	*Yd*	R^2	*F*
5.	Y	-76.30	-50.23	114.09	0.16	-0.19	0.64	6.18***
			(3.98)***	(4.47)***	(0.47)	(2.37)**		

Notes: Refer text for definition of variables and end of Section III for data source.
*** = 1% significance; ** = 5% significance; * = 10% significance.

Source: Author's calculations.

though the overall significance of the estimated regression (F-value) in equation 2 shows a significance at the 5% level.

Equation 3 regresses the percentage reduction in life expectancy shortfall from a maximum of 85 years on the per capita real GDP growth, social expenditure on health and education as percent of GDP and income share of the lowest 40% of the population. The results show, once again, that none of these indicators have had any significant impact on the reduction in life expectancy shortfall. The explanatory power (R^2) and the overall significance of the estimated regression (F) is almost negligible.

Equation 4 regresses the percentage reduction in child mortality rate on the same three indicators of growth as in equation 3 plus the log of child mortality indicating the level of child mortality at a point of time. In this case, the percentage of GDP invested in health and education turns out to be positive and significant at the 10 % level. The level of child mortality rate is also a positive and significant factor at the 5% level. This means that while an increase of 1 percentage point in social expenditure on health and education reduces the child mortality rate by 6.2 percentage points, a 1 percent increase in the initial level of child mortality reduces subsequent mortality rates by 33 percentage points. However, the explanatory power of the variables and the overall significance of the regression, though higher than for equation 3, are still at insignificant levels.

All in all, the results in Table 1 point to the existence of weak links from economic growth to human development since neither the levels nor the changes in the human development indicators are significantly influenced by economic growth.

On the other hand, equation 5 in Table 2, tests the links from human development to economic growth by regressing the rate of growth of real GDP per capita on the log of real GDP per capita, log of life expectancy, gross domestic investment as percent of GDP and income distribution. The results show that the impact of human development on economic growth has been positive and significant. A 10% increase in life expectancy, equal to approximately 5 years in 1980 and 6 years in 1991-92, is estimated to raise per capita GDP growth rate by a whopping 114 percent. The life-expectancy variable (log LE) is significant at the 1% level so also is the overall significance (F) of the estimated regression. The implication is that because of poor human development, it takes almost a decade for India to increase its life expectancy by 5 to 6 percent—from 50 years in 1980 to 55 years by 1991-92 or 60 years in 1991-92 to 66 years by 2001-02 by which time the GDP per capita would have more than doubled.

However, though the income distribution variable (Yd) is significant at the 5% level, it shows a negative sign implying a reducing effect of a more equal income distribution on growth. Does this mean that an unequal distribution of income would lead to rapid economic growth? Then what about an egalitarian society? The proposition needs further investigation and deeper analysis since it seems to support the capitalist theory of relatively higher marginal propensity to save of the rich than the poor and therefore higher savings, higher investments and thus faster growth.

In sum, human development was found to be an important determinant of per capita income growth rate—higher life expectancy has led to higher rate of growth of income. Conversely, social expenditure on health and education as proportion of GDP, though one of the most crucial factor, seems to have had only a marginal impact in reducing child mortality rates and none on reducing life expectancy shortfall, implying the need for a much higher proportion of GDP to be invested in these basic social needs.

These empirical results show that while the links from human development to economic growth are relatively strong, the reverse links from growth to human development are glaringly weak. This points to a serious case of lopsided development—poor human development with good economic growth—which is more difficult to overcome putting the country in a less stable position than the good human development—poor economic growth imbalance.

3. CONCLUSION

The relationship between economic growth and human development is complex. Though it exhibits a degree of independence particularly in the short-term, there are longer-term links—human development helping economic growth and economic growth, in turn, facilitating human development. High levels of human development promote economic growth which in turn helps promote human development. Conversely, weak human development results in low growth which undermines the prospect of future human development. However, there is no automatic link between the two. It is only when the links are forged with policy, commitment and determination, they can be mutually reinforcing and growth will effectively and rapidly improve human development. Most vitally important are government actions and policies.

In principle, governments in wealthier countries are more equipped to lend support to human development since greater the GNP, larger the funds available for government expenditure on human development. Of course, actual spending and the manner in which the funds are utilised vary significantly for countries with similar GNP. At the same time, human development alone cannot transform the economy. Even skilled and healthier people need buildings, machinery and above all, infrastructure. But, here too, human development has its stamp since the quality of investment decisions and policy-making is definitely influenced by the capacity and capability of managers, policy-makers and the governments.

In sum, without economic growth, resources to invest in human development are lacking and with poor standards of health, education and nutrition, rapid economic growth becomes extremely difficult.

Policy Perspectives

The Indian experience with human development as exhibited by the results in Tables 1 and 2 brings out a typical case of a serious imbalance in development. While the links from human development to economic growth are somewhat stronger with human development promoting economic growth (equation 5), the reverse links from economic growth to human development are weak. Income growth does not seem to have translated into either higher levels of or greater advances (progress) in human development (equations 1 to 4) . Such a serious nature of lopsided development is not only difficult to correct but overcoming it requires a much longer-term effort and commitment to human development than the imbalance of good human development and poor economic growth which is relatively much easier to deal with.

From a policy perspective, certain general policy initiatives emerge. The first and the foremost direction is towards attaining minimum literacy and universal primary education. With increasing global integration and global competitiveness, a country like India with a labour force that lacks basic skills will be unable to adapt to changing market conditions and rise up to the challenge. Secondly, the quality of growth needs to be enhanced by improving the income distribution and by focusing on employment creation and reducing poverty. Thirdly, resources also need to be reallocated within sectors, away from high-sounding, capital- and technology-intensive development projects and towards human development priorities that benefit the people broadly.

The most critical area in which the government need to work is towards removing the skewness in government expenditure in favour of the rich. Subsidies to higher (tertiary) education often corner away much of public spending at the expense of primary education. Since the students in the former stream are typically from higher-income category, such spending becomes inequitable. Scarce public money is squandered for purposes that should ideally be covered by private money. Such skewness then becomes absurd and economic 'non'-sense when majority of the population is illiterate. It is important that people are insisted upon to pay for their own higher education.

Finally, public finances are drained away more directly through widespread corruption over and above the skewed government priorities. A government machinery that is more transparent, a judiciary that is quick and strong in punishing those with a corrupted history instead of covering them up due to political pressures and a free press that spreads awareness about such political and economic crimes against the public are the ultimate tools for ensuring faith and trust for the government and instilling a sense of respect and security in the minds of people.

Data Source

The data for the empirical exercise carried out in the paper is collected from Economic Survey, Ministry of Finance, Government of India, various years from 1990 to 1997-98 and Basic Statistics Relating to Indian Economy, Centre for Monitoring the Indian Economy. Data on Income distribution was availed of from various Human Development Reports, 1990-97, of the UNDP.

REFERENCES

Allen, Tim and Alan Thomas (eds.) (1992), *Poverty and Development in the 1990s*, The Open University, Oxford University Press, New York.

Barro, Robert J. and Jong-Wha Lee (1994), "Losers and Winners in Economic Growth", in Michael Bruno and Boris Pleskovic (eds.), *Proceedings of the World Bank Annual Conference on Development Economics*, 1993, Washington, D.C., World Bank.

———, and Xavier Sala-i-Martin (1995), *Economic Growth*, New York, McGraw Hill.

Birdsall, Nancy, David Ross and Richard Sabot (1995), "Inequality and Economic Growth Reconsidered: Lessons from East Asia", *World Bank Economic Review*, Vol. 9, No. 3, pp. 477-508.

Chenery, Hollis, and T.N. Srinivasan (1989), *Handbook of Development Economics*, Vol. 1, North Holland, Amsterdam.

Persson, Torsten and Guido Tabellini (1994), "Is Inequality Harmful for Growth?", *American Economic Review*, 84(3), pp. 600-21.

Reddy, K.N. and V. Selvaraju (1994), *Health Care Expenditure by Government of India: 1974-75 to 1990-91*, New Delhi, Seven Hills.

United Nations Development Programme (UNDP), *Human Development Report, 1990 to 1997*, New York, Oxford University Press.

World Bank (1992), World Development Report, 1992, *Development and the Environment*, New York, Oxford University Press.

———, (1993), World Development Report, 1993, *Investing in Health*, New York, Oxford University Press.

———, (1995), *Global Economic Prospects and Developing Countries*, 1995, Washington, D.C., World Bank.

———, (1996), *Global Economic Prospects and Developing Countries*, 1996, Washington, D.C., World Bank.

———, (1997), *Global Economic Prospects and Developing Countries*, 1995, Washington, D.C., World Bank.

3

Human Resources and Economic Development

R.Y. MAHORE

The development of India is unquestionably a problem of effective Human Resource utilisation. The effective human resource utilisation is primarily a matter of improving productivity and income generation. The State governments have also focused on directly improving the nutritional, health and educational status of the poor who are severely disadvantaged in all these areas. Such efforts are intended both to raise standard of living and to develop greater earning capacity.

Human Resources Development (HRD) encompasses elements of both consumption and investment. High levels of consumption of education and health services are generally associated with quite high income levels.

It must be stressed that effective human resource utilisation is an important concomitant of any human development strategy. Effective utilisation ties the consumption of education and health services to higher levels of productivity in both the formal and non-formal sectors. These conditions can occur in any economy with relatively rapidly expanding economic opportunities. In this case the record of the developing countries is uniformly discouraging. Not only is open unemployment a serious problem but the productivity of the labour force is less than the minimum subsistence level of income. HRD in India must therefore be complimentary with more rapid economic growth even if it is viewed as a direct welfare improving activity.

ENVIRONMENT FOR HRD

The structural characteristics of the population play an important role in determining the stock of potential human resources and the composition of demand for services in health and education.

India's population has already crossed the billion mark. As of 2001, the population of the country was 102.7 crore. The population has multiplied 4 times since 1901 and almost tripled since 1941. The sex-ratio has been declining steadily from 1901 to 1991 except for a small rise in the 1981 census.

The proportion of population living in urban areas increased from 17.3 per cent in 1951 'to 26.1 per cent in 1991. The crude birth rate was 30.5 and 23.1, in 1994, in rural and urban areas respectively. The crude death rate was 10.1 and 6.5, in 1994, respectively in rural and urban areas.

The life expectancy at birth was 62.8 and 65.5 years for males and females respectively in urban areas in 1994. In rural areas it was 57.2 and 57.4 years for males and females respectively.

The number of beds per 10,000 population in public hospitals was 1.9, 21.8 and 7.0 for rural, urban and total respectively in 1991.

CURRENT STATUS OF HRD

Several studies have demonstrated significant linkages between parental education and child health in developing countries.

There are high gender disparities in literacy levels in India. The gross primary school enrolment ratio (GPER) is a flow variable. The National Council for Educational Research and Training has so far undertaken six All India surveys which also present GPER's. These estimates are more dependable than the official statistics. The GPER increased from 64.1 per cent in 1978 to 95.9 per cent in 1993. It is expected that due to relatively longer distance to school, the GPER may be lower in rural areas than urban areas. On the whole, in 1986, the All India Rural GPER was about 6 per cent lower than the urban rate.

Retention rates provide a qualitative dimension to education. For India, as a whole, the proportion of children enrolled in the first standard reaching the fifth standard has improved from 38.9 per cent in 1978 to 54.6 per cent in 1993. While this improvement has been from 42 per cent to 57 per cent for boys and 34 per cent to 52 per cent for girls during 1978-93.

It is observed that the number of teachers has not increased commensurately with the number of students enrolling in primary schools over time. The teacher-student ratio which was 38 in 1981-82 increased to 48 in 1994-95. This works out to an annual growth rate of around 2.1 per cent. It appears that in most States there is a need for fresh recruitment of primary teachers, if TSRs are to be maintained around 50.

India spends about 3.5 per cent of her GDP on education. Larger states spend relatively less per capita than smaller states and the growth rate in expenditure has also been less. Out of 3.5 per cent, one-half is spent on primary and elementary education. The per capita expenditure for enrolled population has worked out be Rs. 798 in 1993-94 as compared with Rs. 398 in 1986-87. Since the expenditure figures are at current prices, any growth rate below 10 per cent has been equal to the average rate of inflation means that there is no change in real terms. About 30 per cent of all children aged 6-14 years are never enrolled in schools in India. If governments wish to enforce compulsory primary education, they have to double their investment in primary education from the current level of 1.8 per cent of GDP to 3.5 per cent of GDP.[1]

PROGRAMMES AND PROCESSES FOR HRD

HRD programmes are being considered in the context of Five Year Plans. The objectives in HRD in education and health will provide a direction and standard for judging financial and administrative commitment. The universalisation of primary education is given prominence in the country. During the last few years Govt. of India has adopted several new programmes for HRD.

In terms of overall development strategy for HRD must be considered in the context of competing investment priorities. Given the levels of poverty and relatively slow growth performance, high priority must be given to increase the rate of growth in the agricultural sector which provides the livelihood for two-thirds of the population. Industrial transformation in the country is also necessary. This will involve public investment in infrastructure. An important aspect of this infrastructure is the stock of human capital.

Human resource development is the process of increasing the knowledge, the skills and the capacities of all the people in a society. In economic terms, it could be described as the accumulation of human capital and its effective investment in the development of an economy. In political terms, HRD prepares people for adult participation in political process, particularly as citizens in a democracy. From the social and cultural points of view, the development of human resources helps people to lead fuller and richer lives, less bound by tradition. In short, the processes of HRD unlock the door to modernisation.

Human resources are developed in many ways. The most obvious is by formal education, beginning with primary or first level education, continuing with various forms of secondary education and then higher education including the colleges, universities and higher technical institutions. Second, human resources are also developed 'on-the-job' through systematic or informal training programmes in employing institutions of adult education programmes and through membership in various political, social, religious and cultural groups. Third process is self-development by acquiring additional knowledge, skills or capacities through preparation on their own initiative by taking formal or correspondence courses by reading or by learning from others in informal contacts.

Two other processes of human resource development are improvements in the health of the working population through better medical and public health programmes, and improvements in nutrition, which increases the working capacity of the people, on a man-hour basis as well as over his/her working life.

BASIC INDICATORS

During the last 40 years, several attempts have been made to determine qualitative relationships between indicators of educational development and economic growth. But there had been no comparative analysis of available data for a larger number of countries at different stages of development.

The basic indicators of human resource development were of two types. Those which measure a country's stock of human capital and those which measure the gross or net additions to this stock, or, more precisely the rate of human capital formation over a specified period. The stock of capital indicates the level of human resource development which has been achieved by a country. The rate of human capital formation indicates its rate of improvement.

The indicators of stock of human capital used by Harbison and Myers were levels of educational attainment and the number of persons in relation to the population or labour force, who are in high level occupations. Both these measures were not available because of the lack of reliable census data on educational attainment and occupational distribution and the absence of special manpower surveys.

Harbison and Myers[2] used the following seven measures in their statistical analysis:

1. Number of teachers (first and second levels) per 10,000 population.
2. Engineers and Scientists per 10,000 population.
3. Physicians and dentists per 10,000 population.
4. Pupils enrolled at first level (primary) education as a percentage of the estimated population aged 5 to 14 years inclusive.
5. The adjusted school enrolment ratios for first and second levels combined.
6. Pupils enrolled at second level (secondary) education as a percentage of the estimated population aged 15 to 19 years inclusive, adjusted for length of schooling.
7. Enrolment in third level (higher) education as a percentage of age group 20 to 24 years.

The first three are partial measures of the stock of human

resources and the last four are measures of addition to the stock.

In addition to these they have also used two other indicators of human resource development which are available for as many as 75 countries. These two indicate the orientation of higher education:

1. The percentage of students enrolled in scientific and technical faculties in a recent year.
2. The percentage of students enrolled in faculties of humanities, fine arts and law in the same year.

They have classified 75 countries into 4 groups on the basis of composite human development index, out of which 17 countries are underdeveloped, 21 are partially developed, 21 are semi-advanced and 16 are advanced countries. India's rank is 35th with HDI 35.2 while United States is ranked 1st with HDI 261.5 in the year 1961.

In the recent years the methodology for the construction of HDI has been modified. The quality of data has been improved. The methodology adopted by UNDP has been explained in their report.

COMPUTATION OF HDI[3]

The Human Development Index (HDI) is based on three indicators:

(1) *Longevity*—as measured by life expectancy at birth;
(2) *Educational attainment*—measured by a combination of adult literacy (2/3rd weight) and combined primary, secondary and tertiary enrolment ratios (1/3rd weight); and
(3) *Standard of living*—measured by real per capita GDP (PPP $).

MINIMUM AND MAXIMUM VALUES OF INDICATORS

(1) Life expectancy at birth	25 years and 85 years;
(2) Adult literacy	0% and 100%;
(3) Combined Gross Enrolment Ratio	0% and 100%;

(4) Real GDP per capita (PPP $) $ 100 and $ 40,000.

The HDI measures the average achievement of a country in basic human capabilities. The HDI indicates whether people lead a long and healthy life, are educated and knowledgeable and enjoy a decent standard of living. The HDI examines the average condition of all people in a country: distributional inequalities for various groups of society.

Human development is the end and economic growth the means. The basic objectives of development as enlarging the choices of people primarily by providing them with education, health and employment opportunities.

ESSENTIAL QUALITATIVE COMPONENTS

The human development has three essential qualitative components:

(1) Equality of opportunity for all people in society;
(2) sustainability of such opportunities from one generation to the next; and
(3) empowerment of people so that they participate in and benefit from development processes.

As a first step towards capturing the combined effect of the above three components, UNDP has developed and advocated a number of indices, the primary one being the Human Development Index (HDI). This index attempts to measure a country's or a region's achievements in the enhancement of human capabilities.

India ranks 138 out of 175 countries. The estimate of HDI for India works out to 0.446. State-wise HDI value is also computed. The highest HDI value is 0.628 for Kerala which is equivalent to 108th rank. China's rank is 108th in the world. The lowest HDI value (0.341) was observed in Bihar which is equivalent to 154th rank, Nepal's rank is 154. The state with an HDI score of more than 0.50 are Haryana, Himachal Pradesh, Kerala, Maharashtra, Punjab and Tamilnadu. The states having score less than 0.40 are Assam, Orissa, Bihar, Madhya Pradesh, Rajasthan and Uttar Pradesh.

HUMAN POVERTY INDEX (HPI)

The HPI concentrates on deprivation in three essential elements of human life already reflected in HDI—longevity, knowledge and a decent standard of living. The first deprivation relates to survival—the vulnerability to death at a relatively early age. The second relates to the knowledge—being excluded from the world of reading and communication. The third relates to a decent standard of living in terms of overall economic provisioning.

The deprivation in longevity is represented by the percentage of people not expected to survive to age 40 (P1), and the deprivation in knowledge by the percentage of adults who are illiterate (P2). The deprivation in a decent living standard in terms of overall economic provisioning is represented by a composite (P3) of three variables—the percentage of people without access to safe water (P31), the percentage of people without access to health services (P32) and the percentage of moderately and severely underweight children under five (P33).

The estimate of HPI for India is 0.3669.

GENDER-RELATED HEALTH INDEX (GHI)

The HDI is the measure of overall levels of human development in society and does not measure the Gender Disparities. The measure used for this is the Gender-related health Index (GHI). The Gender-related Health Index is a measure of the gender inequalities in a state, in selected health and education parameters. On the mortality side, life expectancy at birth (e0) and the infant mortality rate (IMR) have been selected as indicators; and in the sphere of social well-being, educational attainment has been included.

The index compares the disparity between the male and female values of e0, IMR and educational attainment. The method of computation of index is identical to the one used by the UNDP in their 1996 HDR for construction of GDI.

While the GDI uses the above three parameters for the two sexes, the last one has become very difficult to compute in the Indian situation because a large number of women in the rural areas are engaged in the agricultural sector or in the family enterprises without any monetary income. Ultimately, their contribution to the economy has been grossly underestimated. Therefore, income-based index has been omitted and instead of it we have used educational attainment as a proxy for positive health as the third parameter and called the Gender-related Health Index.

The GDI value for the year 1993 was 0.4987 in India with 118th rank in the world. The value was highest for Kerala (0.8812) and the lowest for Orissa (0.3411).

ECONOMIC DEVELOPMENT AND HRD

The development of human resources through directing more resources to health, education, nutrition and other needs of the poor can reduce poverty. Such a strategy might entail increasing non-development consumption expenditure and reducing levels of investment and economic growth. Thus, there might be some sort of trade-off between developing human resources and economic development. On the other hand, these expenditures could be viewed as an investment in human capital having positive returns. Investing in human capital could then have a positive or negative effect on growth depending whether the returns from human capital are greater or lesser than returns from other non-human capital investment.

There have been many attempts to assess the role of human capital in the growth process including the 'growth accounting' approach utilised by Denison and others, and the measurement of social and private returns from investments in education. Both these approaches have tended to indicate positive returns from investments in human capital, but both have been criticised on a variety of theoretical and empirical grounds.

Wheeler's approach allows for the fact that human resource development is both a result of and a cause of economic development and that there will be interactions between the two over time. By using simultaneous equations technique, Wheeler is better able to separate out the cause and effect relationship. He finds that human resource development contributes indirectly by increasing manufactured export goods and the investment rate and lowering the birth rate.

The correct programme of human resource investments will depend on individual country's situation and will have to consider the opportunity cost of capital and the current state of human resources. Nevertheless, it does seem clear that investing in people can be an efficient way of both eliminating poverty and increasing the growth rate of output for many developing countries.

A basic needs approach would also improve the quality of the labour force through the effects of improved health and education. Thus, the emphasis has shifted away from meeting 'needs' towards improving the productivity of human resources, by improving human capital. This revival of interest in human capital approach was pioneered by Schultz and others.

An increase in human resources activities could have little or no direct effect on the level of investments and growth, assuming this, redirection occurs without a deleterious effect on incentives to work. The issue is further complicated by the fact that some human resources activities will be classified as investment (schools, hospital construction) while others will be classified as consumption (teachers' salaries, food subsidies).

Analysis of the role of human resources or human capital in the growth has a long history. The growth accounting approach, for instance, attempts to measure changes in total factor productivity by developing an index of output (generally GNP) and an index of factor inputs. This approach traces its origin to work done by Stigler (1947), Schumacher (1952) and Kendrick (1961), among others, but the definitive work remains that of Dennison (1967, 1974, 1979). Dennison's latest estimates show that 60% of the growth in GNP (1929-1973) in the United States can be attributed to the growth of traditional factors, mainly capital and labour inputs. The remaining growth is a result of economies of scale, improvements in resource allocation and other factors, plus a large residual which is labelled as 'advances in knowledge'.

Education is considered by Dennison to be a factor input and alone accounts for 14% of the growth in GNP during the 1929-1973 period. If education were to be combined with the residual "advances in knowledge", then the human capital component would be about 38%.

The World Development Report (1980) outlines three distinct grounds for the claims of education in scares resources. The first is its direct enrichment of the lives of those who obtain it. The second is its contribution to improvements in nutritional levels and child health and lower fertility. The third is its contribution in incomes and in some but not all circumstances, the greater equality of income.

Herbert Simon often stated that the greatest resource we have is in human heads. Simon Kuznets has laid before us the evidence of labour's dramatically increased share in the production of the GNP with progression from poverty to affluence. T.W. Schultz has led us into increasingly dynamic perceptions of how education may affect productivity in a context of change.[4]

All three of these Nobel laureates, different as their views may be in other respects, have turned a spotlight on the human factor as the generator and implementor of a new knowledge that can be foundation of growth and the explanation of high marginal productivities of both physical and human capital, even as both these forms of capital have increased.

Accordingly to Swami Vivekanand, the end of all education, all training should be man-making. The end and aim of all training is to make the man grow. P.R. Gopinathan Nair opined that by the beginning of 1960's, however, the emphasis shifted from material capital to human capital.[5]

(1) Emphasis on investment in the education, health and skills of people can enable them to participate in growth and to share its benefits, principally through remunerative employment. Such type of investment strategy is in favour of many industrial and developing countries today.

(2) More equitable distribution of income and assets is critical for a close link between economic growth and human development.

(3) Some countries have significantly improved human development through well-structured social expenditures by governments.

(4) Empowering people particularly women is a sure way to link growth and human development.

If people will exercise their choices in the political, social and economic spheres, then there would be a bright prospect for and growth will be strong, democratic, participatory and durable.

ECONOMIC ANALYSIS OF INVESTMENT IN HUMAN BEINGS

Economists have long been aware of the importance of human resource development. Adam Smith, for example, stressed the importance of education at various points in the *Wealth of Nations* and he specifically included the 'acquired' and useful abilities of all the inhabitants or members of society in his concept of 'fixed capital'. Alfred Marshall emphasised the importance of education 'as a national investment' and in his view the most valuable of all capital is that invested in human beings.

Few Economists have been concerned specifically with the relationship of better health and nutrition of the labour force to productivity and economic growth. But the rediscovery of the importance of human resources by Schultz and others has led to more recent efforts to incorporate investment in education into the mainstream of economic analysis.

Human Capital

The first attempt to estimate the monetary value of an entire population was made by Mercantalist writer Sir William Petty in 1691. He used the notion of human capital in attempts to demonstrate the power of England, the economic effect of migration, the value of human life destroyed in war and the monetary loss to a nation owning to deaths.

McCulloch[6] asserted that human beings are the most important of all machines and every investment in their training and education is an "acquisition of the utmost consequence".

Economic Value of Education

Economists have suggested different approaches with regard to the economic value of education in the process of economic development.[7]

(1) Simple Correlation Approach

The approach consists of correlating some overall index of educational activity with some index of the level of economic activity. Svennilson, Edding and Elvin have correlated enrolment ratios and GNP per capita and have found a positive relationship.[8]

(2) The Residual Approach

Kendrick, Solow, Dennison, Mincer and others[9] have used this approach. The approach tries to separate out the share of education in the total increase of output.

(3) Rate of Return Approach

For the calculation of rate of return, we need the cost as well as the yield from education. A number of attempts have been made to estimate the rates of return in India. The first study on this in the Indian context was undertaken by Herberger. He suggested that the economic rate of return to investment in physical capital is higher than economic rate of return to investment in secondary and higher education. This does not mean that investment in education is bad; because it has other advantages than purely economic advantages. The other Indian studies conducted by Miss Ishrat Z. Hussain (1967),[10] Kothari, V.N. (1967),[11] Nalla Gounden (1967),[12] Blaug *et al.* (1969),[13] Pandit H.N. (1972)[14] and Jandhyalaya B.G. Tilak (1980).[15] Almost all the studies unanimously concluded that investment in human beings in India is not as profitable as investment in physical capital from social point of view.

The scholars have found high rates of return from investment in education, particularly primary education in developing countries. The private rates of return for primary education ranges from 7.0% to 25.0%, this is because of the lower rate of earning foregone during the period of primary education.

(4) Forecasting Manpower Needs Approach

Tingberger, Correa, Bos Parnes and Harbison developed this approach. In this approach the attempt is to estimate the future needs of the economy for persons with various kinds of training.[16]

H. Venkateswara Rao[17] has emphasised the importance of economic aspects of education and highlighted a number of approaches for including investment in education.

Kothari, V.N. (1978)[18] discusses various approaches like manpower approach, human capital approach and screening approach for evaluating the role of education in economic development.

EDUCATION AND ECONOMIC GROWTH

T.W. Schultz[19] has given three ratios in relation to education and economic growth:

(1) *Education-labour ratio* to show the amount of human effort going into education relative to the total labour force.
(2) *Education-income ratio* which relates the resources entering into education to consumer income.
(3) *Education-investment ratio* to show the relation between the resources entering into education and the resources going into reproducible physical capital.

V.N. Kothari (1966)[20] mentions Dennison's work about the share of education in the growth rate. Education accelerates human resource development.

Education and development are not two different things but two sides of the same coin. J.P. Naik observed that education should lead to development and development should create the motivation for more education as well as provide tools for it.[21]

Education can help the society to overcome its ills and problems. It has to be made application-*cum*-life oriented and has to be taken to the door-steps of the villages without delay.

According to Rabindranath Tagore,[22] the real ideals of education are not based on mere economic progress. The main purpose behind the system of national movement was to integrate the different currents of Indian culture on the basis of their inherent unity.

M.K. Gandhi[23] was a practical educationists of modern India. He gave a wider meaning to education. His concept of education stands for the balanced and harmonious development of all the aspects of human personality.

In short, economic growth is necessary but not sufficient for human development. Commitment and political will are the constraints of economic growth and human development simultaneously. All countries are facing the problem of integration between economic growth and human development.

Out of 175 countries for which the HDI was calculated, 64 are in the high HDI category (0.800 and above), 66 in the medium HDI category (0.500 to 0.799) and 45 in the lowest HDI category (less than 0.500). The share of population in these categories was 23%, 45% and 32% respectively. The highest HDI value was in Canada (0.960) and the lowest in Sierra Leone (0.176) and the World average (0.764).

The HDI shows the distance a country has to travel to reach the maximum possible value 1.00 and also allows inter-country comparisons. The difference between the maximum possible value of HDI and the HDI value achieved by a country shows the country's shortfall in HDI. A challenge for every country is to find ways to reduce this shortfall.

Notes and References

1. U.N.F.P.A. (1997), *India towards Population and Development Goals*, Oxford University Press, New Delhi.
2. Harbison F. and Myers C. (1970), *Education, Manpower and Economic Growth*, Oxford and IBH Publishing House Co., Calcutta.
3. U.N.D.P. (1995), *Human Development Report*, Oxford University Press, New York.
4. I.B.R.D. (1980), *Education and Income*, Part I, the World Bank, Washington, D.C., U.S.A.
5. Nair, G.R.R. (1981), *Primary Education, Population Growth and Socio-economic Change*, Allied Publishers, New Delhi.
6. Kiker, B.F. (1967), "The Concept of Human Capital in the History of Economic Thought", *The Indian Economic Journal*, Vol. X, Jan.-March.
7. Bowen, W.G., (1969), "Assessing Economic Contribution of Education: An Appraisal of Alternative Approach," M. Blaug (ed.), *Economics of Education*, I, Penguin.
8. Blaug, M., *op. cit.*
9. Bowen, W.G., *op. cit.*
10. Hussain, I.Z., (1967), "Returns to Education in India: An Estimate", Singh, B. (ed.), *Education as Investment*, Meenakshi Prakashan.
11. Kothari, V.N. (1967), "Returns to Education in India", Singh, B. (ed.), *ibid.*
12. Datta, R.C., (1981), *Education and Income Distribution*, Unpublished Ph.D. thesis, University of Bombay.
13. Blaug, *et. al.* (1969), *The Causes of Graduate Unemployment in India*, Allen Lane, The Penguin Press.
14. Datta, R.C., *op. cit.*

15. Tilak, J.B.G. (1983), "Economic Returns to Investment in Education—Regional Level Estimates for Andhra Pradesh", *Anvesak Journal of Sardar Patel Institute of Economic and Social Research*, Ahmedabad, June, Vol. XIII.
16. Bowen, W.G., *op. cit.*
17. Rao, V.H. (1969), "Educational Costs: Concepts and Issues", Pandit, H.N. (Ed.), N.C.E.R.T., New Delhi.
18. Kothari, V.N. (1979), "Employment Dualism and Educational Policy in India", *Manpower Journal*, Vol. XIV, July-Sept.
19. Schultz, T.W. (1971), *Education and Economic Growth*, Bowman, M.J., *et. al.* (Eds.).
20. Kothari, V.N. (1966), "Investment in Human Resources," Rapporteur's Report, *Indian Economic Journal.*
21. Joshi, R.N. (1979), *Education Elsewhere and Here: A Key to Prosperity*, Bharatiya Vidya Bhavan, Bombay.
22. Reddy, V.N.K. (1979), *Men, Education and Values*, B.I. Publishing Corporation, New Delhi.
23. Mangal, S.K. (1984), *The Ground Work of Education*, Arya Book Depot, New Delhi.

4

Human Development: Concepts and International Standards

N.M.P. Verma

The objectives of the present paper are to examine the concepts of human development, to analyse the technique of measurement of human development indices (HDI) and to bring forth the degree of hiatus in different regions of the world and also in different states of India.

CONCEPTUAL ISSUES

The concept of human underdevelopment is related to several types of backwardness and poverty which create hurdles and hindrances for leading a tolerable level of life. It is not just poverty in income or calorie intake for a person but it is an overall poverty in different fields like low income, sub-standard consumption, illiteracy, unhygienic living, improper housing, malnutrition malnourishment, health hazards and poor educational attainments. Thus, unlike poverty human underdevelopment is a broader term and incorporates several dimensions of poverty. "Poverty Line" is also a very lucid and frequently used term. It is normally related to either food poverty or income poverty. The reflections of human underdevelopment is seen through the indices of indicators of human development. According to UNDP criteria (1997) there are several indicators of human development such as life expectancy at birth, educational attainments, real GDP per capita, enrolment ratio, gender-related variables and empowerment of women, share of women in earned income and access to minimum needs like calorie, safe water, child development, health, communication, security, energy, environment and several other related variables.

Thus, human development index attempts to estimate the average achievements in mainly three fundamental dimensions in any economy—longevity, knowledge and per capita income. A composite index that is GDI, therefore, contains three variables: life expectancy at birth, combined educational attainments and real GDP per capita. The human poverty index measures deprivation in basic human development in the same dimensions as HDI. However, the variables used are the percentage of people expected to die before age 40, the percentage of adults who are illiterate, and overall economic provisioning in terms of the percentage of people without access to health service, safe water and the percentage of underweight children under five. Although there is no limit of wants, however, the mechanism of widening people's choices and the level of well-being they achieve are at the core of the notion of human development. Such choices may not be infinite or dynamic. But regardless of the level of development, the three essential choices for people are to lead a long and healthy life, to acquire knowledge and to have access to resources needed for a decent standard of living. Human development does not end there. Income clearly is only one important option that people would like to have. But it is not the sum total of their lives. Income is also a means, the human development the end. 'Poverty line' is based on consumption. Different countries have fixed different norms for defining it. For instance, a poverty line of $ 2 a day is suggested for Latin America and the Carribean, for Eastern Europe the figure is $ 4 and in U.S. it is $ 14.50 (1985). Developing countries have generally used food poverty method for defining national poverty lines. Such poverty lines simply indicate the insufficiency of economic resources to meet basic minimum needs in food. Food poverty is measured through: (a) cost of basic needs method, (b) food energy method, and (c) food share method. Thus, poverty is related to income poverty mainly whereas human development looks at non-income indicators like life expectancy at birth and education, some of the developing nations including India have adopted various economic reforms for human development. Many studies have shown that social sector expenditure declined considerably during the first two years of reform and this could affect human development indicators.

COMPUTATION OF HDI

As mentioned above HDI is an average of three indices, namely, life expectancy index, educational attainment index and an adjusted real GDP per capita (PPP $) index.

In order to construct a specific index as per UNDP criteria, fixed minimum and maximum values have been established for each of these three indicators:

Indicators	*Minimum value*	*Maximum value*
Life expectancy at birth	25years	85 years
Adult literacy	0%	100%
Real GDP per capita (PPP $)	100	40,000

The basic formula for construction of a specific index is as follows:

$$\text{Specific Index} = \frac{\text{Actual Xi value} - \text{Minimum Xi value}}{\text{Maximum Xi value} - \text{Minimum Xi value}}$$

However, in order to construct Income Index Atkinson's formula for utility of income is helpful. In this case the mean value of world income is taken as threshold level (y*) and any income above this level is discounted using the following formulation:

$$W(y) = y^* \text{ for } 0 < y < y^*$$

$$= y^* + 2[(y-y^*)]^{1/2} \text{ for } y^* \leq y \leq 2y^*$$

$$= y^* + 2y^{*1/2} + 3[(y-2y)]^{1/2} \text{ for } 2y^* \leq y \leq 3y^*$$

or $y = y^* + 2y^{*1/2} + 3[(y-2y^*)]^{1/3} + n[|1-(n-1)y^*|]^{1/n}$ for $(n-1)y^* < y < ny^*$

for $(n-1)y^* \leq y \leq ny^*$

In order to estimate the discounted value of say \$ 40,000 (PPP \$), the following form of Atkinson's formula is used:

$$W'(y) = y^* + 2(y^*)^{1/2} + 3(y^*)^{1/3} + 4(y^*)^{1/4} + 5(y^*)^{1/5} + 6(y^*)^{1/6} + 7(y^*)^{1/7} + 8\{40000-7y^*)\}^{1/8}$$

This is because of the fact that \$ 40,000 falls in the range of $7y^*$ and $8y^*$. If the average income of the world is, say, \$ 5815 (PPP \$) in 1994, then the discounted value of the maximum income of \$ 40,000 (PPP \$) is \$ 6154. This way HDI will be equal to indices of:

$$\frac{\text{Life Expectancy} + \text{Education} + \text{Income}}{3}$$

For computation of Gender-related Development Index (GDI), same variables are used. But the GDI adjusts the average achievement of each country in life expectancy, educational attainment and income in accordance with the disparity in achievement between women and men. These indices are added together with equal weights to derive the final GDI value.

In the case of India there are a few rural studies on human development The data relating to human development are published in Economic Survey. In addition, National Council of Applied Economic Research has also estimated for rural India. The indicators of human development in Economic Survey are life expectancy at birth, literacy percentage of male and female, infant mortality rate, death rate and birth rate. In the study of NCAER capability poverty measures are given for different states of India. Even Capability Poverty Measures (CPM) are grouped in two categories. First, CPM deals with 'Stunting' concept and second, CPM deals with 'Wasting' concept. In UNDP criteria also two types of approaches have been taken. One approach is based on three key indicators of human development where life expectancy at birth, educational attainment and per capita GDP have been taken. In the second approach several other indicators of human development have been taken like safe drinking water, enrolment, adult literacy, health services, per capita daily calorie supply, television per 100 people and per capita GNP. But, by and large, there is hardly any important difference in methodology.

HDI: CROSS COUNTRIES COMPARISON

In this section global regional scenario of human development has been discussed in the light of the published data. These data provide a static picture because time series analysis have not been collected here. The data has been published in reports prepared by United Nations Development Programme, National Council of Applied Economic Research and Planning Commission, Govt. of India.

Human Development Index (HDI) has been given below in different tables. Table 1 shows HDI at the global level. Data have been categorised for high, medium and low human development countries, industrial countries, developing countries, least developed countries and Sub-Saharan Africa. Indices are for life expectancy at birth, educational attainment combined and Gross Domestic Product. In addition, aggregative index for these three variables have also been given. It is clear from Table 1 that the diversities are very high in HDI across groups of countries. If the HDI of lowest and highest countries are compared, the range is very wide in respect of all the three indices and more wide in the case of GDP. Countries having highest HDI are basically industrialised countries. Lowest indices of HDI are observed basically in Sub-Saharan African countries and least developed countries. The position of developing countries seems to be slightly better than Sub-Saharan African countries. UNDP data also shows the country-wise indices for selected countries and respective ranks are also given. As per the index rank of aggregated HDI, Canada ranks at the top, USA is at the 4th position, U.K. is on the 15th position. South Asian countries such as China having 108th rank, India having 138th rank, Bangladesh having 144th rank which is followed by Nepal having 154th rank.

The difference in HDI values is almost three times between Canada having first rank and Nepal having 154th rank. The position of India also seems pitiable. Gender-related development index is given in Table 2, shows contrast situation between male and female in industrial countries and least developed/developing countries. Barring the case of life expectancy where females are better placed than males, in both the groups of countries the situation is reverse in the case of adult literacy and earned income share. Female empowerment situation is also very grave in developing and least developed countries. Table 4 shows per capita GDP (1987 US$). According to this data industrial countries are far ahead than least developed countries and developing countries during 1960-94. The overall profile of human development seems very grave in Sub-Saharan Africa, least developed countries and developing countries including South Asia. If a time series analysis is done for showing temporal situation as shown in Table 6, then it may be concluded that human development has been very low especially in Sub-Saharan Africa/South Asian in comparison to industrial nations. In India, human development is highest in Kerala which is followed by Punjab. The position is very critical in U.P., Bihar, Orissa, and West Bengal.

CONCLUSION

To conclude, human development is a broader term. It conveys planning for a tolerable life for human beings. Poverty is a very micro term which is either confined to income poverty or calorie poverty. UNDP has adopted criteria for computation of human development index which was supported by several economists. Human development indices show critical scenario for developing countries, least developed countries, Sub-Saharan African countries, South Asian countries and a few other countries of South-east Asia. In India, human development is satisfactory in Kerala followed by Punjab. But the situation is worse in bigger states like U.P., Bihar, Orissa, West Bengal and a few other states. Therefore, perspective planning in the light of population growth is essential for faster human development.

REFERENCES

Anand, Sudhir and Amartya K. Sen (1993), *Human Development Index: Methodology and Measurement*, Occasional Paper 12, UNDP, New York.

Atkinson, Anthony B. (1970), "On the Measurement of Inequality", *Journal of Economic Theory*, 2(3): 244-63.

Block, Thorsten, (1995), "Human Development and Economic Growth in

Germany," UNDP, New York.

Desai, Meghnad, J. (1991), "Human Development: Concepts and Measurement", *European Economic Review*, 35: 350-57.

Government of India (1995-96), *Economical Survey*, New Delhi.

Haq, Mahbubul (1995), *Reflections on Human Development*, OUP, Karachi.

Human Development Centre (1997), *Human Development in South Asia*, OUP, Karachi.

NCAER (1998), *India: Human Development Report*, New Delhi.

UNDP (1997), *Human Development Report*, OUP.

World Bank (1990), *World Development Report*, OUP.

Regional Aggregates of Human Development Indicators

TABLE 1

Human Development Index

	Sub-Saharan Africa	*Arab States*	*South Asia*	*East Asia*	*East Asia excl. China*	*South East Asia and Pacific*	*Latin America and the Caribbean*	*Least developed countries*	*All developing countries*	*Eastern Europe and CIS*	*Industrial countries*	*World*
Life Expectancy (years)	50.0	62.9	61.4	69.0	71.5	64.3	69.0	50.4	61.8	68.1	74.1	63.2
Adult literacy rate	55.9	54.7	49.7	81.8	96.2	86.3	86.2	48.1	69.7	98.1	98.5	77.1
Combined 1st, 2nd and 3rd level gross enrolment ratio	42	58	53	59	78	61	69	36	56	75	83	60
Real GDP per capita (PPP$)	1,377	4,450	1,686	3,001	9,429	3,638	5,873	965	2,904	4,203	15,986	5,798
Human development index	0.380	0.636	0.459	0.652	0.881	0.672	0.829	0.336	0.576	0.760	0.911	0.764

TABLE 2

Gender-related Development Index

	Sub-Saharan Africa	*Arab States*	*South Asia*	*East Asia*	*East Asia excl. China*	*South East Asia and Pacific*	*Latin America and the Caribbean*	*Least developed countries*	*All developing countries*	*Eastern Europe and CIS*	*Industrial countries*	*World*
Life expectancy (years)												
Female	51.5	64.8	61.2	71.3	74.9	66.5	72.1	51.2	63.5.	72.9	77.8	65.4
Male	48.5	62.0	60.7	66.9	68.0	62.7	65.9	49.1	60.6	63.2	70.2	61.8
Adult literacy rate												
Female	44.4	40.6	34.3	72.0	95.1	82.7	84.9	34.7	60.3	98.1	98.5	70.8
Male	64.3	66.9	61.6	90.0	98.2	91.6	87.3	56.6	78.4	98.1	98.5	83.5
Combined primary, secondary and tertiary gross enrolment ratio												
Female	38.4	53.7	43.2	55.9	76.4	58.9	68.6	30.7	51.6	76.5	83.9	57.1
Male	46.6	63.3	59.6	61.9	82.2	61.8	69.0	40.0	60.3	73.3	81.5	63.9
Earned income share												
Female	35.5	21.7	253	37.7	28.1	349	26.9	33.1	31.7	40.2	37.7	33.3
Male	64.6	78.9	74.8	62.3	72.0	65.2	73.1	67.2	68.4	59.9	62.4	66.9
Gender-related development index	0.374	0.537	0.412	0.626	0.823	0.641	0.729	0.323	0.555	0.749	0.856	0.637

TABLE 3

Gender Empowerment Measure (% Women)

	Sub-Saharan Africa	*Arab States*	*South Asia*	*East Asia*	*East Asia excl. China*	*South East Asia and Pacific*	*Latin America and the Caribbean*	*Least developed countries*	*All developing countries*	*Eastern Europe and CIS*	*Industrial countries*	*World*
Seats held in parliament	..	..	6.9	20.3	..	11.1	9.6	..	12.7	..	13.6	12.9
Administrators and managers	..	..	2.9	11.3	..	14.7	20.0	..	10.0	..	27.4	14.1
Professional and technical workers	..	..	21.3	45.1	..	46.5	49.5	..	36.7	..	47.8	39.3
Earned income share	..	..	30	40	..	30	40	..	30	..	40	40
Gender empowerment measure	..	..	0.231	0.474	..	0.399	0.418	..	0.367	..	0.586	0.418

TABLE 4

Trends in Human Development and Per Capita Income

	Sub-Saharan Africa	*Arab States*	*South Asia*	*East Asia*	*East Asia excl. China*	*South East Asia and Pacific*	*Latin America and the Caribbean*	*Least developed countries*	*All developing countries*	*Eastern Europe and CIS*	*Industrial countries*	*World*
GDP per capita (1987, US$)												
1960	495	989	193	98	..	282	1,122	247	330	658	6,448	2,049
1970	598	1.893	229	135	..	370	1,435	259	461	1,108	9,546	2,756
1980	634	2.757	363	230	2.379	575	1,965	252	671	1,701	11,562	3,205
1990	514	1,740	462	455	4,674	756	1,793	242	723	1,954	14,119	3,470
1994	507	1,595	514	659	5.759	935	1,931	254	823	1,370	14,473	3,402

TABLE 5

Profile of Human Development

	Sub-Saharan Africa	*Arab States*	*South Asia*	*East Asia*	*East Asia excl. China*	*South East Asia and Pacific*	*Latin America and the Caribbean*	*Least developed countries*	*All developing countries*	*Eastern Europe and CIS*	*Industrial countries*	*World*
Life expectancy (years)	50.0	629	61.4	690	71 5	64.3	69.0	50.4	61.8	68.1	74.1	63.2
Access to health services (%)	53	87	78	88	..	85	..	49	80	..	..	..
Access to safe water (%)	51	76	82	68	93	66	75	57	71	..	..	..
Access to sanitation (%)	45	52	35	27	..	56	61	36	39	..	..	..
Daily calorie supply per capita	2.096	2,874	2,367	2,751	3,107	2,541	2,756	2,054	2.553	..	..	..
Adult literacy rate	56.2	55.7	49.7	81.6	96.7	863	862	48.4	69.7	..	..	..
Combined 1st and 2nd level gross enrolment ratio	53	73	67	88	95	78	89	46	74	91	98	78
Daily newspapers (copies per 100)	1.1	4.5	..	4.3	36.4	3.6	7.3	0.8	4.0	19.5	26.4	9.8
Televisions (per 100)	3	12	5	23	26	14	21	2	14	30	50	22
Real GDP per capita (PPP$)	1,373	4,450	1,686	3,001	9,429	3,638	5,873	951	2,908	4,203	15,986	5,806
GNP per capita (US$)	539	1,978	325	904	9,425	1,279	3,188	210	1,053	2,125	17,221	4,797

TABLE 6

Trends in Human Development

	Sub-Saharan Africa	*Arab States*	*South Asia*	*East Asia*	*East Asia excl. China*	*South East Asia and Pacific*	*Latin America and the Caribbean*	*Least developed countries*	*All developing countries*	*Eastern Europe and CIS*	*Industrial countries*	*World*
Life expectancy (years)												
1960	39.9	45.5	43.9	47.5	54.5	45.3	55.3	39.1	46.0	66.6	68.6	50.2
1994	49.9	63.0	61.3	69.0	71.5	64.3	69.0	50.6	62.1	68.0	73.8	63.7
Infant moratality rate												
1960	166	166	163	146	84	127	107	170	149	55	39	129
1994	97	67	73	41	17	50	38	103	64	25	14	58
Access to safe water (%)												
1975-80	24	71	30	..	70	15	60	..	41	..	..	..
1990-96	42	83	76	..	94	67	75	..	69	..	..	..
Underweight children under five (%)												
1975	31	20	69	26	..	46	18	..	41	..	..	..
1990-96	32	14	50	16	..	35	11	..	32	..	..	..
Adult literacy rate												
1970	27	30	32	..	..	65	72	..	43	..	..	..
1994	56	57	49	..	..	87	86	..	64			

Gross enrolment ratio, all levels (age 6-23)												
1980	39	47	37	51	65	51	59	32	46	..	..	..
1994	39	58	53	59	79	61	70	36	56	..	..	..
Real GDP per capita (PPP$)												
1960	990	..	698	729	..	732	2,137	561	915	..	..	..
1994	1,460	..	1,687	2,983	..	4,149	5,933	974	2,923	..	..	..

Source: *Human Development Report, 1997*, UNDP.

TABLE 7

Selected Indicators of Human Development for Major States

States	*Life Expectancy 1988-92*	*Literacy (1991, %)*		*IMR Per 1000 births*	*Death Rate*	*Birth Rate*
		Male	*Female*			
Andhra Pradesh	60.2	55.13	32.72	63	83	23.7
Assam	54.1	61.87	43.03	77	9.1	30.7
Bihar	57.5	52.49	22.89	66	10.4	32.5
Gujarat	59.5	73.13	48.64	64	8.7	27.1
Haryana	62.5	69.1	40.47	67	7.8	30.5
Karnataka	62.2	67.26	44.34	65	8.1	24.9
Kerala	71.3	93.62	86.17	16	6	17.3
Madhya Pradesh	53.4	58.42	28.85	98	11.5	32.8
Maharashtra	63.4	76.56	52.32	54	7.4	24.9
Orissa	55.4	63.09	34.68	103	11.1	28.0
Punjab	66.6	65.66	50.41	53	7.6	25.0
Rajasthan	56.3	54.99	20.44	84	8.9	33.7
Tamil Nadu	61.5	73.75	51.33	59	7.9	19.0
Uttar Pradesh	55.4	55.73	25.31	88	11.0	35.4
West Bengal	61.4	67.81	46.56	61	8.3	25.1
All India	**58.7**	**64.13**	**39.29**	**73**	**9.2**	**28.6**

Source: Economic Survey, 1995-96.

5

Human Development—Conceptual Issues and Realities

P. JEGADISH GANDHI

INTRODUCTION

The roots of the concept of human development can be traced to early periods in human history and can be found in many cultures and religions. In the early period, the concept of development treated income and its growth as a means and directed attention towards a real concern for people in their individuality and collectively, in their commonality and diversity. The central concern of development became the quality of people's lives—what they were capable of doing and what they actually did, the discrimination they faced, the struggles they waged and the expanding choices they enjoyed. The purpose of development is to create an atmosphere to develop people's capabilities, and opportunities, for both present and future generations. The real foundation of human development is universalism in acknowledging the life claims of everyone in society.

There is always a critical trade-off between the human resources growth and material resources potential in every country.

The relation of population and resources has been thought of as one of restricting the size of the former with the availability or possibility of harnessing of the latter. It was about the third century BC that the Greek philosopher Plato established a numerical estimate of population for the city-states of Greece based on the knowledge of the resources likely to be harnessed in each, in terms of the major ones but conceived of as theoretical entities and obtaining a product of the prime members in respect of each. This exercise, however, could attract the attention of only a few within or outside the country. It was long afterwards in the 15th-16th centuries when a similar attempt by an Egyptian philosopher Ibnkhaldun and Italian Govani Botero were known to the world as expounding the limitation of population size and growth set by the availability of resources.

IMPORTANCE OF HUMAN CAPITAL

Not until the late fifties did economists and other social scientists pay much attention to the role of investment in human beings, as an important determinant of economic development. The birth of this idea can be dated from the Presidential Address of Prof. Theodore W. Schultz to the American Economic Association in December, 1960. As a result, the concept of human capital formation came to limelight. Human capital can be defined as the body of knowledge possessed by the population and the capacity of the population to use the knowledge effectively. By the early seventies, the concept of human capital had moved to the centre stage of development priorities. According to Schultz, there are five ways of developing human resources: (i) health facilities and services, broadly conceived to include all expenditures that affect the life expectancy, strength and stamina, and the vigour and vitality of the people; (ii) on-the-job training, including old type apprenticeships organised by firms; (iii) formally organised education at the elementary, secondary and higher levels; (iv) study programmes for adults that are not organised by firms, including extension programmes notably in agriculture; and (v) migration of individuals and families to adjust to changing job opportunities.

ISSUES IN DEVELOPING COUNTRIES

The growth of Western European countries and the USA has been based more on investment in physical capital than in human capital in their earlier phases of development. But in the case of underdeveloped countries, the need for human capital in the form of educated persons in different vocations is greater to provide the missing components in the initial stages of their development. The major problems in human capital formation in developing countries are: (a) rapidly growing population; (b) mounting unemployment in the modern sectors of the economy as well as widespread underemployment in traditional agriculture; (c) shortage of persons with the critical skills and knowledge required for effective national development; (d) inadequate or underdeveloped organisations and institutions for mobilising human effort; and (e) lack of incentives for persons to engage in particular activities which are vitally important for national development. In fact, without an improvement in the quality of human factor, no progress is possible in an undeveloped country. As aptly emphasized by Professor Schultz, "it as if we had a map of resources which did not include a mighty river and its tributaries. The particular river is fed by schooling, learning on-the-job, advances in health, and the growing stock of information of the economy".

HUMAN DEVELOPMENT AND HUMAN SECURITY

While human development is unexceptionably the key element is speedier development of an economy, in itself it cannot provide the full answer to the entire meaning of the quality of life. Just as human development is a necessary but not a sufficient condition for higher quality of life, human security also is a necessary condition for both human development and a better quality of life. It emphasises that human-beings should first live before they can think of any development of the self. Security has for too long been interpreted narrowly as a security of territory from external concerns or as protection of national necessity in foreign policy or as global security from the threat of nuclear holocaust. It has been related more to nation states than to people. The development of human freedom can contribute to loss of security if it is not directed towards human security as such. In the final assessment, human security, "is a child who did not die, a disease that did not spread, a job that was not cut, an ethnic tension that did not explode in violence, a dissident who was not silenced. Human security is not a concern with weapons, it is a concern with human life and dignity" (*Human Development Report*, 1994).

The transition from human development to human security is a matter of universal concern. It is relevant to people everywhere, in rich or poor countries. There are several threats that are common to all people; intensity may differ from one part to another. But these threats to human security are real and growing. In short, human security is people-oriented. Just as development should be around the people, and not the other way, human security must be 'people-centered and not weapon-centered'. If we are to improve the quality of life, people must be protected from economic threat, starvation, ill-health, deteriorating environment, personal insecurity, technological insecurity and political insecurity.

No other aspect of quality of life is so vital for people as their security from physical violence. In developing countries as well as in the rich countries, human life is increasingly threatened by sudden and unpredictable violence. There ought to be safeguards against physical torture, war, ethnic tension, crime and violence, threats directed against women and children as well as the threats from the drug abuse and the like. Technological security has an important bearing on the quality of life. The drudgery of work can be reduced by the gadgets offered by technological advances. It also enhances productivity. At the same time, it can replace labour thereby contributing to unemployment which is nothing but the lack of food and personal security. In addition, political insecurity can affect the quality of people who would otherwise be able to live in a society that honours their basic human rights.

HUMAN RESOURCE DEVELOPMENT (HRD)

The most important indicators of HRD fall in two categories: (i) those which measure a country's stock of human capital; and (ii) those which measure the gross or net additions to the stock or more precisely, the rate of human capital formation over a specified time period. While the stock of human capital indicates the level of HRD which has been achieved by a country, the rate of human capital formation indicates its rate of improvement.

Indicators of HRD

For the purposes of international comparison, the following indicators of the stock of human capital would be useful: (i) level of educational attainment; and (ii) the number of persons, expressed as a percentage of population of the labour force, which is engaged in high level occupations, like scientists, engineers, managers, teachers, doctors, scientific and engineering technicians, nurses and medical assistants and persons in the foreman and skilled worker category. The "second best" measures, indicating the growth of HRD universally recognised, are as under: (i) the number of teachers (primary and secondary levels) per 10,000 population; (ii) Engineers and Scientists per 10,000 population; (iii) Physicians and Dentists per 10,000 population; (iv) Pupils enrolled at the primary level as a percentage of the estimated population in the corresponding age-group; (v) Pupils enrolled at the secondary level as a percentage of the estimated population in the corresponding age-group; (vi) the adjusted school enrolment ratios for primary and secondary levels combined; and (vii) enrolment at the higher level as a percentage of population in the corresponding age-group.

The first three are partial measures of the stock of human resources and the next four are measures of addition to it. Harbison and Myres, using the above indicators of HRD as far as practicable, developed a simple composite index to distinguish among countries in terms of four "levels of human resource development" viz., (i) underdeveloped, (ii) partially developed, (iii) semi-developed, and (iv) advanced. Among these India has been classified as a semi-advanced country in terms of HRD, along with twenty other countries among which the more prominent are Spain, Hungary, Italy, Poland, Yugoslavia, Norway, etc.

Agenda for HRD

The UNDP Human Development Report since 1990 published the Human Development Index which ranks different countries, sexes regions and ethnic groups on the basis of the human development, HDI takes into account longevity (for capability of leading a long and healthy life), educational attainment (for the capability of acquiring knowledge, exercising choice, communicating and participating in the life of the community) and access to resources (for capability for adequate nutrition and other consumption). The actual indicators selected are life expectancy at birth (for longevity), percentage of literate adults and average number of years of schooling for individuals over 25 years (for educational attainments) and real per capita gross domestic product and Purchasing Power Parity (PPP) dollars.

Dr. Mahbub ul Haq, the "guru of human development" and principal author of the United Nations Development Programmes' *Human Development Report, 1993*, had called for six-point agenda of action on human development for the Asia region. The six points are as follows: (1) All Asian governments must immediately prepare human development strategies and, in order to do this, collect and process data which can be used to quantify a variety of HD indicators. (2) Freeze military spending at existing levels if not reduce it, and privatise the public sector to generate resources for retiring public debt. (3) Initiate a sweeping decentralisation of power and financially strengthen local bodies. (4) Create a forum for South-South Co-operation and set-up regional centres for research on and exchange of experience in human development. (5) Form a new partnership with developed world based on a commitment to meeting human development targets and, in turn, demand developed countries to disarm for development. (6) Organise new alliance for change, including non-governmental organisations (NGOs), political parties and so on.

HRD IN INDIA

The Constitution of India, in its various Articles, gives a prominent place to the development of the human factor. The Preamble of the Constitution itself is a recognition of this fact. The Articles of the Constitution relating to 'Fundamental Rights' and 'Directive Principles of State Policy', among others, lay down that the State shall make an effective provision for the development of human resources. Articles 38, 39, 42, 43, 44, 45, 46, 47 and 48 of Part IV of the Constitution are directly relevant to the development of human resources.

Growth with social justice was adopted as the basis for development planning in India. It did not take long for the policy planners to recognise the bi-directional linkages between education and development. Education was viewed as a crucial input in various sectors of the economy. The development of human resources required adequate provision of health services, water supply, education, housing, nutrition and family welfare facilities which are essential determinants of the quality of life. The provision of one without the other is bound to affect the life adversely, hence the strategy of human resources development is to take an integrated view of these factors.

Over the last five decades, a number of measures have been taken to reform the educational system. These various reform measures can be grouped in three parts, viz., (i) equality reforms, (ii) quality reforms, and (iii) reforms for administrative case. However, education has been a low priority area in terms of the resource allocation in our plans. A glance at the percentage share of funds for education in the total plan outlay would reveal that it declined from 7.9 per cent during the First Plan to a low of 3.46 per cent during the Seventh Plan; it is projected to go up to 4.89 per cent during the Eighth Plan.

NEW DIMENSIONS

Human Development Reports added more dimensional riders to understand the dialects in human resources. The HDR for 1996 computes a Capability Poverty Measures (CPM) for different countries. Three indicators are used in constructing the CPM. These are: (a) the percentage of children under five who are underweight, (b) the percentage of births unattended by trained health personnel, and (c) the percentage of women aged fifteen years and above who are illiterate, NCAER (1996) estimated CPM for rural areas in Indian states. Two types of CPMs one using the "stunting" concept, and another using the "wasting" concept have been estimated (Table 1). The diversities are much higher if we look at the human development indicators of rural areas at the district level. For example, the rural female literacy varies from 4 per cent in Barmer district of Rajasthan to 98 per cent in Kottayam district of Kerala. Female literacy seems to be a crucial factor for improving the conditions of the poor. The involvement of women in Panchayats and other decentralized institutions would also improve their position in the society.

TABLE 1

Capability Poverty Measures for Indian States: Rural

States	*CPM$_1$*	*Rank*	*CPM$_2$*	*Rank*
NORTH				
Haryana	46.8	8	38.3	6
Himachal Pradesh	48.4	10	39.4	9
Punjab	35.5	3	29.1	3
UPPER CENTRAL				
Bihar	65.6	15	56.9	15
Uttar Pradesh	60.6	14	53.3	14
LOWER CENTRAL				
Madhya Pradesh	56.3	13	46.3	11
Orissa	55.1	12	49.9	13
Rajasthan	65.8	16	58	16
EAST				
North Eastern Region	40.4	4	36.4	5
West Bengal	53.2	11	46.7	12
WEST				
Gujarat	45.2	6	39.3	8
Maharashtra	46.3	7	39.9	10
SOUTH				
Andhra Pradesh	41.6	5	35.3	4
Kerala	12	1	10.7	1
Karnataka	47.5	9	38.7	7
Tamil Nadu	29.6	2	23.7	2
Rural India	**52.3**		**45**	

CPM$_1$: based on stunting. CPM$_2$: based on wasting.
Source: NCAER (1996), Cf.: *India Development Report, 1997*, p. 71.

In general, India's rank is 138 out of 175 countries of the world. As per the Gender-related Development Index (GDI), which measures the achievements of 146 countries in female life expectancy, educational attainment and income, the country has a rank of 118. While the Gender Empowerment Index (GEM), which examines women's access to professional, economic and political opportunities in 94 countries, places Indian below 86 countries. In terms of the Human Poverty Index (HPI) India ranks 47 out of the 78 countries (Table 2). The HPI reflects three variables: shortness of lifespan (the percentage of population in each country expected to survive to the age of 40); lack of basic education (the percentage of illiterate population); and lack of access to public and private resources (measured as a composite percentage of persons lacking access to health services, safe water and reasonable nutrition). A comparison between the world's two most populous nations—India and China—over a period of time shows India lagging behind in most areas. China brought down adult illiteracy from 34 per cent in 1970 to 19 per cent in1995 as against India's comparative performance of 66 per cent to 48 per cent during the corresponding period. Similarly, the under-five mortality rate in China fell from 209 per 1000 life births in 1960 to 47 in 1995, as against 236 to 115 in India. The real GDP per capita in China rose from $723 in 1960 to $2,604 in 1994 compared, whereas in India it rose from $617 to $1,348.

TABLE 2

Indicators of Human Development

Countries	*Human Development Index*	*Gender Development Index*	*Gender Empowerment Index*	*Human Poverty Index (%)*
Sri Lanka	0.711(91)	0.694 (70)	0.307(70)	20.70 (22)
China	0.626(108)	0.617(90)	0.481 (28)	17.50 (18)
India	0.446 (138)	0.419 (118)	.0.228 (86)	36.70 (47)
Pakistan	0.445 (139)	0.392 (120)	0.189 (92)	46.80 (64)
Bangladesh	0.368 (144)	0.339(128)	0.273 (76)	48.30 (67)

Note: Figures in brackets represent world ranking.

Sources: *Human Development Report, 1997*, Cf. *The Hindu—Business Line*, June 14, 1997.

DISAGGREGATED DERIVATIVES

The basic indicators of human development in India indicate that the birth and death rates have decreased in 1995 over

1994, but the infant mortality rate remained invariant at 74 during the last three years. The overall tentative trends during the 1990s seems to suggest that except the economic crisis years of 1991-92, the subsequent recovery brought about an improvement in living standards. There are, however, wide variations in indicators of human development across different states (Table 3). The life expectancy at birth at 72 years and male literacy rate at 93.6 in Kerala are quite high as compared to States like Bihar, Madhya Pradesh, Orissa, Rajasthan and Uttar Pradesh. The infant mortality rate of 16 per thousand in Kerala is less than a fourth of the All India estimates of 74 and less than one-sixth of rates in Madhya Pradesh and Orissa. It may be noted that the indicators of human development in Kerala are fairly comparable with those in several Asian countries (Table 4). At the same time, the levels of HD indicators are quite low in five states, viz., Bihar, Madhya Pradesh, Orissa, Rajasthan and Uttar Pradesh. If public policy concentrates on these five states, India's human development would increase considerably.

Some of the well-being indicators are poorly correlated with income indicators. For example, the poverty ratios for Uttar Pradesh and Kerala are almost the same but literacy rates are quite different. Similarly, Punjab and Haryana have the highest per capita incomes but literacy rates are relatively lower particularly in Haryana and sex ratio (female to male ratio) is very low in some of the districts in Punjab and Haryana. The child mortality rate is also poorly correlated with poverty. "The point is that many other factors are involved, which tend to weaken the simple correlation between income and health (or other aspects of well-being), when these other factors are not themselves well correlated with income" (Dreze and Sen, 1995). Thus, apart from income poverty, one has to look at non-income poverty indicators like health and education and qualitative changes in the conditions of the poor for better understanding of various facets of poverty. Apart from these, there is also a need to look at the conditions of vulnerable groups such as child labourers, widows, aged population, rural artisans, disabled persons, etc.

POST-REFORM TRENDS

The Indira Gandhi Institute of Development Research,

TABLE 3

Selected Indicators of Human Development for Major States*

States	*Life Expectancy at Birth (years) @ (1989-93)*	*Literacy rate***			*I.M.R+*	*Death rate*	*Birth rate*
		Total	*Male*	*Female*	*(prov. estimates of the SRS-1996) (per thousand)*		
1. Andhra Pradesh	60.6	44.09	55.13	32.72	66	8.3	22.7
2. Assam	54.9	52.89	61.87	43.03	75	9.5	27.7
3. Bihar	58.5	38.48	52.49	22.89	72	10.2	32.1
4. Gujarat	60.1	61.29	73.13	48.64	62	7.6	25.5
5. Haryana	62.9	55.85	69.10	40.47	68	8.1	28.8
6. Karnataka	61.9	56.04	67.26	44.34	53	7.6	23.0
7. Kerala	72.0	89.81	93.62	86.17	13	6.2	17.8
8. Madhya Pradesh	54.0	44.20	58.42	28.85	97	11.1	32.4
9. Maharashtra	64.2	64.87	76.56	52.32	48	7.4	23.2
10. Orissa	55.5	49.09	63.09	34.68	95	10.7	26.8
11. Punjab	66.4	58.51	65.66	50.41	52	7.5	23.5
12. Rajasthan	58.0	38.55	54.99	20.44	86	9.1	32.3
13. Tamil Nadu	62.4	62.66	73.75	51.33	54	7.9	19.2
14. Uttar Pradesh	55.9	41.60	55.73	25.31	85	10.2	34.0
15. West Bengal	61.5	57.70	67.81	46.56	55	7.8	22.8
All India	59.4	52.21	64.13	39.29	72	8.9	27.4

* Major States include States with population of 10 million and above as per 1991 Census.

@ Data relate to average over 1989-93 as estimated by the SRS and centered at 1991.

** Relate to population aged 7 years and above for 1991 and excludes Jammu & Kashmir for All India.

\+ Infant Mortality Rate.

Sources: (1) The data on Life Expectancy are taken from SRS Analytical Studies, Report No. 2 of 1996, whereas IMR, Death and Birth rates are based on the provisional estimates for 1996 from Sample Registration System released by the Office of the Registrar General of India.

(2) Literacy rate is based on Final Population Total of 1991 Census, Series 1, Paper No. 2 of 1992, Registrar General of India.

(3) *Economic Survey, 1997-98.*

TABLE 4

Indicators of Human Development for Some Asian Countries—1994

Country	*Life Expectancy at Birth (Years)*	*Infant Mortality rate (Per thousand births)*	*Adult Literacy (per cent)*
China	68.9	43	80.9
Indonesia	63.5	53	83.2
India	61.3	72	52.2
Kerala State (India)	72.0	13	89.8
Malaysia	71.2	12	83.0
Philippines	67.0	36	94.4
Pakistan	62.3	80	37.1
Republic of Korea	71.5	10	97.9
Singapore	77.1	5	91.0
Sri Lanka	72.2	16	90.1
Thailand	69.5	29	93.5

Source: UNDP—*Human Development Report, 1997*. For India and Kerala State the estimates are from Tables 10.5. But Life Expectancy figure for India for 1994 as per the Planning Commission. Cf. *Economic Survey, 1997-98.*

Mumbai, in its first India Development Report, 1997 made the following observations. It is difficult to say whether reforms have adversely affected human development in the 1990s. One can give broad indications based on public expenditure on health and education. Many studies have shown that social sector expenditure declined considerably during the first few years of the reforms and this could affect human development indicators. Decline in expenditure on important components of health sector, namely, preventive health care, was also noticed. However, the social sector expenditure seemed to have been restored from 1993-94 when the fiscal squeeze had been relaxed. Whether reforms or not, there is a need to increase public expenditure on health and education in the states (Bihar, Madhya Pradesh, Orissa, Rajasthan and Uttar Pradesh) which have low levels of human development.

D.M. Nanjundappa, former Chairman, Indian Council for Social Sciences Research has pointed out that there exists a weak link between the market forces and the improvement in poor person's life. Human development determined by it to emphasise the fact that human development paradigm performs an important service in questioning the presumed automatic link between expanding income and expanding human choices. Such a link depends on the quality and distribution of economic growth and not only on the quantity of such growth. A link between growth and human lives is to be created consciously through deliberate public policy, such public planning of social services and fiscal policy to redistribute income and assets. This link may not exist in the working of the market forces which are generally unfriendly to the poor.

CHALLENGES IN THE 21ST CENTURY

"One of the principal ways of linking economic growth and human lives is to invest liberally in the education and health of the people. Such investment is quite limited in India at present—only $14 a person per annum, compared to $160 in the Republic of Korea. Wherever India has made adequate investment in the education and skill-training of its people and in strengthening its human capital, the strategy has paid rich dividends. For example, India has already emerged as the second larger exporter of computer software as a result of extensive investment in skill formation in Bangalore, which has fast become India's own 'Silicon Valley'. In fact, India enjoys the great advantage of possessing a rich tradition of scientific and technological research, a large reservoir of low-paid hard-working people, the largest middle class in the world, and functioning democratic institutions. Its take-off desperately requires a massive investment in human development" (*Human Development in South Asia Report,* 1997).

To quote *Economic Survey*, 1996-97, "Fifty years after achieving independence, poverty, illiteracy, disease and lack of minimum social services continue to affect hundreds of millions of our people". "The ongoing economic reform process should be re-appraised and revitalised to give the entire national development effort a more human face. The eradication of poverty and unemployment must be the abiding goal of our development policies and programmes. The achievement of this goal will require sustained and rapid economic growth combined with well functioning public programmes for social services, rural development and employment generation to provide an effective safety net for all those millions at the margins of the growth process" (*Economic Survey, 1997-98*). The main purpose of development is to enlarge people's choices. This covers the objective of creating a favourable environment for people to enjoy long, healthy and creative lives. The basic difference between economic growth and human development is that the former focusses exclusively on the expansion of only one choice-income— while the latter encompasses an enlargement of all human choices—economic, social, cultural, or political. Generation of more income for the people and for investment in economic and social infrastructure have a pervasive influence. If higher incomes are available to the people and if basic minimum needs are met, it would provide the pre-conditions for improving the quality of life. The high incidence of poverty in India is an anti-thesis for sustainable human development. In the 21st century, the new paradigm of human development should be systemised around the more than proportionate incremental investment strategy in favour of pro-poor programmes.

References

Ishwar C. Dhingra (1997), *Indian Economy*, Sultan Chand & Sons, New Delhi.

Jegadish Gandhi, P. (1996), *Indian Economic Issues*, Pointer Publishers, Jaipur, Reprinted Edition.

———, (1996), The Concept of Development: Its Dialects and Dynamics, *Indian Journal of Applied Economics*, October-December.

———, (1997): Development: The 21st Century Perspectives, *The Hindu—Business Line*, May 24.

———, Ed., (1998), *Socio-economy of India: The First 50 Years and Beyond*, Deep and Deep Publications, New Delhi.

Jingan, M.L. (1983), *The Economics of Development and Planning*, Vikas Publishers, New Delhi.

Nanjundappa, D.M. (1997), "Formulating a Development Paradigm", *The Hindu—Business Line*, April 22.

Government of India (1996-97 and 1997-98), *Economic Surveys*.

Indira Gandhi Institute of Development Research (1997), *India Development Report*.

UNDP (1994, 1996 and 1997), *Human Development Reports*.

Human Development Centre (1997), *Human Development in South Asia Report*.

6

Concept of Human Development with Special Reference to India

R.S. Mishra

INTRODUCTION

Human development is defined as process of enlarging people's choices. In principle, these choices can be infinite and change over time. But at all levels of development the most critical and essential ones are for people to lead a long and healthy life, to be educated and to have access to resources needed for a decent standard of livings. If these choices are not available, many other opportunities remain inaccessible.[1] Economics has, often, been criticised for its neglect of the human dimension. It is attacked on the score that aggregate or per capita domestic or national product measures have been dominantly and often exclusively used as representing achievements in terms of measures of realized welfare states. The capability Development Theory has been put up sometimes as a complementary and currently as a comprehensive goal pursued by human beings in their economic activities in a country not only by classical but also by post-classical economists. Improvements in human capabilities are deemed to widen the frontier of choices open to them. In the absence of such improvements, capabilities remain undeveloped.[2] Human development is a process which widens people's choices as well as raises the level of well-being. Human development approach concentrates on indicators of levels of capabilities and their development. It is distinguished from the human resource development approach where human beings are treated as inputs in production and not as ends of development. It eschews the instrumentalist view on human beings. It does not estimate the ends other than per capita real income in terms of any type of money measures. It treats the different ends as independent of each other. The ranking in respect of each of the three indicators is ordinal.[3] A higher value of the indicators is preferred to a lower value of the same. Though there is an aggregate Human Development ranking with equal weights for the three component-indicator, we may not treat two similar ranks with different mixes of ranks of individual indicators as being equal in levels of well-being and to be on the same indifference curve.[4]

1. HUMAN DEVELOPMENT AND POVERTY ERADICATION

Poverty has been reduced in many parts of the world but a quarter of the world's population still remain in severe poverty. There are wide inequalities among the people and inexcusable failures of national and international policy to eradicate poverty. The challenge today, is to eradicate not just poverty of income but poverty from a human development perspective—poverty as a denial of choices and opportunities for living a tolerable life. Human poverty is more than income poverty—it is the denial of choices and opportunities for living a tolerable life.[5] There has been remarkable and unprecedented progress in reducing poverty in the 20th century. In the past 50 years poverty has fallen more than in the previous 500 years and it have been reduced in some respect in almost all countries.

The key indicators of human development have advanced strongly in the past few decades. Since 1960 in little more than a generation, child death rates have halved. Malnutrition rates have declined by almost a third. The proportion of children out of primary school has fallen from more than half to less than a quarter. The share of rural families without access to safe water has fallen from nine-tenths to about a quarter.

Components of Human Development

Human development is described as the build-up of capability to enjoy the components of well-being assumed to be normally sought by human beings. The components of the human development, well-being are as under:

1. Longevity,
2. Ability to read and write,
3. Conscious participation in transactions with other human beings in the society,
4. Access to higher education,
5. Learning of crafts and skills, and
6. Capacity to earn and command goods and services.

The index of human development is made up of: (a) longevity, (b) knowledge, and (c) a decent standard of living. A composite index, the human development thus contains three variables, life expectancy at birth, adult literacy rate, combined primary, secondary and tertiary enrolement ratio and real GDP per capita (in PPP).

The process of widening people's choices and the level of well-being they achieve are at the core of the notion of the human development. These choices are to lead a long and healthy life, to acquire knowledge and to have access to resources needed for a decent standard of living. Besides these, there are other choices ranging from political, economic and social freedom to opportunities for being creative and productive and enjoying self-respect and guaranteed human rights. Income is one important option and a means to achieve the goal, i.e. the human development.

Longevity, Educability and Consumption-satisfiability, the three indicators of human development are the goals to be achieved to eradicate human poverty. To live longer, to be educated more and more and to consume more and more, i.e. the decent standard of living.

Human Poverty

There are three perspective on poverty, i.e. (a) Income perspective, (b) Basic needs perspective, and (c) Capabilities perspective. As per Income perspective a person is poor, if, and only if, his income level is below the defined poverty line. According to Basic Needs Perspective poverty is deprivation of material requirements for minimally acceptable fulfilment of human needs including food. It includes the need for basic health and education and essential services that have to be provided by the community to prevent people from falling into poverty. It also recognises the need for employment and participation. According to Capability Perspective poverty represents the absence of some basic capabilities to function a person lacking the opportunities to achieve some minimally acceptable levels of these functionings. The functionings relevant to this analysis can vary from such physical ones as being well nourished, being adequately clothed and sheltered and avoiding preventable morbidity, to more complex social achievements such as partaking in the life of the community. The capability approach reconcile the notions of absolute and relevant poverty, since relative deprivation in incomes and commodities can lead to an absolute deprivation in minimum capability.[7]

Human Development Approach

Human Development approach emphasises providing for all people the basic means of well-being which include among other things, food, health and education. It emphasizes the enlargement of the range of people's choices. It goes much further than the concept of basic needs as it is based on functioning achievement rather than on commodity possession. It encompasses empowerment, co-operation, equity in basic capabilities and opportunities, sustainability and security of the three basic indicators of Human Development, viz. per capita income, educational attainment and life expectancy. Inclusion of income is justified on the ground that it enables the exercise of choice with respect to other two indicators, i.e. education and health which are common to the human resource development.[8] Education may be stressed more for its instrumental role than merely as a means to raise productivity and incomes. Similarly, life expectancy may be stressed more for its basic health services rather than to curative care for the working population. There are several health problems in poverty ridden Indian economy due to poor living. A more holistic approach towards health care encompassing nutrition, water supply and sanitation and housing must be adopted in place of only medical care. For human development emphasis should be on promotion of education, health and nutrition even if the return on investment on them may be zero. Supply of social services plays greater role for human development.

Concept of social security is the most relevant factor aimed at relieving economic and social distress due to specific contingencies such as death, old age and sickness, employment injury, maternity and temporary unemployment to encompass a whole range measures including income generation programme. Pursuit of social justice through social means and maintaining minimum levels of income has become the objective of the welfare governments throughout the world.[9] Concepts of social sectors, social security and human development provide a comprehensive framework which facilitates coordinated policy interventions for improving the state of human development. The aim of human development is to enhance the capabilities of the bottom 40 per cent of the population, viz. income generations and public provision of education, health and nutrition.

Human Development and Human Resource Development

Both the concepts, Human Development and Human Resource Development, represent different approaches. They are linked together by the fact that the broad-based concept of human development provides the necessary conditions that enable human resources to contribute to economic growth. The social capability concept referred to earlier, which emphasizes institutional and attitudinal characteristics in an economy, is a general illustration of this linkage.[10] More specific linkages can be illustrated from the field of education. Productivity increases from education are more pronounced with the attainment of 4-6 years of schooling. East Asian approach of emphasis on universal high quality primary education has important payoffs for economic efficiency as well as for equity. The excess demand for secondary and tertiary education generated by rapid attainment of universal primary was met in these countries. Largely by a meritocracy-oriented public secondary system and a self-financed private system. Vocational training, a facet of education that is emphasized by the human resource development is found to be effective in trainees who have a solid base of primary and secondary education.[11]

2. HUMAN DEVELOPMENT IN INDIA

In order to secure both growth and human development in India, it is essential to create an ideal situation in which economic development and social opportunity may be linked up. There should be political commitment in deliberate policy actions. It is possible to achieve high human development at relatively low levels of income. For example, in Kerala, greater attention is needed to be paid to the pattern of growth to secure both growth and human development. Similar is the case of health. Once the variation in the prevalence of poverty and per capita health expenditure by the government were taken into account, differences in per capita income become unimportant.[12] Thus, poverty reduction and government expenditure seem to be more important than income growth for attaining higher life expectancy. Broad-based increase in primary education could also be growth enhancing.

India has been categorised as a low human development country with HDI rank being 138 among 175 countries in the year 1994. Its rank was 134 in the year 1992 and 135 in the year 1993. It was far behind its neighbouring countries—Sri Lanka and China. The links between growth and social opportunity have been weak in Indian states. In this context, the Indian states can be classified into four categories. In the first category are Kerala and Tamil Nadu which have achieved high levels of human development despite relatively modest levels of income. The second category comprises the states of Punjab and Haryana which despite high levels of per capita income are substantially behind Kerala in terms of crucial social indicators. The third category comprises the states of Bihar, Madhya Pradesh, Orissa, Rajasthan and Uttar Pradesh where neither income nor social opportunities have been realised. The fourth category comprises the remaining states where the difference in their economic and social opportunities are not too large.[13] There has been remarkable attainment in the field of education and health in India. It levels with middle income countries. It has been achieved by incurring relatively low levels of expenditure by the government. The targeting of expenditure towards lower level of facilities, the higher efficiency of such expenditure due atleast in part to greater public vigilance and action, have enabled the state to achieve its pre-eminent position in human development. But in Punjab and Haryana the exemplary performance in economic growth has not been matched by progress in social indicators. The states' record is particularly poor as revealed by relatively low female literacy rates, high infant mortality rates and low female-male ratio. These states also have very low social allocation ratios (i.e. share of social services in total government expenditure) which have been further slashed since the initiation of economic reforms at the Central level in mid-1991. In Bihar, Madhya Pradesh, Rajasthan, Uttar Pradesh and Orissa, there is failure of development in both economic and social fronts. Its reasons are iniquitous production structure, the obsolete value systems and fragmented social structure, the ineffectiveness of various initiatives and isolated manner in which sectoral programmes are devised and implemented. If these states had started-off with Kerala's level of literacy and infant mortality in 1950, rate of rural poverty eradication could have doubled.[14] Maharashtra represents a state in the last category where the attainments in economic and social sectors have been relatively balanced with wide disparities across districts in crucial social indicators. The government action in the field of human development in India is more often inappropriate than inadequate. The constitutional responsibility for many of the sectors that ensure social securities is also with the state government which have different degrees of political commitment as reflected not only in the level of sectoral expenditures but also in their infra-sectoral allocations and the efficiency with which these are spent. The persistence of mass illiteracy, high level of infant mortality and morbidity even as the social infrastructure facilities created at substantial public cost lie unutilised or under-utilised is a paradox that points to the poor quality of services rendered in these institutions. The same factors explain the lack of correspondence between social infrastructure expenditure and attainment in the country.[15] Table 1 indicates the performance of India on the front of human development since 1970.

The Table 1 suggests India's downfall in the HDI rank from 82 in the 1970 to 134 in 1992, 135 in 1993 and 138 in 1994.

According to gender-related development index performance

TABLE 1

Human Development in India

Year	*HDI Value*	*Rank*
1970	0.254	82[15A]
1992	0439	134[16]
1993	0.436	135[17]
1994	0.446	138[18]

of India is again far behind of almost majority of the countries of the world. The gender development index (GDI) value of India was 0.250 in the year 1970, 0.410 in the year 1993 and 0.419 in the year 1994. Similarly, GDI rank of India was 103 in the year 1993 and 118 in the year 1994. Similarly, the gender empowerment index (GEM) rank of India was 93 in the year 1993 and 86 in the year 1994 with GEM value 0.235 in the year 1993 and 0.228 in the year 1994.[19] GDI and GEM rank and value are reproduced in Table 2.

TABLE 2

Indices of Gender Inequalities in India

Year	*GDI*		*GEM*	
	Value	*Rank*	*Value*	*Rank*
1970	0.250	N.A.	—	—
1993	0.410	103	0.235	93
1994	0.419	118	0.228	86

CONCLUSION

A broader perspective towards social sectors needs to be adopted to ensure equity and sustained growth in India. The resource costs of an integrated approach need not be phenomenal if there is a recognition of the interlinked nature of the problem and public action is taken in a manner that maximises synergies.

A retargeting of even the current expenditures being incurred by the government at various levels can lead to sustained gains. The scope for additional resource mobilisation has to be identified. Linkages between various components of promotional and protective social security should be identified alongwith the linkages between social security and economic growth. Various alternatives forms of financing, including social insurance, should be carefully scrutinised and a suitable organisational structure should be devised to ensure wide participation in social and cultural contexts. Urgent and concentrated efforts are essential to belie the UNDP prediction that India will take more than a century (as against China's 25 years) to graduate to a state of high human development. Indian researchers should make efforts to provide policy alternatives in this sphere to initiate not only appropriate public action but also serve to remind all concerned that it is the duty of all the citizens of India to make sincere efforts for Human Development of the country. In the words of Adam Smith, "The progressive state is in reality the cheerful and the hearty state to all the different orders of the society. The stationary is dull; the declining melancholy".

The acceptance of the feasibility of sustained economic growth and its deliberate pursuit as an important objective of social policy is of course, a recognition of the profound social and economic impact of the scientific revolution and the growing momentum of technological advances. Advances in medical sciences and public health measures have reduced the death rate in India without relative decline in birth rate. In this peculiar condition, rapid economic growth is the only foundation of a sustained economic growth and standard of living. But uncritical pursuit of growth can give rise to grave social imbalances such as inacceptably large disparities in income and wealth. In a situation of highly unequal distribution of income and wealth, basic human needs of great mass of people are almost unsatisfied. It generates social tensions and conflicts. Thus, in India, an abiding concern with equity and social justice in development is a vital necessity. Expansion of employment opportunities and provision of social services such as elementary education, primary health care to the poor is essential. We must mobilise all the latent resources of our people to evolve a new sense of social values and incentives. Education in particular is of critical importance both for economic growth and creation of a value system promoting the cause of modernisation, social justice and national integration.

We need to recapture something of the spirit of idealism, adventure, enterprise and endurance and a clear vision of the future which characterized our freedom struggle.[20]

There is a popular belief that education reduces inequalities in the society. There is need for education for all. The education system needs to be programmed to reduce intellectual and economic inequalities.[21] We look forward to make India of our dreams with accelerated economic development with equity and social justice and building our society free from exploitation and suffering.[22]

Notes and References

1. UNDP, *Human Development Report*, 1993 and 1997.
2. Brahmananda, P.R., "The Human Development Report, 1993: A Selective Appraisal", *The Indian Economic Journal*, April-June, 1993, p. 134.
3. *Ibid.*
4. *Ibid.*
5. UNDP, *Human Development Report*, 1997, p. 2.
6. *Ibid.*
7. *Ibid.*, p. 16, Box 1.1.
8. K. Seeta Prabhu, *Social Sectors in Economic Development: Some Issues*, The Indian Economic Association, 79th Conference Volume, 1996.
9. Drez, J., and A.K. Sen, *Hunger and Public Action*, Clarendon Press, Oxford.
10. K. Seeta Prabhu, *op. cit.*, pp. 208-09.
11. World Bank, *East Asian Miracle: Economic Growth and Public Policy*, Oxford University Press, New York, 1993.
12. Anand, S. and M. Ravallion, "Human Development in Poor Countries on the Role of Private Incomes and Public Services", *Journal of Economic Perspectives*, Vol. 7(1), pp. 133-50.
13. K. Seeta Prabhu, *op. cit.*, pp. 211-12.
14. Datt, G. and M. Ravallion, *Why have Some Indian States done Better than Others in Reducing Rural Poverty*, Policy Research Working Paper No. 1594, World Bank, Washington, 1996.
15. K. Seeta Prabhu, *op. cit.*, p. 213.

15a. Tata Services Ltd., *Statistical Outline of India, 1996-97*, p. 252.

16. UNDP, *Human Development Report*, 1995.
17. *Ibid.*, 1996.
18. *Ibid.*, 1997.
19. *Ibid.*
20. Manmohan Singh, "Development, Social Justice and Modernisation", *The Indian Economic Journal*, April-June, 1986, pp. 5-15.
21. Tapas Mazumdar, "Economics of Indian Education for the Next Century", Lecture delivered at the 80th Annual Conference of the Indian Economic Association at Osmania University, Hyderabad, 29-12-1997.
22. D.S. Awasthi, "Erosion of Equity and Social Justice in Indian Economic Development", the Presidential Address at the 80th Annual Conference of the IEA at Hyderabad.

7

Determinants of Human Development

M.S. SUBRAMANIAN

INTRODUCTION

According to the United Nations Development Programme, Human Development is concerned with the process of widening people's choices and the level of well-being they achieve. Such choices are neither finite nor static. But regardless of the level of development, there are three essential choices for people. They are: to lead a long and healthy life, to acquire knowledge and to have access to the resources needed for a decent standard of living. However, Human Development is multi-dimensional. It includes choices ranging from political, economic and social freedom to opportunities for being creative and productive and enjoying self-respect and guaranteed human rights. The objectives of this paper are to identify the important determinants of human development, to estimate their relative effects on the human development and suggest measures to augment human development in the countries with high, medium and low Human Development Index Countries.

METHODOLOGY

Multiple Regression Model has been employed for analysis in this paper. The Human Development Index has been the dependent variable (Y), Life Expectancy at birth in years (X1), Adult Literacy Rate in percentage (X2), Combined first, second and third level gross enrolment ratio in percentage (X3) and per capita real GDP in dollars (X4) have been used as explanatory variables. Linear and Log-Linear Multiple Regression Models have been estimated using Ordinary Least Squares method. The data needed for the study have been collected from Human Development Report, 1997 of UNDP. The cross-section data of 20 leading countries in each of high, medium and low Human Development Indices (HDI) for the year 1994 have been used in this study. The countries with high HDI included in this study are Canada, France, Norway, USA, Iceland, Netherlands, Japan, Finland, Newzeland, Sweden, Spain, Austria, Belgium, Australia, United Kingdom, Switzerland, Ireland, Denmark, Germany and Greece. These selected countries had HDI values ranging from 0.923 to 0.960. The medium HDI countries included in this study are Lebanon, Suriname, Russian Federation, Brazil, Bulgaria, Iran, Estonia, Ecuador, Saudi Arabia, Turkey, Korea, Lithuania, Croatia, Syria, Romania, Macedonia, Tunisia, Algeria, Jamaica and Jordan. These selected countries had HDI values between 0.730 and 0.794. The countries with low HDI included in this study are Myanmar, Ghana, Cameroon, Kenya, Equatorial Guinea, Lao, Lesotho, India, Pakistan, Comoros, Nigeria, Zaire, Zambia, Bangladesh, Cotedvorie, Benin, Togo, Yeman, Tanzania and Mauritania. The HDI values of these selected countries ranged between 0.355 and 0.475.

PRESENTATION AND DISCUSSION OF RESULTS

A. High HDI Countries

The linear regression equation obtained for high HDI countries is given below:

$$Y = 0.1430 + 0.0056{*}X1 + 0.0026{*}X2 + 0.0011{*}X3 + 0.000000411{*}X4$$
$$t\ (65.80) \quad (12.73) \quad (72.18) \quad (10.49)$$

$\bar{R}^2 = 0.99$ $F^* = 2090.08$ $DW^+ = 1.84$

* Significant at 1% level.

\+ Absence of auto-correlation.

All the explanatory variables included are statistically highly significant. An increase in Life Expectancy at birth by one year increases the HDI value in these countries when other variables are constant by 0.0056. An increase in Adult Literacy Rate by one per cent increases the HDI value in these countries by 0.0026 when other variables are held constant. An increase in Combined Enrolment Ratio by one per cent increases HDI value by 0.0011 while an increase in per capita real GDP by one dollar increases HDI value by 0.0000004114.

The estimated double log regression equation for countries with medium HDI values is stated below:

$$\log Y = 0.0256 + \underset{t\,(71.13)}{0.4647^* \log X1} + \underset{(9.88)}{0.2227^* \log X2} + \underset{(77.77)}{0.1021^* \log X3} + \underset{(12.55)}{0.0099^* \log X4}$$

$\bar{R}^2 = 0.99$ $F^* = 2440.49$ $DW^+ = 1.72$

* Significant at 1% level.

\+ Absence of auto-correlation.

B. Medium HDI Countries

The linear regression equation obtained for medium HDI countries is given below:

$$Y = 0.4808 - \underset{t\,(-0.14)}{0.0002\,X1} + \underset{(3.21)}{0.0010^*X2} + \underset{(3.11)}{0.0021^*X3} + \underset{(4.70)}{0.0000153^*X4}$$

$\bar{R}^2 = 0.64$ $F^* = 9.37$ $DW^+ = 1.64$

* Significant at 1% level.

\+ Absence of auto-correlation.

X2, X3 and X4 are found to be highly significant. A one per cent increase in adult literacy rate brings 0.0010 increase in HDI; a one per cent increase in Enrolment Ratio increases HDI by 0.0021 and a one dollar increase in per capita real GDP increases

HDI by 0.0000153 when other variables are constant in middle HDI countries. Life expectancy at birth is found to have a negative influence on HDI but is observed to be statistically insignificant.

The regression results of Double Log model are furnished below:

$$\log Y = 0.0354 + 0.1067 \log X1 + 0.1368^{*} \log X2$$
$$t\ (0.84) \qquad (5.14)$$
$$+ 0.1746^{*} \log X3 + 0.1509^{*} \log X4$$
$$(3.85) \qquad (6.89)$$

$\overline{R}^2 = 0.78$ $\quad F^* = 17.80$ $\quad DW^+ = 1.70$

* Significant at 1% level.

+ Absence of auto-correlation.

From this equation, we infer that a one per cent increase in adult literacy rate increases HDI by 0.1368 per cent; a one per cent increase in combined enrolment ratio increases HDI by 0.1746 per cent and a one per cent increase in real per capita GDP increases HDI by 0.1509 per cent in countries will medium HDI values when other relevant variables are kept at the same level. Combined Enrolment ratio is found to be the dominant variable influencing HDI in countries with medium HDI values.

C. Low HDI Countries

The results of the linear regression equation fitted for the low HDI countries are presented below:

$$Y = -0.1438 + 0.0055X1 + 0.0022^{*}X2 + 0.0011^{*}X3 + 0.000056^{*}X4$$
$$t\ (388.94) \qquad (466.95) \qquad (132.88) \qquad (436.86)$$

$\overline{R}^2 = 0.99$ $F^* = 149891.4$ $DW^+ = 2.05$

* Significant at 1% level.

+ Absence of auto-correlation.

According to this equation, a one year increase in Life Expectancy at birth increases HDI by 0.0055; a one per cent increase in Adult literacy rate increases HDI by 0.0022; a one per cent increase in combined enrolment ratio increases HDI by 0.0011 and a one per cent in per capita real GDP increases HDI by 0.00056 when other relevant variables are kept constant.

Following is the double log regression equation obtained for Low HDI countries.

$$\log Y = 0.0015 + \underset{t\,(12.14)}{0.7170^{*}} \log X1 + \underset{(14.78)}{0.3190^{*}} \log X2 + \underset{(2.28)}{0.0721^{**}} \log X3 + \underset{(12.80)}{0.1633^{*}} \log X4$$

$\bar{R}^2 = 0.97$ $F^* = 139.11$ $DW^+ = 2.34$

** Significant at 5% level.

* Significant at 1% level.

+ Absence of auto-correlation.

This equation indicates that a one per cent increase in life expectancy at birth increases HDI by 0.7170 per cent; a one per cent increase in adult literacy rate increases HDI by 0.3190 per cent; a one per cent increase in combined enrolment ratio increases HDI by 0.0721 per cent and one per cent increase in per capita real GDP increases HDI by 0.1633 per cent when other variables are held constant. Life expectancy rate has been the dominant variable in determining HDI in these countries.

D. All Countries

The linear regression equation estimated for the combined data of 60 sets of observations for all the countries included in this study is as under:

$$Y = -0.5067 + \underset{t\,(11.99)}{0.0128^{*}X1} + \underset{(3.46)}{0.0016^{*}X2} + \underset{(41.66)}{0.0033^{*}X3} + \underset{(0.62)}{0.00000073^{*}X4}$$

$\bar{R}^2 = 0.97$ $F^* = 465.33$ $DW^+ = 1.60$

* Significant at 1% level.

+ Absence of auto-correlation.

According to this equation an increase in the life expectancy rate by one year increases HDI by 0.0128; a one per cent increase in adult literacy rate increases HDI by 0.0016; and a one per cent increase in enrolment ratio by 0.0033 while other explanatory variables are kept constant. it is to be noted that the per capita real

GDP variable is found to be statistically insignificant.

The estimated double log equation for all the 60 countries is given below:

$$\log Y = 0.00076 + 1.0238^{*} \log X1 + 0.2591^{*} \log X2$$
$$t\ (8.55) \qquad (5.50)$$
$$+ 0.1771^{**} \log X3 + 0.0731^{*} \log X4$$
$$(2.36) \qquad (3.84)$$

$\bar{R}^2 = 0.97$ $F^* = 492.24$ $DW = 0.93$

** Significant at 5% level.

* Significant at 1% level.

All the explanatory variables included in this model are statistically significant. According to this model, an increase in life expectancy at birth by one per cent increases HDI by 1.0238 per cent; an increase in adult literacy rate by one per cent increases HDI by 0.2591 per cent; an increase in combined enrolment rate by one per cent increases HDI by 1.1771 per cent and an increase in per capita real GDP increases HDI by 0.0731 per cent, keeping all other relevant variables constant. Life expectancy at birth is observed to be the dominant variable in determining the values of HDI in the category of all 60 countries.

CONCLUSION

Life expectancy at birth has been the dominant variable in determining the value of Human Development Index in countries with high HDI and countries with low HDI. Combined enrolment ratio is found to be the dominant variable in the determination of Human Development Index in countries with medium HDI. Life expectancy at birth, Adult Literacy rate and Combined enrolment ratio had the greatest influence on HDI in countries with low HDI, per capita real GDP had the greatest influence on HDI in countries with medium HDI. For the world as a whole, Life Expectancy at birth is to be given the top most priority in enhancing HDI. This is followed in order by literacy rate, combined enrolment ratio and per capita real GDP in importance in enhancing HDI. This analysis thus brings out the importance of expenditure on social sectors such as Health and

Education apart from taking measures for economic development in augmenting Human Development.

References

Human Development Report (1997), Published for the United Nations Development Programme by Oxford University Press, New York, 1997.

Aggarwal, J.C. (1997), *Human Development in India: 50 Years of Data Handbook*, Shipra Publications, Delhi.

Gujarathi Damodar, (1988), *Basic Econometrics*, McGraw Hill Book Company, New York.

Anand, Sudhir and Amartya K. Sen (1993), *Human Development Index: Methodology and Measurement*, Human Development Report Office, Occasional Paper 19, UNDP, New York.

8

A.K. Sen's Contribution to Human Development

S. NARAPA REDDY, A. RAJASEKHAR AND P. KODANDARAMI REDDY

The award of Nobel Prize for Economics to A.K. Sen in 1998, though belated, brings to light his remarkable contribution to development of economics on the one hand and welfare economics on the other. Human development may be regarded as a blend of both development economics and welfare economics. A.K. Sen probed into choice of techniques in development planning and subsequently moved to issues of social welfare including poverty and famines. The human development index constructed by the UNDP under the leadership of Mahbub-ul-Haq of Pakistan has derived roots from the writings of A.K. Sen as well as his personal advice to the UNDP. Through his writings and speeches A.K. Sen has brought the human touch to the science of Economics. Like Alfred Marshal, he has put human well-being as the main focus in the study of Economics. His explorations into issues of poverty and famine, *inter alia*, bear ample testimony of his concern for the welfare of the deprived segments of society. In this paper it is proposed to highlight some of the contributions of A.K. Sen to human development theory and practice.

SOCIAL CHOICE AND INDIVIDUAL VALUES

The impossibility theorem posed by Kenneth Arrow that there is no aggregation rule that fulfils the five conditions, each of which appears very reasonable on its own. Sen's work not only enriched the social choice theory but also opened up new and important fields of study. His monograph Collective Choice and Social Welfare was influential and inspired many scholars to renew their interests in basic welfare issues. In this book as well as many articles Sen treated problem of majority rule, individual rights and the availability of information about individual welfare ; a minimal requirement for protecting individual preferences. Sen's finding that no collective decision rule can fulfil such a minimal requirement on individual rights in Arrow's impossibility theorem initiated an extensive debate and discussion leading to the extent to which a collective decision rule can be made consistent with individual rights.

INDEXES OF WELFARE AND POVERTY

The construction of a welfare index is an important application of the theory of social choice. Inequality indexes are closely linked to welfare functions representing the values of society. Following the line of thinking initiated by Serge Kolm and Anthony Atkinson, Sen elucidated the relation between Lorenz curve and Gini coefficient and made valuable contributions to poverty indexes and welfare indicators. In order to overcome the shortcomings of the H measure of poverty, Sen postulated five reasonable axioms from which he derived his poverty index $P=H[1+(1-I)].G)$.[1] His poverty index has been applied extensively and some of the axioms he postulated have been used by others who have proposed alternative indexes. UNDP's human development index is constructed on the basis of the actual capabilities in addition to income. These capabilities pertain to health, education and nutrition. His analysis of famines is in line with his theoretical framework to welfare measurement. He has challenged a common view that a shortage of food is the most important explanation for famine through his empirical work on famines in the Indian sub-continent and Saharan Africa. He arrived at the conclusion that more than a shortage of food, it is lack of entitlement that causes starvation at the time of famine.

ECONOMIC DEVELOPMENT AND HUMAN DEVELOPMENT

Economic Development is measured in a variety of ways and we do not have an index of economic development as in the case of human development. However, real GDP per capita in PPP $ is considered to be a better index of economic development as it embraces GDP in the aggregate and population stock. It has been argued by the critics of development economics that the benefits of economic development may not percolate to the bottom strata of society. They question the trickle down theory of development because of widespread primary poverty in the developing world. Therefore, development is viewed from the human side and not from the side of goods and services. A healthy, educated population with access to sanitation and drinking water and communication without gender discrimination, regional disparity, and environmental degradation provide a strong foundation for sustainable human development which will ensure economic development and not *vice versa*. The new economic policy regime advocates liberalisation, privatisation and globalisation which are not necessarily consistent with the indicators of human development. It is in this context that the contribution of A.K. Sen to welfare indicators and the need for social investment in education, health, nutrition and sanitation assumes great significance. There are various inadequacies in educational and health policy including low levels of public expenditure on education, elitist biases of Indian planning and a deep absence of accountability on the part of the establishment and limited power of disadvantage groups contribute to this social failure as against the remarkable success of Sri Lanka in human development indicators.[2] Table 1 incorporates some of the major indicators of human development for the countries of the Indian sub-continent and Sri Lanka.

It may be noted from Table 1 that the gap between the rank of economic development and human development is zero in Bangladesh, -19 for Pakistan, 5 for India and 9 for Sri Lanka. The higher the rank in gender-related development index and gender empowerment measure, the greater is the level of social development and Sri Lanka leads in this respect as also in life expectancy at birth, adult literacy rate, gross enrolment ratio, safe

TABLE 1

Human Development Indicators

Sl. No.	*Indicator/Index*	*Ranks*			
		India	*Bangla Desh*	*Pakistan*	*Sri Lanka*
1.	Economic Development as measured by Real GDP per capita PPP $, 1994	143	144	120	100
2.	Human Development	138	144	139	91
3.	Real GDP per capita (PPP $) rank minus HDI rank	5	0	-19	9
4.	Gender-related Development	118	128	120	70
5.	Gender Empowerment Measure	86	76	92	70
6.	Life expectancy at birth (years) 1994	61	56	62	72
7.	Adult Literacy Rate (%) 1994	51	37	37	90
8.	Combined first, second and third gross enrolment ratio (%) 1994	56	39	38	66
9.	Rural-Urban disparity in services*				
	(a) Health (1985-95)	80	—	35	—
	(b) Safe water (1990-95)	93	98	74	56
	(c) Sanitation (1990-95)	20	40	31	90
10.	Female life expectancy at birth (years) 1994	61	63	57	75
11.	Maternal mortality rate 1990 (Per 1 lakh live births)	570	850	340	140
12.	Annual population growth rate (%) 1960-94	2.2	2.4	2.9	1.7
13.	Infant mortality rate (per thousand live births) 1994	74	85	80	16
14.	Public expenditure on health as of GDP 1990	1.3	1.4	1.8	1.8
15.	Food consumption (As % of total household consumption) 1980-85	52	59	37	43
16.	Public expenditure on primary and secondary education (As % of all levels) 1990-94	64	88	67	72
17.	Labour force in agriculture (percentage) 1990	64	65	52	48

18. Percentage of people in poverty*				
(a) Urban	38	56	20	15
(b) Rural	49	51	31	36
19. Income share of lowest 40% households (%) 1981-93	21	23	21	22
20. Urban population (As % of total) 1994	27	18	34	22
21. Percentage of population with access to a sanitary means of excreta disposal*	3	3	3	2

Sources: UNDP, *Human Develoment Report, 1997*, pp. 146-87.
UNDP, *Human Development Report, 1996*, pp. 152-70.
UNICEF, *The Progress of Nations, 1997*.

drinking water, female life expectancy at birth, maternal mortality rate, annual population growth rate, infant mortality rate, public expenditure on health, labour force in agriculture, percentage of urban people in poverty and access to sanitation. That is why Dreze and Sen have remarked that Sri Lanka's health indicators rival to those of many middle income economies and the decline in population growth rate to 1.7% has challenged the wide-spread view that high levels of income are a pre-requisite for favourable demographic change. This is primarily due to advanced indicators of education as a result of a traditionally strong emphasis on social sector policies.[3] In respect of urbanisation, incidence of rural poverty and food consumption, Pakistan has a lead over the rest of the countries, while Bangladesh leads in the income share of the lowest 40% of households. India lags behind in respect of all the indicators.

CONCLUSION

Amartya Sen, the nobel laureate in Economics for 1998 through his outstanding contributions to development economics as well as welfare economics has made Economics a social science. From the choice of techniques in the theory of development, he has travelled a long way to the construction of poverty and welfare indices. He has emphasised that social choice cannot be inconsistent with human values and rights. His measure of poverty is more relevant because its focus is on the poorest of the poor and ways and means of their empowerment. Economic development will not automatically ensure equity and social justice. Consequently, the deprived segments of society remain at the margin of subsistence. During periods of famine, starvation deaths are not uncommon. It is not the shortage of food supply but lack of entitlement which causes human suffering due to famine. Due to elitist bias, social investment on primary education and primary health has been limited in Indian sub-continent though increasing in recent years. The human development index is based on social welfare indicators rather than purely economic betterment. Mahbub-ul-Haq was the architect of UNDP's human development index. The concern for poverty and its alleviation are the common threads in the fabric of Haq and Sen. Measured in terms of the basic indicators of human development Sri Lanka has recorded a remarkable success in relation to the countries of the Indian sub-continent. Dreze and Sen opine that Sri Lanka's record in human development can rival most of middle income and some of the high income economies. This is due to a long tradition of commitment of the governments in Sri Lanka for social sector investment. India's new economic policy might prove to be fatal if social sector investments are neglected. Sen's contributions to welfare economics have more relevance for India than elsewhere because of the persistence of absolute poverty and wide-spread underemployment.

Notes and References

1. *The Hindu*, 15-10-1998,
2. Jean Dreze and Amartya Sen (1995), Basic Education as a Political Issue, *Journal of Educational Planning and Administration*, New Delhi, January, pp. 1-17.
3. *Ibid.*

9

Development Planning and Grass-root Level Democracy in India: Need for a Development Index

ARABINDA GHOSH

INTRODUCTION

India, the largest democratic country in the world today accounts for 14 percent of the World's population and about 25 percent of that of developing countries. At the time of independence in 1947, India was faced with the problems of rehabilitating the economy, which was disrupted by the World War II and partition of sub-continent and of achieving rapid economic growth and alleviating wide-spread poverty, hunger and malnutrition. The economy was predominantly agrarian, with large imbalances in resource endowments amongst regions and people, high unemployment and under-employment, low levels of saving and capital formation and low incomes and living standards.

Independent India adopted central planning to remove the structural constraints on its growth process through five year plans. The central purpose of planning was identified as that of initiating a process of development which will raise living standards and open out to the people new opportunities for a richer and more varied life. The manner in which this purpose has been translated into specific objectives has varied from plan to plan.

Alleviation of rural poverty has been one of the primary objectives of planned development in India. Ever since the inception of planning, the policies and programmes have been designed and redesigned with this aim. The problem of rural poverty has been brought into a sharper focus during 80's. It was stated in the plan document that a substantial increase in the overall rate of growth of the economy will no doubt create favourable conditions for a reduction in poverty. However, in the light of past experience, it is understood that it will not be realistic to rely solely on the growth process to find a solution to this problem. It is necessary to formulate specific poverty alleviation programmes. It is now widely believed that increased participation of people in the rural development process together with decentralisation of planning will go a long way in providing the rural people with better prospects for development. But a meaningful decentralisation needs to be backed by a constitutional guarantee in a country like India. The 73rd Amendment of Indian Constitution which came into force with effect from April 24, 1993 provides the necessary constitutional guarantee. The Act provides with for a uniform three-tier system of panchayat at village level, the intermediate level and the district level throughout the country. This amendment of Indian constitution mandates the entrustment of the following functions commensurate with authority to the three-tier structure of panchaysts at village, block and district levels:

'Subject to the provision of the Constitution the legislature of a state may, by law endow the panchayats with such powers and authority as may be necessary to enable them to function as institutions of self-government and such law may contain provisions for the devolution of the powers and responsibilities upon panchayats at the appropriate level, subject to such conditions as may be specified therein, with respect to:

(a) the preparation of plan for economic development and social justice, and
(b) the implementation of schemes for economic development and social justice . . .'

So panchayats in India are to play an important role in human development in rural areas. They are to prepare plans sitting with the common people at the grass-roots level. They will monitor the plan and evaluate the same. At this moment, it is of paramount importance for all these grass-root level institutions to use a Development Index, which will lead them to put necessary emphasis, to encourage a pattern of growth that increases the efficient use of assets owned by the poor, to expand the access of the poor to land, credit, infrastructure and productive inputs, education, etc. The commitment for delivering social services to the poor is intended to develop the human resource. The Human Development Index (HDI) has been developed by UNDP to have development with a human face. The HDI includes three key components—longevity, knowledge and income. Longevity is measured by life expectancy at birth as the sole unadjusted indicator. Knowledge is measured by two educational stock variables: adult literacy and mean years of schooling. The measure of educational achievement is adjusted by assigning a. weight of two-thirds to literacy and one-third to mean years of schooling. Income is measured by adjusted real GDP per capita.

But it cannot be denied that it is very difficult to use such an index at grass-root level to motivate the rural people. On the other hand, at this moment there is a crying need for a development index to sensitise the decision-makers and local leaders at the grass-root level in India. Otherwise we may move towards the same direction of development in rural areas having inequality as the inevitable consequence. It is also widely accepted that there is a strong adverse impact of inequality on well-being.

OBJECTIVES OF THIS STUDY

The objective of the study is to develop an index which satisfies the following conditions:

(i) it is easily understood and operated,
(ii) it reflects the well-beings, seen in terms of basic capabilities of the rural people, and
(iii) it sensitises the rural leaders to adopt policies for development with a human face.

THE STUDY

Under five mortality rate (U5MR) may be used as an alternative index. U5MR means number of deaths of children under five years of age per thousand live births. In this study U5MR and HDI for 100 countries have been chosen to verify whether U5MR can be used as an alternative to HDI in measuring the well-being of the rural people.

The correlation co-efficient between U5MR and HDI for 100 countries has been calculated. It is found that this correlation co-efficient is (-)0.918 and their rank correlation is (-)0.949.

The correlation co-efficient for the same 100 countries between U5MR and longevity a component of HDI, is (-)0.994.

The correlation co-efficient for the same 100 countries between U5MR and literacy rate a component of HDI is (-)0.857.

The correlation co-efficient for these 100 countries between U5MR and mean year of schooling—a component of HDI is (-)0.792.

The correlation co-efficient between U5MR and adjusted GNP per capita is (-)0.674.

The correlation co-efficient between U5MR and HDI for 30 countries having HDI below 0.400 is (-)0.883.

The correlation co-efficient between U5MR and HDI for 36 countries having HDI between 0.400—0.800 is (-)0.698.

The correlation co-efficient for 54 countries having HDI above 0.800 in (-)0.822.

It is revealed that under five mortality rate reflects the core of the human development index. On the other hand, this indicator is simple and can be measured by any person responsible for development administration irrespective of his/her educational status. Now the educational status of rural leaders of the lowest tier of Panchayati Raj Institutions (PRIs) of West Bengal (India) have been analysed. Gram Panchayat is the lowest tier of village self-government. Educational status of elected representatives of Gram Panchayats of three districts of West Bengal, i.e. Burdwan, North 24-Parganas and Hooghli have been analysed. Rural population of these three districts is 10.48 million which is 1.67 percent of the total population in rural India.

It is revealed from Table 1 that 0.63 percent of the Gram Panchayat leaders are illiterate, 5.87 percent of them are neo-

TABLE 1

Educational Status of Elected Members of Gram Panchayats West Bengal (India)

Educational Status	*Districts*			*Total*
	Burdwan	*Hooghli*	*North 24-Parganas*	
Illiterate	52	16	18	86(0.63)
Neo-literate	513	162	127	802(5.87)
Literate	462	325	269	1,056(7.73)
Primary	1,382	1,023	1,050	3,455(25.29)
Secondary	2,276	1,864	1,876	6,016(44.03)
Graduate	510	585	576	1,671(12.25)
Post-Graduate	117	146	200	463(3.39)
Technical	49	22	42	113(0.83)
Total	5,361	4,143	4,158	13,662(100.00)

Figures in the parenthesis indicate percentage.

literate, 7.73 percent are only literate, 25.29 percent of them have educational qualification upto primary level, 44.03 per cent of them have educational qualification upto secondary level, 12.23 percent of them are graduate, 3.39 percent of them are post-graduate. Considering this level of educational status of rural leaders of local democracy, U5MR may be used as a development index. Further, U5MR measures an end result of the development process rather than an input such as mean year of schooling. The U5MR is known to be the result of the variety of inputs: the nutritional health, the health knowledge, availability of health facility and access to this health service, income and food availability in the family and gender disparity in its sharing, educational status, awareness and access to information, availability and access to other social services.

CONCLUSION

As the concept of development has shifted from economic development to human development, local level institutions of rural India are to prepare plans for rural areas and low level of educational status of large number of local leaders, it is the need of the day to use U5MR as a development index for grass-root level democratic institution, particularly in the developing countries.

References

UNDP, *Human Development Report, 1993*, New York, Oxford University Press (1990).

UNICEF, *The State of the World Children, 1994*, Oxford University Press (1994).

Jean Dre'ze and Amartya Sen, *India, Economic Development and Social Opportunity*, New Delhi, Oxford University Press (1995).

Streeten, Paul with Burki, S.J., Mahbub-ul-Haq, Hicks, N. and Stewart F., *First Things, First—Meeting Basic Needs in Developing Countries* (New York. Oxford University Press), 1981.

Bardhan, Pranab K. and T.N. Srinivasan, ed., *Rural Poverty in South Asia*, New York, Columbia University Press, 1988.

World Bank, *World Development Report, 1992*, New York, Oxford University Press, 1992.

10

Returns to Investment in Human Capital: Indian Evidence

P. DURAISAMY

Investment in human capital refers to any spending on persons that raises productive skills and this may take several forms such as schooling, on-the-job training, migration, health and job search (Schultz, 1963). As research proceeded, education emerged as a key form of investment in human beings. In fact, the 'hard core' of human capital theory has turned out to be education and the human capital theory is used synonymously with the theory of investment in education. Recently, health is also recognised as an important form of human capital investment. In fact, the human development index constructed by the UNDP makes use of these two indicators besides the per capita income. The human development index is now being increasingly used as a development indicator to monitor the progress of welfare of the people of a nation and of global society.

This paper first examines the evolution of the concept of human capital. Next we examine the contribution of human resources to the economic growth of nations. Another approach to assess the impact of education on economic development is to estimate the private and social rate of returns to education. The methodology and the available rate of return estimates are summarised. We also present the returns to education in India based on our works. The impact of human capital on several development issues are also discussed. The conclusions are presented at the end.

CONCEPT OF HUMAN CAPITAL IN THE HISTORY OF ECONOMIC THOUGHT

Perhaps the first attempt to estimate the value of the stock of human capital was made in 1691 by William Petty. Adam Smith in his classical work on '*Wealth of Nations*' tried to include the acquired abilities and skills, not human beings, *per se*, as capital. Though some economists like Irving Fisher differ from Smith, Smith's followers like McCulloch supported his view and the concept of human capital flourished. However, Ricardo failed to include human beings in his definition of capital. The concept of human capital was somewhat prominent in economic thinking until Marshall discarded the notion as 'unrealistic'. Economists who considered human beings or their acquired abilities and skill as a component of capital include such well-known names in the history of economic thought as William Petty, Adam Smith, Jean-Baptiste, Say, Nassau Senior, Friedrich List, Johann H. Von Thunen, William Roscher, Walter Bagehot, Ernst Engel, Henry Sidgwick, Leon Walras and Irving Fisher (*Kiker*, 1968). Attempts have also been made to estimate the money value of the aggregate stock of human capital, human beings, loss of human capital due to war, cost of preventable diseases and premature deaths, etc.

The scientific inquiry on the role of human capital on development started with the intellectual inspiration given by the late Nobel Laureate T.W. Schultz (1961, 1963), the father of economics of education. His Presidential address to the American Economic Association (*Schultz*, 1961) on the 'investment in human capital' motivated several young economists and resulted in a voluminous literature on human resources. He rightly points out that the investment in human capital rests on the proposition that "people enhance their capabilities as producers and as consumers by investing in themselves" (*Schultz*, 1963). Thus, investment in human capital is undertaken for investment and consumption benefits. Investment in human capital is expected to enhance the skills and abilities of the individuals and thus result in productivity increase which can be measured through growth in national incomes and higher earnings in the labour market. The works of Denison (1967) on the growth analysis and the methodologies developed by Becker (1965) and Mincer (1974) on the rate of returns to education provided impetus for further work in this area. Attempts to examine the consumption benefits of education took place later with the development of the new theory of consumer behaviour or the new household economics during the 70s.

HUMAN CAPITAL AND ECONOMIC GROWTH

Denison (1967) tried to examine the factors responsible for the growth of modern economies and found that the conventional inputs such as labour and capital could explain only 60% of the total growth of United States' real national income during the period 1948-63. The remaining 40% growth in real national income could be attributed to improvements in human capital. It is estimated that the direct benefit of education accounts for 11% and the remaining 29% is due to the indirect influence in the form of advances in knowledge. Psacharopoulos (1985) based on a study of 29 countries found that the average direct effect of education is 8.7% of the total growth of national income. Similar estimates on the contribution of human capital to the economic growth of India is not available.

RETURNS TO EDUCATION AND HEALTH

Methodology

One of the earliest attempts in the modern literature on the human capital is the estimation of private and social rate of returns to education. Becker (1964) provided the methodological foundation by applying the cost-benefit techniques to compute the returns to education and also estimated the returns using U.S. population census data. This methodology is often referred to as 'elaborate method' as it requires large volume of data to construct the age-earning profiles and cost of education for each level of education. Closely following this and using earnings growth pattern, Mincer (1974) developed a procedure to compute the returns to investment in education and it is called the 'earnings function' method. The earnings function method is not only applied in the returns to education studies but also in addressing a wide range of issues such as wage differentials and discrimination by sex, sector of employment, caste, race, religion, migrant and non-migrant status, union-non-union membership, etc., returns to training, health and so on (see *T.P. Schultz* (1986) for a review).

Returns to Education: Global Estimates

Using the above methodologies, a number of studies have estimated the private and social returns to education. In fact, studies on returns to education now exist for almost all countries of the World. In a recent review, Psacharopolous (1993) summarises comparable studies for about 78 countries based on elaborate method. The average returns to education for different regions of the world are given in Table 1. The table shows that in all the regions of the world, the social and private returns are the highest for primary education. The private returns are much higher than social returns for all levels of education. The higher the level of education the greater the difference between social and private returns. In general, the returns to education declines with the level of education and by the level of development of the country/region.

TABLE 1

Private and Social Rate of Returns to Education by Level of Education and Region

Region	*Social*			*Private*		
	Primary	*Secondary*	*Higher*	*Primary*	*Secondary*	*Higher*
Sub-Saharan Africa	24.3	18.2	11.2	41.3	26.6	27.8
Asia, Europe/Middle	19.9	13.3	11.7	39.0	18.9	19.9
East/North Africa	15.5	11.2	10.6	17.4	15.9	21.7
Latin America/Caribbean	17.9	12.8	12.3	26.2	16.8	19.7
OECD	14.4	10.2	8.7	21.7	12.4	12.3
World	18.4	13.1	10.9	29.1	18.1	20.3

Source: Psacharopolous (1994).

Returns to Education: Indian Estimates

Returns to education in India have been estimated since the early 60s. The estimates of the returns to education in India using the elaborate method are shown in Table 2. We observe more or less similar pattern as seen in the above table. That is, primary education exhibits the highest profitability and the returns decline with increase in the level of education. The available Indian estimates for the whole country is based on the data for the year 1960. The other and more recent studies are based on samples from small geographical regions (from a city or a district).

TABLE 2

Private and Social Rates of Returns to Investment in Education in India

Author	*Blaug et al. (1969)*		*Tilak (1987)*	
Year	*1961*		*1978*	
Coverage;	*All Urban India*		*West Godavari District*	
Educational Level	*Social*	*Private*	*Social*	*Private*
Primary	20.0	25.0	23.0	33.0
Matriculation/Secondary	17.0	19.0	18.0	23.0
Higher	15.0	19.0	11.0	12.0

Source and Note: As given in Psacharopolous (1987). Blaug *et al.* estimates refer to males in urban India and Tilak's estimates are for both males and females in West Godavari district.

We have estimated the private rate of returns to higher education using a large survey data, namely, the Degree Holders and Technical Personnel (DHTP) survey covering all of India for the year 1981. The survey collected information from 1.96 million persons with post-secondary education. The earnings function method is followed in this study and the estimates of the marginal and average rate of returns to higher education are given in Table 3.

In general, the marginal rate of return declines with increase in the level of education. The post-graduate (PG) diploma and degree-holders earn 33% and 18% respectively more than their counterparts with under-graduate (UG) degree. An M.Phil degree fetches 11% higher returns compared to a PG degree while a Ph.D. degree confers 16% higher returns than M.Phil. degree.

TABLE 3

Private Rate of Return to Higher Education by Discipline in India, 1981

Education Level	*All*	*Scientific and Technical Fields*	*Social Science, Arts and other Fields*
PG Diploma *Versus* UG Degree	32.5	30.2	29.9
	(32.5)	(30.2)	(28.9)
PG Degree *Versus* UG Degree	17.5	19.7	17.7
	(8.8)	(9.9)	(8.9)
M.Phil *Versus* PG Degree	11.1	2.9	19.2
	(11.1)	(2.9)	(19.2)
Ph.D. *Versus* M.Phil	15.5	16.2	11.9
	(7.8)	(8.1)	(6.0)

Source and Note: Duraisamy and Duraisamy (1995a). Figures in parenthesis are average returns per year of additional Education.

We also find striking differences between the scientific and technical (S & T) education and social science, arts and other (SS&O) fields. The estimates show that the S&T persons earn higher compared to SS&O persons at any given level of education except M.Phil since M.Phil programmes are not popular in many S&T fields such as engineering, medicine, etc.

Returns to Education: Gender Differences

It has been observed in several studies that the returns to female education are higher than those to male education. We also estimate the gender specific returns to higher education based on the DHTP data and these are provided in Table 4. Women's education is found to be more profitable compared to men's education for all except M.Phil and Ph.D. degrees since the number of females in these two levels are small. For instance, women with PG diploma/degree earn 40 and 24% more than UG degree while men with comparable level of education earn only 26 and 12% more than UG degree.

TABLE 4

Gender Specific difference in Private Rate of Returns to Higher Education in India

Education Level	*All Technical Fields*		*Scientific and Other Fields*		*Social Science, Arts*	
	Male	*Female*	*Male*	*Female*	*Male*	*Female*
PG Diploma *Versus* UG Degree	26.3	40.0	23.1	43.8	29.6	16.6
	(26.3)	(40.0)	(23.1)	(43.8)	(29.6)	(16.6)
PG Degree *Versus* UG Degree	12.4	23.6	13.6	24.6	13.6	24.0
	(6,2)	(11.8)	(6.8)	(12.3)	(6.8)	(12.0)
M.Phil *Versus* PG Degree	16.4	12.2	-0.6	5.8	14.8	17.1
	(16.4)	(12.2)	(-0.6)	(5.8)	(14.8)	(17.1)
Ph.D. *Versus* M. Phil	20.0	19.8	21.1	18.0	13.5	22.5
	(10.0)	(9.9)	(10.6)	(9.0)	(6.8)	(11.3)

Source and Note: Duraisamy and Duraisamy (1995a). Figures in parenthesis are average returns per year of additional education.

Returns to Health

The earning function methodology is applied to study the impact of health on wages in the labour market and to estimate the returns to health status indicators. In a recent study, we have estimated the impact of health on wages in the rural agricultural labour market using household level data from two districts of Tamil Nadu. The estimates are given in Table 5. Two health indicators namely ill-days and body mass index are used. The body mass index is defined as a ratio of weight over height's square. The results indicate that a unit (one day) increase in ill-days reduces the daily wage of males and females by 0.18 and 0.16% respectively. Similarly, a unit increase in the body mass index of males and females increases their daily wage by 3.3 and 1.1% respectively. Thus, the impact of health on the wages of males seems to be about three times that of females. From the same data, we also estimated the returns to education and found that one year increase in the education of adult males and females results in 1.65% and 0.87% increase in daily wages in the rural labour market.

TABLE 5

Returns to Education and Health in the Rural Agricultural Labour Market, Tamil Nadu, 1994-95

Human Capital Variable	*Adult Males*	*Adult Females*
Health Indicator: Ill-days	-0.18	-0.16
Body Mass Index	3.31	1.13
Education (average per year)	1.65	0.87

Source and Notes: Duraisamy and Sathiyavan (1998). The figures are in percentage terms. See text for explanation.

TABLE 6

Effect of Education on Agricultural Production in India

Year and Region	*Source*	*Co-efficient of Education*	*Measurement of Education*
1961-64 Punjab, Haryana and UP	Chaudhri (1979)	0.114 (3.65)	Years of Schooling
1977 Tamil Nadu	Kalirajan & Shand (1985)	0.102 (2.54)	Years of Schooling
1980-81 Tamil Nadu	Duraisamy (1992)	0.043 (2.23)	>4 years (dummy)
1980-81 Tamil Nadu	Duraisamy (1990)	0.198 (2.93)	>4 years (dummy)

Notes: a. 't'-statistics in parenthesis.

Returns to Education in Farm Production

Another area in which the human capital has a strong positive impact is on the agricultural production (Table 6). These effects are called technical (or worker) and allocative effects of education. Chaudhri (1979) using agricultural production function shows that the education enhances farm output by 11% and the marginal value product of education is Rs. 150 while Duraisamy (1992) found that the marginal value product to be Rs. 356. In another study using the profit function approach,

Duraisamy (1990) shows that the educated farmers are more technically and allocatively efficient than their uneducated counterparts (illiterates). His estimates indicate about 20% higher profit for the educated farmers.

Non-Market Benefits of Human Capital

Studies show that education yields substantial benefits other than the higher returns in the labour market. These benefits take the form of reduction in fertility or family size, infant and child mortality, increases in children's schooling, better allocation of non-market time, etc. Duraisamy and Malathy (1990) using district level data for all major states show that an increase in the percentage of adult males and females with secondary education significantly reduces the fertility and increases the investment in child schooling. Duraisamy and Duraisamy (1995b) based on household level data from Tamil Nadu show empirical evidence on the impact of parental education on child survival and preventive health care measures.

CONCLUSION

The concept of human capital was known in the early economic literature dating back to Adam Smith. However, the scientific inquiry and the treatment of human capital as an investment gained currency only since the intellectual inspiration given by the late Nobel Laureate Theodore W. Schultz in the 1960s. Among various forms of investment in human capital, education emerged as a key form of investment and recently health is also recognised as an important form of human capital. Attempts have been made to estimate returns to education and health and non-market benefits of education, particularly women's education in the Indian context.

We have presented the estimates of rate of return to education in India and for higher education based on the DHTP survey data. The results are in line with the stylized facts that primary education continues to be the most profitable and private returns are higher than social returns. The marginal rate of return to education declines with increase in the level of education. In higher education, scientific and technical education is more rewarding than the social science, arts and other fields. The returns to female education is higher than those to male education except at M.Phil and Ph.D. level.

This paper also presents our estimates on the returns to health and the finding that good health pay-off in the form of higher wages in the labour market. The other benefits of investment in human capital include increased agricultural production and also educations effect on household decisions such as family size, child schooling, infant and child mortality, labour supply, allocation of time to non-market work, etc.

In sum, the available evidence in the Indian context points to the fact that the investment in human capital is rewarding both for the individuals as well as to the society. Much work is needed on the role of other forms of human capital such as training, information, health, migration, etc. and further work in this fascinating area of research would be rewarding.

References

Becker, G.S. (1964), *Human Capital: A Theoretical Analysis with Special Reference to Education*, New York, Columbia University Press for NBER.

Blaug, M., R. Layard and M. Woodhall (1969), *Causes of Graduate Unemployment in India*, London, Penguin Press, 1969.

Chaudhuri, D.P. (1979), *Education, Innovations and Agricultural Development*, London, I.L.O.

Denison, E.F. (1967), *Why Growth Rates Differ: Post-War Experience in Nine Western Countries*, Washington, D.C. : Brookings Institute.

Duraisamy, P. (1990), Technical and Allocative Efficiency of Education in Agricultural Production: A Profit Function Approach, *Indian Economic Review*, Vol. XXV, No. 1.

——— (1992), Effects of Education and Extension Contacts on Agricultural Production, *Indian Journal of Agricultural Economics*, Vol. 47, No. 2.

——— and Malathy Duraisamy (1995a), Returns to Higher Education in India, *Journal of Educational Planning and Administration*, Vol. IX, No. 1, January, 1995.

——— (1995b), Determinants of Investment in Health of Boys and Girls : Evidence from Rural Households of Tamil Nadu, India, *Indian Economic Review*, Vol. 30, No. 1.

Duraisamy, P. and R. Malathy (1990), Impact of Public Programs on Fertility and Gender Specific Investment in Human Capital of Children in Rural India : Cross Sectional and Time Series Analyses, *Research in Population Economics*, Vol. 7.

Duraisamy, P. and D. Sathiyavan (1998), Impact of Health Status on Wages and Labour Supply of Men and Women: Evidence From a Rural Household Survey, *Indian Journal of Labour Economics*, Vol. 41.

Kalirajan, K.P. and R.T. Shand (1985), Type of Education and Agricultural Productivity : A Quantitative Analysis of Tamil Nadu Rice Farming, *The Journal of Development Studies*, Vol. 21, No. 2.

Kiker, B.F. (1968), Human Capital: In Retrospect, *Essays in Economics*, No. 16, University of Southern California, USA.

Malathy, R. and P. Duraisamy (1993), Returns to Scientific and Technical Education in India, *Margin*, Vol. 25, No. 4.

Mincer, J. (1974), *Schooling, Experience and Earnings*, New York, Columbia University Press for NBER.

Psacharopolous, G. (1985), Returns to Education: A Further International Update and Implications, *Journal of Human Resources*, Vol. 20, No. 4.

——— (1987), Economic Development and Investment: The Role of the Work Force, *Journal of Educational Planning and Administration*, Vol. 1, Nos. 3-4.

——— (1993), Returns to Investment in Education: A Global Update, *Policy Research Working Paper No. 1067*, The World Bank.

Schultz, T.P. (1988), Educational Investments and Returns, *Handbook of Development Economics*, Vol. 1, H. Chenery and T.N. Srinivasan (eds.), Amsterdam: North Holland.

Schultz, T.W. (1961), Investment in Human Capital, *American Economic Review*, Vol. 51, No. 1.

——— (1963), *The Economic Value of Education*, New York: Columbia University Press.

Tilak, J.B.G. (1987), *The Economics of Inequality in Education*, New Delhi : Sage Publications.

11

Human Development and Poverty: Some Policy Issues

G. Karunakaran Pillai

The average income of a country does not, *per se*, say anything about the quality of life of its citizens. There is no automatic link between income and human lives, as higher income does not automatically translate into better human lives. Accumulation of wealth may not necessarily fulfil several kinds of human choices. The main purpose of development is to enlarge people's choices. This covers the objective of creating a favourable environment for people to enjoy a long and healthy life, to be educated and to enjoy a decent standard of living, political freedom, other guaranteed human rights, dignity, self-respect and respect of others. Thus, the process of widening people's choices denotes human development. If human development is about enlarging choices, poverty means the opportunities and choices most basic to human development are denied.

Development is analysed in terms of people. The touchstone of the success of development policies becomes the betterment of people. Human development fosters the formation of human capabilities, such as improved health, knowledge and skills. People are the means and ends of development. People are not the mere instruments for producing commodities through the augmentation of human capital. Human beings are the ultimate end of development. Human development has important components of productivity, equity, sustainability and empowerment. Human development is a holistic concept.

Poverty is too complex to be reduced to a single dimension of human life. There are three perspectives on poverty: (1) Income perspective—income level below a defined poverty line, (2) Basic needs perspective—deprivation of material requirements for minimally acceptable fulfilment of human needs, and (3) Capability perspective—absence of some basic capabilities to function. Poverty in human development approach draws particularly on the capability perspective.

HUMAN DEVELOPMENT INDEX (HDI)

Since 1990, UNDP has constructed HDI for various countries of the world. In essence the index combined three aspects: health, education and per capita income. These three elements of the index represent the achievements in basic human capabilities in three fundamental dimensions, viz., a long and healthy life; knowledge and a decent standard of living.

In Human Development Report (1997) the HDI is based on four variables; life expectancy at birth; adult literacy; combined first, second and third level enrolment ratio; and adjusted real GDP per capita in terms of purchasing power parity measure of 1994. These four indicators are reduced to three indices : the life expectancy index, education index and the GDP index. The health status is measured by life expectancy, knowledge is represented by literacy and the school enrolment ratio and per capita income by the GDP at PPP rates in US dollars. 175 countries have been ranked on the basis of composite HDI. These countries are grouped under three heads as high (HDI value of 0.80 and above), middle (HDI value of 0.5 to 0.79) and low (HDI value below 0.5) income human development countries.

The HDI value ranging from 0.96 to 0.80 to the developed countries and countries like Singapore, Hong Kong, Republic of Korea, Thailand and Malaysia and also most Latin American countries. In medium human development countries, the rank ranging from 0.67 to 0.50 such in Russia, Brazil, Srilanka, the Philippines, China, Egypt and Iraq. In low human development countries the rank ranging from 0.48 to 0.18, we have Kenya, India, Pakistan, Bangladesh, Uganda, etc.

GENDER-RELATED DEVELOPMENT INDEX

Human Development Report, 1995 focussed on the dimensions of gender inequality in development and introduced two development measures. Gender Development Index (GDI) and Gender Empowerment Measure (GEM) GDI measures achievements of a country in basic human capabilities like health, education and standard of living, taking note of inequality in the achievement between men and women. GEM focuses on three variables : income earning power; share in managerial, administrative and professional employment; and share of seats in parliament.

In Human Development Report (1997), GDI was calculated for 146 countries. Canada tops the GDI rankings. The second and third ranking countries are in the Nordie belt—Norway and Sweden. The Scandinavian countries do exceptionally well in terms of GDI, implying that women enjoy relatively far higher social, economic and political status. India performs extremely poorly in ranking—86th barely ahead of Pakistan (ranked 92) and well behind China ranked (28) Indian women face poorly *vis-a-vis* men not only in health, but also in education and income levels. Several developing countries do well in GDI ranking : Barbados (17), Singapore (27), Hongkong (28), Uruguay (31), the Republic of Korea (35), and Thailand (39). These countries have succeeded in enhancing basic capabilities of women. The bottom places are occupied by Sierra Leone, Niger, Burkina Faso, Mali and Ethiopia, in ascending order. Women in these countries face deprivation.

Human Development Report (1997) ranked 116 countries in terms of GEM. Sweden tops the list where 34% of Parliamentarians, 39% of administrators and managers and a whopping 63% of all professional and technical workers are women. Further 50% of the cabinet ministers are women. While India performs poorly in the sense that only 7% of Parliamentarians, 2% of administrators and managers and 21% of professionals are women.

Like GDI ranking GEM ranking demonstrates the non-correspondence between national income and women status. UAE ranked 4th in GDP, it ranked 94th in GEM. Incongruence between GEM and real GDP can be seen in Singapore, South Korea, France and Turkey, while China, Cuba, Sri Lanka and Hungary do far better in GEM than in GDP. Gender gap in health, education and political and economic participation shows the long way to go in the struggle for gender equality.

Several conclusions can be drawn from the gender disparity. First, the GDI value for every country is lower than HDI value showing that no society treats its women as well as its men. Secondly, gender inequality is strongly associated with human poverty. Finally, gender equality can be achieved at different income levels and stages of development, which means that it can be achieved across a range of cultures and political ideologies.

HUMAN POVERTY INDEX (HPI)

The *Human Development Report (1997)* introduced a new measure of deprivation among nations—Human Poverty Index (HPI). HPI attempts to bring together in a comprehensive index the different features of deprivation in the quality of life to arrive at an aggregate judgement on the extent of poverty in a community. This has been attempted in the Human Development Report, 1996 through a particular version of the "capability poverty measure". The HPI pursues the same approach, focusing on a broader and more representative set of variables, in a consistent relation to HDI. HPI in a sense measures the extent to which the country falls short in human development. It is the opposite of HDI. It looks at shortcomings in health and educational status of each country's citizens, the actual data used are different.

HPI concentrates on deprivation in three essential elements—longevity, knowledge and decent living standard. The first deprivation relates to survival—vulnerability to death at a relatively early age. It is the percentage of people expected to die before age 40. The second dimension relates to knowledge—being excluded from the world of reading and communication. It is measured by the percentage of adult who are illiterate. The third aspect relates to a decent standard of living. This is represented by a composite of three variables—the percentage of people without access to safe water, the percentage of people without access to health services, and the percentage of moderately and severely underweight children under five. The HPI, in general, measures the extent of deprivation in each country. It is estimated as one value in percentage terms, which shows what proportion of the population suffers from 'human poverty'.

The *Human Development Report, 1997* estimates the HDI for 175 developed and developing countries. However, HDI has been estimated only for developing countries. Owing to the non-availability of data for all developing countries, HPI has been calculated for only 78 countries. At the top of the rankings are Trinidad and Tobago, Cuba and Chile. These countries have reduced human poverty to the point at which it affects less than 10% of the population. At the bottom are countries like Niger, Sierre Leone, etc. whose HPI exceeds 50%. In India, it is 36.7%. In almost half of the 78 countries, HPI exceeds 34%, implying that about a third of their people suffer human poverty.

Let us examine how does the HPI compare with income-based poverty measures: (1) Some countries have relatively high income, where human development is high and human poverty is low. (2) Some countries with abysmally low per capita income and low human development and very high human poverty. (3) There are countries like India with fairly low per capita income rank and low levels of achievement in human development and high incidence of human poverty. (4) Countries like Egypt, Pakistan, Namibia and Morocco rank higher in HDI than in HPI, signalling the need for greater attention to human development for the most deprived. (5) Countries like Zimbabwe, Cuba, China and Vietnam rank much higher in HPI than in HDI, which shows that in these countries overall progress in human development was pro-poor. (6) Countries at the bottom of HPI ranking also rank near the bottom in HDI. (7) HPI estimates at regional and global level show that human poverty affects a quarter of developing world, while income poverty affects a third. Human poverty is widespread in Sub-Saharan Africa and South Asia, affecting about 40% of people.

INDICATORS OF HUMAN POVERTY

(1) Short Life

One major indicator of human poverty is short life. Deprivation in years of life is reflected in dying before age of 40. Nearly fifth of the people in developing countries die before age of 40, which is four times the proportion in industrial countries. Child mortality also represents a severe deprivation. In Sub-Saharan Africa child mortality rate is 100 per 1,000 live births as against 112 per 1000 in East Asia which is nearly 6 times that in industrial countries. Similarly, maternal mortality rate in developing world is 471 per 100,000 live births, more than 15 times the rate in industrial countries.

(2) Deprivation in Health

In developing world, around 17 million people die each year from curable infections and parasitic diseases. Nearly 50% of people in Sub-Saharan Africa do not have access to health services, as against 20% for the developing world. Nearly 31% of the people in developing world do not have access to safe water, it is 42% in Sub-Saharan Africa. The share of underweight children under five in South Asia is 50%. About 78% of pregnant women in South Asia suffer from anaemia, it is 50% for the developing world. Thus, the health backlog in the developing world is enormous.

(3) Housing Deprivation

More than a billion people in developing world live without adequate shelter. Poor housing is often connected with poor sanitation that exposes people to infection.

(4) Knowledge Backlog

The developing world has more than 840 million illiterate adults, 538 of them are women. Female illiteracy is 40% in developing world. Nearly half the developing world's illiterates (407 million) are in South Asia. Nearly half the children (50 million) are out of school in South Asia. This may be viewed against the background of near universal education and close to 100% literacy in industrial countries. Developing world has about 200 radios per 1000 people, a fifth of the ratio in industrial countries, and 140 televisions per 1000 people, a little more than a fourth of that in industrial countries.

(5) Lack of Personal Security

Crime and violence are on the rise, and most of the victims are poor. The worst threats of violence are those against women. A third of married women in developing world are battered by their husbands. Dowry deaths and rapes show shocking figures. Children are also subject to many abuses. 25 million children aged 10-14 labour in developing countries (45 million of them in Asia) are working in slavery, prostitution and hazardous conditions. Each year 1 million girls in Asia are forced into prostitution.

(6) Environmental Deterioration

Continuing environmental deterioration is a source of continuing impoverishment. Half of a billion poor people in developing world live in ecologically fragile regions. Water supply per capita in developing countries is only a third of what it was in 1970, more than 55% of the people in the Arab States suffer from serious water scarcity. Some 8-10 million acres of forest land are lost every year in developing countries. Air pollution is serious, as 700 million people, in poor rural areas inhale indoor smoke from burning bio-mass fuel. In developing countries, a third to a half of urban solid wastes go uncollected with serious health implications.

The trend analysis of human poverty shows that human poverty affects more than a quarter of the population in developing countries. Sub-Saharan Africa and South Asia has the highest incidence of both income poverty (the World Bank uses a poverty line of $ 1 at 1985 PPP $ a day per person) and human poverty at about 40%. South Asia is the home of two-fifths of income poor of developing countries and almost half of those in human poverty. We are living in a world where 1.3 billion people struggling to survive on less than the equivalent of $ 1 a day, 160 million children are malnourished, 840 million live without secure source of food and 1.2 billion lack access to safe water.

SIX-POINT ACTION PLAN

The UNDP set out six actions required to eradicate poverty in the 21st century. (1) Empower people to gain greater control over their life by ensuring access to assets, food security, education and health and building social safety nets; (2) strengthen gender equality; (3) Accelerate pro-poor growth, i.e., growth restores full employment, creates an enabling environment for small farmers and enterprises, restructure fiscal policy and reverse environmental degradation; (4) Improve the management of globalisation; (5) ensure an active state; (6) Special actions for special situations, i.e., more effective support to Sub-Saharan Africa and other LDC's.

UNDP places the costs of eradicating poverty at about 1% of global income, no more than 2-3% of national income of all developing countries. The cost of achieving basic social services for all in the developing world is estimated at about $ 40 billion a year over the 10 years to 2005, to provide basic education for all ($6 billion) basic health and nutrition ($13 billion), reproductive health and family planning ($12 billion) and low cost water supply and sanitation ($9 billion). Less than 0.2% of world income, this sum is about 1% of developing country income—or half the GNP share of the United States transferred each year to Europe during 1948-52 as part of the Marshall Plan for post-war reconstruction.

The world summit for Social Development, 1995 endorsed the 20:20 development agreements, i.e., governments should allocate 20% of their budgets and the donors 20% of their aid budget, to basic social services, sufficient for universal coverage.

GENERATION OF RESOURCES FOR HUMAN DEVELOPMENT EXPENDITURE

Poverty of resources is often suggested as a cause for the neglect of investments in human development. The following are the avenues for major improvements in the spending of existing resources:

(1) *Cut in military spending*: Many countries are mortgaging their development options with huge military expenditure. It is estimated that both India and Pakistan together spend $ 20 billion a year on defence. There is immense scope for cut in military spending and channelisation of the savings to poverty reduction and pro-poor growth.

(2) *Privatisation of public sector assets*: Public sector enterprises are crowding out much needed social investment. Many public sector assets such as public industries, nationalised banks, power stations,

telecommunications, etc. can be privatised and high cost domestic debts wiped out.

(3) *Inject pro-poor bias in social sector investment through efficient and equitable reduction*: Budgetary resources shall be spent on essential development needs—Development Report, 1991 shows that 34% total social sector spending in India and only 14% in Pakistan is earmarked for priority human needs in basic education, rural health care and water supply, family planning and nutrition programmes. The rest is earmarked for projects benefiting a tiny minority of privileged groups. There are many avenues for efficient and more equitable re-allocation of resources.

(4) *Continue anti-poverty programmes with better management and accountability*: Anti-poverty and human development programmes have found problems like leakages, corrupt practices and over-inclusion and under-inclusion of beneficiaries. Management, accountability and transparency and community involvement are improved in anti-poverty programmes.

(5) *Balancing social sector reform with economic reforms*: Economic reforms have focussed on industry and trade but a clear agenda has not yet been articulated for social sector. The dynamism evident in economic sector reforms is not matched by similar momentum in social sector. Hence, reforms should be focussed on social sector.

The International community can lend a helping hand for achieving the human development goals in the following ways:

(1) *By restructuring existing aid allocation*: The per capita aid received by South Asia accounts for only $ 5 as against $ 55 by countries of Middle-east, despite their per capita income more than three times that of South Asia. India receives less than 5% of total CDA, yet it has nearly one-third of world's absolute poor.

(2) *Prioritisation of aid for human development expenditure*: At present less than 5% of bilateral aid and less than

10% of multilateral aid is earmarked for priority expenditures like education, primary health care and safe water.

(3) *Dismantle all trade barriers so as to enable the developing countries to share more of the global economic opportunities*: Developing countries suffer a potential annual loss of at least $ 500 billion from restriction in global market for goods and services and for capital and labour as per the calculation of Human Development Report, 1992. The market loss of developing countries accounts for as large on 10 times the total foreign assistance they receive each year.

According to a World Bank study, two-thirds of the sources of growth are human and social capital. Thus, human development permits a faster and larger economic development.

References

Ahmed, E.J., Dreze, J. Hills and A. Sen (eds.) (1991), *Social Security in Developing Countries*, Oxford : Clarendon Press.

Arthreya, V.B. and S.R. Chunkath (1996), *Literacy and Empowerment*, New Delhi: Sage Publications.

Dreze, J. and A. Sen (1989), *Hunger and Public Action*, Oxford: Clarendon Press.

Haq, Mahabubul (1995), *Reflection on Human-Development*, Oxford : Oxford University Press.

———, (1996), "Human Development Paradigm", D.T. Lakdawala Memorial Lecture, *Institute of Social Science*, New Delhi, February 7.

Human Development Centre (1997), *Human Development in South Asia, 1997*, Karachi: Oxford University Press.

Nanjundappa, D.M. (1997), "Formulating a Development Paradigm", Paper presented at the Fourth Asian Conference on Scientific Co-operation, Tokyo, February 3-7.

Parikh, Kirit (Ed.) (1997), *India Development Report, 1997*, New Delhi : Oxford University Press.

Sen, Amartya, K. (1983), "Poor, Relatively Speaking", *Oxford Economic Papers*, 35.

——— (1992), *Inequality Re-examined*, Oxford: Clarendon Press.

——— (1993), "Life Expectancy and Inequality: Some Conceptual Issues", in P.K. Bardhan, M. Dattachaudhuri and T.N. Krishnan (eds.), *Development and Chance*, Bombay: Oxford University Press.

UNDP (1997), *Human Development Report, 1997*, New York: Oxford University Press.

——— (1996), *Human Development Report, 1996*, New York: Oxford University Press.

——— (1995), *Human Development Report, 1995*, New York: Oxford University Press.

——— (1992), *Human Development Report, 1992*, New York: Oxford University Press.

World Bank (1995), *Economic Development in India: Achievements and Challenges*, Washington, D.C.: The World Bank.

12

Human Development through Poverty Alleviation

KASTURI BAI DHANASEKARAN

INTRODUCTION

UNDP defines human development as a process of enlarging people's choice, including to live a long and healthy life, to be educated and to have access to resources needed for a decent standard of living. The premise of this approach is that people are beneficiaries of development. National income and economic growth are not automatically translated into the betterment of life. The focus of development is on people and how people benefit from development. Income is a means and not an end. The attainment of high levels of income in itself is not important. What is more important is how income is spent to benefit people. In an attempt to measure and monitor human development, UNDP constructed a human development index, incorporating a wide range of indicators, focussing on three essential elements of human life, namely, longevity, knowledge and decent living standard.

Poverty is a reflection of shortfalls and deprivation in various indicators of human development such as life expectancy, educational and nutritional levels, per capita income and access to various goods and services. It also signifies lack of progress in human development, inadequacy and under-attainment in the desired levels of human development indicators. Alleviation of poverty will no doubt contribute significantly towards human development. With increased incomes and improvements in basic needs, people's access to better educational, nutritional and health services will increase and contribute significantly towards human development. Reduction in poverty is expected to contribute positively towards improving health, education, population growth and economic performance.

The problem of poverty is massive and there is a need to improve the conditions of the poor with appropriate public policies. Poverty alleviation is considered core to India's planning philosophy. Poverty alleviation programmes are directed towards massive employment generation and direct transfer programmes through subsidized consumption and delivery of basic services including education, health, etc. Effective implementation of these programmes is crucial to attack poverty on the frontline and to promote human development. Hence, an attempt is made in this paper to assess the effectiveness of poverty alleviation programmes in promoting human development.

This paper has been divided into three sections. The first section deals with the human resource development of India in the global context. Incidence of poverty before and after economic reforms have been discussed in the second section. Effectiveness of the public policy as an anti-poverty measure is being analysed in the last section.

Human Resource Development in the Global Context

The human development index introduced by UNDP combines life expectancy, educational attainments and income indicators to give a composite measure of human development. India occupies a very low position in this ranking 121, next to Pakistan which is at 120. Ten top positions go to Canada, Japan, Norway, Switzerland, Sweden, USA, Australia, France, Netherland and UK. Among Asian countries Sri Lanka occupies highest ranking (76) and Bangladesh lowest (135).

TABLE 1

Human Development Indicators (Selected Countries)

Country	*Life Expectancy in years (1990)*	*Adult Literacy rate in % (1990)*	*Real GDP per capita in dollars (1989)*	*Ranking (1990)*
Canada	77.0	99	18,635	1
Japan	78.6	99	14,311	2
Norway	77.1	89	16,838	3
Switzerland	77.4	99	18,590	4
Sweden	77.4	89	14,817	5
USA	75.9	99	20,998	6
Australia	76.5	99	15,266	7
France	76.4	99	14,164	8
Netherlands	77.2	99	13,351	9
U.K.	75.2	99	13,732	10
Sri Lanka	70.9	88.4	2,253	76
Pakistan	57.7	34.8	1,789	120
India	59.1	48.2	910	121
Bangladesh	51.8	35.3	820	135

HRD in India and Developing Countries

The extent of human deprivation in India at the beginning of 1990s could be assessed from Table 2.

TABLE 2

Human Deprivation in 1990 (Millions)

Deprivation	*India*	*All Developing Countries*
Without access to safe water	220.0	1,325
Malnutrition in children under 5	46.9	180
Children not in schools	75.4	325
Illiterate adults	280.0	950
Illiterate females	180.0	600

Expenditure on HRD

The expenditure on HRD has been low in India. The public expenditure on health and education were respectively 0.9% and 3.2% of GNP in 1990 in India, against 1.4% and 3.6% respectively in all developing countries. The daily calorie supply per capita was 2,014 in 1988 as against 2,440 in all developing countries. The social security benefits stood at 4.3% of GDP in 1980 in India as against world average of 10% and developing countries average of 5%.

Table 3 portrays the information regarding HRD in India and developing countries. The achievements during the last three decades on HRD in India has been moderate. Life expectancy at birth has gone up from 44 years to 59 years and mortality rate has been reduced from 282 in 1960 to 142 in 1990, population with access to safe water has increased from 31 in 1975-80 to 75% in 1989-90 and daily clorie supply has increased from 89 to 90% of requirement during 1965 to 1988. The adult literacy rate has increased from 34% in 1970 to 48% in 1990. The combined primary and secondary enrolment ratio has gone up from 49 to 67 during 1970 to 1989. The real GDP per capita has increased from $ 530 in 1960 to $ 910 in 1989. In comparison to all developing countries India's achievements have been above average in reducing mortality rate and increasing daily calorie supply. The growth in real GDP per capita has however, been much below the average.

Incidence of Poverty in India

Several estimates on poverty are available for pre- and post-economic reform periods. Poverty indicator given in Table 4 is being based on Planning Commission's all India poverty line of monthly per capita total expenditure (MPCTE) of Rs. 49.90 (Rural) and Rs. 56.65 (Urban) at 1973-74 levels.

Turning to the trends in the pre-reform period, rural poverty has shown a consistent reduction during the period 1970-71 to 1989-90 before showing a mild increase in 1990-91. The rate of decline was faster in 1980s. The decline in poverty in 1980s could be attributed to stable agriculture growth and the impact of official poverty alleviation programmes. Till 1987-88 rural poverty ratios were fluctuating with agricultural output. In other words, poverty increased (decreased) during bad (good) agricultural periods. In 1987-88, however, rural poverty declined inspite of significant

TABLE 3

Human Resource Development in India and Developing Countries

Countries	*Life Expectancy at birth in years*		*Mortality under five*		*Population with access to safe water (%)*		*Daily Calorie supply (%) of requirement*		*Adult Literacy rate (%)*		*Combine Primary & Secondary enrolment ratio*		*Real GDP per capita (US $ PPP)*	
	1960	*1990*	*1960*	*1990*	*1975*	*1989*	*1965*	*1988*	*1970*	*1990*	*1970*	*1989*	*1960*	*1989*
India	44	59	282	142	31	75	89	94	34	48	49	67	530	910
All Developing Countries	46.2	628	233	112	40	68	90	109	46	64	55	72	784	2296

TABLE 4

Poverty Indicators

Year	*People below the poverty line in %*	
	Rural	*Urban*
1970-71	57.33	45.89
1972-73	57.21	47.00
1973-74	56.71	49.20
1977-78	54.47	42.86
1983-84	49.02	38.33
1986-87	45.21	35.39
1987-88	44.88	36.52
1988-89	42.23	35.07
1989-90	36.69	34.76
1990-91	37.48	35.04
1991-92	40.07	34.79
1992-93	46.07	36.37
1993-94	39.65	30.94

decline in agricultural production. In this year, the public distribution system and the special employment programmes of some state governments have helped in arresting the increase in poverty in a drought year. The point is that public action in the form of employment generation makes a greater impact on alleviating when the real value of wage payment in cereal units is not eroded by the increase in rural prices of cereals. The non-farm employment also increased during the 1980s and helped in reducing rural poverty.

The urban poverty registered an increase between 1970-71 and 1973-74 and showed a decline between 1977-78 and 1986-87. It remained unchanged between 1986-87 and 1990-91. It may be noted that unlike in rural areas there has not been any major anti-poverty programmes in urban areas. High growth in 1980s, however, would have its impact on the demand of the unorganised sector. Public policy in food management via buffer stock and PDS also had a poverty reducing impact in urban areas. It may be noted that the delivery systems for urban PDS are much better than those for rural areas. The rural-urban migration also seemed to have declined during the 1980s which could be due to the higher growth in rural areas.

When examining the trends in poverty after the reforms, rural poverty increased significantly in the first two and a half years of reforms (1991, 1992 & 1993). In 1992, it was around 46% but declined to 40% in 1993-94. As compared to 1990-91 (the pre-reform years) rural poverty was higher in 1993-94. Urban poverty increased in 1992 and 1993 before declining significantly to 31% in 1993-94. In other words, a comparison of 1990-91 and 1993-94 shows that rural poverty increased by about 2% while urban poverty declined by 4%.

There are three main factors that caused an increase in the incidence of rural poverty in the post-reform period, namely, stabilisation measures, poor agricultural performance and increase in food prices. A more moderate rise in urban poverty in the first two years of the reform period and a decline in 1993-94 was attributable to the slower pace of reform in the industrial and public sector along with the relaxation of fiscal contraction.

EVALUATING POVERTY ALLEVIATION PROGRAMMES

Social safety measures such as public distribution system (PDS) and expansion of employment schemes like Employment Guarantee Scheme (EGS), Integrated Rural Development Programme (IRDP) have been undertaken on a large scale. Effectiveness of these programmes in reducing poverty has been evaluated and measures for strengthening these programmes have been suggested.

Public Distribution System (PDS)

As an anti-poverty device, PDS aims at transferring incomes to low income persons and the programme becomes more targeted towards poor persons and regions. It aims at raising nutritional standards of vulnerable groups of persons and ensuring household level food security. The average quantity of both rice and wheat distributed through fair price shops during 1965-67 was about 9 million tonnes (19% of the net availability) which went upto 16 million tonnes during 1989-90 (15% of net availability). There are, however, many problems with the present PDS viz., (1) PDS supplies are supplemental in nature and do not aim at meeting the total requirement of all families. Therefore, open market remains as the primary source of supplies for the poor consumers. The dependence of the poor on the PDS in rural areas for many commodities is less than 16%. (2) There are considerable regional disparities of foodgrains under PDS. The pattern of distribution does not seem to be related to the extent of poverty. The correlation between shares in PDS and shares in population below poverty line across the states is as low as 0.25 but the correlation is high with 0.56 with respect to shares in urban population, implying urban bias in PDS. (3) Many empirical studies based on 1986-87 NSS data have shown that the poor were not benefitting much from the PDS. For every rupee spent, less than 22 paise reach the poor in all states. The cost effectiveness of reaching the poorest 20% of households through PDS is small. (4) PDS also suffers from leakages of foodgrains in the form of losses in the transport and storage and diversion to the free market. Leakages are estimated to be about one-third of the quantity supplied into the PDS. Nearly one-half of rice procured from surplus states is of superfine variety but such rice is rarely available in fair price shops. It leaks into open market where prices are higher than at fair price shops. (5) Inefficiencies in the operation of Food Corporation of India (FCI) has been remarked by the Bureau of Industrial Costs and Prices. The economic cost of FCI foodgrain operation has been rising both on account of increase in procurement as well as the distribution incidentals and the subsidized credit given to FCI and preference given by the railways in handling freight. (6) Another problem seems to be the narrowing down of the gap between the PDS prices and the open market prices. As a result, PDS off-take declined in recent years. (7) The role of PDS in containing inflation appears to be somewhat limited. Parikh has found that free market prices are not lower where PDS exists. In any case, the quantities distributed through PDS are no more than 15-16% of total availability. (8) It may be also noted that the Central Government issues foodgrains to states for PDS at a uniform common issue price, whereas the consumer and retail price fixed by the state governments for PDS varies considerably between states.

The following strengthening measures could be taken to restructure PDS: (1) there seems to be two solutions for targeting of PDS to the poor. The first one is to target PDS to wage employment programmes like JRY and EGS as it leads to self-targeting. (2) The panchayats should be given the responsibility of identifying the poor and managing the PDS. (3) Buffer stock should be managed efficiently for stabilizing the prices and steps could be taken to reduce FCI's overheads. (4) Plugging leakages in the issue points, at the retail shop or during the transit or because of bogus ration cards could save 35% of foodgrains distributed.

Rural Works Programmes (RWPs)

There has been much enthusiasm for employment programmes. RWPs such as Employment Guarantee Scheme (EGS) in Maharashtra, and the Central Government Programmes like Jawahar Rojgar Yojana (JRY) and Employment Assurance Schemes (EAS) have been tried in India. One of the strong points of RWPs is that they are self-targeting, (i.e.) only the target group of unskilled manual workers are likely to participate. Leakages to the non-poor are expected to be minimum due to self-targeting.

The contribution of EGS in reducing underemployment in Maharashtra varies from 10% to 30% of the total person days of underemployment. The micro-evidences show that the employment provision of person days per person in a year varies from 23 to 170. There are also several secondary benefits of EGS, viz. (1) EGS projects contribute to the creation of rural assets and they can have substantial impact on agricultural growth. (2) EGS puts an upward pressure on agricultural wages. (3) It can act as an insurance for the rural workers and can prevent acute distress and avoid the need for costly form of adjustment such as selling productive assets or livestocks. (4) It does not discriminate between men and women while paying wages and it has expanded the right to work for the rural women.

A close and critical look at the EGS reveals the following: (1) since about 1988, there has been a very sharp drop in employment created under the EGS. From 180 million mandays per annum, it has come down to about 90 million mandays in the last five or six years. (2) While considering the coverage of unemployment under the EGS, it covers only about 2.5% of unemployment among rural workers and about 3.6% of unemployment in the case of agricultural workers and it comes to only 7% among wage employment in agriculture. When analysing the targeting efficiency in the EGS, the best estimate shows that 80 to 90% reaches the poor. But the actual transfer of outlay to the poor is very low. For Rs. 100 spent overall, only Rs. 40 goes to the actual beneficiary as gross benefit and Rs. 24 as net benefit. Applying the 90% targeting efficiency for Rs. 100 spent on the EGS, the final transfer to the poor is about Rs. 24. Hence, the benefit-cost ratio is as low as around 20%. (3) EGS alone is not a blue-print for poverty alleviation, as even if workers work full time on EGS, they cannot earn enough to cross the poverty line. (4) EGS has impact on the intensity of poverty as the gap between the ultra poor and the poor has been narrowing in recent times. (5) The macro-level of poverty ratios do not fully capture the impact of EGS on the poor because EGS is concentrated in a few districts. (6) Many macro-level studies reveal that impact of EGS on incomes among the poor was substantial and income were enhanced by 21 to 65%.

Strengthen the RWPs we note that : (1) There is scope for labour-intensive land development schemes which could generate employment in rural areas. For effectiveness, such schemes must be well engineered, relevant to the needs of the people and efficiently executed. (2) Technical experts are needed to prepare well engineered projects. (3) Local panchayats should be involved in the selection of schemes which are relevant to the needs of the area. (4) Cost effectiveness and efficiency of execution of the schemes are to be evaluated by the introduction of a scheme of engineering audits. Chartered engineers could be recognised for the purpose by professional institutions.

Coming to specific anti-poverty measures, IRDP is the oldest and best known, of which, there are numerous evaluations. It is in a complete mess for the following reasons: (1) IRDP is very inefficient as it lacks horizontal and vertical efficiency. It is not vertically efficient as it is not able to differentiate the poor from the non-poor so that there is infiltration of the non-poor into the targeted group of poor. It is also not horizontally efficient as it fails to capture almost all the poor and leaves out too many of them. (2) The externalities are missing as it is a micro-level household approach. The infrastructures for translating the household assets into dependable streams of income is missing. (3) Its benefits do not really go to the poorest; the beneficiaries cluster around the poverty line. (4) There is also a lot of politicisation of leakage, handouts, and so on. So, IRDP could be scrapped and a durable, large scale, viable credit system could be created in rural areas.

Credit should be made available for assets, not target-based, not without subsidy or only a limited subsidy but with a very broad access insisting on a better repayment record.

Poverty alleviation is not just simply about delivering of benefits. It is about empowerment and involving people in the process of development. This requires "bottom up" measures where beneficiaries have a choice and design of projects intended to benefit them. Past experiences indicate that poverty alleviation strategies need to play heavy reliance on employment generation and not merely on income growth. Increased public spending on aspects of human development is more likely to have a greater impact on poverty reduction and at the same time improve human development.

References

Parikh, K.S. (ed.) (1997), *India Development Report, 1997*, Oxford University Press, Delhi.

Raghuram, S. Heikosievers and Vinod Vyasulu (ed.) (1995), *Structural Adjustment*, Macmillian India Limited, New Delhi.

Roy, K.C., Hans, C. Blomqvist and Iftekhar Hossain (ed.) (1997), *Development that Lasts*, New Age International Publishers, New Delhi.

Sharma, P.K. (1997), *Foodgrain Economy of India*, Shipra Publications, Delhi.

Singh, B. and Prem Kumar (ed.) (1995), *Current Trends in Human Resource Development*, Deep and Deep Publications, New Delhi.

World Bank (1990), *World Development Report, 1990, Poverty*, Oxford University Press, New York.

13

Human Capital Development: Towards a New Approach in Research and Intervention

Arindam K. Sen and Mausumi Manna

INTRODUCTION

Intergenerational transmission of resources and culture is an essential prerequisite for development of human capital. Evidences have suggested that inequity is transmitted intergenerationally, affecting private (parental) investment on human capital development of the younger generation. Underdevelopment in terms of resources (material and cultural) in the previous generation act as a detrimental factor in inducing investment on successive generations. In a planned economy, such conditions necessitate thoughtful and timely intervention to help the underdeveloped section of the population to come out of the low-investment low-income trap.

This paper presents a new approach to look into the various requirements for a successful policy initiative. For this purpose, it draws attention to the need for people's participation in both construction of baseline information with regard to the nature of underdevelopment and need assessment, as well as framing and implementation of policies. It argues, with the help of two case studies from the field experience of the organisation, that direct and participatory research provides useful inputs to frame a bottom-to-top policy in economic development.

In order to develop the most appropriate investment strategy for human capital formation in a backward area, the most appropriate data-base is that which is generated through participatory quantitative and qualitative research and not the one provided by non-participatory outside observation. A successful development initiative should come from within, specially when cultural constraints are a major barrier to development, and should not be imposed from outside. This involves a new approach towards understanding the gap in human capital formation within the cultural specificity of a region.

To substantiate our argument, we have taken up an important aspect of human capital formation : investment on education which is the most basic precondition for human capital formation. We have discussed the problem of investment in education in two tribal areas: Jhargram in West Bengal and Dimapur in Nagaland. These two areas are selected simply because of our association with the people in the area in course of our field research in these two areas. The experiences of these areas are not supposed to generalise the problem of human capital formation either within the tribal communities, or within any backward area. Our experience is expected to strengthen our arguments through case study analysis. But we do not claim to have provided a general policy framework even to address all the problems specific to the selected areas.

The paper is structured in three parts. In the first part we discuss the constraints in investment on education within an underdeveloped (backward) area and community and the need for proper need assessments. In the second part we discuss the methodology of participatory research and its usefulness in framing appropriate development strategy. In the last and concluding section we present two case studies from Jhargram and Dimapur to substantiate the arguments built so far.

I. CONSTRAINTS IN INVESTMENT ON EDUCATION WITHIN A BACKWARD COMMUNITY

Investment in not only elementary and secondary education, but also in higher education is considered a principal vehicle to judge the performance of human capital development (Mc Mohan, 1991). Education is expected to enhance labour productivity through skill formation (Ali, 1985). Investment on general and technical education is a pre-requisite to reduce dependancy on outside agents and develop self-reliance.

The prime problem of increasing investment on education within a backward community is the lack of economic resources, as well as lack of awareness towards the use value of education. The level of investment on children's education is directly linked to family's endowments. Birdshall and Meesook (1986) highlight the link between children's education and inter-generational transmission of inequality. This aspect is further clarified by Becker (1991).

"Some children have an advantage because they are born into families with substantial ability, a strong emphasis on childhood learning and other favourable cultural and genetic attributes" (p. 241).

Investments during childhood are crucial to children's later development (Bloom, 1976). The total amount of human capital accumulated is proportional to the amount accumulated during childhood. Rates of return to a person depend on the amount invested on him as well as on aggregate stock of human capital (Becker, 1991).

Thus, parents' play a crucial role in influencing children's development in the initial years. However, parents' motives and interest in investing on children depend crucially on their expected rate of return from children. This· is more important, given the fact that poorly endowed parents are required to sacrifice substantial amount of personal consumption in order to invest on children. Not only do parents pass on some of their endowments to children, they also influence adult earnings of their children by expenditures on their skills, health, learning motivation and many other characteristics. Parents influence the economic welfare of their children primarily by influencing their potential earnings. Parents are assumed to maximise the welfare of children when no reduction in their own consumption or leisure is entailed. In that case expenditure on human capital of children is equal to the marginal rate of return on children (Becker, 1991). If we add the cost of parental sacrifice to the total expenditure on human capital of children, parents will not be motivated to invest on children unless the expected rate of return on children is high enough to equate expenditure to rate of return.

In a situation of large-scale educated unemployment in the job market, expected rate of return on children's education is low. This works as a disincentive to invest on children's education. However, we may observe that under similar situation of expected low return from investment on education in the job market, parents with higher educational attainment invest more on children's education in comparison with parents with lower educational attainment. Thus, parents' investment on human capital on children are not entirely motivated by economic logic, and cultural background of the parents play an important role.

A further economic logic overlooked here is the contribution made by children's labour. The neo-classical theory of human capital as postulated by Becker *et al.* makes the crucial assumption of absence of child labour. While this assumption remains valid for parents from educated middle or upper class whose living comes from the service sector (paid job, trade and business) or organised manufacturing sector, the assumption becomes unrealistic in an agrarian or tribal economy, and also for parents engaged in home-based manufacturing. Here children are expected to make significant contribution in the family farm, home-based manufacturing unit or family trade, as well as through paid child labour.

Investment on human capital of children within these classes/categories of parents therefore involves two additional costs, —apart from the actual expenditure on children's education, training, etc. First, since the physical endowments of the parents are not adequate enough, parents have to make sacrifice of own personal consumption in order to support children's education. Second, the income forgone through not allowing children to work must be included in the cost of education.

Thus, we observe that parents with poor physical endowment and with low educational attainment have poor motivation to invest on children's education for both economic and cultural causes. However, education not only increases the expected future earning potentials, it also develops other human qualities. Exposure to knowledge can improve the quality of living through more efficient and proper use of available civic and public amenities including health services, sanitation, legal provision, etc. Education is expected to better equip a citizen to demand and enjoy his/her civic, political, legal and social rights. These use values of education are difficult to be perceived by parents with low educational attainment, unless a felt need exists among themselves.

It is an important component in policy formation, therefore, to include not only the felt need of the people, but also the unfelt need which the people themselves fail to perceive. A proper need assessment is crucial in policy formulation. Before we go into the argument why participatory research methodology can serve the purpose of need assessment in a better and effective way, let us briefly point out a few weaknesses in our educational policy, which is somewhat insensitive to culture-specific need for education.

An important illustration of such weakness is made by the following quotation from the editorial of the *Weekly Young Indian*, September, 1997.

"Any farmer would tell you that his children are given holidays when there are no activities on farms and fields. But there are examinations and reopening of schools when there is a need for another helping hand at the farm. Such an academic calendar is perhaps the single largest contributory factor to early and heavy drop-outs in rural areas of the country" (p. 2).

While the above paragraph speaks for itself, some other insensitivity is observed in syllabus for curriculum, nutritional requirement and health education of school children, environment at home conducive to education, etc. We have taken note of the need of the backward communities while formulating our employment policies, but very little practical attention has been paid to frame suitable educational policies to suit their need. Reservation and quota are not enough to make the children interested in education where those coming to school are the first generation in their community/area. However, formation of appropriate policy is not possible unless the planners and policy-makers have adequate knowledge regarding the felt and unfelt needs and problems of the people.

In many tribal communities, parents' drinking habits act as

serious impediment to children's school education. Given the continuously falling teacher-student ratio in our schools, individual attention to students, especially the first generation students who need more care and attention than usual, is becoming an impossible task. Environment at home and facilities for home tuition is becoming more and more important. Drinking, which has been an important part of the tribal culture linked to the normal way of life in rhythm with their economic and social activities is becoming problematic for the system of school education their children are exposed to. Educational strategy for these children thus need to be more sensitive to their specific requirements for intervention.

II. THE NEED FOR PARTICIPATORY FIELD RESEARCH TO DEVELOP STRATEGY FOR INTERVENTION

The essential underlying principle of participatory field research is capacity building of the population in question, i.e., strengthening local capacity to conduct problem analysis on its own. The major focus of participatory research is on users' involvement in the data collection process. In participatory data collection, the main goal of the research process is to ensure that all data will be used appropriately. Users' involvement increases interest and commitment to the study and its result. This method also uses an important resource in the sense that it uses the expertise of the non-experts, the ability, intelligence and knowledge of the community.

There are mainly two broad approaches to research—conventional research and participatory research. In conventional research, data are collected by experts who are outsiders or external to a situation. In contrast, participatory research embodies an approach to data collection which is two-directional—from the researcher to the subject and from the subject to the research. This method is therefore more dynamic, demand-based and change-oriented (Narayan, 1996).

The first thing that needs to be kept in mind in any data collection process is how sensitive the information is within local cultural context. The research must take note to which degree the method is obtrusive or unobtrusive, direct or indirect, closed or open-ended.

Sensitive information is broadly defined as information that cannot be obtained from people directly or indirectly because people's responses to questions are influenced by factors or motives which result in strategic bias. Collection of sensitive information, therefore, require more acquaintance and involvement with the subject difficult to be attained in conventional research.

Planners and policy-makers in our country mostly base their strategy on data generated through conventional techniques. There are several arguments used in favour of conventional data collection methodology. This method is quicker, cheaper and technically more superior as the investigation is done by trained field investigators. Moreover, collection of large numerical data on cross-sectional evidences is possible only through conventional strategy. Participatory techniques are thought to be more useful in anthropological studies and less useful in fields such as economic surveys.

It is a popular misconception that participatory research is compatible only with socio-anthropological surveys where the investigator researcher spends years with the subject. A skilled field researcher can gather information more useful and appropriate in shorter time frame through active involvement and participation of the subject in generation of data. Innovative data collection methods include small-group interaction, listening surveys, walking surveys, mapping, collection of stories and folk tales, utilisation of indigenous knowledge system, pictures, drawings and photographs, games and simulations, etc. Structured and semi-structured interviews in focus groups, participatory workshops and discussion groups can produce quantitative and qualitative evidences far superior than closed and quantitative surveys. Software technology in today's world is fast developing to facilitate analysis of qualitative evidences with near accuracy. There is no need to feel constrained in data analysis methods to confine ourselves to numerical exercises alone.

Moreover, a multi-disciplinary field methodology is becoming immensely popular which has the advantage of combining the knowledge and efforts of researchers from various disciplines. The span of research in Economics is expanding to include topics and subjects conventionally left outside the scope of Economics.

Proper need assessment of the subjects requires ready-to-change and ready-to-adopt field research methodology. Collection of micro-level information is absolutely preconditioned by sensitivity to local cultural context which is more easy to exercise through participatory research technology. While universal and standard structured questionnaire enables comparison across groups and across countries, many useful insights are lost. Attempts should be made to compare the data *ex-post* rather than *ex-ante* use of rigidly structured data collection methods.

Policy intervention in our country is over-depended on numeric target-based approach where the success of a development programme is judged by numeric figures. For example, school enrolment is usually conceived as a performance indicator of educational attainment. But number of years of schooling hardly tell us of the quality of education and extent of knowledge (Jeffry & Basu, 1996). Culture specific action research through direct involvement of the subjects can produce better result than bureaucratic policy interventions.

We conclude our arguments by referring to two case studies based on our field experiences in two tribal areas of Jhargram and Dimapur.

III. PARTICIPATORY ACTION RESEARCH IN DEVELOPING HUMAN CAPITAL IN TWO TRIBAL AREAS

The table in the appendix gives the state-wise enrolment of tribal children as a percentage of total enrolment in various stages at school. As it appears from the table, enrolment in Classes I-V is congruous with the proportion of tribal population in the respective state. In fact, in the states where tribal population forms the majority of the state population, e.g., in Arunachal Pradesh, Meghalaya, Mizoram, Nagaland, the percentage of enrolled tribal children in total enrolment is higher than the general share of tribal population in total population. This shows that in the states where tribal population forms the majority, the enrolment ratio of non-tribal children is very poor. On the other hand, in states like Himachal Pradesh, Karnataka, Orissa, Rajasthan, Sikkim, West Bengal, Rajasthan, Sikkim, West Bengal and Andaman and Nikobar Island. The enrolment ratio of tribal children in Classes I-V is below the ratio of tribal population in total population.

While the performance in terms of enrolment in the primary and middle level of schooling of the tribal children is quite satisfactory, the enrolment ratio in higher classes gradually declines, indicative of drop outs at later phases. This ratio improves for Classes XI-XII for Arunachal Pradesh and Bihar, which may reflect in-migration of tribal students from neighbouring regions. Except these two, the enrolment ratio drops drastically in Classes XI-XII, with Mizoram and Nagaland experiencing almost hundred per cent drop outs, in all the states. In both Nagaland and West Bengal, the two states under special focus in our study, drop-out rates in the higher classes is quite evident. Let us probe into the causes behind such evidence through our field experience.

The Experience of Psycho-social Research Centre, Jhargram

The Psychosocial Research Centre is a voluntary organisation involved in health and education of tribal children in a small Santhal village in Jhargram, West Bengal. The school is run by Sokol Tudu, a young and enthusiast worker who himself could not complete his college education. Being a good organiser, Sokol could mobilise pre-school and school children from the adjacent villages. The training in his school is informal, which combines fun with education. Yet Sokol had to face the inevitable problem of running a school among children from very poor Santhal families, viz., high drop-outs. Deforestation and the spread of urbanisation has been affecting the economic life of the tribal population in the area for many years. Once the forest ceased to be the major source of livelihood, to find alternative sources of living became the main problem. The difficulty, as Sokol observed, came not only from outside, from want of adequate jobs, but also from within. A cultural as well as psychological barrier prevented the local inhabitants to switch over the alternative occupations. Sokol himself is an ardent and enthusiast farmer, who loves to experiment in cultivation. He developed this interest in farming from his father, who worked in the farm for many years.

Sokol initially identified poverty to be the major reason for drop-outs. He tried to share his knowledge in farming with the guardians of his pupils. But hardly anyone showed the necessary interest. Besides, his school is open in the morning when the young children usually play around and do not do any work. He decided to try out other options.

Consumption of alcohol is integral to the tribal way of life. But Sokol's close interaction with the families of his pupils taught him that the habit of drinking is difficult to be associated with the enterprising attitude the local youth need to survive in the fast changing surroundings. Under strong influence of modernisation, the indigenous life knowledge and culture are endangered. At the same time, economic well-being at the face of growing competition demands more commitment and interest in non-traditional occupations.

Sokol's school attempted to preserve the tradition and culture at one level, by organising sports and festivals that encourage traditional games, dance and music. But at a different level; his mind was busy probing ways to combat the habit of alcoholism among the elders. He then came up with an innovative and brilliant idea. He composed anti-alcoholism songs in both Bangla and Santhali. He received help in the composition of both verses and tunes from others. Next, he taught these songs to his pupils and asked them to sing them at home when their fathers were sober.

This idea soon became a big hit and many fathers came to complain to Sokol about the songs. He knew he had been able to hit the right chord. He could not cure the habit of drinking of all of them, but he could sense that a consciousness is growing in the area against the habit, especially among the younger people.

Soko's school is still struggling to survive, mainly for economic reasons. But he is also growing beyond the school. He has already started a local youth group. Recently the group has conducted a socio-economic survey of 14 villages entirely on their own initiative. This has been a baseline survey for them to assess the developmental need of the area. These data were collected and compiled by the villagers themselves, under the guidance of Sokol and Srimat Tundu, another local youth who has a post-graduation degree, and other members of their youth group.

In the case cited above, Sokol has been a participatory researcher for many years. But his method has been slow, experimental and lacking proper methodology. The gap in his endeavour has been the lack of expertise and guidance. Also there has been no proper documentation of the discussions he had with his subjects, the findings from his walking and listening surveys, which he has unknowingly conducted many times in his desperate attempt to learn the problem. The end product of his research was an effective Action Research Programme, but the stages through which the ideas developed are missed, and, therefore, lost. If a replication of his ideas fails in another village and in another school, it will be difficult to pin point what exact local contexts helped him to gain success.

On the other hand, routine development works are also in progress in the area. There are many formal schools in the area attended by Santhali students, and also drop-outs. In the absence of any opportunity for skill training, these huge number of dropouts in their later years have no option but to join the army of unskilled manual workers.

A proper co-ordination between the official educational programme and individual or group efforts as made by Sokol and his friends could have given a proper direction to human capital formation in the area. The authorities in the area perhaps have little systematic knowledge regarding the felt and unfelt needs for human capital formation in the area. At the same time, Sokol and his friends have also been trying to understand these felt and unfelt needs, but unsystematically. A combined effort by the two, through a properly co-ordinated participatory research should have resulted in a more appropriate need-based approach to human capital formation in the area.

Experience of Field Research Operation Network in Dimapur

In Dimapur, another tribal area in the North-East India, the problem of human capital formation involves different, yet similar aspects. As the table in the appendix shows, Nagaland has high enrolment ratio upto Class X, but the rate drops to zero beyond that.

The field experience in Dimapur has been drawn from a collaborative study by FRON and Prodigal's Home, a Dimapur-based NGO, 'On the Drug using Patterns and Factors in Kohima and Dimapur Districts of Nagaland for Developing an Appropriate Strategy for Prevention'. This study used both quantitative and qualitative field research techniques and covered over 5,000 drug users in the two districts.

The analysis completed so far clearly indicates a close link between the use of human resources with prevalence of drug use among youths. Spread of Christianity and availability of English medium schooling facilities have resulted in school enrolments in lower classes among the local tribal communities. But the scope of higher education is limited. On the other hand, the ten years spent at school are dissociating the children from traditional skills and knowledge. An antipathy towards manual work is also observed to have developed. There is also very little scope for technical training after school. Even if there was a scope, there is not much opportunity to utilise the training owing to absence of industrial base in the state.

All these are making them easy victims of drugs. Among the drug users interviewed by us, teachers of private schools for children are found to be a high risk group. These young teachers have completed their school education, some have also attended college and consider themselves educated and worthy of dignified jobs. They work against very low pay in these private schools and suffer from acute depression.

Thus, we find that there has been investment in school education in the Dimapur area. But without proper need assessment and planning, the human resources developed remain under-utilised and get mis-directed. Nagaland being a very small state, creation of adequate jobs for all those passing out of school is a near impossible task within the state in the service sector. Yet the curriculum in school education leaves no scope for the students to be prepared for alternative occupations. Rather it creates a cultural gap in the minds of the students, unsuitable to the local solo-economic contents. Only a minor section of the school-leaving children can avail the opportunity of higher education and technical training outside the state. Those who are left behind suffer from an emotional setback, making then easy victims to drugs.

The two cases discussed above highlight the need for a new approach to planning for investment in human capital formation in a country like ours, where education is highly subsidised and supported through tax payers' contributions. The tax structure in our country is rather regressive whereby those endowed with less resources are made to bear proportionately higher tax share, through the indirect taxes. On the other hand, it is the children from the less endowed families who receive proportionately less opportunities for education and skill training. While these facts reveal the unethical side of the existing system of school and higher education, under-utilisation of the human resources developed leads to sub-optimal use of capacity generated. A resource-scarce country can hardly afford such inefficient use of human resources, calling for more efficient planning and investment strategy. In order to undertake this task, the planners need to be more equipped with knowledge of culture-specific micro-problems of the vast and diverse population.

References

Ali, M.S. (1985), Contribution of Education Towards Labour Productivity: A Cross Cultural Study, *Pakistan Economic and Social Review*, 23(1), pp. 41-54.

Becker, G.S. (1992), 'Education, Labour Force Quality and the Economy', *Business Economics*, 27(1), pp. 7-12.

Becker, G.S. (1991), 'Human Capital and the Rise and Fall of Families' in *A Treatise on the Family*, Harvard University Press, Massachussettes, pp. 238-76.

Birdshall, N. and Meesook, O.A., 'Children's Education and Inter-generational Transmission of Inequity: A Simulation', *Economic Education Review*, 5(3), pp. 239-56.

Dunlop, J.T. (1998), 'The Challenge of Human Capital Resources Development', *Industrial Relations*, 11(1), pp. 51-60.

Jeffry, R. and Basu, A.M. (eds.) (1996), *Girl's Schooling, Women's Autonomy and Fertility Change in South Asia*, Sage Publication, New Delhi.

Jennifer, R.M. and Narayan, O. [compiled] (1998), *Participation and Social Assessment, Tools & Technique*, The World Bank, Washington, D.C.

McMahon, W.W. (1991), 'Relative Returns to Human and Physical Capital in the U.S. and Efficient Investment Strategies', *Economic Education Review*, 10(11), pp. 283-96.

Narayan, D. (1996), Towards Participation Research, *World Bank Technical Paper No. 307*, World Bank, Washington, D.C.

Norton, A., Owen, D., Miline, J.T. (1994), *Participatory Poverty Assessment Draft Results*, World Bank, Washington, D.C.

Weekly *Young Indian*, Sept. 13, 1997, New Delhi.

APPENDIX

State-wise Enrolment of Tribal Children in Class I-XII*

State	*Percentage of Tribal Population to Total Population*	*I-V % of ST Population in Total Enrolment*	*VI-VIII % of ST Population in Total Enrolment*	*IX-X % of ST Population in Total Enrolment*	*XI-XII % of ST Population in Total Enrolment*
Andhra Pradesh	5.93	5.76	3.37	2.87	1.00
Arunachal Pradesh	69.82	74.41	75.93	66.1	68.26
Assam	10.99	14.58	13.18	11.10	7.25
Bihar	8.31	8.52	6.79	5.68	6.99
Gujarat	14.22	14.47	11.05	9.58	8.57
Himachal Pradesh	4.61	3.89	3.05	2.58	1.77
Karnataka	4.91	3.52	2.99	2.82	3.11
Kerala	1.03	1.13	0.77	0.55	0.60
Madhya Pradesh	22.97	18.53	12.49	10.43	7.94
Maharashtra	9.19	9.13	5.78	4.92	1.95
Manipur	27.3	33.63	22.29	19.74	5.22
Meghalaya	80.58	91.11	89.22	85.43	84.27
Mizoram	93.55	100.00	100.00	100.00	0.00
Nagaland	83.99	97.78	97.18	96.17	0.00
Orissa	22.43	18.52	10.13	8.56	1.79
Rajasthan	12.21	10.52	8.45	8.03	5.63
Sikkim	23.27	21.26	20.36	23.14	28.59
Tamil Nadu	1.03	0.95	0.62	0.66	0.48
West Bengal	5.63	5.05	3.33	2.45	1.31
Andaman & Nicobar	11.85	9.09	9.57	8.84	4.82
Tripura	28.44	28.8	20.84	17.13	6.64

* We have excluded the Union Territories and the states with Tribal Population below one percent of total population.

Source: *Fifth All-India Educational Survey*, (Volume II), National Tables, National Council of Educational Research & Training, 1992 (Reference Date 30, 1986).

14

"Well-being" of People—A Journey from Per Capita Gross National Product to Human Development Index

SWAGATA DAS BHOWMICK

I. INTRODUCTION

Since the Second World War, independent Asian and African countries began to put economic development in their political agenda. But at that time growth and development were regarded as synonymous. The policy-makers had the impression that if the country grew in terms of per capita gross domestic product (PCGDP) or per capita gross national product (PCGNP), the effect of economic growth would trickle down to the masses and the problems of poverty, illiteracy, unemployment, etc. would gradually be eliminated. But the experience of the 1950s and 1960s, when a large number of countries achieved the overall growth targets of the United Nations with the levels of living of the masses remaining mainly unchanged, signalled that something was wrong with the narrow definition of well-being.

Gradually, development began to be considered "as a multi-dimensional process involving major changes in social structures, popular attitudes and national institutions, as well as the acceleration of economic growth, the reduction of inequality and the eradication of absolute poverty."[1]

The limitations of the use of PCGNP as a measure of national well-being are many.

Some importance ones are given below:

First, the coverage of GNP excludes non-marketed and non-priced production. Moreover, it gives more weight to the production of defence articles having more money value than the production of basic necessities.

Another very important problem of the PCGNP approach lies in the comparison of PCGNP of different countries. Such comparisons become very difficult due to conceptual differences, exchange rate problems and the difference in domestic price structures among the countries.

Thirdly, PCGNP does not take account of the income-distribution aspect.

The last problem is slightly deeper. It relates partly to somewhat philosophical distinction between income and well-being—the notion that income does not necessarily measure well-being. Hence, non-monetary measures of well-being require to be taken into account.

An increase in the PCGNP does not necessarily mean a higher level of development in terms of socio-economic aspect of life or a higher level of social development does not necessarily mean a higher level of PCGNP. For example, China and Sri Lanka with less than a seventh of PCGNP of Brazil or Mexico have achieved similar life expectancy. Again, South Korea with magnificent growth and five times PCGNP than China and Sri Lanka has not been able to reach the level of life expectancy achieved by China and Sri Lanka.

II. BIRTH OF ALTERNATIVE MEASURES OF "WELL-BEING"

The dissatisfaction with the PCGNP as an index of national

well-being led the development economists to search for an alternative yardstick for measuring human well-being. Consequently, a number of approaches such as social indicators, physical quality of life, basic needs, commodities and capabilities and human development emerged.

Indicators that attempt to define non-monetary measures of social progress are called social indicators. These social indicators attempt to measure the development of health, nutrition, housing, income distribution as well as other aspects of cultural and social development.

As measures of well-beings social indicators have some advantages over PCGNP. They are concerned with intermediate ends nearer to the ultimate end of a full and healthy life. Even those social indicators that measure inputs (e.g. hospital beds per thousand of population, school enrolment ratios, etc.) rather than results (life expectancy, adult literacy, etc.) attempt to capture inputs that are nearer to the desirable results than PCGNP. The PCGNP measure points to catching up and suggests a race. Social indicators point to common shared values and problems of alternative styles of development, to the opportunities of learning from one another. Reducing or closing the international "gap" in life expectancy, infant mortality, morbidity or literacy would appear to be a more sensible objective and can be achieved at even a relatively lower level of PCGNP, and, therefore, much sooner than reducing the income gap.

Morris D. Morris developed a composite indicator that measures economic development in terms of "quality of life". He used three indicators—life expectancy at age one, infant mortality and literacy and constructed a simple composite index known as Physical Quality of Life Index (P.Q.L.I.). For each indicator, he rated the performance of all the individual countries of the world on a scale of 1 to 100, with '1' representing the worst performer and '100' the best one. This study revealed that though usually there was a positive relation between PCGNP and PQLI, yet there were some significant exceptions. Though PQLI had many limitations, it was taken as a far more reliable measure of development.

Greater attention of the economists on the socio-economic aspects gave birth to the basic needs approach. This approach requires first the identification of basic needs. Most experts agree that essential basic needs cover health, basic education, nutrition, water supply, sanitation and housing. The basic needs approach is practically a human development approach.

Prof. Amartya Sen is critical of the use of both income and commodities relevant for assessment of the living standard. To Sen the "value of the living standard" lies in the living and not on the possessing of commodities. The standard of living, according to him, is a matter of people's functionings, that is, what they succeed in 'doing' or 'being' or their capabilities to function. While some functionings are very elementary such as being adequately nourished, being in good health, etc., others are more complex such as achieving self-respect or being socially integrated. Functionings and capabilities refer to human flourishing and well-being rather than mere-survival in the biological sense. Capabilities reflect an individual's freedom of choosing among various commodity bundles. Poverty, according to Sen, is a matter of 'capability deprivation'.

Sen and Dreze observed: "Expansion of basic human capabilities, including such freedoms as the ability to live long, to read and write, to escape preventive illness, to work outside the family irrespective of gender and participate in collaborative as well as adversarial politics, not only influence the quality of life . . . but also affects the real opportunities . . ."[2]

Thus when well-being is seen in terms of basic capabilities, PCGNP requires to be regarded as one among several relevant means of increasing well-being. In a nutshell, economic development is seen in terms of expansion of opportunities of an individual.

III. HUMAN DEVELOPMENT PARADIGM

Following the line of reasoning of Sen and a host of other economists in the 1980s, UNDP offered a broader perspective of human well-being and the consequent human development. The basic premise underlying the UNDP's approach to evaluation of the alternative paths of development is that development should provide basic capabilities to the people which enhance the quality of their lives. This philosophy finds support in Aristotle's view. "Wealth is evidently not the good we are seeking for, it is merely useful for the sake of something else."

The Human Development Report, 1990 defined human development as a process of enlarging people's choices. The most critical ones are to lead a long and healthy life, to be educated and to enjoy a decent standard of livings. Additional choices include political freedom, guaranteed human rights and self-respect—what Adam Smith called the ability to mix with others without being 'ashamed to appear in public'.

"The term human development here denotes both the process of widening people's choices and the level of their achieved well-being. It also helps to distinguish between two sides of human development. One is the formation of human capabilities such as improved health or knowledge. The other is the use that people make of their acquired capabilities, for work or leisure."[3]

This way of looking at development where people are taken as the 'real wealth of a nation' differs from the conventional approaches to economic growth, human capital formation, human resource development or basic needs.

While PCGNP growth is necessary, it is not sufficient condition for human development. Theories of human capital formation and human resource development took human beings as instruments for increasing commodity production. They look upon human homes as means and not as ends. Thus, it captures only one side of human development.

Human welfare approaches look at human beings more as beneficiaries of the development process rather its participants.

The basic needs approach concentrates on the bundle of goods and services that the deprived population groups need: food, shelter, clothing, health care and water. It gives no importance to the role of human choices.

Human development approach brings together production and distribution of commodities and the expansion and use of human capabilities. It also focuses on choices. It applies equally to the less developed and highly developed countries.

The Human Development Report, 1991 opines that most developing countries have achieved some sort of development within three decades which the industrial countries took nearly a century to accomplish.

"Judged by the basic indicators of human development, it has succeeded beyond any reasonable extent. Average life expectancy has increased by 16 years, adult literacy by 40%, and per capita nutritional levels by over 20%. And child mortality rates have been halved during this period."

"... The income disparity between the North and the South is still very large : the South's per capita income is only 6% of the North's. But in human terms, the gap is closing fast. Average life expectancy in the South is 84% of the North's average, adult literacy 61% and nutrition measured by daily caloric supply 80%."[4]

The essential components of human development paradigm are: equity, sustainability, productivity and empowerment.

When development is defined in terms of enlarging people's choices, people should enjoy equitable access to opportunity.

The concept of sustainability means sustaining all forms of capital—physical, human, financial and environmental. This is important because the essence of human development is that everyone should have equal access to development opportunities—now and in the future.

Productivity requires investment in people. Economic growth is, therefore, a subset of human development model.

Empowerment implies that people are in a position to exercise choices of their own free will. This aspect distinguishes human development paradigm from other development concepts. Investment in people is required as a prelude to equal access to market opportunities. Thus, human development models are not basic needs models. Moreover, human development paradigm embraces all choices—particularly political, social and cultural—while the basic need concept is generally centred on economic aspect.

The basic needs concept of human development is a holistic development paradigm, which includes both ends and means, both productivity and equity, both economic and social development, both material goods and human welfare. The main features of this approach are:

(a) People are moved to the centre stage—development is understood in terms of betterment of people's lives.
(b) Human development is assumed to have two sides—one is the formation of human capabilities and other is the use that people make of their capabilities.
(c) A careful distinction is made between ends and means. People are regarded as both ends and means.

(d) Human development paradigm embraces total society—not just the economy. The political, cultural and social factors are given as much importance as the economic factors.

Some important advantages of this paradigm over other measures are:

As indicator of human development, this paradigm has taken income along with health and literacy. Here income is taken as a proxy for bundles of goods and services needed for the best use of human capabilities. This paradigm considers the troubles of both over-development and under-development. Diseases of affluence can kill as the diseases of poverty can. The income statistics do not reveal this destructive aspect of wealth. Moreover, the distribution of income is much more skewed than the distribution of literacy and life expectancy. There is a maximum of 100% literacy and maximum life span is also limited. But for income, sky is the limit. A very few high income earners can raise the average.

The average of human development indicator tells us something about the distribution. There cannot be high averages if many people do not participate. Any upward movement in human development indicator can be taken as an overall improvement.

Whereas high income for someone can cause relative deprivation for others, that is not true for human development. Improvement of health and education of anyone benefits the entire society.

Any country aiming at reducing international gap in human development can do so to a considerable extent if public policy is so formulated.

IV. HUMAN DEVELOPMENT INDEX

The discussion remains incomplete without a brief reference to the Human Development Index (HDI).

For construction of the HDI, it has taken—

(1) the log of PCGDP, calculated at the real purchasing power, not at exchange rate upto the international poverty line (after 1990, this has been modified) as a

measure of income or entitlement;

(2) literacy rates (and since 1991 mean years of schooling) as measure of knowledge; and

(3) life expectancy at birth as measure of health.

With these three basic variables HDI is constructed in three simple steps.

The first step is to define a country's measure of deprivation for each of the three basic variables. Minimum and maximum values are defined for the actual observed values of each of the three variables in all countries. The deprivation measure then places the county in the 0-1 range, where '0' is the minimum observed value and '1' is the maximum.

The second step is to compile an average indicator by taking a simple average of the three indicators.

The third step is to measure the HDI as one minus the average deprivation index. The value of HDI shows a country's place relative of other countries. The closer the value of the HDI to '1', the higher is the country's human development.

The concept of human development is much broader and richer than what can be caught in one indicator. Practically, a vector has been tried to be caught in one single number.

Such indicators are useful for focussing attention and simplifying problems. They are eye-catching and have considerable political appeal. Such single indicators have stronger impact and draw public attention more powerfully than the list of indicators having qualitative dimensions.

The great advantage of this methodology is that every country's actual progress is measured in relation to a goal. Merging of economic and social indicators in one index is the chief strength of the HDI.

The record of the developing world is uneven. There is still a large unfinished agenda of human development—with one-fourth of the people in developing countries still deprived of basic human necessities, minimum incomes and decent social services. Hence, every country should properly choose its development priorities.

It is true that economic growth is necessary for sustained improvement in human welfare, though high economic growth does not automatically translate into high human development. It has been found that developing countries do not always lack considerable resources to address their human development. Restructuring the present priorities in their national budgets can increase their human development to a great extent. As market alone cannot deliver balanced patterns of economic growth and human development, there must be a judicious mix of market efficiency and social compassions. It is not wealth but what people make use of it is important. Moreover, accumulating wealth is not necessary for the fulfilment of many choices. A nation does not require to be rich either to afford democracy or to treat its men and women equally.

The Human Development Report, 1997 reveals the following important observations regarding the ranking of 175 countries by their HDI values:

The HDI ranking of countries differ significantly from their ranking by real PCGDP. Ten countries including Costa Rica, Vietnam and Zaire have an HDI rank at least 20 places higher than their PCGDP rank. For 17 countries including Kuwait, Oman and Namibia, the PCGDP rank is higher than HDI rank. Thus,

Similar HDI but different incomes			**Similar incomes, different HDI**		
Country	*HDI Value*	*Real PCGDP (PPP $) 1994*	*Country*	*Real PCGDP (PPP $) 1994*	*HDI Value*
New Zealand	0.937	13,350	France	20,510	0.943
Sweden	0.936	25,530	Kuwait	21,875	0.844
Barbados	0.907	6,560	Spain	14,324	0.934
Singapore	0.900	22,500	Baharin	15,321	0.870
Brazil	0.783	2,970	Georgia	1,585	0.637
Bulgaria	0.780	1,250	Mauritania	1,593	0.355
South Africa	0.716	3,040	Tajikistan	1,117	0.580
Sri Lanka	0.711	640	Guinea	1,103	0.271
Zambia	0.281	330	Madagaskar	694	0.350
Mozambique	0.281	90	Sierra Leone	693	0.176

Source: *Human Development Report, 1997.*

countries can have similar incomes but different human development achievements—or similar HDI's but very different incomes.

The HDI can be disaggregated by gender, ethnic groups or geographical regions or in many other ways. The construction of gender-adjusted development index known as GDI makes considerable differences in the ranking of countries.

CONCLUDING REMARKS

The HDI is still evolving. It was decided to keep the coverage and methodology of the HDI quite flexible subject to gradual refinements as analytical critics emerged and better data became available. It is neither perfect nor fully developed.

It requires continuous analysis and refinements. This dynamic character is an entirely new and revolutionary way to recast the conventional approaches to development. The establishment of supremacy of people in economic development is a great challenge. This human dimension of development is not just another addition to the development dialogue.

Notes and References

1. Todaro, M.P. (1987), *Economic Development in the Third World*, Orient Longman Ltd., New Delhi, p. 85.
2. Dreze, Jean and Sen Amartya (1995), *India: Economic Development and Social Opportunity*, Oxford University Press, Delhi, Preface VII.
3. UNDP (1990), *Human Development Report*, Oxford University Press, New York, Oxford, p. 10.
4. UNDP (1991), *Human Development Report*, Oxford University Press, New York, Oxford, p. 14.

References

Morris, Morris D. (1979), *Measuring the Conditions of World's Poor: The Physical Quality of Life Index*, Oxford University Press, New York.

Streeten, Paul, *et al.* (1981), *First Things First: Meeting Basic Needs in Developing Countries*, Oxford University Press, New York.

Sen, Amartya (1984), *Resources, Value and Development*, Oxford University Press, Delhi.

Sen, Amartya (1985), *Commodities and Capabilities*, North Holland, Amsterdam.

Todaro, H.P. (1987), *Economic Development in the Third World*, Orient Longman Ltd., New Delhi.

Griffin, Keith (1987), *World Hunger and the World Economy*, The Macmillan Press Pvt. Ltd., Houndmills etc.

Dreze, Jean and Sen, Amartya (1989), *Hunger and Public Action*, Clarendon Press, Oxford.

Dreze, Jean and Sen, Amartya (1995), *India: Economic Development and Social Opportunity*, Oxford University Press, Delhi.

Haque, Maqbul (1996), *Reflections on Human Development*, Oxford University Press, Delhi.

Kakwani, N.K. (1993), Performance in Living Standards, *Journal of Development Economics*, Vol. 41.

UNDP (1990, 1991, 1995, 1997), *Human Development Reports*, Oxford University Press, New York, Oxford.

15

Concept and Estimation of Human Development Index

R. ANNAPOORANI

Human resources are by far the most important wealth of a nation. There is a growing realisation that rapid rate of human capital formation is the most important precondition of economic growth. The experience of advanced countries suggests that the crucial factor responsible for their economic advancement has been human capital, rather than physical capital. In this context, Kuznets observes: "the major capital stock of an industrially advanced country is not its physical equipment. It is the body of knowledge amassed from tested findings and discoveries of empirical science and the capacity and training of its population to use this knowledge effectively."

The term human capital formation refers to the process of acquiring and increasing the number of persons who have the skills, education and experience which are critical for the economic and political development of a country. In order to accelerate economic growth, the existing supply of trained people must be capable of providing dynamic leadership. This may take the form of improvements and radical adaptations in the administrative and organised framework, increasing its capacity to absorb capital for development or it may take the form of technical innovations, research and new application of existing knowledge to local problems.

Schultz (1960) was a pioneer in studying economic process leading to human capital formation and its impact on economic growth. Subsequently, a number of economists like Becker (1964), Denison (1962) have recognised that expenditure on education, health, etc., were not mere consumption outlay, but also means of growth promoting factors. Desai (1979) has argued that it is human knowledge in its entirety which determines the pace of technical knowledge and economic progress rather than a part of it.

World organisations such as the World Bank, Asian Development Bank, etc., applied some broad parameters to consider the quality of human resources in a country. The World Bank highlights four different aspects such as longevity, literacy, infant mortality and Gross National Product.

The physical quality life index is generally based on three indicators:

1. Infant mortality : IM
2. Life expectancy : e
3. Basic literacy : L

Therefore, PQLI = f (IM, e, L).
To construct the PQLI we can write

$$PQLI = (IMI, eI, LI)/3$$

where IMI is an index of IM, eI is an index of e and LI is an index of L.

The last equation could be written as:

$$PQLI = .33\ IMI + .33\ eI + .33\ LI$$

where .33 is the equal weight applied to each of the separate indicator indices.

In 1990, the United Nations Development Programme (UNDP) published a Human Development Index (HDI)—a new yardstick that provides a broad method by which inter-country and inter-temporal comparisons of living standards can be undertaken.

In the HDI proposed by the UNDP, we have

$$HDI = g\ (Y, L, e)$$

where Y is per capita income, L is the literacy rate and e is life expectancy at birth. Thus, the HDI, according to UNDP, comprises GNP per capita, longevity and education. The Index varies between 0 and 1 : the nearer to 1, the higher the level of human development.

According to United Nations Development Programme, human development has two facets:

1. Actual achievement, and
2. A measure of deprivation - shortfall from a target or an index which emphasises the magnitude of the tasks that lie ahead.

The construction of the index of deprivation indicator (DI) is as follows:

$$DI_{yj} = \frac{\text{Max } y - Y_j}{\text{Max } y - \text{Min } y}$$

$$DI_{ej} = \frac{\text{Max } e - e_j}{\text{Max } e - \text{Min } e}$$

$$DI_{Lj} = \frac{\text{Max } L - L_j}{\text{Max } L - \text{Min } L}$$

where DI_{yj} DI_{ej} and DI_{Lj} are the DI for the jth country for income, life expectancy at birth and literacy respectively. Max Y, Max L and Max e are the maximum values for Y, L and e respectively. Y_j, e_j and L_j are the actual values for income, life expectancy at birth and literacy respectively for the jth country.

For example, we can calculate the DI_y for jth country. Let the highest per capita GDP is \$ 10,000 and the lowest be \$ 2,000. The per capita GDP is \$ 5,000.

Now

$$DI_{yj} = \frac{10,000 - 5,000}{10,000 - 2,000} = \frac{5,000}{8,000} = .63$$

An average DI has been constructed by the UNDP as follows:

$$DI = .33\ DI_{yj} + .33\ DI_{ej} + .33\ DI_{Lj}$$

Finally to obtain the HDI the value of DI is subtracted from 1.

Therefore, HDI = 1–DI

Indicators of Human Development

Table 1 presents the indicators of human development for some Asian Countries.

TABLE 1

Indicators of Human Development for Some Asian Countries, 1992

Country	*Life expectancy (years)*	*Infant mortality rate (per thousand births)*	*Adult literacy (per cent)*
China	70.5	27	80.0
Indonesia	62.0	66	84.4
India	60.8	74	52.2
Malaysia	70.4	14	80.0
Philippines	64.6	40	90.4
Pakistan	58.3	99	36.4
Republic of Korea	70.4	21	96.8
Singapore	74.2	8	92.0
Sri Lanka	71.2	24	89.1
Thailand	68.7	26	93.8

Source: UNDP, *Human Development Report, 1994.*

However, human capital formation takes place in India very slowly. A comparison of rates of growth of the stock of human capital in India with the advanced countries revealed that in the three developed countries, human capital has increased faster than physical capital. In Japan 3.3 times faster, in U.S.A. 1.9 times faster and in Germany 1.5 times faster. But in India, the trend is reversed, physical capital growing at a faster rate than human capital.

Table 2 represents the trends in indicator of human development in India from 1951-1993.

TABLE 2

Basic Indicators of Human Development in India

Year	*Life Expectancy of birth (years)*	*Literacy rate 1991 (per cent)*	*Birth rate*	*Death rate*	*Infant Mortality rate*	*Per capita NNP at 1980-81 prices (Rs.)*
			Per thousand			
1951	32.1	18.3	39.9	27.4	146	1,127
1961	41.3	28.3	41.7	22.8	146	1,350
1971	45.6	34.5	41.2	19.0	129	1,520
1981	50.4	43.6	37.2	15.0	110	1,630
1982	NA	NA	33.8	11.9	105	1,693
1983	55.4	NA	33.7	11.9	105	1,691
1984	NA	NA	33.9	12.6	105	1,790
1985	NA	NA	32.9	11.8	97	1,811
1986	NA	NA	32.6	11.1	96	1,841
1987	NA	NA	32.2	10.9	95	1,870
1988	57.7	NA	31.5	11.0	94	1,901
1989	NA	NA	30.6	10.3	91	2,059
1990	NA	NA	30.2	9.7	80	2,157
1991	NA	52.2	29.5	9.8	80	2,223
1992	60.8	NA	29.2	10.1	79	2,178
1993	NA	NA	28.5	9.2	74	2,226

Source: Documents of the United Nations Development Programme.

In India, there exist inter-state variations in human development index. In the report on India, 'The road to human development' prepared by the United Nations Development Programme, it is mentioned: "Certain States in India report levels of human development similar to those of leading industrialised countries. Others report achievement levels which are worse than the average of the poorest countries. And the gender-related development index for Indian States reveals not only the extent of gender inequalities within India but also the country's poor performance *vis-a-vis* other countries.

TABLE 3

HDI and GDI for Major States of India

State	*Life Expectancy of birth (years) (1989-93)*	*Literacy rate 1991 (per cent)*	*State domestic product (Rs.) at current prices (1992-93)*	*Human development Index (HDI) (1991-92)*	*Gender development Index (GDI) (1991-92)*
Kerala	72.0	90	5,768	.603	.565
Punjab	66.4	59	11,217	.529	.424
Maharashtra	64.2	65	9,795	.523	.492
Haryana	62.9	56	9,037	.489	.370
Gujarat	60.1	61	8,045	.467	.437
West Bengal	61.5	58	5,633	.459	.399
Himachal Pradesh	63.6	64	6,390	.454	.432
Karnataka	61.9	56	6,331	.448	.417
Tamil Nadu	62.4	63	6,809	.400	.402
Andhra Pradesh	60.6	44	5,718	.400	.371
Assam	54.9	53	4,973	.379	.347
Orissa	55.5	49	4,114	.373	.329
Rajasthan	58.0	39	5,086	.356	.309
Bihar	58.5	38	3,053	.354	.306
Madhya Pradesh	54.0	44	4,558	.349	.312
Uttar Pradesh	55.9	42	4,345	.348	.293
India	59.4	52	—	.423	.388

Source: Document of the United Nations Development Programme.

Table 3 helps to analyse the inter-state variations in human development Index for India.

Ranking of Countries based on Human Development Index

However, a big gap emerges in rankings of the same country according to the HDI and GNP per capita index. This is evident from Table 4.

TABLE 4

Ranks Based on HDI and GNP Per Capita

Countries	*Ranks on HDI*	*HDI*	*Rank on GNP per capita*	*Ranks based on 160 Countries*	
				HDI	*GNP per capita*
Japan	1	.981	1	2	3
United Kingdom	2	.962	3	10	21
Germany	3	.955	2	12	10
Republic of Korea	4	.871	6	34	39
Singapore	5	.848	4	40	25
Brazil	6	.739	7	59	54
Saudi Arabia	7	.687	5	67	33
Thailand	8	.685	8	69	79
Srilanka	9	.651	10	76	120
China	10	.612	11	79	130
Cameroon	11	.313	9	118	88
Tanzania	12	.268	14	126	158
Uganda	13	.192	13	133	141
Sierra Leone	14	.062	12	159	145

Source: UNDP: *Human Development Report (1992)*.

China, Srilanka and Tanzania are ranked much more highly interms of the HDI than on GNP per capita basis. On the other hand, Cameroon and Saudi Arabia are the countries where HDI lags behind GDP per capita.

CONCLUSION

The analysis reveals that corresponding to each stage of development in a country it is necessary to evolve a new package for achieving the highest state of development. The identification and the servicing of an ideal package of inputs in consonance with the social, economic and technological development of the region is essential for attaining a satisfactory level of human development.

REFERENCES

Jayagopal, R. (1992), *Human Resource Development: Conceptual Analysis and Strategies*, Sterling Publishers Private Limited, New Delhi, pp. 90-96.

Krishna Majumdar and Mahabendra Patel (1991), *Human Capital Formation*, Mittal Publications, New Delhi, pp. 1-12.

Shri Bhagroan Dehiya (Ed.) (1996), *Theoretical Foundations of Development Planning*, Volume 3, Sectoral and Regional Planning, pp. 136-42.

Subrata Ghatak (1995), *Introduction to Development Economics*, Routledge, London, pp. 37-40.

Uma Kapila (1995), *Recent Development in Indian Economy—After 4 Years of Economic Reforms*, Academic Foundation, Delhi, pp. 250-60.

Varughese, K.V. (1993), *Indian Economy: Programmes and Prospects*, Ashish Publishing House, New Delhi, pp. 115-23.

Southern Economist, September 15, 1997.

16

Economic Growth and its Impact on Human Development in the Indian Economy

KEYA SENGUPTA

Development of an economy over the years has focussed attention to the growth rate of various macro-economic variables such as the GNP, balance of payments, savings rate, fiscal deficits, assigning a secondary role to human being and his needs in this process of development. Emphasis on the growth rate of such variables relating to the macro-economic indicators has over the years been accepted as the yardstick of progress of a nation. However, it is often overlooked that it is the human being who is the real initiator and engine of the process of growth and development of an economy and therefore deserves to be the main beneficiary of economic growth. In other words, man is not only the means but also the need of all forms of economic growth. It is thus postulated that since growth and development of an economy is by the people, it should also be for the people, in the absence of which increasing the macro-economic indicators of growth will not only be meaningless, but will serve the interest of only a small segment of the population. Growth of this nature will fail to achieve any purpose, if it cannot improve the living condition of the masses. The crucial issue that needs to govern the policy-makers in taking any vital decisions concerning the economy is: What should be the end of all economic policies and programmes? Is it merely improving the economic indicators of growth or the living condition of the people, who actually constitute a nation?

1. NEED FOR THE STUDY ON HUMAN DEVELOPMENT

Development experience of an economy both developed as well developing, were governed by various growth models and other theories of economic growth, which often failed to focuss attention, to any form of social indicators of development associated with growth experience. Comparison of growth among nations or the criteria of success of growth of a nation revolves only around some vital economic yardsticks, irrespective of the living conditions of their people. It was very naively assumed that the benefits of economic growth were automatically transferred into better living conditions of its people, since the fruits of economic development are bound to be shared by the people of the nation. It was, therefore, considered unnecessary to make human-being the main focuss of economic growth. However, experience of growth revealed a wide gap between theoretical expectations and empirical reality. Benefits of economic growth in most nations resulted in unequal distribution of income and concentration of wealth in a few hands. As a result, economic growth failed to improve the living conditions of the masses. Consequently, developmental theories and models of economic growth which were able to achieve some success as for as economic indicators of growth were concerned were unable to incorporate all aspects of development of an economy, especially the 'human beings' and their condition of living. This necessitated restructuring the entire objective of growth and reformulating the entire process of economic growth, making the Pure Growth Theories redundant to a large extent.

All these issues which have recently been the subject of heated debate have resulted in the emergence of the concept of *Human Development.* Rapid rate of economic development, particularly in the post-Second World War, has revealed that economic development has resulted in a burgeoning middle class with a high propensity to consume. This has given rise to a distorted pattern of investment programme, while the living condition of the masses has rapidly deteriorated. An attempt at rapid growth of the economy has resulted in massive industrialisation programmes, which in most nations was unplanned and unsystematic. Consequently, migration to towns and cities, unplanned urbanisation with unhygienic and slum conditions of living, pollution, over-population, poverty and unemployment were the common features characterising the lives of the masses, resulting in a deterioration in the quality of life.

2. STUDIES ON HUMAN DEVELOPMENT UNDERTAKEN BY INTERNATIONAL ORGANISATIONS

As a result of all these disturbing trends witnessed in many nations of the world, human development as highlighted by the various social indicators of growth, seemed to be attracting the attention of the researchers and policy-makers. In recent years, a number of pioneering studies have been undertaken by various international organisations in this connection.

The post-Second World War period witnessed diminishing role and importance of merely the economic indicators to assess the extent of development of a nation. This trend was particularly evident from the 1960's onwards, when experience revealed that the application of the Received Theories of pure growth models failed to have any favourable impact on the living conditions of the people. As an alternative to modernisation, theories of development, which put total emphasis merely on GNP and other related economic indicators of development, a number of research studies have been undertaken with the purpose of investigating the real meaning of development. It was increasingly realised that economic indicators may reflect the strength of an economy, but may not be sufficient to indicate the quality of living of the people, and may thus fail to capture the real essence of development.

Most of these studies maintained that social indicators are to be used for assessing the real meaning of development. One of the first work that had been undertaken in this connection was in 1954, by United Nations on defining and measuring the levels of living. However, the work that deserves attention by all serious workers in this field is the one undertaken by the United Nations

Research Institute for Social Development (UNRISD) founded in 1960. Levels of living were defined with reference to social indicators relating to health, education and nutritional levels. UNRISD Report highlighted for the first time the effect of the level of living on economic growth and pointed out that inequalities in the level of living may pose serious threats to economic growth, particularly in modern times (UNRISD Report, 1960). UNRISD idea of measuring social development in conjunction with economic growth and economic development became one of the main objectives of its study. The indicators of Human Development adopted by them are more comprehensive in comparison to the ones developed by the western industrialised nations.

The World Bank has also undertaken work regularly on Human Development issues relating to education, health, nutrition and fertility. UNESCO has also been a pioneering agency, which has shifted its focus of attention from 'Human Resource' indicators to 'Socio-economic indicators', and to the linkage of social and economic indicators relevant to measuring trends and disparities within countries. The joint study by the World Bank and the Institute of Development Studies at the University of Sussex, namely, *Redistribution with Growth* incorporated employment and the distribution of household income and employment into the conventional economic growth models.

As Nancy Baster (1985) in her work reveals that the general direction of international research on social indicators and human development over the past twenty years can be illustrated by taking four examples. First among them is the Report of the United Nations Expert Group on the international definition and measurement of the levels of living (United Nations, 1954). Second was the work of Jan Drewnowski on the measurement of the levels of living and welfare (Drewnowski, 1974). The third in the series was the OECD research programme on the measurement of the social well-being and lastly was the Lisk's categories of basic needs (Lisk, 1979), reflecting the orientation of programmes launched by the International Labour Office in 1976 (ILO, 1976).

Latest among the studies undertaken by International Organisations in the *Human Development Report* prepared every year from 1990 onwards by UNDP. The reports try to interlink the various aspects of human development with economic growth. The important feature highlighted by their studies focusses attention on the fact that link between human development and economic growth is not automatic, since high rate of economic growth manifested by high GDP, may reveal a low level of Human Development or in other cases even a low level of economic development may be associated with a high level of human development.

3. DISTINCTION BETWEEN HUMAN RESOURCE DEVELOPMENT AND HUMAN DEVELOPMENT

It is necessary to draw the distinction between Human Resource Development and Human Development, since these two concepts are not synonymous, though highly inter-related, and considerable confusion may arise particularly for policy formulation due to a failure in grasping the difference between these two important terms. Though both HRD and HD consider people to be the main asset of an economy and put human being at the centre stage of all developmental process, the concept of HRD considers the role of human being as a resource for the purpose of development of the economy. The capability and the ability acquired by human being through better education and health facilities are used as a means for the attainment of rapid economic growth which is the ultimate aim of the nation. Investment in human being is undertaken, not for the development of the human being for his own welfare, but purely from the point of view of the economy. Human being here is treated on par with other inputs, like capital or machine and therefore all efforts are directed to improve his conditions not for his own welfare but for the economic betterment of the nation.

The concept of human development is much broader. It considers human being not as a means but as an end of all development process. All efforts at economic development are directed towards the people and their well-being who are considered to be the main objective of economic growth, and are treated merely as agents of economic development of a nation. The concept of human development encompasses the welfare of not only the present generation, but the future generation as well. Attempts are made to uplift the economic, cultural and political environment of a society with the ultimate aim of improving the welfare of the people. Highlighting the importance of HD, the *Human Development Report* (1995) opines: "Human Development . . . brings together the production and distribution of commodities and the expansion and use of human capabilities. Encompassing these earlier concerns, human development goes beyond them. It analyses all issues in society—whether economic growth, trade, employment, political freedom or cultural values—from the perspective of people. It thus focusses in enlarging people's choices—and it applies equally to developing and industrial countries." Human Development, therefore, maintains that not merely economic development, but also its qualitative and distributive aspects and more importantly, the relationship of economic development with human beings and the quality of their life.

4. RELATIONSHIP BETWEEN ECONOMIC GROWTH AND HUMAN DEVELOPMENT

Economic growth and human development are not contradictory and cannot be viewed in isolation, and the achievement of one is impossible without the achievement of the other. Attainment of human development is impossible without economic growth, just as economic growth by itself is meaningless without human development. Therefore, achieving these two goals simultaneously should form part of every developmental goal and effort. This is particularly because experience has revealed that economic growth does not automatically transform itself into human development. All depends on the nature and extent to which policies and programmes of an economy are geared to harmonise economic growth with human development. Concepts of economic growth and human development are thus not contradictory, rather they are more of a complementary nature. It is essential to overcome the misconception as is harboured by the critics of Human Development, that stress on human development may be at the cost of economic growth. At the same time, it is also crucial to focusses attention on the fact that too much of emphasis on either economic growth or only human development may result in unbalanced growth of the economy, which may jeopardise the very process of long-term development.

High GNP, has often failed to transform into better living

conditions of the masses, particularly where the fruits of development and the distribution of income have been uneven. Absence of such coordinated policy measures, which ensures uneven distribution of income may fail to establish a relationship between economic growth and human development. Such was the developmental experience witnessed in countries like Brazil, Nigeria and Pakistan. On the other hand, some nations like China, Japan, Republic of Korea have adopted such growth models, which emphaize the role of human beings in the development process. Consequently, these nations have devoted a significant proportion of their investment in improving human capacities and ensured their participation in the process of economic development through remunerative jobs, and the sharing of the fruits of economic development.

5. HUMAN DEVELOPMENT AND GOVERNMENT POLICIES IN INDIA

It is with this aim of improving the condition of living of the masses, who fail to be the direct beneficiaries of economic development that the government of India has undertaken certain measures from time to time to sustain a decent living standard. Social justice has always been a strong pillar of the successive Five Year Plans in India. Among the recent measures adopted by government in this connection is the "Basic Minimum Services" to provide basic facilities to the deprived section of the society. This may go a long way in improving the Human Development Index in the country. Some of the steps undertaken in July, 1996 deserve a brief mention:

(i) Provision of *Safe Drinking Water* to all the people in urban as well as in rural areas. It is realised that water and sanitation facilities are basic requirements for leading a decent life and poor people are often not in a position to provide these facilities themselves, particularly in the rural areas. Accelerated Rural Water Programmes and National Drinking Water Mission are some of the other schemes that attempt to assist people in providing drinking water to the entire rural population. Sanitation facilities under various central and state sector programmes are also undertaken in rural areas.

(ii) Provision of *Primary Health Service Facilities* in rural and urban areas to cover cent per cent of the population. The recent economic reforms have given special importance to medical care in the nation by not only increasing the outlay in the different sectors of health care, but has also adopted many new schemes like the Social Safety Net Schemes, in an attempt to ensure that the reforms do not lead to any adverse effect on health care of the poor people.

(iii) *Universalisation of Primary Education* is the other important objective of the programme. The government has initiated concerted efforts for raising the gross enrolment ratio, particularly in those states where the ratio is lower than the average. Total Literacy Campaign has become the principal strategy of the National Mission in eradication of illiteracy throughout the country.

(iv) *Provision of Housing Facilities* to the poor. Among the various schemes on housing for the poor, the Indira Awas Yojana (IAY), which was originally meant for the poorest of the poor belonging to SC and ST and free bonded labour in rural areas had been extended further to assist the poor non-SC and ST. The National Housing Bank was set-up to enhance the flow of funds for rural housing.

(v) Extension of *Mid-day Meal Programme* in primary schools to all rural blocks and urban slums and disadvantaged sections.

(vi) Streamlining the Public Distribution System targeted to families below the poverty line are some of the other steps adopted for improving the living condition of the people, living below the poverty line.

6. METHODOLOGY OF THE STUDY

Studies on Human Development have witnessed numerous debates on the choice of indicators for the exact assessment of human indicators. The UNDP Report on Human Development widely used for the purpose of inter-country comparison, used indicators like life expectancy, literacy rate and the per capita income for the construction of the Human Development Index. However, the use of these indicators alone for a country like India characterised by over-population and poverty can neither fully capture the essence of the quality of life nor the level of living. For instance, long life expectancy, in the midst of poverty, illness and the deprivation of the basic needs of life can be more painful rather than indicate a positive aspect of the quality of life. High literacy rate indicates the abilities and the capabilities acquired by an individual but such abilities may fail to transform into earning capacities, when the individual fails to secure a remunerative job. This is a common feature in an over-populated nation like India, where unemployment among the educated may mean more frustration, crime and social unrest bringing down the level of human development as a whole. Similarly, per capita income alone may fail to convey the true meaning of the quality of life of an individual in a nation where there is widespread inequality in the distribution of income.

It is due to all these factors that though we retain literacy and life expectancy as indicators of human development, as they reflect the overall condition of the level of living, we also include a few more indicators to make the index of human development more comprehensive. Some of the other indicators adopted for the purpose of our study are the accessibility to the basic amenities of life like, clean drinking water, sanitation facilities and good housing facilities, accessibilities to facilities like electricity, TV and newspapers. Added to these additional indicators we have also retained the economic indicator of per capita income, since the amount of income earned by an individual can be considered as a proxy for the quality of life. It is true that the expenditure incurred by the government on social sectors can go a long way in raising the index of human development, but government funding and subsidy can only improve the HDI temporarily, but is surely not a permanent solution for raising the quality of life and improve the index of human development.

For each of the selected indicators we have constructed an index, following the methodology adopted by the UNDP by choosing the highest and the lowest value for each of the indicators, with the exception of life expectancy, for which we have used 25 years and 85 years as the lowest and the highest values. Individual indices have been computed according to the following:

$$I_{ij} = \frac{X_{ij} - \min X_{ij}}{\max X_{ij} - \min X_{ij}}$$

where

X_{ij} = actual value of the ith indicator of the jth group of indicators.

Min X_{ij} = minimum value of the ith indicator.

Max X_{ij} = maximum value of the ith indicator.

The overall index is computed as follows:

$$HDI = \frac{1}{n}.I_{ij}$$

Computation of HDI was undertaken for the 15 major states of the country in terms of the indicators discussed above for the period 1991-93. Data for the purpose are obtained only from the secondary sources like the Census Report and Statistical Abstract. After Computation of the HDI for the respective states, ranking of the states in terms of their HDI is made. The states are also ranked in terms of their State Domestic Product Index. Difference in ranking between the two indices would indicate, whether the economic growth of the state concerned signifies equal level of human development or the absence of any kind of relationship between economic development and human development.

7. FINDINGS AND ANALYSIS

As a first step towards analysing the position in respect of their achievement in human development, we have firstly computed the HDI of the fifteen states using the same indicators as adopted by the UNDP for the preparation of their Human Development Report. Our findings (Table 1) according to this analysis reveal that Punjab tops the list among the states in India in terms of HDI followed by Maharashtra, Kerala, Haryana and Tamil Nadu, whereas among the states which fall at the bottom of

TABLE 1

Human Development Profile of India

(Using the Selected Indicators of UNDP)

Sl. No.	*States*	*Human Development Index (HDI)*	*Per Capita SDP Index*	*HDI Rank*	*SDPI Rank*	*SDPI Rank Minus HDI Rank*
1.	Andhra Pradesh	.459	.346	9	7	-2
2.	Assam	.429	.261	10	10	0
3.	Bihar	.314	.011	15	15	0
4.	Gujarat	.551	.456	6	4	-2
5.	Haryana	.655	.774	4	3	-1
6.	Karnataka	.521	.389	7	6	-1
7.	Kerala	.660	.299	3	8	5
8.	Madhya Pradesh	.379	.212	12	11	-1
9.	Maharashtra	.715	.844	2	2	0
10.	Orissa	.398	.197	11	14	-3
11.	Punjab	.991	.690	1	1	0
12.	Rajasthan	.372	.181	13	12	-1
13.	Tamil Nadu	.559	.427	5	5	0
14.	Uttar Pradesh	.352	.126	14	13	-1
15.	West Bengal	.487	.277	8	9	-1
	India	.439	.210			

the list are Bihar, preceded by Uttar Pradesh, Rajasthan, Madhya Pradesh and Orissa. An overview of the HDI turned for the nation as a whole reveals an interesting picture. The cluster of states consisting of Bihar, UP, Madhya Pradesh and Rajasthan have very poor record in terms of human development. The Eastern states of India consisting of Assam, Orissa and West Bengal are the group of states which follow next, though West Bengal fares much better in comparison to Assam and Orissa. Western region consisting of Gujarat and Maharashtra fare relatively better, whereas the four southern states are on an average level, though the HDI of Kerala is one of the best. It is interesting here to review the HDI of these states as against the HDI for India as a whole computed by the UNDP on Human Development for the corresponding period. The HDI for India for the period was .439 and the states which record HDI that exceeds the all-India average are Andhra Pradesh, Gujarat, Haryana, Karnataka, Kerala, Maharashtra, Punjab, Tamil Nadu and West Bengal. The states which are below the all-India HDI index, which is already extremely low by the world standards are Assam, Bihar, Madhya Pradesh, Rajasthan and Uttar Pradesh.

We have then ranked the states in terms of their per capita state domestic product index. The two rankings have then been compared—one indicating the achievement in terms of human development and the other index signifying economic achievement (Table 1). Cases where we derive a positive figure, by deducting HDI ranking from the per capita SDP ranking would imply that the state registers a satisfactory HDI in comparison to its economic growth. A negative sign, on the other hand, would indicate that the human development of the state lags behind its economic growth. This method of assessing the progress of the state in terms of human development is based on the pattern followed by UNDP Report. The result of this kind of analysis reveals that out of the fifteen states, the ranking of five states match with the rankings of the state's domestic product. This is, however, a highly unrealistic situation, particularly for a nation characterised by widescale inequality in income distribution, even to assume that the benefits of economic growth are transformed totally for human development, is to ignore the empirical reality. It may however, be true in case of extremely high or low per capita income which may also result in extremely high or low HDI ranking, resulting in same ranking between HDI and economic ranking. It is, therefore, evident that the indicators adopted for assessing human development, by most international organisations and applied uniformly to all nations, irrespective of their individual characteristic problems may not provide us with realistic conclusion about the progress of human development. This method of assessment further implies a very dismal situation of human development, since the extent of human development in all the states with the exception of Kerala lags much behind their economic achievement.

Keeping all these factors in mind, we switched over to a

more comprehensive measurement of HDI for India, which may be able to capture the real essence of the progress of human development in India. It is, therefore, essential that attention be drawn to the fact that for a poor nation with low per capita income and GDP growth rate, compounded with high growth rate of population, the right choice of indicators for evaluating human development assumes a great significance and plays a crucial role in taking stock of the real development of a nation. In such a situation, only literacy rate, life expectancy and the per capita income, by themselves may fail to capture the essence of reality relating to human development.

Due to all these factors we have expanded the horizon of our indicators by incorporating the accessibility to housing facilities, safe drinking water, sanitation facilities, consumption of electricity, TV sets, newspapers. For each of these items we have constructed an index, and then computed the overall HDI for these fifteen states, following the methodology outlined above. On the basis of these findings our analysis reveals that by broadening the concept of HDI, the HDI of eleven states out of the fifteen has experienced a decline while the index of only four states have improved (Table 2). This may indicate that when we go a little deeper in an attempt to assess the quality of life of an average Indian, the empirical reality reveals a picture much worse than the one drawn by any study conducted by various international organisations. Methodology followed for a nation where the HDI already begins at a high level cannot be applied with the same degree of satisfaction for another nation where the basic amenities for a decent life are also missing. It is thus evident that by including indicators that may be considered as a basic right of leading a decent life in a western nation, may be grossly absent in another nation, with its own characteristic problems. Consequently, by taking these factors into account, the HDI declines even further. Inter-country comparison of HDI, therefore, with vast differences in economic, sociological and other impediments to growth may fail to convey the true picture of HDI of the nations.

Analysis of HDI by this method reveals that Punjab tops the list and Bihar occupies the bottom-most position in terms of HDI index. As hypothesised earlier, the reason could perhaps be explained by the highest or the lowest per capita SDP respectively of these two states. Too high or low an economic index of the state

TABLE 2

Profile of Human Development Index (Method II)

Sl. No.	States	Human Development Index (HDI)*	Per Capita SDP Index	HDI Rank	SDPI Rank	SDPI Rank Minus HDI Rank
1.	Andhra Pradesh	.440	.346	9	7	-2
2.	Assam	.377	.429	13	10	-3
3.	Bihar	.349	.314	15	15	0
4.	Gujarat	.549	.456	5	4	-1
5.	Haryana	.608	.774	2	3	1
6.	Karnataka	.490	.389	8	6	-2
7.	Kerala	.587	.299	4	8	4
8.	Madhya Pradesh	.369	.212	14	11	-3
9.	Maharashtra	.601	.844	3	2	-1
10.	Orissa	.437	.197	10	14	3
11.	Punjab	.728	.991	1	1	0
12.	Rajasthan	.430	.181	11	12	1
13.	Tamil Nadu	.521	.427	6	5	-1
14.	Uttar Pradesh	.427	.126	12	13	1
15.	West Bengal	.504	.277	7	9	2

* HDI here includes indicators such as literacy rate, life expectancy, use of electricity, TV sets, newspaper, safe drinking water, sanitary facilities and housing facilities.

is bound to have some reflection on its human development. However, incorporation of some additional indicators have changed the HDI ranking of the other states. Assam which occupied 10th position in terms of our earlier findings, has now gone down to 13th in terms of the new methodology. Madhya Pradesh's rank has gone down from 12th to 14th. Ranking of Haryana has improved from 4th to the 2nd position. Rajasthan and Uttar Pradesh are the two states whose ranking, though has improved by two positions, continue to occupy the lower most grades as far as and Human development is concerned. For most other states rankings have either improved or gone down by only one position. On the basis of regional analysis the position of the Central states consisting of Bihar, Madhya Pradesh, Rajasthan and U.P. continue to be the worst in India. This is followed by the states belonging to the Eastern region consisting of Assam, Orissa, with the exception of West Bengal, whose position has actually improved to 7th position. In contrast, the northern region of the country, consisting of the states of Punjab and Haryana experiences the highest level of human development. This is followed by the western and the southern region, whose HDI has now improved, in terms of the new methodology followed.

The above findings prompt us to highlight the crucial reality of human development of a country like India, that merely literacy rate and life expectancy alone are insufficient to convey the achievement as far as human development is concerned. Kerala, for instance, has the best index in terms of its literacy rate as well as life expectancy, the two important variables which are often highly correlated. Notwithstanding this fact, the state does not occupy the highest ranking in terms of Human development as would have been normally expected. Assam has a satisfactory literacy index, yet it occupies the 13th position in terms of HDI ranking. Punjab and Haryana do not witness a very high literacy rate in comparison with the other states, yet these are the two states in India with the highest HDI ranking. As against this, the literacy rate in Bihar witnesses a very low index, inspite of a high life expectancy rate, though her overall HDI ranking in India is the lowest.

We have next ranked the states in terms of their economic achievement. Though the ranking of Punjab and Bihar coincide with their human development ranking, it is, however, different in case of their other states. The state of Kerala enjoys HDI ranking which exceeds its economic development. Kerala is followed by West Bengal and Haryana whose human development achievement is far better than its economic development. It is surprising to note that U.P. and Rajasthan which fare very poorly both in terms of human development and economic development, yet their human development is marginally ahead of her economic development. With a very low literacy index and a low life expectancy, such an experience is, however, contrary to reality. One of the possible reasons could be the extremely unequal distribution of income, resulting in the concentration of wealth in a few hands. This may give rise to high conspicuous consumption by a few individuals, due to which the HDI is marginally better than the economic growth concealing to a large extent the real picture of the Human development. As far as the states of Assam, Orissa and Madhya Pradesh are concerned, human development in these states is miserably below its economic growth.

It is therefore maintained that the fruits of economic growth have failed to transform automatically into better living conditions of its people which may be due to:

(i) Inequality in income distribution, poverty or high unemployment rate, and/or
(ii) Failure to give adequate importance to human development and to incorporate it as an indicator in the growth models.

It is, therefore, evident that achievement in terms of economic growth alone is not sufficient for a decent level of living. Planning era in India over the years in its urgency to achieve rapid economic growth, has considered achievement of various economic indicators as the main objective of growth, and the efforts at raising the GDP rate has thus failed in raising not only the HDI of India as a whole in comparison to the world standard, but has also resulted in a wide disparity among the individual states which is also highly disturbing.

It is therefore, postulated that human development needs to be given immediate attention in all types of policy formulations for economic development. Decline in the role of the Received Theories on economic growth in improving the living conditions of the masses, should prompt the planners and policy-makers to shift the emphasis of treating human being merely as human resource for the purpose of economic development to the development of the 'human beings'. Human development should, therefore, be treated as a major field of study in its own right, as is revealed by the developmental experience of some of the nations of the world.

Implication of the Study and Policy Consideration

Examination of the level of HD in the various states of India reveals certain relevant issues which are highly pertinent from the point of view of policy considerations. If the deteriorating condition of the level of living is to be immediately arrested, planners and policy-makers need to reformulate the growth models and develop a new paradigm of growth, by incorporating human development in all growth models. Economic growth coupled with HD, should be considered as the end of all developmental programmes. This is particularly crucial of an economy like India, marked by widescale dualism, where technological and economic growth results in further widening the social and economic gap, with its consequent adverse effect on HD.

There is often a dangerous tendency for planners and policy-makers in developing nations, including India to achieve rapid economic growth by adapting the growth models of developing nations, where GNP or GDP or GNP per capita and GDP per capita, which are easily quantifiable and measurable fits perfectly into the growth models. Inter-county comparison is also facilitated by this method. India like the other developing nations has adopted the common practice of applying such models by importing foreign technology and foreign capital by overlooking entirely the goal of HD in our growth models which could also be possible reason for the low level as well as wide diversity in HD in India. Such a strategy of growth on the other hand might have resulted only in widening the GNP gap between the different states as well as the extremely low level of HD in India as a whole. Case studies in respect of other nations have also revealed that absolute poverty and economic inequality have actually increased in those nations due to economic growth:

(i) The behavioural pattern of HDI across the nations may also be explained by the fact that there is the presence of a strong traditional sector along with a modern sector which is likely to be the root cause of wide disparity as well as low HDI in India. Absence of land tenure system in India which is dominated by rural agricultural sector results in massive unequal distribution of income and widescale poverty. All these factors in turn combine to pull down the HDI.

(ii) Another disturbing factor characteristing the Indian economy is the dominance of a large informal sector. A major proportion of the production in the subsistence agricultural sector as well as informal urban sector is not exchanged for cash and, thereby, remains outside the purview of any calculation. As a result, the state domestic product by itself is not only inadequate to reflect the condition of living of the people uniformly over the states, but an equal amount of per capita income may fail to mean an equal level of HDI in these states.

(iii) It is also apparent that for a country like India, marked by large scale inequality in the distribution of income as well as differences in economic and other related conditions in different states, per capita income may fail to reflect the actual living condition of the people. An increase in per capita income by an equal percentage may mean higher welfare for the poor, whose marginal utility of money is higher than that of the rich. Lower marginal utility of money to the rich results in conspicuous consumption, while the poor continue to survive at the level of subsistence and the economy is shaped by the purchasing power of the rich which may thus fail to convey the true scenario of HDI.

All these factors prompt us to conclude that improving the HDI in India as well as attempting to close the wide gap in HDI across the country is not only called for, but is also one of the most difficult tasks for planners and policy-makers, particularly for a vast country like India marked by wide economic, sociological, geographical and institutional diversity and constraints. At the same time, no nation can be oblivious of the poor living conditions of the masses, since all development in the economy is ultimately meant for the people. It is therefore essential that HD should be made an integral part of all growth models.

References

Baster, Nancy (1985), "Social Indicator Research: Some Issues and Debates" in *Social Development in the Third World: Level of Living Indicators and Social Planning*, J.C.M. Hilhorst and M. Klatter, London, Croom, Helm.

Burgess, G. Robert (ed.), *Key Variable in Social Investigation*, London, Routledge and Kegan Paul.

Census of India (1991), "Housing and Amenities", Occasional Papers.

Drewnowski, J. (1966), "Social and Economic Factors in Development: Introductory Consideration on the Meaning, Measurement and Interdependence", UNRISD, Geneva.

Economic Survey, 1996-97, Govt. of India, New Delhi.

Fox, Karl A. (1985), "Social System Accounts: Linking Social and Economic Indicators through Tangible Behaviour Settings", Dordrecht, Reidel.

Human Development Report, 1990-97, UNDP, Oxford.

Koskiaho, B. (1985), "Social Indicators as Applied in Planning: Notions, Criteria and Methods" in *Social Development in Third World: Level of Living Indicators and Social Planning*, J.C.M. Hilhorst and M. Klatter (Eds.), London, Croom, Helm.

Miles, Ian (1985), *Social Indicators for Human Development*, London, Frances Pintes.

Statistical Outline of India, 1996-97, Tata Services Ltd., Department of Economics and Statistics, Mumbai.

United Nations (1954), *Report on the International Definition and Measurement of Levels of Living*, New Delhi.

United Nations (1971), *Social Development in Asia: Retrospect and Prospects*, New York.

17

Role of Investment in Human Capital on Human Development: An Empirical Study on Developing Society

Kaushal K. Srivastava and Tanuja Srivastava

Jaunsari Tribe, which has been chosen for this study, is found concentrated in the area of Jaunsar-Bawar of Chakrata tehsil of Dehradun District. While the Jaunsaris are those who inhabit Jaunsar, the southern part of Chakrata tehsil, Bawaris (sharply distinguishable from Bawaria nomads found in the plains) live in the northern part of Chakrata tehsil. However, both the groups are clubbed together under the common classification of Jaunsaris. This tribe is sharply distinguishable from majority of Indian tribes due to the prevalence of caste as well as the fraternal polyandry system (Srivastava *et. al.*, 1996). Considering their social hierarchy, all the castes, among Jaunsaris, are generally sub-grouped into three different categories. These are upper castes (*Brahmins* and *Rajputs*), intermediate castes (*Badi, Sunar, Jagdi, Nath, Lohar* and *Bajgi*), and lower castes (*Darn* and *Chamar*). The objective of the present paper is to identify the role of human capital investment on human development in a peculiar tribal setting.

For this study, necessary information has been collected through primary survey. 310 households were randomly selected and interviewed with the help of a pre-tested interview schedule. The selection of the sample for each region, however, has been made on the basis of socio-economic and demographic characteristics of both the regions under study. The information pertaining to the mean and standard deviation values for different variables are summed up in Table 1. As is evident from Table 1 in appendix, children belonging to farmers have obtained higher level of schooling in relation to those belonging to non-farming households.

The description of each variable for children's schooling is being given below:

MEOC	=	Mean education of children
CFAG	=	Father's age (in years)
CFEDU	=	Father's education (in years)
CMEDU	=	Mother's education (in years)
CMAG	=	Age of head of the household's spouse
HFSXC	=	Family size excluding children
NCSF	=	Total female children survived
NCSM	=	Total male children survived
HIXC	=	Earning excluding children (in Rs.)
NFHIXC	=	Non-farm earning excluding children (in Rs.)
FASI	=	Farm size (in hect.)
FSN	=	Dummy variable for nuclear family
RGDV	=	Dummy variable for regions
DVUC	=	Dummy variable for upper castes
DVIC	=	Dummy variable for Intermediate caste
EOS	=	Dummy variable for outside contacts
DVPF	=	Dummy variable for polyandrous family
COFED	=	Education of other father's education (in years)
CFAG (SQ)	=	Father's age in square (in years)
NCBF	=	Number of Children (age below 5)

The analysis of the regression results has been undertaken. The regression analysis is preceded by the computation of the correlation matrix to get information about the probable existence

TABLE 1

Mean and Standard Deviation Values for Different Variables and Occupational Groups

Variables	*All*		
	All	*Farmers*	*Non-farmers*
N	310	162	148
MEOC	3.01	3.52	2.21
	2.12	*2.31*	*2.11*
FASI	0.34	0.64	0.04
	0.52	*0.63*	*0.05*
CFEDU	2.19	3.10	1.18
	2.92	*3.29*	*2.06*
CMEDU	0.49	0.57	0.42
	1.30	*1.25*	*1.21*
FSN	0.58	0.49	0.71
	0.49	*0.52*	*0.42*
HIXC	11,217	14,678	7,378
	10,123	*12,876*	*4,447*
COFED	0.59	0.81	0.21
	1.80	*2.39*	*0.79*
DVPF	0.23	0.27	0.16
	0.41	*0.47*	*0.39*
NCBF	1.29	1.21	1.39
	1.07	*1.11*	*1.06*
CFAG	37.13	38.11	36.07
	8.08	*8.31*	*7.60*

Figures in the italics are the standard deviations of the respective mean values.

of the problem of multi-collinearity. The matrix highlighted a high degree of correlation between HIXC and NFHIXC. Hence, out of these two variables, HIXC was retained on account of high R^2 value when regressed against all other independent variables in comparison to R^2 calculated when NFHIXC was regressed against other explanatory variables. The results of the regression analysis are given in Table 2.

The insignificance of the regression coefficient for the farm size appears to be pointing towards the weak relationship it has

TABLE 2

Regression Estimates for Demand for Schooling

	1st Iteration			*Final Iteration*		
	COEF	*T-ratio*	*STDEV*	*COEF*	*T-ratio*	*STDEV*
Constant	-3.007	-3.012	1.031	-3.015	-2.862	0.974
FASI	0.291	1.101	0.291	0.289	1.059	0.269
CFAG	0.069*	3.412	0.021	0.071*	3.419	0.022
CFEDU	0.129**	2.563	0.048	0.127*	2.589	0.051
CMEDU	0.078	0.745	0.076	0.054	0.665	0.078
FSN	0.698**	2.411	0.287	0.684**	2.512	0.278
NCSF	0.229**	2.067	0.112	0.218**	2.064	0.113
NCSM	0.732*	7.013	0.105	0.732*	7.015	0.106
HIXC	0.000	0.340	0.000	0.000	0.203	0.000
RGDV	0.187	0.901	0.223	0.211	0.929	0.234
DVUC	0.542***	1.748	0.317	0.539***	1.721	0.322
DVIC	0.837*	3.334	0.253	0.811*	3.221	0.243
COFED	-0.055	-0.789	0.059	-0.061	-0.812	0.071
EOS	0.928*	2.686	0.347	0.959*	2.793	0.348
DVPF	0.035	0.089	0.347	0.051	0.141	0.339
NCBF	-0.149	-1.240	0.122	-0.154	-1.334	0.119
F = 14.914	R^2 = 0.512 s = 1.716			F = 14.732 R^2 = 0.542		
Rho = -0.052	DW=1.869			s = 1.689 Rho = -0.005		
N = 310				DW = 1.989		

Dependent variable is MEOC
* Significant at 1% level
** Significant at 5% level of probability
*** Significant at 10% level of probability.

with the dependent variable. However, the positive regression coefficient brings to fore the positive association of farm size (FASI) with the schooling of children (Singh, R.D., 1978).

The father's age (CFAG) in linear form has had a positive and statistically significant influence on schooling of the children.

This implies that as the age of the father increases the child schooling increases. The reason for this could mainly be a possible positive correlation between the age of father and the age of the child. This result, however, needs to be interpreted with great caution for the fact when the father and children grow older, the utility of later's education to the former may decline as he may need his children for carrying out the farming/non-farming operations. This is evident from the fact that when father's age squared (CFAG^2), its influence turns out to be negative and significant. The negative relationship is expected for the reason that with the growing age, the demand for labour, to be provided by the household children, as a substitute for the labour of head of the household, increases. This substitution seems to have led to a negative, yet statistically significant regression co-efficient.

The regression coefficient for CFEDU shows a strong and positive relationship between father's education and the schooling of his children (Wolfe, 1984, Singh, H., 1987). This is also indicative of the important role that father's education can play in improving the schooling of the children. This result also highlights the impact of past investment in human capital on the education of present generation (Singh, 1978, 1988, Gronau 1973).

The variable CMEDU has, on the other hand, been found to be insignificant. The relationship between MEOC and CMEDU, however, is positive. In view of the low level and little variability of mother's schooling among Jaunsari households, one may reasonably expect that education of the mother might exercise a relatively weak influence on the education of children.

The regression coefficient of the dummy variable representing family structure (FSN) has been found to be positive and statistically significant. It reveals that children belonging to the nuclear families get more opportunities of schooling in comparison to the joint families. In other words, regression result shows that, other things remaining the same, nuclear families have certain attributes which have had promoting influence on the education of the children.

The regression coefficient for both the variables NCSF and NCSM, display a positive association with the dependent variable. However, much greater t values for NCSM seems to be indicating towards a strong and positive association between the average education (MEOC) and survival of the male children (Behrman, 1986, Resenzweig, 1977). Relatively weak association between the dependent variable and the explanatory variable (NCSF) may be attributed to the possibility that the economic value of female children, at least at school-going age, is higher than that of male children. In fact, females play highly important role in the hill agriculture, at least in this area. They have not only to perform the routine domestic chores but have also to bear most of the burden of the jobs of agricultural and non-agricultural nature. The routine domestic chores, to be performed by the females, also include the collection of fodder, fuelwood and fetching of water generally from far off places and looking after the cattle, in addition to the cooking, washing, cleaning and looking after the old and younger ones. Female child is generally relied upon for assisting her mother in carrying out all these operations. This dependence on female children can be attributed to the perception of traditional societies towards the future role of a female child in a family. The female child in fact, is seen only in the role of a housewife. Hence, she needs to learn all the household chores and her assistance to mother is seen as a kind of training. This training gets priority over all other things, including education. Keeping in view this backdrop, it is not at all surprising to find a relatively weak, though statistically significant relationship of NCSF while strong association of NCSM with the dependent variable.

In case of the variable HIXC, it was expected that this income variable would have a positive effect on the household demand for children's schooling. The relationship has been found to be positive but the regression coefficient is not statistically significant.

The insignificance of dummy variables for the regions (RGDV) indicates that Chakrata is not different from Kalsi region as far as the factor endowments and regional characteristics influencing child schooling are concerned.

Among the three classifications of the castes, the regression coefficient for upper castes (DVUC) and intermediate caste (DVIC) have been found to be positive and statistically significant. It implies that children belonging to upper castes and intermediate castes are better-off in terms of schooling when compared to the children of lower castes. This difference is attributable to the differences in the caste characteristics that were not included as explicit variables in the schooling model.

The negative yet statistically insignificant sign of the variable representing the education of other male members of a polyandrous family (COFED) is difficult to be interpreted. However, one probable reason for this phenomenon could be that with the attainment of education, the member/members of the family may try to part with the practice of polyandry. A number of such cases have been reported in both the regions. This, in turn, might lead to the development of an indifferent attitude towards the children from wife being shared by brothers because as per traditions, the children from the eldest wife, in principle, belong to eldest brother. Higher is the level of education obtained by other male members (fathers of the children), stronger may be such tendency.

The positive and significant regression coefficient for the variable representing outside contacts (EOS) indicates towards the favourable impact of this explanatory variable on the schooling of the children. It seems that such contacts exert powerful and positive influence on the attitude and outlook of a household towards schooling of the children. In fact, increasing outside contacts might provide the family with the opportunity to earn more apart from acquiring new ideas and concepts. All these may play a conducive role in promoting the schooling of the children.

The regression coefficient of dummy variable representing polyandrous/non-polyandrous (DVPF) families is not statistically significant and bears positive sign. While the polyandrous families were hypothesized to be partially relieving the work pressure of the children, it, however, does not seem to be playing an important role in promoting the education of the children. This result is quite consistent with the significant and positive regression coefficient for FSN.

The variable NCBF representing the children below 5 years in a household bears a negative sign and has emerged as statistically significant. The statistically significant and negative sign for the variable implies that with rise in the number of children below 5, the MEOC tends to become lower. It is consistent with the hypothesis that with a greater number of children below 5, relatively older children would also be of lesser age and would be studying in the lower standard. This would, undoubtedly, find reflection in the lower value of MEOC for such a household.

Since the Durbin-Watson statistic falls in the inconclusive range, it is difficult to accept or reject the hypothesis of no serial correlation in the model. Hence, Cochrane-Orcutt iterate procedure was adopted to estimate p. This helped in estimating the coefficients afresh. Durbin-Watson statistic obtained in the third iteration satisfies the condition $d_u < d < 4 - d_u$. Hence, the hypothesis of no serial correlation (positive or negative) is accepted in this case. No additional variable has emerged as statistically significant in the final iteration. There has, however, been a change in the level of statistical significance of some of the variables.

Since the F-statistics for the sample regression is larger than the critical F-value for the 1% significance level, the hypothesis of independence between the dependent and explanatory variables can be rejected. It can further be inferred that the regression model provides a significant explanation of variation in the depended variable, i.e., MEOC.

Following conclusions can be drawn on the basis of analysis performed above:

(A) The father's age and education have had a positive and statistically significant influence on schooling of the children. This conclusion also highlights the impact of past investment in human capital on the education of present generation.

(B) The schooling level of the children is basically governed by the presence of the male children in the household. It implies that parents take little interest to educate the female children.

(C) Nuclear family structure has been found to be positively influencing schooling of the children. It shows that children belonging to the nuclear families get more opportunities of schooling in comparison to the joint families.

(D) The positive and significant regression coefficient for the variable representing outside contacts indicate toward the favourable impact of this explanatory variable on the schooling of the children. It seems that such contacts exert powerful and positive influence on the attitude and outlook of a household towards schooling of the children.

Finally, the variable representing the number of children below the age of five years bears negative relationship with children's schooling.

REFERENCES

Garry S. Becker (1964), *Human Capital : A Theoretical and Empirical Analysis*, With Special Reference to Education, NBER, New York.

Gronau, R. (1973), "The Intra-Family Allocation of Time: The Value of the Housewives Time", *American Economic Review*, Vol. 63, pp. 634-50.

Gujrati, Damodar N. (1988), *Basic Econometrics*, McGraw-Hill Book Company, Singapore, p. 436.

Hanushek, E.A. (1992), "The Trade-off Between Child Quantity and Quality", *Journal of Political Economy*, pp. 84-117.

Makhija, I. (1974), *The Economic Contribution of Children and Its Effect on Fertility and Schooling : Rural India*, Ph.D. Thesis, Department of Economics, The University of Chicago.

Michael, R.T. (1975), "Education and the Derived Demand for Children", *Economics of the Family: Marriage, Children and Human Capital*, ed. Schultz, T.W., The University of Chicago Press, Chicago.

Nauriyal, D.K. and Srivastava Kaushal, K., *An Explorative Study of Selected Socio-Economic and Demographic Indicators in Tribal Society : A Case Study of Jaunsari Tribe*, communicated.

Rosenzweig, M.R. and Evenson, R.E. (1977), "Fertility Schooling and the Economic Contribution of Children in Rural India", *Econometrica*, Vol. 5.

Schultz, T.W. (1961), "Investment in Human Capital", *The American Economic Review*, Vol. LI.

Singh, R.D., Schuh, G. Edward and Kehrberg, E.W. (1978), *Economic Analysis of Fertility Behaviour and the Demand for Schooling among poor households in Rural Brazil*, Purdue University, West Lafayette, Indiana, Station Bulletin, No. 214.

Singh, R.D. (1988), *Economics of Family and Farming Systems in Sub-Saharan Africa*, Westview Press, Colorado.

Srivastava, Kaushal, K., *An Economic Analysis of Central Himalayan Tribals in India: A Human Capital Approach*, Ph.D. Thesis (Submitted in 1993), University of Roorkee.

Srivastava, Kaushal, K., Nauriyal, D.K. and Srivastava, Tanuja (1996), "Economic Composition of Work Force and Educational Status of Tribals of Central Himalaya in India", *Status of Tribals in India: Health, Education and Employment*, edited by Amar K. Singh & M.K. Jabbi, Council for Social Development, New Delhi.

PART B

INTER-STATE COMPARISONS AND MEASUREMENT OF HUMAN DEVELOPMENT

18

Interstate Comparison of Human Development in India—An Alternative Measure

DEBABRATA MANDAL

Human progress is conditioned by our conception of development. Until the end of 1980s development is often viewed as growth in income. The human development approach receiving emphasis since 1990 views economic development as the enhancement of certain basic capabilities and social opportunities rather than growth of income *per se*. This view denies the relevance of income growth as an end in itself. Poverty in the human development perspective means not only 'income poverty' but it includes curtailing of capabilities—denial of opportunities and choices to lead a long, healthy and active life without being constrained by illiteracy, to enjoy a decent standard of living with freedom and dignity and to take part in communal life. The basic goal of development is the expansion of these choices and opportunities by eliminating basic human deprivations.

The pace of human development in various Indian states has been extremely disparate. The majority of the rural poor (as measured by the head-count ratio) are in eastern and central India, gender disparities are most acute in the north-west, while south Indian states are doing better in terms of literacy, life expectancy and fertility. As there is no single problem region in India, public policy has to be designed to meet different kinds of challenges that arise in different parts of the country. All this provides the motivation to undertake a disaggregative exercise to capture enormous variations in human development. But still one sometimes feels the need for overall ranking of the states in order to evaluate their overall performance.

The objective of this paper is to generate an overall ranking of major Indian states in terms of levels of human development as indicated by certain indicators. Then it seeks to analyse the human development experience in India, to make an empirical assessment of the stark contrasts in the levels and trends of human development across major Indian states and examine how state-level indicators of well-being are correlated with each other.

Our interstate comparisons are based on four state-level indices: per capita net state domestic product (PCNSDP-Y) at factor cost at constant 1980-81 prices to measure command over resources, life expectancy at birth (E) to measure health status and literacy rate (L) to represent educational attainment, female-male ratio (F) as an indicator of gender differences (and poverty ratio). We have taken sixteen major Indian states, each having a population of 5 million or more (1991 Census).The basic data relate to two periods—early 80s: Period I and early 90s Period II and are presented in Table 1.

These state-level indicators are highly aggregative and conceal tremendous regional diversities. Further state-level data on such variables as life expectancy at birth and literacy rate are well-known to be defective. For several states the data are not strictly comparable; they were not collected in the same year and the methods of collection were also different. Nevertheless, we concentrate on state-level comparisons rather than at the regional-level because each state in the Indian federal structure is an important political and administrative unit and a wide range of activities related to well-being, e.g. health, education, etc., are either in state list or in the concurrent list of our constitution. Given the quality of data being what it is for many states, it will be wise to rely on ordinal measures of the four components of well-

TABLE 1

Basic Data Relating to Sixteen Indian States

States	Per Capita Net State Domestic Product (Rs.) (a)		Life Expectancy years (b)		Literacy Rate per cent (c)		Female-Male Ratio (d)		Poverty Ratio (HCR) Expert Group Estimate (e)	
	1981-82	1993-94	1983	1990	1981	1991	1981	1991	83-84	93-94
	(1)		(2)		(3)		(4)			
Andhra Pradesh	1,494	1,808	58.4	60.2	35.7	44.09	.977	.972	29.9	22.19
Assam	1,428	2,157	51.9	54.1	43.6	52.89	.896	.923	40.9	40.86
Bihar	933	1,122	52.8	57.5	32.0	34.48	.954	.911	62.5	54.96
Gujarat	2,011	2,351	57.6	59.5	52.2	61.29	.934	.9335	33.3	24.21
Haryana	2,419	3,479	60.3	62.5	43.9	55.85	.867	.865	21.2	25.05
Himachal Pradesh	1,718	2,141	60.4	63.3	51.2	63.86	.958	.976	16.4	28.44
Karnataka	1,572	2,357	60.6	62.2	46.2	56.04	.957	.960	38.5	33.16
Kerala	1,487	2,043	68.4	71.3	81.6	89.81	1.20	1.040	40.9	25.43
Madhya Pradesh	1,370	1,744	51.6	53.4	34.2	44.20	.941	.931	50.1	42.52
Maharashtra	2,452	3,901	60.6	63.4	55.8	64.87	.930	.9344	43.6	36.86
Orissa	1,265	1,578	53.0	55.4	41.0	49.09	.988	.971	65.3	48.56

(Contd.)

TABLE 1 *(Contd.)*

	(1)		*(2)*		*(3)*		*(4)*			
Punjab	2,818	4,055	63.1	66.6	48.1	58.51	.865	.882	16.3	11.77
Rajasthan	1,261	1,760	53.5	56.3	30.1	38.55	.911	.910	35.0	27.41
Tamilnadu	1,555	2,410	56.9	61.5	54.4	62.66	.978	.974	52.4	35.03
Uttar Pradesh	1,299	1,605	50.0	55.4	33.3	41.60	.879	.879	47.2	40.85
West Bengal	1,605	2,106	57.4	61.4	48.6	57.70	.891	.917	54.7	35.66
India			55.4	58.7	43.6	52.21	.930	.927	44.8	35.97

Notes and Sources:

(a) Data on NSDP per capita at factor cost at constant 1980-81 prices are from the Report of UNFPA (1997).
(b) Figures on life expectancy at birth are from the Report of UNFPA (1997).
(c) Figures of literacy rate are from the Census of India, 1991, Series 1, Paper 2, of 1992, Final Population totals, Brief Analysis of Primary Census Abstract, 1981 and 1991: as reported in UNFPA (1997) except Assam. The national growth rate in adult literacy between 1971 and 1981 has been used to project Assam's literacy for 1981.
(d) Female-Male ratio figures from the Census of India, 1991, as reported in UNFPA (1997).
(e) Figures of Head Count Ratio are from the *Report of the Expert Group on Estimation of Proportion and Number of Poor*, July 1993, Planning Commission, Govt. of India.

being, rather than their cardinal magnitude. This will enable us to avoid systematic biases in claims about achievements across states.

We would use a modified Human Development Index based on the well known Borda Rule for our broad inter-state comparisons. The Borda rule is a rank-order method of ordinal aggregation. We award each state a point equal to its rank in each of the four indicators (excluding poverty ratio) and then add up these scores for each state to obtain its aggregate Borda Score. Finally, we rank (Borda Rank) each state on the basis of their Borda Score. Ranking goes up from the worst (1) to the best (16). Table 2 provides the ranking of 16 states in term of 4 indicators and the Borda index. Next we use these rankings to conduct an empirical investigation of differences in the quality of life across the states. We intend to look at a snapshot of the quality of life in each state in period II, i.e., early 90s.

The disparities across states can be well examined by classifying them into groups, depending on their levels of human development. The grouping is done according to the Borda Scores in Period II (Col. 5 of Table 2): lower category of states with Borda score below 30, middle category with the score between 30 and 40 and the upper category with the scores above 40. First, we look at the worst-off and best states: six in each category in terms of Borda Rank, as shown in Table 2A.

Our Borda rank brings out the marked difference between the levels of well-being among the northern and southern states. Four out of the six worst-off states at the bottom in ascending order are UP, Bihar, Rajasthan and MP—the so-called BIMARU states; all of them are from the Hindi-speaking region of north India. They account for 40% of the total Indian population and 50% of India's rural poor live in Bihar, UP and MP. These states also turn out to be those with the lowest literacy rates ranging from 38% in Bihar to the maximum of 44% in MP. This is in sharp contrast to an overall 59% literacy rate in south India. Bihar has the lowest SDP per capita (28% of Punjab's) as well as lowest literacy rate and MP has the lowest life expectancy at birth among all Indian states. UP records the second lowest female-male ratio (next only to Haryana). On the other side, four out of the six highest ranked states are from south India. Punjab would be relegated to the middle rank category if we exclude its rank of income from its Borda score. That is, in terms of non-income

TABLE 2

Borda Index—Interstate Ranking

States	NSDP Per Capita Rank		Life Expectancy Rank		Literacy Rank		Female-Male Ratio Rank		Borda Rank Period I	Borda Rank Period II	Head-Count Ratio Rank
	1981	1993-94	1983	1990	1981	1991	1981	1991	1993-94		1993-94
	(1)		(2)		(3)		(4)		(5)		
Andhra Pradesh	8	6	10	8	5	4	13	13	9	7	15
Assam	6	10	3	2	7	7	4	7	5	6	4
Bihar	1	1	4	6	2	1	10	5	3	2	1
Gujarat	13	11	9	7	13	12	9	9	12	10	14
Haryana	14	14	11	12	8	8	1	1	7	9	13
Himachal Pradesh	12	9	12	13	12	14	12	15	14	14	10
Karnataka	10	12	13	11	9	9	11	11	10	11	9
Kerala	7	7	16	16	16	16	16	16	16	16	12
Madhya Pradesh	5	4	2	1	4	5	8	8	4	4	3
Maharashtra	15	15	14	14	15	15	7	10	15	15	6
Orissa	3	2	5	4	6	6	15	12	6	5	2
Punjab	16	16	15	15	10	11	2	3	10	12	16
Rajasthan	2	5	6	5	1	2	6	4	2	3	11
Tamilnadu	9	13	7	10	14	13	14	14	12	14	8

Uttar Pradesh	4	3	1	3	3	3	3	2	1	1	5
West Bengal	11	8	8	9	11	10	5	6	8	8	7

Note: Borda Ranking is based on the aggregate Borda Score of each state obtained by adding the rank scores in each of the 4 indicators: Income, Life Expectancy, Literacy and Female-Male Ratio. Ranking goes up from the worst (1) to the best (16). Borda Score does not include HCR.

social indicators, Punjab's performance is the worst among the top six states. The north-south divide among major states in respect of well-being becomes most conspicuous if we consider gender disparities, especially in sex ratio and literacy rate. The greatest disparity exists between the north-west and the south, with eastern states somewhere in the middle. On the whole, therefore, the Borda pattern that becomes visible is that a west-east boundary could be drawn along the line of the Bindhya scarp in the centre of the Indian map to demarcate northern and southern India between which differences in well-being show a marked dissimilarity.

The presence of the north-western state of Himachal Pradesh in the list of top-ranking states needs to be explored. The remarkable achievements of Himachal Pradesh in human development are comparable to those of southern states in the group in spite of cultural and ethnic differences. In respect of female-male ratio, Himachal Pradesh is next only to Kerala (where the ratio exceeds unity). This is in line with the general pattern prevailing in the smaller hilly states in north-eastern India. The literacy rate in Himachal Pradesh (3rd from the top) and life expectancy at birth are also appreciably higher as compared with other Indian states.

The list of top six states remains the same regardless of whether poverty ratio is incorporated in our ranking or not. For example, Kerala remains way ahead of others in spite of its poor growth performance. However, the relative ranking of the remaining five states will change. Maharashtra with the second highest per capita income would then lag behind both Punjab and Himachal Pradesh. This reflects the fact that poverty ratio (expert group estimates) in Maharashtra is the highest (36.86%) among the top six states. Kerala and UP are to the opposite poles in the scale of all indicators of well-being. Kerala has a population size of 30 million and its income growth is one of the poorest in India. Nevertheless, Kerala's human development outstrips those of all states in India. On the other hand, Uttar Pradesh, with a population size of more than 156 million suffers from endemic and persistent human deprivation. Kerala's performance in near-universal literacy, high gender equity, health standards and demographic factors are in stark contrast with UP's extremely low levels of literacy, life expectancy and oppressive gender relations.

Kerala's experience provides a glowing testimony of highly significant role played by public action, political initiative and education-oriented popular movements in the sphere of human development. In sharp contrast with this, we observe in UP an astonishingly resilient inertia of public action and weak socio-cultural movements [Dreze & Sen (eds.) 1996] amidst appalling social backwardness.

Now we turn to four middle ranking states, Gujarat, Haryana, West Bengal and Andhra Pradesh in descending order of Borda Ranking, as shown in Table 2A. Despite having a relatively high per capita income, Gujarat, lags behind the high ranking states mainly because of its low life expectancy and female-male ratio. Haryana, a relatively prosperous state with the third highest per capita income (next to Punjab and Maharashtra), has the worst figure for the sex ratio. This along with the low level of literacy is responsible for its low overall ranking. It is the fast growth of income which acts as the driving force behind the expansion of life expectancy at birth (62.5) in Haryana. But gender inequality cannot really be explained by income. The same is also true for educational deprivation as illustrated by the low literacy rank (8) of Haryana. The closeness of ranking between Andhra Pradesh and West Bengal deserves scrutiny. Andhra Pradesh, the largest state in south India beats West Bengal only in one respect. The former has a higher female-male ratio (972 against 917 in West Bengal)—a

TABLE 2A

Ranking of States in Period II

Borda Rank	*State* (Rank without P.C. NSDP)
Low Borda Score (Below 30)	Uttar Pradesh (1), Bihar (3), Rajasthan (2), Madhya Pradesh (4), Orissa (6), Assam (11)
Borda Score (between 30 and 40)	Andhra Pradesh (7), West Bengal (7) Haryana (5), Gujarat (9)
Borda Score (above 40)	Karnataka (12), Punjab (10), Himachal Pradesh (15), Tamilnadu (14), Maharashtra (14), Kerala (16)

Tying Rule: If two states for example, tie for 3rd place (of badness) both are given the rank number 3 and the next state is ranked 5.

basic indicator of gender inequality. This is in line with the common features of better equity in all southern states and the declining relative position of Eastern states and to a lesser extent of West Bengal in the scale of female-male ratio. But in terms of the other three social indicators, Andhra Pradesh is closer to the large north Indian states than to southern state like Kerala or Tamilnadu. On the other hand, West Bengal is much ahead of Andhra Pradesh in terms of educational attainment. The life expectancy at birth and per capita income are also higher in West Bengal compared to those in Andhra Pradesh.

Another two-way comparison may be made between Bihar and Rajasthan which are next to each other at the bottom. Equal weights have been assigned to income and each of the non-income social indicators in our ranking. If we exclude income, the two-way ranking between Bihar and Rajasthan is reversed. However, such two-way ranking between any two states could go either way if we had included other smaller states or union territories in our sample. The position of two states relative to each other depends on our choice of the indices of well-being as well as on how others are performing. The Borda rule violates the axiom of the independence of irrelevant alternatives.

So far we have reached a number of qualitative conclusions regarding the human development experience of Indian states. We now turn to a quantitative assessment of the relationships between Borda rank and other indices, as well as those between pairs of other indices of income, health, education and gender equality. For this we look at Table 3 which presents the Spearman's rank correlation coefficient for each pair of ranks from the six ranking of states. The first column of Table 3 shows that the highest correlation is between Borda index and literacy (.95). Next in order of strength is the correlation between Borda rank and life expectancy. Thus, educational attainment and health seem to be the most important determinants of well-being. The second column of Table 3 shows the correlations between income and each of the three non-income indicators of well-being, i.e., health, education and gender equality. The correlations of income with these non-income indicators are not substantially high, as those between non-income indicators themselves. The degree of association between life expectancy and literacy (.75) is higher than those of both income with life expectancy (.65) and with literacy

TABLE 3

Correlation Matrix of Constituent Ranking in Period II

	Borda	*NSDP Per capita*	*Life Expectancy*	*Literacy*	*Female-Male Ratio*
	(1)	*(2)*	*(3)*	*(4)*	
NSDP Per Capita	.7294*				
Life Expectancy	.8676*	.6529*			
Literacy	.9529*	.7059*	.7529*		
Female-Male Ratio	.5735	.0029	.2941	.5352	
Poverty Ratio (HCR)	.6735*	.6044*	.5574	.4764	.1044

* Correlation is statistically significant at 1% level (for n = 16, the critical value of the rank correlation coefficient being .601 at 1% level).

(.71). The correlation of per capita income with the female-male ratio (.0029) is negligible and not statistically significant even at 5% level.

It may seem that Kerala alone is responsible for the low observed correlation between income and non-income indicators of well-being because of its high achievements in social development in spite of its low income level. We give below the correlation between income and indicators of health and education excluding Kerala:

Rank Correlation Excluding Kerala : Period II

	Life Expectancy	*Literacy*	*Female-Male Ratio*
Income	.7232	.7875	-.0732

As the above figures indicate, the correlation between income and life expectancy (.72) is still lower than that between life expectancy and literacy (.79)

So far we have examined similarities and differences in the levels of well-being of different states in terms of indicators of health, education and gender disparity. We now turn to Table 2 which presents together the ranks of the states by all the different indicators for the two periods under consideration. The table clearly shows that the relative rank of different states of the Borda Index is by and large unchanged over 80s—the decade under consideration. This leads us to the most important conclusion that the pattern of human development in India is not only uneven but it has remained stagnant over the last decade. Uttar Pradesh, Bihar, Rajasthan and Madhya Pradesh were the worst performers in life expectancy and literacy in both periods and these four states also belong to the bottom rung by the Borda Index, although they interchange their positions among themselves in the two periods.

Uttar Pradesh remains stuck to the bottom in both periods while Bihar and Rajathan have inter-changed their ranks in the early 90s compared with early 80s. Also there has been no improvement in the rank of Madhya Pradesh (4). The rank of Rajasthan has improved marginally due to its relatively higher growth in per capita income in the late 80s. The rank of Orissa has, however, receded because of further deterioration in its female-male ratio over the decade (from .988 to .971). On the other hand, Kerala has been consistently at the top of the list in both periods, leading in all the indicators except per capita income. The ranks of Himachal Pradesh and Maharashtra remain the same while that of Tamilnadu has improved from the fifth to the third position from the top over the decade mainly because of improvement in its PCNSDP and life expectancy. Gujarat's rank has deteriorated (from 5th to the 7th from the top) owing to its poor performance in terms of all indicators and also because Tamilnadu which had the same rank (12) and Punjab which was lagging behind (10) in early 80s have moved ahead during the early 90s.

A similar pattern also emerges from the income ranking as well. Punjab, Maharashtra and Haryana respectively, occupy the top three positions in the list, while Bihar persistently remains at the bottom in both the periods. Kerala's performance, at least in terms of its income (ranked 7) does not seem to have improved. However, it remains to be explored what would be the result if large remittances into the state from abroad are taken into consideration in the computation of its SDP. Even in 1993-94, all the major states except Maharashtra and Haryana had per capita SDP values less than what Punjab had in 1981, (and per capita SDP values of at least eight major states e.g., BIMARU states along with Orissa, Andhra Pradesh, Kerala and Himachal Pradesh during

1993-94 were lower than even what Punjab had as far back as during 1970-75). Thus, the non-convergent pattern of income growth of different states seems hardly to have changed over the decade.

We summarise below the results relating to interstate comparison of human development experience of sixteen major states:

- Human development requires much more than growth of income. The correlation between income and non-income indicators such as life expectancy, literacy rate and female-male ratio is lower than the correlation between the non-income indicators. Gender inequality, one important aspect of human deprivation has little to do with income. Gender equality can also be achieved across a range of cultures and political commitments.
- The progress in human development in India is marked by unevenness and stagnation. There are wide disparities in achievements and improvement among northern and southern states over the two sides of the Bindhyas.
- Public policy both at the state and at the central level has to be designed to meet different kinds of challenges in different parts of the country. For this, it is necessary to compile and analyse data on well-being indicators, based on non-linear achievements and improvement at the district level.

References

Anand, S. and Ravallion, M. (1993), "Human Development in Poor Countries: On the Role of Private Incomes and Public Services", *Journal of Economic Perspectives*, 7 (Winter).

Dasgupta, P. (1993), *An Inquiry into Well-being and Destitution*, Clarendon Press, Oxford.

Dreze, J. and Sen, A.K. (1995), *India: Economic Development and Social Opportunities*, Oxford University Press, Delhi.

——— (eds.) (1997), *Indian Development: Selected Regional Perspectives*, Oxford University Press, Delhi.

Dutta B., Panda, M. and Wadhwa, W. (July 1994), *Human Development in India: An Interstate Analysis*, mimeo, Indian Statistical Institute, New Delhi.

Government of India (1997), *Economic Survey, 1996-97*, New Delhi : Ministry of Finance.

Harriss, B., Guhan, S., and Cassen, R. (eds.) (1992), *Poverty in India: Research and Policy*, Delhi, Oxford University Press.

Kumar, A.K. Shiva (1991), UNDP's Human Development Index: A Computation for Indian States, *Economic and Political Weekly*, October 12

UNDP (1996), *Human Development Report, 1996*, Oxford : Oxford University Press.

——— (1997), *Human Development Report, 1997*, Oxford : Oxford University Press.

UNFPA (1997), *India: Towards Population and Development Goals*, Oxford University Press, Delhi.

19

Human Development in India—A Study of Interstate Disparity

BISWAJIT GUHA

I

The concept of Human Development throws light on total development of human beings by considering within its fold the improvement of economic, social, cultural, educational, health and civic conditions of human beings residing in a definite territory. Mere consideration of economic development and neglect of non-economic promotion of human beings cannot be regarded as development in true sense. Here lies the significance of the term Human Development. During last few years, the United Nations has been publishing its Report on Human Development. Its "Human Development Report, 1997" published a detailed analysis of human development of 175 countries of the world including India. In the year 1997, the UNFPA also published a report on human development in India in a book entitled "*India: Towards Population and Development Goals*". Mahbub-ul-Haq also wrote a book entitled "*Human Development in South Asia, 1997*" on behalf of the "Human Development Centre". This book also carried out a study of human development in India. A careful review of both these reports shows that these studies have covered only limited areas of human development in India. This paper has aimed at analysing the human development in India by considering a few more areas in order to provide a much wider study of human development in India.

The UNFPA considered only three types of indices of human development in India: (i) The index of life expectancy; (ii) The index of per capita income, i.e. per capita state domestic product; and (iii) The index of education considering literacy rate and school enrolment ratio, Mahbub-ul-Haq also considered similar three types of indices of human development in India with a minor difference in the sense that he considered only literacy rate in his study while neglecting the element of school enrolment ratio in the study of the index of education.

It is worth mentioning that both these studies have failed to provide a clear state-wise information of human development in India by neglecting many important aspects of human development. The present study is an attempt to overcome this inadequacy by including three additional elements of human development, such as, the quality of life, poverty eradication and urbanisation within the fold of the study of human development. The study of the index of quality of life has included the following different elements, such as, the percentage of households with access to the safe drinking water, electricity connection, enjoyment of two square meals a day throughout the year and residence in "pucca" houses along with the per capita availability of beds in public hospitals.

The present study of human development in India has the following objectives: (i) To analyse the different aspects of human development in the form of a state-wise comparative study ; (ii) To determine the different state-wise index numbers of the following different items such as life expectancy, per capita income of the state, education, quality of life, poverty eradication and urbanisation; (iii) To carry out a separate analysis of quality of life of the people in details with respect to the access of the people towards the primary amenities of daily life in both rural and urban areas of each state; (iv) To examine the nature of eradication of poverty in rural and urban areas separately as well as in the combined form of both rural and urban areas of each state; (v) To examine the nature of disparity in the quality of life of rural and urban population of each state; and (vi) To analyse a comparative study of human development in all the states of India in a general manner.

The present study has considered the following methodology and design : 1. The nature of human development of 15 major states of India has been considered where in each state, population has exceeded a number of 10 millions. 2. The study is based on secondary data collected from different published reports of different departments and organisations of the Government of India, such as, different reports of the C.S.O., C.M.I.E., N.S.S., Planning Commission, Ministry of Finance, Ministry of Education, Ministry of Health, and the Census Report of 1991. It has also considered different reports of different organisations of the United Nations in the similar context. 3.This study has considered the period of 1988-94 for the purpose of construction of different index numbers based on the data collected for the said period since all the different statistical data required for the purpose of a state-wise comparative study of human development during the post-1994 period are not available in an organised manner. 4. The different index numbers constructed in the study have followed the internationally accepted procedure which has been adopted and used by the UNDP. 5. In order to understand the nature of inter-state disparity in human development, each separate value of coefficient of variation with respect to each separate index has been determined. 6. In order to understand the degree of association between different attributes, the rank correlation coefficients have been determined. 7. The quality of life and poverty eradication index numbers of rural and urban population have been compared along with a study of urban-rural disparity in the field of quality of life index. 8. Following the UNDP's procedure, the following different index numbers have been constructed:

(i) Index of Life Expectancy is given by:

$$I_1 = \frac{(\text{actual value of } X_i \text{ of the state}) - (\text{minimum value of } X_i)}{(\text{maximum value of } X_i) - (\text{minimum value of } X_i)}$$

where X_1 refers to the state-wise figure of life expectancy at birth in years. The UNDP has assumed the minimum and maximum values of life expectancy to be 25 and 85 years respectively.

(ii) Actual value of PPP is given by:

$$PPP = \frac{\text{per capita income of the State}}{\text{per capita GDP}} \times 1{,}240$$

Here, PPP refers to the purchasing power parity of rupee equivalent to dollar. The per capita GNP at the all India level is considered as $US 1,240 as given by the UNDP. The per capita GDP of India at current price stood at Rs. 6,262 in the year 1992-93.

(iii) Index of per capita income of the state is given by:

$$I_2 = \frac{(\text{actual value of PPP of the state}) - (\text{minimum value of PPP})}{(\text{maximum value of PPP}) - (\text{minimum value of PPP})}$$

Here the UNDP assumes the minimum and maximum values of per capita GNP at PPP to be $US 100 and 5,448 respectively.

(iv) Index of 'education is given by :

$$I_3 = [2 \times (\text{literacy rate}) + (\text{school enrolment ratio})] \div 3$$

(v) Index of any item of quality of life is given by:

$$I_4 = \frac{(\text{actual value}) - (\text{minimum value})}{(\text{maximum value}) - (\text{minimum value})}$$

Here, and for indices given in (vii) and (viii) below UNDP assumes minimum and maximum values to be 0 and 100 percentages respectively, which makes actual value of any item to be equal to Index of that item.

(vi) Index of quality of life is given by:

$$I_4 = \frac{\text{sum of index numbers of all items of quality of life}}{\text{number of items of quality of life}}$$

(vii) Index of poverty eradication is given by 15.

(viii) Index of urbanisation is given by : $I_6 \cdot I_5$ and I_6 are given by the same formula as given in (v).

The final study of Human Development Index in the present paper is divided into four separate parts of estimate such as HDI_1, HDI_2, HDI_3 and HDI_4. The UNFPA and Mahbub-ul-Haq estimated only HDI_1 while the present paper has considered all these four separate estimates following the UNDP's procedure as follows:

$$HDI_1 = \left[\frac{1}{3}\sum_{j=1}^{3} I_j^3\right]^{\frac{1}{3}} \qquad HDI_2 = \left[\frac{1}{4}\sum_{j=1}^{4} I_j^4\right]^{\frac{1}{4}}$$

$$HDI_3 = \left[\frac{1}{5}\sum_{j=1}^{5} I_j^5\right]^{\frac{1}{5}} \qquad HDI_4 = \left[\frac{1}{6}\sum_{j=1}^{6} I_j^6\right]^{\frac{1}{6}}$$

Here, I_j refers to I_1, I_2, . . . I_6, respectively.

II

The study of human development reveals the true picture of socio-economic development of population residing in a definite territory. Mere consideration of life expectancy, per capita income of the state and education is not enough. We must know the actual quality of life being maintained by the population at a decent standard of living, i.e., quality of life is an important indicator of human development. We should also know what percentage of population could exceed the so-called "poverty line'. Since urbanisation gives rise to a lot of dynamism in social life, it should also be accordingly considered. The present study has accordingly considered all these elements together.

The non-availability of some important official statistical data, say, on sanitation, per capita availability of food, clothing and footwear, etc. of all the states separately could not represent the true picture of quality of life of rural and urban population as well as that of entire population of each separate state in the present study. On account of similar non-availability of official statistical data of all the states, it was not possible to consider the factors like state-wise growth of employment opportunities, progress of land reform, etc. However, it can also be mentioned that it is very difficult to offer a complete as well as true picture of human development of any country mainly on account of non-availability of all types of required statistical data and partly on account of failure to include all types of required items to reveal the nature of human development. So, there are always some conceptual and practical limitations involved in this type of analysis. However, in spite of all these limitations, it can be stated that even if some factors are excluded from the analysis of human development, these will have some impact upon the per capita state domestic product. So, per capita income will still act as an important index of development.

In order to confine the present study strictly within the limit of measuring Human Development Index, the present study has refrained from estimating the following related items of human development in India: (i) gender-disparity, (ii) gender-empowerment, (iii) food security, and (iv) human deprivation and poverty.

The entire study has considered and analysed the data collected for this purpose. Accordingly, the following different index numbers have been constructed for each separate state:

1. The Census Report, 1991, mentions that India is primarily dominated by rural population (74.3%). So, human development in India depends mostly upon the all-round improvement of the socio-economic condition of the rural population.
2. The Index of Life Expectancy of all the states has been prepared on the basis of the state-wise actual data on life expectancy.
3. The Index of Per Capita Income of the state, i.e.. Per Capita State Domestic Product of all the states has been prepared on the basis of the state-wise data on per capita state domestic product.

4. The Index of Education of all the states has been prepared on the basis of the state-wise data on literacy rate and school enrolment ratio.
5. The Index of Quality of Life of all the states has been prepared separately for rural population, urban population and total population. The Index of Quality of Life of each state has been prepared on the basis of the state-wise data on percentage of households with access to: (a) safe drinking water, (b) electricity connection, (c) enjoyment of two square meals a day throughout the year, and (d) residence in "pucca houses" along with the state-wise data on availability of beds in public hospitals.
6. The Index of Poverty Eradication of each separate state has been prepared with respect to the eradication of poverty among total population. The index has been prepared on the basis of the estimates of poverty in India as prepared by the Expert Group of the Planning Commission.
7. The Index of Urbanisation of each separate state has been prepared on the basis of the state-wise data derived from the Census Report of 1991. All the results mentioned in 1-7 are reported in Table 1.
8. A separate state-wise study of Quality of Life Index Numbers of total population is reported in Table 2. The similar state-wise index numbers of rural and urban population and the urban-rural disparity in this context is reported in Table 3. In this context, a separate study of dwellers of slums/*bustees* is reported in Table 4. We can observe the alarmingly deplorable condition of these people who live mostly in "kutcha" houses.
9. Figures in Table 5 report about the study in terms of HDI, by UNFPA, Mahbub-ul-Haq and the present author.
10. Figures in Table 6 report about the three alternative studies of HDI_2, HDI_3 and HDI_4 conducted by the present author.
11. In both Tables 5 and 6, the state-wise results and ranks of human development are mentioned by these

TABLE 1

Major State-wise Index Numbers of Human Development in India (1988-94)

Sl. No.	States	Index Number of					
		Life Expectancy (1)	Per Capita Income of the Sate (2)	Education (3)	Quality of Life (4)	Poverty Eradication (5)	Urbanisation (6)
1.	Andhra Pradesh	59.17 (8)	19.33 (9)	45.38 (12)	49.77 (8)	73.9 (4)	26.9(7)
2.	Assam	49.83 (4)	17.81 (10)	50.72 (9)	37.79 (14)	70.4 (6)	11.1 (15)
3.	Bihar	55.83 (11)	9.56 (15)	36.76 (15)	39.47 (13)	47.0 (14)	13.1 (14)
4.	Gujarat	58.33 (9)	24.73 (4)	60.38 (4)	58.87 (2)	78.0 (3)	34.5 (2)
5.	Haryana	63.58 (4)	32.13 (3)	56.12 (7)	58.21 (3)	82.7 (2)	24.6 (9)
6.	Karnataka	61.33 (6)	22.01 (6)	57.12(5)	52.82 (7)	60.5 (10)	30.9 (4)
7.	Kerala	78.00 (1)	19.51 (8)	90.85 (1)	55.07(5)	71.5 (5)	26.4 (8)
8.	Madhya Pradesh	48.33 (15)	15.67 (12)	46.19 (11)	45.25 (11)	53.8 (12)	23.2 (10)
9.	Maharashtra	65.33 (3)	33.82 (2)	67.39 (3)	57.00 (4)	64.2 (9)	38.7 (1)
10.	Orissa	50.83 (13)	13.32 (14)	47.60 (10)	36.27 (15)	42.1 (15)	13.4 (13)
11.	Punjab	68.83 (2)	39.30 (1)	56.41(6)	70.53 (1)	85.7 (1)	29.5 (5)
12.	Rajasthan	54.83 (12)	16.98 (11)	39.48 (14)	48.41 (10)	68.0 (7)	22.9 (11)
13.	Tamilnadu	62.33 (5)	22.83 (5)	68.19 (2)	53.58 (6)	59.3 (11)	34.2 (3)
14.	Uttar Pradesh	57.33 (10)	13.97 (13)	41.14 (13)	43.17 (12)	52.4 (13)	19.8 (12)

15. West Bengal	60.83 (7)	19.54 (7)	55.75 (8)	49.28 (9)	66.5 (8)	27.5 (6)
Coefficient of Variation (in Percent)	13.45	38.37	25.22	18.24	19.52	32.54

Note: Figures in parenthesis indicate respective state-wise ranks.

Sources: (1) Government of India : *Census Report, 1991*;

(2) Registrar General, India : *Abridged Life Tables, 1989-93*;

(3) Government of India : *Health Information of India, 1993*;

(4) *6th All India Education Survey, 1995*;

(5) National Sample Survey: *Report of 48th Round, 1994*;

(6) Planning Commission: *Report of the Expert Group on Poverty Estimates, 1993*; and

(7) UNFPA : India : *Towards Population and Development Goals*, OUP, 1997.

TABLE 2

Major State-wise Quality of Life Indicators of Population in India, (1991-94)

Sl. No.	*States*	*Percentage of Households with*				
		Access to Safe Drinking Water	*Electricity Connection*	*Enjoyment of Two Square Meals a Day Throughout the year*	*Residence in Pucca Houses*	*Percentage of Availability of Beds in Public Hospitals*
1.	Andhra Pradesh	66.3	48.3	93.9	40.3	0.04
2.	Assam	63.6	17.5	94.0	13.8	0.056
3.	Bihar	65.9	13.6	86.7	31.1	0.034
4.	Gujarat	76.2	65.8	95.6	56.6	0.143
5.	Haryana	75.1	69.7	96.9	49.3	p.043
6.	Karnataka	78.3	52.2	91.4	42.1	0.084
7.	Kerala	75.3	49.7	93.3	56.8	0.265
8.	Madhya Pradesh	62.6	44.0	88.4	31.2	0.027
9.	Maharashtra	73.6	68.2	92.9	50.2	0.1
10.	Orissa	52.0	24.2	85.8	19.3	0.046
11.	Punjab	95.4	82.3	98.0	76.9	0.072
12.	Rajasthan	60.6	33.2	93.4	54.8	0.047
13.	Tamilnadu	74.7	55.8	90.6	46.7	0.087
14.	Uttar Pradesh	66.2	22.4	85.8	41.4	0.034
15.	West Bengal	87.3	33.6	92.1	33.3	0.08
Coefficient of Variation (in percent)		15.21	46.11	4.17	37.2	78.52

Sources: 1. Government of India : *Census Report, 1991.*

2. U.N.F.P.A.: India : *Towards Population and Development Goals,* OUP, 1997.

3. National Sample Survey : *Report of 48th Round, 1994.*

4. Directorate of Health Services, Ministry of Health and Family Welfare, Government of India : *Health Information of India, 1993.*

TABLE 3

Major State-wise Quality of Life Index Number of Rural and Urban Population in India and their Disparity, (1991-94)

Sl. No.	*States*	*Quality of Life Index Number*		
		Rural	*Urban*	*Urban-Rural Disparity*
1.	Andhra Pradesh	44.16 (8)	62.84 (10)	18.68 (10)
2.	Assam	35.50 (14)	58.37 (14)	22.87 (6)
3.	Bihar	35.80 (13)	60.11 (13)	24.31 (5)
4.	Gujarat	52.73 (3)	70.25 (4)	17.52 (12)
5.	Haryana	54.14 (2)	73.82 (2)	19.68 (9)
6.	Karnataka	47.72 (6)	64.75 (8)	17.03 (13)
7.	Kerala	52.02 (4)	62.27 (11)	10.25 (14)
8.	Madhya Pradesh	39.62 (11)	62.10 (12)	22.48 (7)
9.	Maharashtra	49.66 (5)	70.59 (3)	20.93 (8)
10.	Orissa	32.38 (15)	58.21 (15)	25.83 (2)
11.	Punjab	68.44 (1)	75.38 (1)	6.94 (15)
12.	Rajasthan	43.32 (9)	68.82 (5)	25.50 (3)
13.	Tamilnadu	47.32 (7)	65.15 (7)	17.83 (11)
14.	Uttar Pradesh	37.90 (12)	64.15 (9)	26.25 (1)
15.	West Bengal	41.84 (10)	66.55 (6)	24.71 (4)
Coefficient of Variation (in percent)		20.34	8.07	28.16

Note: Figures in Parenthesis indicate respective State-wise Ranks.

Sources: (1) Government of India : *Census Report, 1991*;
(2) Government of India : *Economic Survey, 1996-97*;
(3) Government of India : *Health Information of India, 1993*;
(4) National Sample Survey : *Report of the 48th Round, 1994*;
(5) UNFPA : India : *Towards Population and Development Goals*, OUP, 1997.

alternative studies,

12. Glaring inter-state disparity is observed with respect to some items as revealed from their figures of coefficient of variation. These are, for example, per capita income of the state (38.37%), index of education (25.22%), index of urbanisation (32.54%), index of electricity

TABLE 4

Major State-wise Distribution of Households Living in Slums/ Bustees

Sl. No.	*States*	*Percentage of Households living in Slums/Bustees*		*Percentages of Dwellers of Slums/ Bustees living in Kutcha Houses*	
		Rural	*Urban*	*Rural*	*Urban*
1.	Andhra Pradesh	6.68 (6)	18.23 (3)	65.12 (4)	48.00 (4)
2.	Assam	15.03 (1)	12.02 (8)	72.99 (2)	66.64 (1)
3.	Bihar	6.81 (5)	15.72 (7)	53.30 (6)	36.64 (5)
4.	Gujarat	4.65 (10)	10.86 (9)	15.05 (15)	15.93 (12)
5.	Haryana	2.03 (14)	4.90 (14)	15.27 (14)	19.18 (10)
6.	Karnataka	7.38 (4)	16.94 (6)	41.06 (8)	26.56 (6)
7.	Kerala	1.67 (15)	4.28 (15)	28.17 (10)	20.09 (9)
8.	Madhya Pradesh	8.09 (3)	18.09 (4)	22.25 (12)	20.51 (8)
9.	Maharashtra	12.49 (2)	25.42 (1)	26.74 (11)	14.04 (13)
10.	Orissa	6.38 (7)	19.07 (2)	79.47 (1)	49.92 (3)
11.	Punjab	3.47(13)	6.28 (13)	20.75 (13)	8.76 (15)
12.	Rajasthan	5.36 (9)	8.06 (12)	39.74 (9)	16.75 (11)
13.	Tamilnadu	6.27 (8)	9.23 (11)	62.36 (5)	58.83 (2)
14.	Uttar Pradesh	3.66 (12)	9.53 (10)	50.55 (7)	26.34 (7)
15.	West Bengal	3.95 (11)	17.60 (5)	71.90 (3)	13.64 (14)
Coefficient of Variation (in percent)		57.75	47.09	50.6	61.62

Note: Figures in parenthesis indicate respective state-wise ranks.

Sources: 1. Government of India : *Census Report, 1991.*
2. National Sample Survey : *Report of 44th Round, 1988-89.*
3. Government of India : *Census Report, 1991.*
4. U.N.F.P.A. : India : *Towards Population and Development Goals*, OUP, 1997.

connection to households (46.11%), index of residence in *pucca* houses (37.2%), per capita availability of bed in public hospitals (78.52%), urban-rural disparity in quality of life index (28.16%), percentage of households living in slums in rural areas (57.75%) and

TABLE 5

Major State-wise Alternative Studies of Human Development in India (HDI_1)

Sl. No.	*States*	*Value of HDI_1 as studied by*		
		UNFPA	*Haq*	*Guha*
1.	Andhra Pradesh	41.28 (9)	39.3 (9)	46.82 (9)
2	Assam	39.48 (10)	37.4 (10)	44.25 (10)
3	Bihar	34.05 (15)	35.04 (12)	42.14 (13)
4	Gujarat	47.82 (6)	45.8 (5)	52.48 (6)
5	Haryana	50.56 (5)	47.6 (4)	53.75 (5)
6	Karnataka	46.83 (7)	44.2 (7)	52.24 (7)
7	Kerala	62.79 (1)	59.7 (1)	74.33 (1)
8	Madhya Pradesh	36.71 (11)	34.1 (15)	41.56 (14)
9	Maharashtra	55.49 (2)	51.3 (3)	59.24 (2)
10	Orissa	37.25 (12)	36.8 (11)	43.18 (11)
11	Punjab	54.86 (3)	51.6 (2)	57.36 (4)
12	Rajasthan	37.11 (13)	35.03 (13)	42.56 (12)
13	Tamilnadu	51.11 (4)	43.2 (8)	57.53 (3)
14	Uttar Pradesh	35.51 (14)	34.3 (14)	41.06 (15)
15	West Bengal	45.37 (8)	45.2 (6)	51.33 (8)
Coefficient of Variation (in percent)		19.20	17.93	18.02

Note: Figures in parenthesis indicate respective state-wise ranks.

Sources: 1. U.N.F.P.A. : India : *Towards Population and Development Goals*, OUP, 1997

2. Mahbub-ul-Haq : *Human Development in South Asia*, OUP, 1997.

3. Calculations of Index by B. Guha are based on Figures used in Table 1.

in urban areas (47.09%), percentage of dwellers of slums living in *kutcha* houses in rural areas (50.6%) and in urban areas (61.62%), etc. Thus, in most of the items, the figures of coefficient of variation exceeded 20%. But when all these items are put together the four alternative values of coefficient of variation related to the study of HDI_1, HDI_2, HDI_3 and HDI_4 are found to be at 18.02, 17.11, 16.17 and 16.26 percentages respectively. These figures are also

TABLE 6

Major State-wise Alternative Extensive Studies of Human Development in India (1988-94)

Sl. No.	States	HDI_2	HDI_3	HDI_4
1.	Andhra Pradesh	48.85 (9)	58.51 (7)	58.07(6)
2.	Assam	43.95 (11)	54.71 (10)	54.49 (10)
3.	Bihar	43.24 (13)	45.12 (14)	44.61 (14)
4.	Gujarat	55.24 (6)	63.3 (4)	62.47 (4)
5.	Haryana	55.78 (5)	65.78 (3)	65.11(3)
6.	Karnataka	53.52 (7)	55.79 (9)	54.64 (9)
7.	Kerala	73.14 (1)	74.47(1)	73.54 (1)
8.	Madhya Pradesh	43.45 (12)	46.74 (12)	45.81 (12)
9.	Maharashtra	59.67 (3)	61.27(5)	60.02 (5)
10.	Orissa	42.92 (14)	43.5 (15)	42.77 (15)
11.	Punjab	62.16 (2)	70.29 (2)	69.26 (2)
12.	Rajasthan	45.43 (10)	54.08(11)	53.64(11)
13.	Tamilnadu	57.99 (4)	59.07(6)	57.99 (7)
14.	Uttar Pradesh	42.72 (15)	45.91 (13)	45.08 (13)
15.	West Bengal	52.07(8)	56.84 (8)	55.84 (8)
Coefficient of Variation (in percent)		17.11	16.17	16.26

Note: Figures in parenthesis indicate respective state-wise ranks.

Source: Calculations of Index by B. Guha are based on Figures used in Table 1.

moderately high though these are very close figures. The figures of coefficient of variation with respect to the study of HDI_1 by UNFPA, Mahbub-ul-Haq and the present author are also similarly very close and moderately high and found to be at 19.2, 17.93 and 18.02 percentages respectively. These three different studies of HDI_1 are found to be very much mutually consistent. It is also worth-mentioning that in all these three studies, the state of Kerala occupies the highest rank.

13. It is observed that the index of per capita income of the state varies from 9.56% in Bihar to the maximum of

TABLE 7

Rank Correlation Coefficients in the Study of Major State-wise Human Development in India (1988-94)

Sl. No.	*Nature of Items in the Determination of Rank Correlation Coefficient*	*Mentioned in Table No.*	*Nature and Size of the Rank Correlation Coefficient*
1.	State-wise Index Numbers of Life Expectancy (I_1) and Per Capita Income of the State (I_2)	1	+0.77
2.	State-wise Index Numbers of Education (I_3) Per Capita Income of the State (I_2)	1	+0.75
3.	State-wise Index Numbers of Quality of Life (I_4) and Per Capita State Domestic Product (I_2)	1	+0.91
4.	State-wise Index Numbers of Quality of Life of Rural and Urban types of Population	1	+0.81
5.	State-wise Index Numbers of Urbanisation (I_2) and Per Capita Income of the State (I_2)	1	+0.82
6.	State-wise Index of Urban-Rural Disparity in Quality of Life and the Study of HDI_2	3 and 6	-0.82
7.	State-wise Index of Urban-Rural Disparity in Quality of Life and the Study of HDI_4	3 and 6	-0.80
8.	Study of HDI_1 by UNFPA and Haq	5	+0.91
9.	Study of HDI_1 by UNFPA and Guha	5	+0.97
10.	Study of HDI_1 by Haq and Guha	5	+0.93
11.	Guha's Study of HDI_1 and HDI_2	5 and 6	+0.96
12.	Guha's Study of HDI_1 and HDI_3	5 and 6	+0.89
13.	Guha's Study of HDI_1 and HDI_4	5 and 6	+0.86

Source: Figures used in Tables 1, 3, 5 and 6.

39.3% in Punjab. The index of education varies from the minimum of 36.76% in Bihar to the maximum of 90.85% in Kerala. The index of urbanisation varies from the minimum of 11.10% in Assam to the maximum of 38.70% in Maharashtra. The index of life

TABLE 8

Major State-wise Percentages of Population and Seats in Lok Sabha and their Ranks in Human Development in India

Rank according to HDI_4	*States*	*Percentage of Total Population*	*Total Seats in Lok Sabha*	
			In Number	*In Percent of Total*
1.	Kerala	3.4	20	3.7
2.	Punjab	2.4	13	2.4
3.	Haryana	1.9	10	1.8
4.	Gujarat	4.9	26	4.8
5.	Maharashtra	9.3	48	8.8
	Sub-Total	21.9	117	21.5
6.	Andhra Pradesh	7.9	42	7.7
7.	Tamilnadu	6.6	39	7.2
8.	West Bengal	8.0	42	7.7
9.	Karnataka	5.3	28	5.2
10.	Assam	2.6	14	2.6
	Sub-Total	30.4	165	30.4
11.	Rajasthan	5.2	25	4.6
12.	Madhya Pradesh	7.8	40	7.4
13.	Uttar Pradesh	16.4	85	15.7
14.	Bihar	10.2	54	9.9
15.	Orissa	3.7	21	3.9
	Sub-Total	43.3	225	41.5

Sources: 1. Figures used in Table 6.
2. Government of India, *Census Report, 1991.*
3. Government of India, *India 1996.*

expectancy varies from the minimum of 48.33% in Madhya Pradesh to the maximum of 78% in Kerala. The index of rural quality of life varies from the minimum of 32.38% in Orissa to the maximum of 68.44% in Punjab, the index of urban quality of life varies from the minimum of 58.21% in Orissa to the maximum of 75.38% in Punjab and the index of quality of life of total population varies from the minimum of 36.27% in Orissa to the maximum of 70.53% in Punjab. The index of poverty eradication varies from the minimum of 42.1% in Orissa to the maximum of 85.7% in Punjab.

14. The urban-rural disparity in terms of quality of life index varies from the minimum of 6.94% in Punjab to the maximum of 26.25% in Uttar Pradesh.
15. The final study of human development in terms of the HDI_4 shows that it varies from the minimum value of 42.77% in Orissa to the maximum value of 73.54% in Kerala. Two results are specially worth-mentioning. The states of Kerala and West Bengal maintained consistently their ranks as 1 and 8 respectively in all the different alternative studies of human development in the estimates of HDI_1, HDI_2, HDI_3 and HDI_4. The respective ranks of other states changed slightly in these successive estimates. It is also observed that some states consistently maintained their ranks between 10 to 15. These states are Orissa, Bihar, Uttar Pradesh, Rajasthan and Madhya Pradesh.
16. Figures in Table 7 show a long list of rank correlation coefficients. These show that there exists high positive rank correlation between the index of per capita income of the states (12) and different other types of index like I_2, I_3 and I_4. A high negative rank correlation is quite reasonably observed between urban-rural disparity and estimates of human development. However, it is worth-mentioning that all the different alternative estimates of human development have a very high degree of positive rank correlation since such coefficients vary from +0.86 to +0.97. So, the values of these rank correlation coefficients are highly significant. The respective ranks of states with respect to different items of index as well as in case of the total index of each separate HDI are, therefore, examined and it is found that in all the alternative studies of HDI, the ranks of states have minor variations which is accurately pointed out by the range of high positive

rank correlation between 0.86 and 0.97. It is further observed that as the number of items of index in the study continues to rise in the estimate of HDI, the size of the rank correlation coefficient continues to fall.

17. Figures in Table 8 report the state-wise distribution of percentage of population and seats in the Lok Sabha. It is observed that the states occupying ranks 1 to 5 constitute 21.9% of total population of India and these represent 21.5% of total number of seats in Lok Sabha. On the other hand, the states occupying ranks 11 to 15 constitute 43.3% of total population of India and these represent 41.5% of total number of seats in Lok Sabha. The Lok Sabha is the highest legislative body in the country which indirectly rules the country through the Council of Ministers most of whom are also its members. This should be considered as a paradox in the arena of economics and politics in India since in spite of enjoying a large majority of total population as well as the same of total seats of Lok Sabha, the 5 states like Orissa, Bihar, Uttar Pradesh, Rajasthan and Madhya Pradesh continue to be the most backward states. On the other hand, the 5 states belonging to a minor percentage of total population as well as that of total seats in Lok Sabha in the county, such as the states like Kerala, Punjab, Haryana, Gujarat and Maharashtra, lead the country in the field of human development.

To conclude, however, it can be stated that we should assign high importance to all aspects of human development in India. In this context, the state governments have to play the major role. The central government should play an active role in removing all forms of inter-state disparities in the field of human development. A nation cannot develop without adequate provision for public health, education, food, clothing, shelter and a decent standard of living.

References

Atkinson, Anthony B. (1970), "On the Measurement of Inequality", *Journal of Economic Theory*, 2(3), pp. 244-63.

Anand, Sudhir (1993), *Inequality between and within Nations*, Harvard University, Centre for Population and Development Studies.

Anand, Sudhir and Sen, Amartya Kr. (1992), Human Development Index: Methodology and Measurement, *Occasional Paper 12*, U.N.D.P.

Dreze, Jean and Sen, Amartya Kr. (1998), *India—Economic Development and Social Opportunity*, OUP.

———, (1998), *Indian Development—Selected Regional Perspectives*, OUP, 1998,

Government of India, *Census Report*, 1991.

———, *Registrar General : Abridged Life Tables, 1989-93.*

———, Ministry of Finance (1997), *Economic Survey, 1996-97.*

———, National Sample Survey, *Reports of 44th Round (1988-89) and 48th Round*, (1994).

———, Planning Commission (1993), *Report of the Expert Group on Poverty Estimates.*

———, *Sixth All India Education Survey, 1995.*

———, *India, 1996.*

Mahbub-ul-Haq (1997), *Human Development in South Asia*, 1997, OUP.

U.N.D.P. (1997), *Human Development Report, 1997*, OUP.

U.N.F.P.A. (1997), *India: Towards Population and Development Goals*, OUP.

20

A Modified Measure of Human Development

INDERJEET SINGH AND REENA SINGH

INTRODUCTION

Labour and capital alone cannot explain the process of economic development. To explain the process of economic development different factors have been identified as determinants of growth in different growth models. According to some descriptive theories, a purely structural change will raise the level of per capita income when there is a shift from sectors of the economy which require more of labour per unit of output to sectors that require less of it, other things being equal (Clark, C., 1957, Kuznets, S., 1963, Lewis, 1963). Some other theories found capital formation as the main key to development (Heller, W., 1954, Myrdal, G., 1958, Nurkse, R., 1953). Many theories have emphasized the role of investment as a generator of employment and income (Keynes, 1939, Harrod, 1949, Domar, 1946, Kindleberger, 1958). Post-World War experience has underscored the fact that growth of output is not explained fully by the growth of capital and labour alone. There is always an unexplained gap.

This gap is explained by the contributions of human capital by its productivity effects (Leontief, 1953).

Resources, which highlight the nature's power to regenerate are those materials capable of economic exploration through the application of human knowledge and skill. This has underscored the need for development of human resources. Human resource development is concerned with the development of skill, energy, talent and attitude of human beings which can be used for productive purposes. The UNDPs '*Human Development Report, 1990*' states, "Human development is a process of analysing people's choices. In principle these choices can be infinite and change over time. But at all levels of development, the essential ones are for people to lead a long and healthy life to acquire knowledge and to have access to resources needed for decent standard of living. If these choices are not available, many more opportunities remain inaccessible".

So the concept of economic development is a broad one and encompasses all types of economic, social, cultural and political changes leading to human welfare. That is why there is a need to have a better and more comprehensive socio-economic measure. Various studies have measured human development in different ways. This has led to the development of UNDP's Human Development Index (HDI). We have attempted a modification in HDI in the light of limitations and criticism of UNDP's index. Present work is an attempt to construct and analyse a modified HDI, an income disparity adjusted HDI and a gender adjusted HDI for the Indian states,

MODEL

UNDP has combined three indicators, i.e., life expectancy, educational attainment (defined as adult literacy, mean years of schooling) and per capita income into a composite HDI. UNDP's HDI defines a country's measure of deprivation for each of these variables. For calculation of a deprivation measure, the maximum and minimum values have to be identified for actual values for each of these variables. For calculating the minimum value that value is taken which is observed historically going back by about 30 years and the maximum values are limits of what can be envisioned in the next 30 years.

The deprivation measure places a country in the zero to one range defined by the difference between the maximum and minimum. The deprivation measure, I_{ij} showing deprivation indicator for the jth state with respect to ith variable is defined as:

$$I_{ij} = \frac{\left(\max X_{ij} - X_{ij}\right)}{\left(\max X_{ij} - \min X_{ij}\right)}$$

Average deprivation indicator I_{ij} is computed by taking a simple average of the three indicators:

$$I_j = \frac{1}{3}\sum_{i=1}^{3} I_{ij}$$

Human development index is defined as one minus average deprivation indicator as:

$$HDI = (1 - I_j)$$

Several studies have been done on the Indian economy using the UNDP methodology (Shivakumar, A.K., 1991). Some modifications in UNDP methodology have been proposed. First modification proposed in the Indian context relates to inclusion of population living below the poverty line as a fourth variable (Nair, N.K., Prakash, M.K. and others, 1992). Pritosh Banerji (1996) has suggested a simple formula for adjusting the real per capita GDP.

UNDP's index has assumed a constant marginal significance of longevity but it diminishes as human beings become older. In the same way, increase in educational attainment does not necessarily fill the same additional gap in educability. It has also been criticised for assuming that the three indicators taken in HDI exclusively cover all aspects of human development. A big criticism which has been levelled against UNDP's methodology is that it gives same weight to all the three indicators in HDI computation. Many other studies, based on this methodology, too assume a unit weighting scheme for the three indicators of human development. In the wake of this, our study is an attempt to present a modified HDI with a dynamic weighting scheme. Instead of superimposing an extraneous unitary weighting scheme, there is a need to determine the weighting scheme endogenously. Now the question is how to determine this weighting scheme for the three human development indicators endogenously. Several alternatives are there to the unit weighting scheme. First one can go for a geometric mean rather than the arithmetic mean as:

$$I_j = (I_{ij} \times I_{2j} \times I_{3j})^{½}$$

Secondly, weighted average of the deprivation indicators, W (I_i), of human development can be obtained by taking ranks (R_{1j}) of individual indicators as weights, i.e.,

$$W(I_j) = \frac{R_{ij}I_{ij} + R_{2j}I_{2j} + R_{3j}I_{3j}}{R_{ij} + R_{2j} + R_{3j}}$$

and

$$WHDI = 1 - W(I_j)$$

This model can be suitably applied to capture the disparities in human development in the country. Such disparities provide us an income distribution adjusted HDI and a gender disparity adjusted HDI.

EMPIRICAL PROGNOSTICATION OF THE MODEL

The Human Development Index (HDI) and Weighted Human Development Index (WHDI) for 15 states of India have been constructed for the years 1981 and 1991. For computing these indices data regarding three development indices have been obtained from K.R. Shah, A. Suba Rao and others (1993).

The HDI for 1981 (Table 1) is an indicative of the fact that Kerala has the highest place in terms of human development. It is followed by Punjab, Maharashtra, Haryana and Gujarat in order. U.P., Bihar, Rajasthan and Madhya Pradesh are on the lowest rank in terms of human development index. But WHDI depicts a little bit different picture. In terms of WHDI, in the years 1981, Maharashtra is at rank one. It is followed by Punjab, Gujarat and West Bengal in order of ranking. But U.P., Rajasthan and Bihar are characterised by a lower ranking in terms of human development. The difference between HDI and WHDI ranking is pronounced

TABLE 1

Human Development Index (HDI) and Weighted Human Development Index (WHDI) for the Indian States, 1981

States	Level of Deprivation			Average depriv. level	HDI	WHDI	Difference (HDI-WHDI)
	Life Expectancy	Adult Lit. Level	Real PCI (Rs.)				
Andhra Pradesh	0.378 (6)	0.736 (10)	0.561 (7)	0.558	0.442 (9)	0.411 (9)	0
Assam	0.590 (13)	0.672 (8)	0.626 (10)	0.629	0.371 (10)	0.377 (10)	0
Bihar	0.567 (12)	0.805 (12)	0.728 (15)	0.700	0.300 (14)	0.298 (13)	1
Gujarat	0.404 (7)	0.628 (6)	0.416 (4)	0.483	0.517 (5)	0.514 (3)	2
Haryana	0.316 (5)	0.691 (9)	0.346 (2)	0.451	0.549 (4)	0.469 (7)	-3
Karnataka	0.306 (3.5)	0.656 (7)	0.535 (6)	0.499	0.501 (6)	0.462 (8)	-2
Kerala	0.052 (1)	0.274 (1)	0.579 (8)	0.302	0.698 (1)	0.504 (5)	-4
Madhya Pradesh	0.599 (14)	0.814 (14)	0.660 (13)	0.691	0.309 (12)	0.308 (12)	0
Maharashtra	0.306 (3.5)	0.548 (2)	0.391 (3)	0.415	0.585 (3)	0.607 (1)	2
Orissa	0.554 (10)	0.745(11)	0.694 (14)	0.664	0.336 (11)	0.330(11)	0
Punjab	0.225 (2)	0.615 (4)	0.240 (1)	0.360	0.640 (2)	0.550 (2)	0
Rajasthan	0.537(11)	0.911 (16)	0.644 (11)	0.697	0.303 (13)	0.275 (14)	-1
Tamil Nadu	0.427 (9)	0.585 (3)	0.606 (9)	0.539	0.461 (8)	0.474 (6)	2
UP	0.717 (15)	0.806 (13)	0.657 (12)	0.727	0.273 (15)	0.272 (15)	0
West Bengal	0.410 (8)	0.627 (5)	0.470 (5)	0.502	0.498 (7)	0.513 (4)	3

for some states like West Bengal, Haryana and Kerala.

HDI and WHDI for the year 1991 are presented in Table 2. An analysis of the ranking on the basis of HDI underscores the fact that after a decade Kerala, Punjab, Maharashtra and Haryana continue to occupy the same leading position, as in the year 1981, in terms of human development index, HDI. During this decade Gujarat has shifted from fifth rank to eighth. U.P., Bihar and Madhya Pradesh occupy the same lower rank. In terms of WHDI Maharashtra at first place is followed by Haryana and Punjab.

Above analysis shows that WHDI, because of its endogenous weighting scheme, automatically brings forth that sector which is least developed and thereby needs a higher attention. Development is an ongoing process. The importance of the three indicators taken in the HDI ranking changes. The indicator with a highest deprivation level needs highest attention and is automatically ensured if the ranks of deprivation indicators are used as weights. As level of development in terms of a development indicator is achieved, its weight is automatically reduced. Thus, the Weighted Human Development Index can be used as the best guide mark for investment allocation in the state planning applications.

As already said that the HDI is an average index and it hides considerable differences in the distribution of the basic indicators like income, gender, race, region, ethnicity, etc. Two out of the three indicators, i.e. life expectancy and educational attainment are generally normally distributed. But the inequalities in Per Capita Income (PCI) are too sharp. So HDI is very sensitive to income distribution while interpreting the achieved well-being for the people of a country. For adjusting inequalities in the distribution of income the ranking of the states by PCI is adjusted by a factor indicating distributional inequality (1-Gini Coefficient). It represents the ratio of income shared by the highest 20% to the lowest 20%. The adjusted income, W(Y) (1-G), is then used as the third component in addition to life expectancy and educational attainment to compute the Income Distribution Adjusted Index (IDA-HDI). Such an index is presented in Table 3. Due to paucity of data, in calculating IDA-HDI, PCI data has not been adjusted for the local cost of living as suggested in the UNDPs methodology. The comparison of HDI and IDA-HDI highlights that Kerala and Panjab's rank in terms of human development remains unaltered. Human development index is very sensitive to

TABLE 2

Human Development Index (HDI) and Weighted Human Development Index (WHDI) for the Indian States, 1991

States	*Level of Deprivation*			*Average depriv. level*	*HDI*	*WHDI*	*Difference (HDI-WHDI)*
	Life Expectancy	*Adult Lit. Level*	*Real PCI (Rs.)*				
Andhra Pradesh	0.338 (7)	0.619 (10)	0.719 (8)	0.559	0.441 (9)	0.428 (8)	1
Assam	0.459 (13.5)	0.580 (9)	0.804 (12)	0.614	0.386 (10)	0.389 (9)	1
Bihar	0.407 (11)	0.743 (14)	0.866 (15)	0.672	0.328 (14)	0.303 (15)	-1
Gujarat	0.369 (9)	0.509 (5)	0.678 (4.5)	0.519	0.481 (8)	0.518 (4)	4
Haryana	0.287 (4)	0.533 (6)	0.487 (2)	0.436	0.565 (4)	0.557 (2)	2
Karnataka	0.288 (5)	0.484 (4)	0.706 (7)	0.493	0.507 (6)	0.480 (7)	-1
Kerala	0.089 (1)	0.115 (1)	0.784 (10)	0.329	0.671 (1)	0.330 (13)	-12
Madhya Pradesh	0.459 (13.5)	0.735 (12)	0.817 (13)	0.670	0.330 (13)	0.334 (12)	1
Maharashtra	0.282 (3)	0.395 (2)	0.588 (3)	0.422	0.578 (3)	0.575 (1)	2
Orissa	0.440 (12)	0.624 (11)	0.828 (14)	0.631	0.369(11)	0.359(10)	1
Punjab	0.235 (2)	0.536 (7)	0.277(1)	0.349	0.651 (2)	0.550 (3)	-1
Rajasthan	0.394 (10)	0.764 (15)	0.785 (9)	0.648	0.353 (12)	0.339(11)	1
Tamil Nadu	0.337 (6)	0.401 (3)	0.692 (6)	0.477	0.523 (5)	0.508 (5)	0
U.P.	0.556 (15)	0.739 (13)	0.803 (11)	0.699	0.301 (15)	0.313 (14)	1
West Bengal	0.366 (8)	0.547 (8)	0.678 (4.5)	0.530	0.470 (7)	0.495 (6)	1

TABLE 3

Income Distribution Adjusted Human Development Index (IDA-HDI), 1991

States	*Level of Deprivation*			*Average depriv. level*	*HDI*	*WHDI*	*Difference (HDI-WHDI)*
	Life Expectancy	*Adult Lit. Level*	*Real PCI (Rs.)*				
Andhra Pradesh	0.338	0.619	0.861	0.606	0.394 (9)	0.441 (9)	0
Assam	0.459	0.580	0.891	0.643	0.357 (10)	0.386 (10)	0
Bihar	0.407	0.743	0.937	0.696	0.304 (13)	0.328 (14)	-1
Gujarat	0.369	0.509	0.792	0.557	0.443 (7)	0.481 (8)	-1
Haryana	0.287	0.533	0.669	0.496	0.504 (3)	0.565 (4)	-1
Karnataka	0.288	0.484	0.835	0.536	0.464 (5)	0.507 (6)	-1
Kerala	0.090	0.116	0.905	0.370	0.630 (1)	0.671 (1)	0
Madhya Pradesh	0.459	0.735	0.911	0.702	0.298 (14)	0.330 (13)	1
Maharashtra	0.282	0.395	0.967	0.548	0.452 (6)	0.578 (3)	3
Orissa	0440	0.624	0.913	0.659	0.341 (11)	0.369 (11)	0
Punjab	0.235	0.536	0.512	0.428	0.572 (2)	0.651 (2)	0
Rajasthan	0.394	0.764	0.899	0.686	0.314 (12)	0.353 (12)	0
Tamil Nadu	0.337	0.401	0.836	0.525	0.475 (4)	0.523 (5)	-1
U.P.	0.556	0.739	0.898	0.731	0.269 (15)	0.301(15)	0
West Bengal	0.366	0.547	0.832	0.582	0.418 (8)	0.470 (7)	1

TABLE 4

Gender Disparity Adjusted Human Development Index (GDA-HDI), 1991

States	*Female HDI*	*Male HDI*	*HDI*	*GDA-HDI*	*Difference*
Andhra Pradesh	0.305 (7)	0.417 (9)	0.441 (9)	0.323 (7)	2
Assam	0.262 (10)	0.388 (11)	0.386 (10)	0.261 (10)	0
Bihar	0.196 (13)	0.355 (13)	0.328 (14)	0.181 (13)	1
Gujarat	0.332 (6)	0.476 (8)	0.481 (8)	0.336 (6)	2
Haryana	0.304 (8)	0.574 (3)	0.565 (4)	0.299 (8)	-4
Karnataka	0.365 (4)	0.503 (6)	0.507 (6)	0.368 (4)	2
Kerala	0.590 (1)	0.634 (2)	0.671 (1)	0.625 (1)	0
Madhya Pradesh	0.191 (14)	0.352 (14)	0.334 (13)	0.178 (14)	-1
Maharashtra	0.410 (2)	0.562 (4)	0.578 (3)	0.422 (2)	1
Orissa	0.229 (11)	0.400(10)	0.369 (11)	0.212 (11)	0
Punjab	0.350 (5)	0.666 (1)	0.651 (2)	0.342 (5)	-3
Rajasthan	0.210 (12)	0.366 (12)	0.353 (12)	0.202 (12)	0
Tamil Nadu	0.372 (3)	0.519 (5)	0.523 (5)	0.375 (3)	2
U.P.	0.130 (15)	0.349(15)	0.301 (15)	0.112 (15)	0
West Bengal	0.299 (9)	0.482 (7)	0.470 (7)	0.291 (9)	-2

income distribution for Maharashtra. Its rank has turned out to be six in place of three.

The most striking feature of inequality in human development is along gender lines. Men generally fare better than women on almost every socio-economic indicator except life expectancy. Thus, there is urgent need to analyse a gender adjusted HDI. For this purpose, data regarding life expectancy and educational attainment is readily available for each state but the data on PCI are not available properly. Main problem relating to such data is that most of the women are engaged in unpaid or under-paid jobs.

For calculating the ratio of female income to male income, two factors are significant. First is the relative ratios of labour participation rate and the second is the relative wage rate ratio. Women constitute roughly half of the population but female work participation rate is only 22.27% as against 51.61% of the male.

All the more, 1991 Census data depicts that only 4% women workers are employed in the organised sector. Hence, a Gender Disparity Adjusted HDI (GDA-HDI) is essential to understand the true picture. Following the UNDPs methodology, the PCI of each state has first been discounted on the basis of relative ratio of labour force participation. The derived income is then again discounted on the basis of existing wage differentials.

The gender sensitive HDI is presented in Table 4. In almost all the states male HDI has higher value than the female HDI. This shows that the gains of socio-economic development have not reached equally between both the sexes. Gender disparity is there. A major benefit of the development has gone to males and females are lagging behind. Many of the states face a decline in their HDI due to high gender disparity. States like Kerala, Assam, Orissa, Rajasthan and U.P. shows no change in the HDI ranking due to gender sensitivity. On the other hand, Punjab and Haryana display a marked decrease in both absolute and relative value of HDI ranking due to gender sensitivity.

Hence, to conclude we can say that the process of human resource development in India is characterised by an uneven development pattern. There are marked differences in human development level in both temporal and special dimension. Income and gender disparities in a particular state have also a strong bearing on the human development level of a state.

References

Brahmananda, P.R. (1993), "The Human Development Report, 1993: A Selective Appraisal", *Indian Economic Journal*, Vol. 40, No. 4.

Chaudhary, Uma Datta Ray (1992), "Inter-State and Intra-State Variations in Economic Development and Standards of Living", *Economic and Political Weekly*, Dec. 5-12.

Clark, C. (1957), *The Conditions of Economic Progress*, Macmillan, London.

Hague, M. (1996), *Reflections on Human Development*, Oxford University Press, New York.

Harrod (1949), *Towards a Dynamic Economics*, Macmillan, London.

Heller, W. (1954), "Fiscal Policies in Underdeveloped Countries" in Wald, H. (ed.), *Agricultural Taxation and Economic Development*, Cambridge Mass.

Joseph, K.P. (1987), Human Development through Literacy, *Yojana*, Vol. 31, June.

Kindleberger (1958), *Economic Development*, McGraw Hill, New Delhi.

Kuznets, S. (1963), *Modem Economic Growth, Rate, Structure and Spread*, Vakil Feffer and Simons.

Leontief (1953), *Studies in the Structure of American Economy*, Oxford University Press, New York.

Lewis (1963), *The Theory of Economic Growth*, George Allen & Unwin.

Mehta, M.M. (1976), *Human Development with Special Reference to Asia and the Far East*, Macmillan, New Delhi.

Myrdal, G. (1958), *Economic Theory and Underdeveloped Regions*, Vora.

NCAER (1993), "Human Development", *Margin*, Vol. 25, Jan.

Nair, N.K., Prakash, M.K. and others (1992), "Human Development in Indian States", *Productivity*, Vol. 37, No. 2.

Nurkse, R. (1963), *Problems of Capital Formation in Underdeveloped Countries*, Bassil Blackwell & Mott.

Parikh, K.S. and Sundaram, R. (1993), *Human Development and Structural Adjustments*, Macmillan, New Delhi.

Pritosh Bannerji (1996): "Human Development Index", *India Journal of Economics*, Vol. LXXVI, No. 302, Jan.

Shah, K.R. and Suba Rao, A. and others (1993), "Human Development and Economic Growth", in NCAER, Human Development, *Margin*, Vol. 25, Jan.

Shivakumar, A.K. (1991), "UNDPs Human Development Index: A Computation for Indian States", *EPW*, Vol. 26, No. 41.

21

Measuring Human Resource Development

S.S. DHILLON AND JASMEET KAUR

Country's potential for economic growth is greatly influenced by its physical resource endowment as well as by its human resource endowment. William Petty, one of the first development economists, was interested not only in national income but also in such factors as "the common safety" and "each man's particular happiness" (Sen, 1988). The assessment of development achieved cannot be a matter only of quantification of the means of that achievement. The concept of development has to take note of actual achievements themselves. These achievements include the length of life (life expectancy) and the nature of life and what people value as important to their well-being in the form of nourishment, good health, clean air and water, and the ability to move about freely. According to the concept of human development, income clearly is only one option that people would like to have though certainly an important one, but it is not sum total of their lives. The purpose of development is to enlarge all human choices, not just income.

In this paper effort has been made to measure human

resource development through alternative measures like human development index, composite index and per capita income. Attempt has also been made to compare the position of countries with respect to human resource development based on these measures. Human development index has been developed by following the United Nations Development Programme (UNDP) methodology. Composite index of human development has been developed by using 15 socio-economic and demographic indicators. Specifically analysis has been carried out to see whether there occurs any change in the ranking of the countries with different measures of human resource development. Various publications of World Bank like World Development Reports, World Tables, Social Indicators of Development and World Development Indicators were consulted for data purposes. The analysis was carried out at three points of time, one for the earliest possible year for which the data were available, i.e. 1970 and second for the year 1980 and 1993, the year for which the latest data were available. As the data were not available for certain countries and certain variables either at the initial point or later point, the number of countries for analysis varied between 54 and 65 for the three years of the study. For this purpose, the paper has been divided into three sections. In Section I, human development index is developed and ranking of countries with HDI is compared with ranking according to PCI. Composite index is developed in Section II and the comparison of position of countries with per capita, HDI and composite index is taken up.

I

Per capita income is most widely used method for measuring economic development. Per capita income as an index of development has been widely criticised by Bauer (1973) and as such is not a fit indicator for measuring human resource development. One important measure of human resource development is Human Development Index (HDI). The HDI has been constructed to reflect the most important dimensions of the human development. The HDI is developed following the UNDP methodology based on three indicators: longevity, as measured by life expectancy at birth; educational attainment as measured by a combination of adult literacy and combined primary, secondary enrolment ratio; and standard of living, as measured by GNP per capita (UNDP, 1995). Countries are ranked according to PCI and human development index and the ranks are then compared with each other. Per capita GNP and Human Development Index along with ranking of countries according to PCI and HDI for the year 1970, 1980 and 1993 are presented in Tables 1, 2 and 3 respectively.

Table 1 shows that in the year 1970, when countries were ranked according to HDI, Spain had the maximum HDI followed by Italy among the countries whereas Ethiopia had the minimum HDI. There was improvement in the ranks of 33 countries and fall in the ranks of 25 countries. There was only one country for which position remained unchanged. Of the 33 countries whose ranks improved, there were 8 countries, where the ranks improved by 10 or more points. There were another 9 countries where ranks improved between 5 to 9 points and for remaining 16 countries ranks improved by less than 5 points. Of the 25 countries whose ranks deteriorated, there were 10 countries where ranks deteriorated by 10 or more points. For another 6 countries for which ranks deteriorated by 5 to 9 points and for remaining 9 countries ranks came down by less than five points.

Table 2 shows that in the year 1980, U.S.A. had the highest HDI as well as per capita income followed by Netherlands whereas Sierra Leone had the lowest HDI when the countries were ranked according to HDI. There was improvement in ranks of 28 countries and fall in the ranks of 22 countries. There were four countries for which position remained unchanged. Of the 28 countries with improved ranks, there was one country whose rank improved by 10 or more points. There were 14 countries where ranks improved between 5 to 9 points and for remaining 13 countries the ranks improved by less than 5 points. Of the 22 countries for which ranks deteriorated, there were five countries where ranks deteriorated by 10 or more points, for another 7 countries for which ranks deteriorated by 5 to 9 points and for remaining 10 countries.

Table 3 explains the ranking of countries on the basis of per capita income (PPP) and HDI for the year 1993. It is seen that with ranking of countries according to HDI *vis-a-vis* PCI (PPP), there was an improvement in the ranks of 29 countries and fall in the ranks of another 31 countries. There were five countries for

TABLE 1

Per Capita Income, Human Development Index (HDI), Composite Index and Ranking of Countries, 1970

Sl. No.	*Countries*	*PCI*	*Rank*	*HDI*	*Rank*	*Composite Index*	*Rank*
1.	Ethiopia	60	59	.119	58	11.23	56
2.	Rwanda	100	58	.241	51	13.30	45
3.	Burkina Faso	120	57	.151	56	10.73	57
4.	Pakistan	140	56	.272	49	12.04	54
5.	Bangladesh	150	55	.169	54	14.08	44
6.	Haiti	160	54	.271	50	12.96	49
7.	India	180	53	.432	36	14.11	43
8.	Benin	220	52	.167	55	12.61	52
9.	Niger	230	50.5	.106	59	10.17	58
10.	Indonesia	230	50.5	.354	43	12.79	51
11.	Sierre Leone	240	49	.192	53	12.25	53
12.	Sudan	280	48	.197	52	11.94	55
13.	Madagascar	300	47	.374	42	15.22	38
14.	Ghana	303	46	.520	31.5	13.20	47
15.	Mauritania	330	45	.140	57	10.07	59
16.	Cameroon	340	43.5	.346	44.5	15.04	40
17.	Egypt	340	43.5	.413	39	16.63	34
18.	Syrian Rep.	350	42	.406	40	16.45	36
19.	Philippines	370	41	.556	28	16.82	33
20.	Thailand	390	40	.522	30	14.65	41
21.	Bolivia	400	39	.385	41	15.15	39
22.	Liberia	450	38	.284	48	12.93	50
23.	Jordan	530	37	.596	24	21.69	11
24.	Congo	550	36	.511	33	18.83	23
25.	Papua New Guinea	570	35	.326	47	13.21	46
26.	Cote d' Ivoire	580	34	.334	46	14.18	42
27.	Zimbabwe	590	33	.427	37	16.58	35
28,	Paraguay	600	32	.346	44.5	13.10	48
29.	Ecuador	610	31	.563	27	17.13	32
30.	Korea Rep.	640	30	.637	19	21.44	12
31.	Nicaragua	680	29	.425	38	16.00	37
32.	Dominician Rep.	720	28	.592	25	18.40	25
33.	Mauritius	770	26.5	.672	18	18.36	26

34. Tunisia	770	26.5	.503	34	17.90	30
35, Malaysia	890	25	.707	16	18.19	28
36. Turkey	900	24	.602	22	18.26	27
37. Chile	920	23	.729	14.5	21.08	13
38. Costa Rica	1028	22	.769	12	20.21	17
39. Peru	1090	21	.613	21	19.09	22
40. Fiji	1130	20	.733	13	19.74	18
41. Panama	1140	19	.729	14.5	20.25	16
42. Brazil	1170	18	.460	35	19.62	19
43. Uruguay	1410	17	.817	7	23.85	6
44. Iran	1320	16	.553	29	17.38	31
45. Iraq	1375	15	.584	26	18.61	24
46. Jamaica	1380	14	.784	11	20.37	15
47. Bahrain	1520	13	.629	20	28.02	3
48. Mexico	1590	12	.682	17	19.21	21
49. Poland	1755	11	.853	5	24.84	5
50. Libya	1870	10	.520	31.5	19.56	20
51. Trinidad & Tobago	1910	9	.788	10	23.70	9
52. Greece	2590	7.5	.900	3	22.51	10
53. Venezuela	2590	7.5	.800	9	21.07	14
54. Argentina	2680	6	.862	4	23.82	7
55. Singapore	2770	5	.806	8	23.73	8
56. Spain	3000	4	.932	1	25.32	4
57. Italy	4020	3	.923	2	29.30	1
58. Saudi Arabia	6240	2	.599	23	18.09	29
59. Kuwait	10140	1	.852	6	28.05	2

which position remained unchanged. Of the 29 countries whose ranks improved, there were 7 countries where the ranks improved by 10 or more points. There were another 9 countries where ranks improved between 5 to 9 points and for remaining 13 countries the ranks improved by less than 5 points. Of the 31 countries whose ranks deteriorated, there were five countries where ranks deteriorated by 10 or more points. For another 7 countries ranks deteriorated by 5 to 9 points and for remaining 19 countries ranks came down by less than 5 points.

TABLE 2

Per Capita Income, Human Development Index (HDI), Composite Index and Ranking of Countries, 1980

Sl. No.	Countries	PCI	Rank	HDI	Rank	Composite Index	Rank
1.	Ethiopia	110	54	.197	48.5	12.63	54
2.	Bangladesh	150	53	.197	48.5	14.10	48
3.	Burkino Faso	160	52	.089	53	14.55	46
4.	Central Africa	270	51	.179	52	12.85	51
5.	Benin	280	49.5	.503	38	12.33	53
6.	India	280	49.5	.312	45	16.45	39
7.	Kenya	300	48	.372	41	15.66	43
8.	Sierra Leone	320	45	.050	54	15.72	42
9.	Cape Verde	350	45.5	.369	42	15.25	44
10.	Zambia	350	45.5	.341	44	15.86	41
11.	Pakistan	360	44	.212	47	12.97	50
12.	Sudan	362	43	.192	50	15.97	40
13.	Mauritania	380	42	.182	51	12.41	52
14.	Guyana	490	41	.533	34	18.43	30
15.	Philippines	520	40	.531	35	18.34	31
16.	Indonesia	520	39	.438	39	14.21	47
17.	Zimbabwe	620	38	.415	40	17.94	33
18.	Papua N. Guinea	720	37	.284	46	13.64	49
19.	Dominician Rep.	760	36	.513	37	17.59	36
20.	Nicaragua	760	35	.520	36	17.89	34
21.	Thailand	810	34	.572	31	17.66	35
22.	Jamaica	930	33	.681	28	20.03	26
23.	Botswana	1020	32	.559	33	16.79	37
24.	Nigeria	1020	31	.356	43	14.88	45
25.	Turkey	1060	30	.565	32	20.16	25
26.	Ecuador	1150	29	.632	30	18.99	29
27.	Romania	1230	27.5	.770	19	23.50	15
28.	Colombia	1230	27.5	.655	29	19.88	27
29.	Hungary	1880	26	.714	26	24.69	8
30.	Malasiya	1910	25	.721	24.5	18.22	32
31.	U.A.E.	2010	24	.740	21	23.55	14
32.	Mexico	2180	23	.789	18	20.53	22

33. Portugal	2220	22	.828	17	21.29	21
34. Korea Rep.	2260	21	.838	14	20.39	23
35. Panama	2290	20	.833	16	20.38	24
36. Poland	2470	19	.834	15	24.41	9
37. Greece	2590	18	.910	6	23.98	10
38. Argentina	3050	17	.872	11	23.46	16
39. Syrian A. Rep.	3257	16	.722	23	19.39	28
40. Barbados	4490	14.5	.901	8	21.79	20
41. Ireland	4490	14.5	.876	10	23.68	11
42. Hong Kong	6080	13	.908	7	23.18	17
43. Trinidad & Tobago	6140	12	.880	9	23.57	13
44. Oman	6430	11	.768	20	16.78	38
45. Singapore	7350	10	.923	5	28.06	3
46. Italy	7480	9	.928	4	23.58	12
47. Bahrain	8130	8	.739	22	24.78	7
48. Saudi Arabia	8300	7	.702	27	22.99	18
49. Libya	8420	6	.721	24.5	22.09	19
50. Austria	8740	5	.852	13	24.86	6
51. Netherlands	9190	4	.943	2	26.35	4
52. Sweden	11550	3	.941	3	29.78	2
53. Kuwait	14910	2	.862	12	25.83	5
54. U.S.A.	16200	1	.945	1	30.87	1

II

Human resource development depends upon many factors, therefore, a single indicator cannot be used to measure human development. Human resource development can only be explained by number of economic, social, and demographic indicators. In this section, attempt has been made to measure human resource development which is representative of broad spectra of indicators with the help of a composite index. In order to develop a composite index of human resource development, the following 15 indicators have been used in the present study : (1) Per Capita Income, (2) Combined School Enrolment Ratio, (3) Adult Literacy Rate, (4) Life Expectancy at Birth, (5) Infant Mortality Rate, (6) Crude Birth Rate, (7) Crude Death Rate, (8) Energy Consumption Per Capita, (9) Number of Physicians Per Lakh of Population, (10) Number of Hospital Beds Per Lakh of Population,

TABLE 3

Per Capita Income (PPP), Human Development Index (HDI), Composite Index and Ranking of Countries, 1993

Sl. No.	*Countries*	*PCI (PPP)*	*Rank*	*HDI*	*Rank*	*Composite Index*	*Rank*
1.	Tanzania	620	65	.311	52	14.14	52
2.	Rwanda	710	64	.274	55	13.78	53
3.	Burundi	720	63	.193	59	11.33	62
4.	Bhutan	750	62	.190	61	12.06	59
5.	Angola	751	61	.163	64	13.31	55
6.	Afghanistan	819	60	.171	63	11.03	64
7.	Niger	820	58.5	.122	65	12.59	57
8.	Guinea Bissau	820	58.5	.181	62	12.39	58
9.	Uganda	860	57	.235	58	11.20	63
10.	Vietnam	1010	56	.537	45	16.06	45
11.	Haiti	1046	55	.304	53	12.01	60
12.	Nepal	1170	54	.247	57	11.90	61
13.	India	1230	52.5	.375	49	19.40	27
14.	Bangladesh	1230	52.5	.290	54	13.72	54
15.	Comoros	1350	51	.350	51	13.52	56
16.	Kenya	1400	50	.360	50	15.37	50
17.	Cape Verde	1750	48.5	.488	46	15.78	47
18.	Senegal	1750	48.5	.256	56	17.20	37
19.	Guyana	1800	47	.605	39	17.21	36
20.	Burkina Faso	1810	46	.191	60	11.01	65
21.	China	1950	45	.622	38	18.17	32
22.	Cameroon	2390	44	.455	47	15.45	49
23.	Papua N. Guinea	2410	43	.417	48	14.68	51
24.	Mongolia	2790	41.5	.558	43	19.53	25
25.	Nicaragua	2790	41.5	.583	42	15.69	48
26.	Romania	2840	40	.718	37	20.90	20
27.	Indonesia	2950	39	.592	40	16.15	44
28.	Jamaica	3200	38	.785	26	18.71	29
29.	Peru	3300	37	.821	21	18.20	31
30.	Paraguay	3390	36	.723	35	16.23	43
31.	Iraq	3413	35	.584	41	16.8	41
32.	Domician Rep.	3526	34	.761	31	18.18	30

33. Egypt	3540	33	.543	44	15.94	46
34. Bulgaria	4250	32	.798	22	22.09	16
35. Jordan	4270	31	.741	34	17.76	34
36. Ecuador	4350	30	.795	24	17.61	35
37. Qatar	4830	28.5	.796	23	25.91	9
38. Poland	4830	28.5	.866	17	23.52	11
39. Algeria	4870	27	.719	36	19.55	24
40. Tunisia	5160	26	.762	30	16.99	28
41. Turkey	5230	25	.794	25	16.26	42
42. Venezuela	5410	24	.865	18	19.44	26
43. Iran	5420	23	.768	28	16.96	39
44. Thailand	5950	22	.771	27	16.93	40
45. Hungary	6580	21	.879	16	26.05	8
46. Malaysia	7790	20	.845	19	17.96	33
47. Greece	8310	19	.919	11	21.60	17
48. Kuwait	8326	18	.822	20	21.50	18
49. Chile	8410	17	.899	13	20.12	22
50. Argentina	8860	16	.887	15	23.25	13
51. Korea Rep.	9280	15	.753	33	20.40	21
52. Trinidad & Tobago	9760	14	.893	14	21.35	19
53. Libya	9782	13	.760	32	20.04	23
54. Saudi Arabia	9880	12	.767	29	19.13	28
55. Ireland	12830	11	.923	9	23.68	12
56. Spain	13400	10	.926	7.5	23.04	15
57. Sweden	17200	9	.920	10	23.12	14
58. U.K.	17210	8	.902	12	24.98	10
59. Italy	18090	7	.926	7.5	27.14	6
60. Singapore	18330	6	.960	1	30.36	3
61. Denmark	19560	5	.939	5	31.43	2
62. Norway	19780	4	.947	2.5	32.62	1
63. Canada	20230	3	.930	6	26.76	7
64. Japan	20850	2	.942	4	27.23	5
65. U.S.A.	24740	1	.947	2.5	28.03	4

(11) Access to Safe Water, (12) Urban Population as Percentage of Total Population, (13) Road Length, (14) Pupil-Teacher Ratio (Primary), and (15) Pupil Teacher Ratio (Secondary).

The statistical technique employed to develop the weighted composite index consists in finding out the principal component of the groups consisting of various variables and derive the implicit weights based thereon. Technique applied here is known as "principal component analysis" popularly known as factor analysis which is a branch of well known multivariate analysis (Adelman and Morris, 1967, Harman, 1967). The composite index is then constructed by combining various indicators whose implicit weights are already determined.

Composite index for ith country in term of the first principal component is expressed as:

$$\sum_{j=1}^{n} a_{ji} Z_{ji}$$

where a_{ji} denotes the factor loading of jth variable and i indicates the factor number (j = 1, 2,...n).

Z_{ji} the standardised jth variable on ith country and is expressed as:

$$Z_{ji} = \frac{X_{ji}}{S.D.X_j}$$

where X_{ji} = Value of X_i variable on ith country, $S.D.X_j$ = Standard deviation of X_j variable. Composite index has been prepared for 59, 54 and 65 countries for the year 1970, 1980 and 1993 respectively. Composite Index and ranking of countries are presented in Tables 1, 2 and 3 for the years 1970, 1980 and 1993 respectively. In this section the ranking of countries according to composite index is also compared with ranking as per PCI and HDI.

Table 1 shows that when countries are ranked according to composite index *vis-a-vis* per capita income there was improvement in ranks of 24 countries, deterioration in ranks for 30 countries and ranks remained same for 5 countries. Of the 24 countries which improved in ranks, there were 10 countries where ranks improved by 10 or more points. In other six countries ranks improved by 5 to 9 points and for remaining 8 countries ranks improved by less than 5 points. Of the 30 countries with deterioration in position, there were 7 countries where ranks came down by 10 or more points. There were another 7 countries where the ranks deteriorated by 5 to 9 points and for remaining 16 countries ranks decreased by less than 5 points.

Table 2 shows that for the year 1980, when countries are ranked according to. composite index there is improvement in the ranks of 27 countries, deterioration in ranks for another 21 countries and the ranks remained same for 6 countries. Of the 27 countries with improved ranks, for nine countries ranks improved by 10 or more points. In other 8 countries ranks improved by 5 to 9 points and for remaining 10 countries ranks improved by less than 5 points. Of the 21 countries with deterioration in position there were 6 countries where ranks came down by 10 or more points, there were 5 countries where ranks deteriorated by 5 to 9 points and for remaining 10 countries ranks decreased by less than 5 points.

Table 3 shows that for the year 1993, when composite index is used to rank the countries, there was improvement in ranks of 31 countries, deterioration in the ranks for 33 countries and ranks remained same for one country *vis-a-vis* ranking with PCI (PPP). Of the 31 countries with improved ranks, for 13 countries ranks improved by more than 10 points. In case of three countries ranks improved by 5 to 9 points and for remaining 15 countries ranks improved by less than 5 points. Of the 33 countries with deterioration in position, there were 8 countries where ranks deteriorated by 10 or more points. There were another 15 countries where the ranks deteriorated by 5 to 9 points.

Table 1 further explains that when ranking of countries according to composite index and HDI for the year 1970 are compared, there was improvement in ranks of 27 countries, deterioration in the ranks of another 28 countries and ranks remained same for 4 countries. Of the 27 countries with improved ranks, in case of 8 countries ranks improved by 10 or more points. In another four countries ranks improved by 5 to 9 points and for remaining 18 countries ranks improved by less than 5 points. Of the 28 countries with deterioration in position there were 3 countries where ranks came down by 10 or more points. There were another 13 countries for which ranks deteriorated by 5 to 9 points and for remaining 12 countries ranks decreased by less than five points.

Table 2 shows that when ranking of countries according to composite and HDI are compared for the year 1980, there was improvement in ranks of 27 countries, deterioration in ranks of 26 countries and rank remained same for U.S.A. only. Of the 27 countries whose ranks improved there were 3 countries where ranks improved by 10 or more points. There were another 10 countries where ranks improved by 5 to 9 points and for remaining 14 countries ranks improved by less than 5 points. Of the 26 countries with deterioration in position, there were 5 countries where ranks came down by 10 or more points. There were 8 countries where ranks deteriorated by 5 to 9 points and for remaining 13 countries ranks decreased by less than 5 points.

Table 3 shows that when countries are ranked according to composite index *vis-a-vis* HDI for the year 1993, there was improvement in ranks of 26 countries, deterioration in ranks for 33 countries and ranks remained same for 6 countries. Of the 26 countries with improved position, ranks improved by 10 or more points in case of 7 countries for another 7 countries ranks improved by 5 to 9 points and for remaining 12 countries ranks improved by less than 5 points. Of the 33 countries with deterioration in positions, ranks deteriorated by 10 or more points in case of 7 countries there were another 11 countries where ranks deteriorated by 5 to 9 points and for remaining 15 countries ranks decreased by less than 5 points.

Over time (1970-80; Tables 1 and 2) comparison of ranks on the basis of HDI's shows that there was improvement in ranks for 44.11% of countries, deterioration in the ranks for 52.94% of countries and for 2.94% of the countries ranks remained same over the time. Further with composite index as basis, the ranks for 52.94% of countries improved, for 45.11% countries deteriorated and for 2.94% remained same. Over time (1980-93: Tables 2 and 3) comparison of ranks on basis of HDI's shows that there was improvement in ranks for 64.28% of countries, deterioration in the ranks for 28.57% of countries and for remaining 7.14% the ranks remained the same. When composite index was taken as basis for ranking, the ranks for 64.28% of countries, deterioration in the ranks for 28.57% of countries and for remaining 7.14% the ranks remained the same. When composite index was taken as basis for ranking, the ranks for 64.28% of countries improved, for 17.87% of countries deteriorated and for 17.85% of countries the ranks remained the same.

Analysis of the ranks on the basis of HDI—based on life expectancy, education attainment and income—and Composite

Index—based on different socio-economic and demographic indicators—shows that composite index definitely has an edge in explaining the human resource development of different countries. The main reason for this is the broad-based nature of the composite index which covers many aspects of human welfare.

References

Adelman, I. and C.T. Morris (1967), *Society, Politics and Economic Development*, Baltimore : John Hopkins University Press.

Bauer, P.T. (1973), *Dissent on Development Studies and Debates in Development Economics*, Delhi, Vikas.

Harman, H.H. (1967), *Modern Factor Analysis*, Chicago: Chicago University Press.

Sen, A. (1988), "The Concept of Development," in Hollis Chenery and T.N. Srinivasan (eds.), *Handbook of Development Economics*, Vol. 1, Amsterdam : North Holland.

UNDP (United Nation Development Programme) (1995), *Human Development Report, 1995*, New York, Oxford University Press.

World Bank (1997), *World Development Indicators*, Washington, D.C.

———, *Social Indicators of Development*, Baltimore: Johns Hopkins University Press, Various Issues.

———, *World Development Report*, New York: Oxford University Press, Various Issues.

———, *World Tables*, Baltimore: John Hopkins University Press, Various issues.

22

Measuring Human Well-being of the Countries: Achievement and Improvement Indices

KRISHNA MAZUMDAR

1. INTRODUCTION

Human well-being has been defined by Professor Sen (1985, 1987) in terms of 'functioning' and 'capability'. Functioning denotes 'achievement of different attributes' such as education, health, nutrition, etc. and capability indicates 'ability to achieve' these attributes. In a pioneering paper Kakwani (1993) has introduced a class of 'achievement indices' to represent the actual 'levels' of standard of living and a class of 'improvement indices' to represent the improvement in the standard of living of a country over a period.

This paper attempts to provide an overview of the changing pattern of human well-being of the countries over the period 1960 to 1994. In this context the overall achievement indices representing overall human well-being for the sample countries have been estimated for five points of time: 1960, 1970, 1980,

1990 and 1994. The improvement indices for the periods 1960-94, 1960-70, 1970-80, 1980-90 and 1990-94 have been derived. A comparison of the relative position of a country is attempted on the basis of the overall achievement index and other composite indices used to measure human well-being, e.g. Weighted index formed with the same indicators (Wtd8), Physical Quality of Life Index (PQLI) introduced by Morris (1979), Human Development Index (HDI) introduced by United Nations Development Programme (UNDP) in 1990. Also comparison of relative position of a country has been attempted for Per Capita Real Gross Domestic Product (PCRGDP).

2. CHOICE OF INDICATORS

In welfare analysis, the basic notion that welfare (*human well-being*) should be measured on the basis of as large a number of attributes as is relevant and feasible, has enjoyed widespread support. (For example, see Slottje, 1991; Hirschberg, Maasoumi and Slottje, 1991; Sen, 1985, 1987; Maasoumi, 1986; Atkinson and Bourguignon, 1982; and Kolm, 1977). At the same time the selection of appropriate indicators to represent *human well-being* or *social indicators of development* requires attention to comprehensiveness and comparability. The basic requirements of a particular society may not tally with the basic requirements of another society. Therefore, one should be careful when choosing indicators for any cross-country analysis. However, a wider breadth of agreement is possible if indicators of social life which are directly related to the provision of long-life, health and education are used.

In this study choice of indicators is governed by two apparently conflicting principles: wide coverage of various aspects of human development, and parsimony regarding the number of indicators. The indicators chosen are:

Life expectancy at birth (LIFE), Infant survival rate as per 1,000 of live births (INFS), Adult literacy rate as percentage of total population over age 15 years (ADLI), Calorie supply per capita as percentage of requirement (CALO), Physician per 1,000 of population (PHYS), Urban population as percentage of total population (UPOP), Teacher-pupil ratio in primary schooling (TPRP), Passenger car per 1,000 of population (PCAR).

These indicators are considered to be representative of the

Broad group	Variable	Variable name used in the study
1. Population	Urban population (% of total)	UPOP
2. Demographic characteristics	Life expectancy (years)	LIFE
3. Health and nutrition	Calorie supply per capita (% of requirement)	CALO
	Infant survival rate (per 1,000 of live births)	INFS
	Physician per 1,000 of population	PHYS
4. Education	Adult literacy rate (% of total population over age 15 yrs.)	ADLI
	Teacher-pupil ratio primary level	TPRP
5. Consumption	Passenger car per 1,000 of population	PCAR

list of indicators within the broad group. Some of these indicators are also listed as representative variables in Hicks-Streeten (1979) study.

Broad group	Variable
Health	LIFE
Education	ADLI
Food	CALO
Water supply and sanitation	INFS

Rationale Behind Choice of Each Indicator

LIFE

Life expectancy at birth is the number of years a random newborn baby can expect to live, on the assumption that current age-specific mortality rates will persist. It is mathematical expectation of a person's longevity as seen from the vantage point of his date of birth if age-specific mortality rates are not expected to alter. LIFE directly reflects the levels of health, nutrition and income and thus indirectly links employment and shelter. A low figure usually shows there is a sizeable percentage of the population facing poor living conditions and there is a lack of proper health facilities in the country.

INFS

Infant mortality rate is the number of babies who die before reaching their first birthday out of every 1,000 of live born babies during a year. Infant survival rate is obtained by 1,000 minus infant mortality rate. Plainly, this is not unrelated to LIFE, but it focuses on something quite different—nutrition and hygiene at the earliest stage of life. This indicator also reflects the degree of existence of contagious disease in a country, as infants are more susceptible to these diseases. It is also closely related to the health of the mother and to the duration of lactation. It is also related to the educational attainment of the mother because literate women are more likely to know how to protect their infants' lives. Moreover, literate women possess higher status in the family than the illiterate women, which helps to advance interests of the infants in the family. The infant survival rate reflects nutrition and sanitary conditions of the country. This indicator shows very rapid response to many health policies. It is obvious that where the infant mortality rate is very high, there are many people living in conditions under which basic health needs are not met.

ADLI

Adult literacy rate is percentage of literate population above age 15. This is a direct measure of achievement of one basic right of the human beings, minimum education. This indicator is also well correlated with many other indices of quality of life such as measures of employment, income or health and therefore, adult literacy can be considered the most excellent overall quality of life indicator.

According to Professor Das Gupta (1992) LIFE, INFS and ADLI along with income are key indicators of general well-being. This study considers LIFE, INFS and ADLI as the 'core indicators' of human well-being. Five other background indicators have been incorporated in this study in order to have better idea about the inter-country inter-temporal pattern of human well-being.

CALO

Calorie intake per capita as percentage of requirement is an indicator of level of nutrition of a country. Of the various social indicators that can be used to describe the conditions of life, the standard of nutrition is the most fundamental. Food is the most basic need for survival and in many cases the definition of poverty is based on nutritional level of the households. Also the problem of malnutrition is closely associated with the problem of low productivity and ultimately low national income. And the countries where the available calories per person fall short of the required calories per head, almost certainly there exists a significant problem of malnutrition. The problem of malnutrition is closely associated with the problem of low productivity and ultimately low national income.

UPOP

The indicator used to represent urbanization of a country is, percentage of total population residing in the urban areas. Although increasing urbanization is widely accepted as a natural phenomenon, the justification of inclusion of this indicator is that it carries profound implications for both the immediate well-being of citizens and the prospects of a nation for future welfare gains. In reality, more is the percentage of total population residing in the urban areas, more is the people (at least some of) with urban facilities such as better sanitation, medical and educational facilities, better communications, access to safe water, etc. There is a close association between urbanization and industrialization. Moreover, "urbanization promotes values favourable to participation, entrepreneurship and industrial growth; in particular, cities typically tend to innovate and accept change, since in the relatively impersonal and fragmented setting of urban life the all embracing bonds of traditional community systems are difficult to maintain".

PHYS

The health situation of population depends mainly upon the health services available. The old industrialized countries have experienced slow but steady progress in regard to health services. In the newly independent poor countries, it is an enormous task to build up health services approaching the levels now existing in the rich countries. Education and various kinds of paramedical personnel on a large scale are required. It is expected that there are many more patients to share the service of one physician or nursing person in the poor countries than in the rich ones. Physician per thousand of population, therefore, provides a general picture of the quality of health care available in a country.

TPRP

Teacher-pupil ratio in the primary level of education gives an indication of quality of educational care available in the primary level of education. The higher the number of pupils per teacher, the lower is the quantity and quality of personal care available for each pupil.

PCAR

The passenger car per thousand of population reflects the level of communication and transportation in the country. In fact, better the transportation system in a country, more widespread is the medical and educational facilities and more mobile is the population.

PCRGDP

The standard measure of *economic growth* is per capita gross domestic product (PCGDP). No doubt, it is an acceptable indicator for measuring a specific country's economic performance, but its utility in cross-country study is not beyond question. The major problem associated with the choice of PCGDP as an indicator for comparing the level of economic development of a number of countries is the conversion of each country's PCGDP to a common currency. The most widely used method is to convert the PCGDP of each country to US dollars using exchange rates between the country's currency and the US dollar. This method implicitly assumes that the purchasing power parity of US $1 is equivalent in all the countries being compared. This assumption may not be correct. For the purpose of comparison, the indicator used to measure economic growth should be adjusted for purchasing power parity. Therefore, the indicator chosen in this study to measure economic well-being of the countries is the Per Capita Real Gross Domestic Product (PCRGDP) which is adjusted for purchasing power parity.

3. DATA

The data for 1960, 1970, 1980, 1990 and 1994 on all the indicators representing human well-being considered in this study have been obtained from different issues of *World Tables, World Development Reports* published by the World Bank and *Human Development Reports* published by the UNDP. Figures not available for these five years have been imputed in some cases by figures from around these years. The data for per capita calorie intake as percentage of requirement for 1990 and 1994 are not available. These figures are approximated using the ratio between percentage of requirement and actual supply for the year 1980.

A few indicators incorporated in this study are required to be transformed to make all the indicators move in the same direction. Data obtained from the official sources mentioned are infant mortality rate, population per physician, pupil-teacher ratio. These variables are negatively related with the level of development while other variables have positive correlations with the level of development. These variables are transformed as follows:

(a) Infant survival rate (INFS) = 1,000 – Infant mortality rate
(b) Physician per 1,000 of population = 1,000/population per physician.
(c) Teacher-pupil ratio = 1/pupil-teacher ratio.

The data for per capita real gross domestic product (PCRGDP) have been taken from Summers and Heston (1984, 1988, 1991).

4. SAMPLE

The principle followed in choosing the sample countries is wide representation of countries from various income levels and various geographical regions. At the same time the study attempts to obtain uniform sample for five years under study and to have all the variables for all samples. Consequently, the sample consists of 92 countries. Broadly these countries may be divided into three income groups: high, middle and low following the World Bank classification of countries for 1990 per capita gross domestic product. A list of the sample countries is provided below:

High Income Group

Australia, Austria, Belgium, Canada, Denmark, Finland, France, Federal Republic of Germany, Hong Kong, Iceland, Italy, Japan, Netherlands, New Zealand, Norway, Singapore, Spain, Sweden, United Kingdom, United States of America (20).

Middle Income Group

Algeria, Argentina, Barbados, Bolivia, Brazil, Cameroon, Chile, Colombia, Congo, Costa Rica, Cyprus, Dominican Republic, Ecuador, El Salvador, Greece, Guatemala, Guyana, Iran, Iraq, Ireland, Israel, Jordan, Korea Republic, Malaysia, Mauritius, Mexico, Morocco, Panama, Papua New Guinea, Paraguay, Peru, Philippines, Portugal, Suriname, Syrian Arab Republic, Thailand, Trinidad and Tobago, Turkey, Uruguay, Venezuela (40).

Low Income Group

Bangladesh, Benin, Burundi, Central African Republic, Egypt, Ethiopia, Gambia, Ghana, Guinea, Haiti, Honduras, India, Kenya, Liberia, Madagascar, Malawi, Mozambique, Myanmar, Nicaragua, Niger, Nigeria, Pakistan, Rwanda, Sierra Leone, Sri Lanka, Sudan, Tanzania, Togo, Upper Volta, Zaire, Zambia, Zimbabwe (32).

5. TIME FRAME

Our choice of the points of time are restricted by the availability of data. Unfortunately, suitable data is not available for most of the countries and indicators prior to 1960. Year 1994 is the latest available year for which data for all the variables and sample countries could be gathered. Most of the analysis have been carried out for five points of time, i.e. 1960, 1970, 1980, 1990 and 1994.

6. CONSTRUCTION OF ACHIEVEMENT INDICES AND IMPROVEMENT INDICES

The achievement function is derived as an univariate function of the indicators representing well-being of the nation and the aggregate achievement index for a particular country for a particular point of time is the simple arithmetic mean of the achievement indices of the constituent indicators. In fact, the weighting pattern has greater significance in formulation of any index. Flexible weighting is better in this respect, as in reality some countries may prefer LIFE to ADLI, some others may have choice for ADLI over LIFE. But in practice, flexible weighting is likely to be complicated. If constant weights are to be used, then the obvious candidate is equal weighting since it is difficult to rationalize a greater valuation being placed on achievement in one particular indicator. In order to form the achievement indices, the maximum and the minimum values of the particular indicator have been taken from the data set at particular point of time. In some other similar studies, arbitrary values have been chosen for the maximum and minimum. For such choice the justification offered is that if one chooses maximum and minimum values from the sample set, the improvement in the highest and the lowest performing country would affect performance of all other countries in the sample. In reality, however, choice of an arbitrary value depends on the value judgement of the particular researcher and obviously this choice varies from person to person. Whereas, choice of value of the maximum and minimum for a definite data set would be impartial. Moreover, biological and physical maximum and minimum varies with region, climate, time and other conditions of life . Therefore, this study uses actual maximum and minimum values for each indicator as are obtained from the values of the sample countries. The assumption behind is that the maximum and the minimum obtained for a particular point of time is the possible maximum and possible minimum value for the respective indicator at that point of time for the given set of countries. The achievement index thus obtained leads to give an impression of the relative position of a country at a particular point of time in respect of a particular indicator of well-being.

The overall achievement index provides the overall standard of living of the country. This is estimated as a composite index formed with the achievement indices derived from the indicators of well-being. The overall improvement indices for a period of time are derived as the difference between the overall achievement indices of two points of time.

The estimation procedure precisely is as follows:

The achievement index for a particular indicator of well-being for a country at a point of time is:

$$A_{ij} = \frac{X_{ij} - X_{i\,min}}{X_{i\,max} - X_{i\,min}}$$

where X_{ij} = value of the ith indicator for jth country,
X_{imin} = minimum value of the ith indicator, and
X_{imax} = maximum value of the ith indicator.

The overall achievement index for the jth country at any point of time is obtained as:

$$A_j = \frac{1}{n}\sum_{i=1}^{n} A_{ij}$$

where, n = Number of constituent indicators.

The improvement index over a period $(t_2 - t_1)$ for the ith indicator is derived as:

$$I_{ij}\,(t_2 - t_1) = A_{ij}\,(t_2) - A_{ij}\,(t_1)$$

The overall improvement index of well-being is obtained as:

$$I_j\,(t_2 - t_1) = A_j\,(t_2) - A_j\,(t_1)$$

7. OBSERVATIONS

The general observations regarding the achievement and improvement indices of 92 countries have been summarised in the following paragraphs. Table 1 presents overall achievement indices and overall improvement indices for the sample countries over the period 1960 to 1994. It has been observed from the table that there is wide variation in the achievement levels among the sample countries considered. It is a useful exercise to look at the best and the worst performers of the set. Looking at the achievement indices (first five columns of the table) it has been observed that the lists of the highest performers and the lowest performers are not the same for five years under study but they are strikingly similar. Among the ten highest ranked countries for five years (1960, 1970,

TABLE 1

Overall Achievement and Improvement Indices: 1960-94

Country	*Achievement Indices*					*Improvement Indices*				
	1960	*1970*	*1980*	*1990*	*1994*	*1960-94*	*1960-70*	*1970-80*	*1980-90*	*1990-94*
1	*2*	*3*	*4*	*5*	*6*	*7*	*8*	*9*	*10*	*11*
Algeria	27.48	28.19	33.25	38.33	45.78	18.30	-7.68	5.06	5.08	7.43
Argentina	61.81	70.35	68.31	64.51	63.58	1.77	1.96	-2.04	-3.80	-1.07
Australia	73.36	77.05	80.63	78.38	76.66	3.30	-0.06	3.58	-2.27	-1.70
Austria	67.34	72.73	76.20	73.39	72.90	5.56	0.02	3.47	-2.81	-0.43
Bangladesh	15.07	19.91	20.06	17.94	21.38	6.31	-1.36	0.15	-2.12	3.43
Barbados	43.42	56.77	58.70	59.66	58.41	14.98	3.22	1.93	0.96	-1.40
Belgium	57.19	76.19	79.90	81.64	82.36	25.17	13.51	3.71	1.74	0.79
Benin	9.46	18.12	21.64	21.87	24.34	14.88	4.08	3.52	0.23	2.37
Bolivia	15.64	30.30	35.40	31.03	38.38	22.74	6.88	5.10	-4.37	7.38
Brazil	35.36	46.34	49.67	49.94	50.44	15.08	2.61	3.33	0.27	0.50
Burundi	17.34	20.08	20.47	20.83	15.69	-1.65	-2.04	0.39	0.36	-5.12
Caf. Rep.	14.58	20.28	22.08	28.39	23.55	8.97	1.53	1.80	6.31	-4.82
Cameroon	16.09	21.59	28.30	29.95	22.90	6.82	0.24	6.71	1.65	-7.11
Canada	72.71	77.14	77.39	77.35	76.08	3.37	4.43	0.25	0.04	-1.31
Chile	43.17	51.87	55.25	56.95	55.58	12.41	8.70	3.38	1.70	-1.37
Colombia	35.48	47.23	49.07	50.87	52.21	16.73	3.42	1.84	1.80	1.20
Congo	19.11	32.17	34.01	28.63	28.96	9.85	5.39	1.84	-5.38	0.30

Costa Rica	34.53	51.99	54.65	54.52	50.35	15.82	7.64	2.66	-0.13	-4.10
Cyprus	43.84	58.66	60.49	60.82	68.71	24.87	2.55	1.83	0.33	7.87
Denmark	68.01	84.43	84.38	76.88	76.27	8.26	12.22	-0.05	-7.50	-0.56
Dom. Rep.	28.66	40.92	42.91	45.25	46.99	18.33	4.11	1.99	2.34	1.60
Ecuador	28.68	39.39	42.81	44.83	47.51	18.83	0.91	3.42	2.02	2.68
Egypt	29.00	35.95	40.01	37.56	40.63	11.63	0.74	4.06	-2.45	3.04
El Salvador	26.49	38.10	39.48	40.54	41.43	14.94	1.70	1.38	1.06	0.83
Ethiopia	14.66	18.25	16.94	17.92	14.21	-0.45	-4.18	-1.31	0.98	-3.70
Finland	56.42	67.43	73.15	71.75	69.04	12.62	4.80	5.72	-1.40	-2.65
France	66.56	75.33	76.05	75.66	76.42	9.85	4.41	0.72	-0.39	0.80
FRG	67.34	76.17	79.62	80.04	79.07	11.73	4.67	3.45	0.42	-0.98
Gambia	16.86	16.86	15.95	15.57	17.06	0.20	-2.17	-0.91	-0.38	1.38
Ghana	22.59	29.99	31.32	30.30	29.47	6.88	0.94	1.33	-1.02	-0.79
Greece	49.56	62.67	68.33	66.97	66.94	17.38	2.81	5.66	-1.36	-0.18
Guatemala	28.72	36.69	36.71	37.21	36.31	7.59	0.96	0.02	0.50	-0.90
Guinea	12.34	16.84	16.86	11.61	13.23	0.89	0.41	0.02	-5.25	1.51
Guyana	37.71	47.79	48.75	41.27	41.78	4.07	0.41	0.96	-7.48	0.56
Haiti	14.76	23.96	26.06	24.78	25.94	11.19	1.20	2.10	-1.28	1.24
Honduras	24.99	35.19	35.94	37.01	39.95	14.96	2.96	0.75	1.07	2.86
Hong Kong	49.58	61.19	63.05	62.35	60.90	11.32	1.24	1.86	-0.70	-1.49
Iceland	67.64	76.12	79.55	82.93	83.12	15.48	1.29	3.43	3.38	0.17
India	19.07	26.45	26.10	27.26	30.23	11.16	0.38	-0.35	1.16	2.98
Iran	21.52	33.56	35.89	39.07	42.05	20.53	3.51	2.33	3.18	2.99

(Contd.)

TABLE 1 *(Contd.)*

1	*2*	*3*	*4*	*5*	*6*	*7*	*8*	*9*	*10*	*11*
Iraq	25.32	37.98	44.69	48.04	40.02	14.70	6.11	6.71	3.35	-7.92
Ireland	58.84	66.22	67.05	65.33	63.79	4.95	0.20	0.83	-1.72	-1.56
Israel	65.66	75.90	74.69	70.53	69.67	4.01	2.17	-1.21	-4.16	-0.82
Italy	62.44	75.24	80.96	80.14	80.40	17.96	5.22	5.72	-0.82	0.33
Japan	53.15	68.00	69.62	68.94	67.51	14.37	4.73	1.62	-0.68	-1.45
Jordan	26.36	40.11	44.19	49.11	52.70	26.34	6.05	4.08	4.92	3.67
Kenya	18.25	27.89	30.08	29.97	31.78	13.54	3.44	2.19	-0.11	1.70
Korea Rep.	31.50	47.61	51.97	60.60	61.99	30.48	6.25	4.36	8.63	1.36
Liberia	20.81	24.97	28.00	22.57	19.53	-1.28	-0.56	3.04	-5.44	-3.17
Madagascar	20.86	28.40	30.26	24.55	21.11	0.25	3.42	1.86	-5.71	-3.34
Malawi	13.26	18.52	17.03	15.13	13.59	0.33	-0.45	-1.49	-1.90	-1.52
Malaysia	35.09	42.73	44.45	49.76	52.78	17.69	-0.09	1.72	5.31	3.01
Mauritius	36.29	47.29	50.50	49.44	49.58	13.29	1.58	3.21	-1.06	-0.02
Mexico	40.74	49.23	52.74	55.91	55.69	14.95	1.84	3.51	3.17	-0.38
Morocco	20.30	30.06	32.16	35.42	36.83	16.53	2.62	2.10	3.26	1.46
Mozambique	12.48	19.60	19.19	14.53	11.47	-1.01	2.23	-0.41	-4.66	-3.03
Myanmar	18.92	32.70	37.15	38.31	35.33	16.42	6.17	4.45	1.16	-2.97
Netherlands	64.17	71.88	74.49	75.14	73.74	9.57	1.12	2.61	0.65	-1.33
Newzealand	73.71	78.03	77.09	75.29	74.79	1.08	0.43	-0.94	-1.80	-0.52
Nicaragua	32.29	41.22	43.61	47.07	40.78	8.49	4.09	2.39	3.46	-6.28
Niger	12.65	17.68	16.81	13.26	12.53	-0.12	0.37	-0.87	-3.55	-0.68

Nigeria	14.00	22.07	24.21	22.18	24.73	10.73	2.27	2.14	-2.03	2.57
Norway	58.80	69.98	78.78	83.36	79.94	21.15	3.60	8.80	4.58	-3.36
Pakistan	18.34	25.34	26.09	24.63	26.74	8.40	-0.93	0.75	-1.46	2.20
Panama	40.00	53.26	55.69	54.27	51.35	11.34	3.13	2.43	-1.42	-3.06
Papua NG	15.69	24.91	26.05	27.18	30.34	14.65	1.95	1.14	1.13	3.26
Paraguay	41.38	48.60	50.38	49.54	48.99	7.61	-0.74	1.78	44.16	-44.52
Peru	34.05	43.85	45.43	44.88	45.98	11.92	4.18	1.58	-0.55	1.06
Philippines	31.96	43.10	43.32	42.98	43.96	12.00	1.93	0.22	-0.34	0.87
Portugal	40.11	52.39	60.31	61.30	61.60	21.49	3.11	7.92	0.99	0.34
Rwanda	14.47	21.26	21.62	16.08	15.23	0.76	-0.09	0.36	-5.54	-0.83
Siera Leone	10.27	17.45	16.83	13.54	10.23	-0.04	0.44	-0.62	-3.29	-3.41
Singapore	49.08	62.91	63.77	61.56	60.93	11.85	3.39	0.86	-2.21	-0.62
Spain	51.95	64.43	73.43	73.72	73.29	21.34	2.98	9.00	0.29	-0.43
Sri Lanka	34.70	48.20	44.51	45.33	42.21	7.51	2.53	-3.69	0.82	-3.15
Sudan	13.59	21.06	25.41	31.42	22.79	9.20	1.11	4.35	6.01	-8.55
Suriname	41.92	51.59	54.01	50.48	53.44	11.52	0.07	2.42	-3.53	2.96
Sweden	74.86	77.93	79.41	74.68	75.96	1.09	-1.83	1.48	-4.73	1.35
Syrian AR	25.69	37.64	45.09	44.11	44.57	18.88	4.43	7.45	-0.98	0.49
Tanzania	13.59	28.22	30.07	31.88	24.37	10.78	7.15	1.85	1.81	-7.48
Thailand	28.91	39.88	41.92	42.94	42.91	14.01	1.58	2.04	1.02	0.03
Togo	14.22	22.25	22.84	24.36	24.95	10.73	1.47	0.59	1.52	0.60
Trin. & Tob.	44.46	51.01	52.65	61.28	57.76	13.30	-1.62	1.64	8.63	-3.55
Turkey	26.73	37.60	41.69	44.36	47.39	20.67	5.17	4.09	2.67	3.00

(Contd.)

TABLE 1 *(Contd.)*

1	*2*	*3*	*4*	*5*	*6*	*7*	*8*	*9*	*10*	*11*
UK	71.41	75.42	74.45	73.20	71.09	-0.32	0.16	-0.97	-1.25	-2.06
Up Volta	7.01	12.18	12.12	13.59	16.89	9.88	-0.76	-0.06	1.47	3.32
Uruguay	56.62	62.53	65.68	62.40	61.44	4.82	-2.01	3.15	-3.28	-0.99
USA	80.45	82.55	81.54	77.34	76.09	-4.36	2.12	-1.01	-4.20	-1.26
Venezuela	45.51	54.88	58.91	58.39	63.19	17.68	4.00	4.03	-0.52	4.64
Zaire	21.03	12.17	30.56	25.34	25.56	4.53	-14.92	18.39	-5.22	0.27
Zambia	19.13	29.00	30.37	33.78	27.08	7.94	3.58	1.37	3.41	-6.70
Zimbabwe	29.18	34.24	34.23	38.75	34.77	5.59	-1.03	-0.01	4.52	-3.98

1980, 1990, 1994) five countries are same: Australia, Canada, Denmark, Iceland and USA. It has also been found that among the ten toppers of 1994, Belgium, France and Italy were outside the orbit of first ten in 1960 while among the ten performers of 1960 Israel, New Zealand and Sweden fail to retain their position among the first ten in the latter years. The table shows that among the ten lowest ranked countries for the five years six common names occurred are : Benin, Guinea, Malawi, Sierra Leone, and Upper Volta (Burkina Faso). It is of interest to have a picture of the countries belonging to different ranges of achievement. If the countries are grouped on the basis of their overall achievement indices, it has been observed that for all the five points of time considered in the study a tri-polar picture is observed where most of the countries of North America, Western Europe and Australia are found to have high human development, most of the countries from Central and South America and East Asia have obtained middle level of human development and the rest are characterised by the low human development. For example, Australia, Canada, New Zealand, Sweden, UK and USA have achievement indices above 70.00, while Bangladesh, Benin, Burundi, Central African Republic, Congo, Ethiopia, Gambia, Haiti, India, Malawi, Mozambique, Niger, Nigeria, Pakistan, Papua New Guinea, Rwanda, Sierra Leone, Sudan, Tanzania, Togo and Upper Volta have achievement indices below 30.00 and Argentina, Barbados, Cyprus, Greece, Finland, Ireland, Hong Kong, Japan, Panama, Suriname, Trinidad and Tobago, Uruguay and Venezuela have value of the overall achievement indices between 50.00 to 69.99. It has been observed that most of the countries having achievement indices below 30.00 belong to Africa. Only Bangladesh, India and Pakistan are from (South) Asia, Haiti from Latin America and Papua New Guinea from the Australia-New Zealand zone. In this context it is worthy to note that the improvement indices of these countries are not significant.

It is very surprising to find that the region which had the rich heritage of Indus Valley Civilization is lagging behind the other regions of the World in respect of human development! In reality, the annual additions to the South Asian population exceed the total population of fifty of the smaller UN member countries. This population could have become the real wealth of these nations, if sufficient investment had been made in human development. But South Asia spends very little on the education and health of its people less than five percent of its combined GNP. And that is why rapidly multiplying populations have become a major liability rather than an asset. In case of Haiti and Papua New Guinea, it may be noted that these countries are suffering from continuous political and economic turmoil.

It has further been observed from the table that the overall improvement indices for the period 1960-94 is very high (above 15.00) for some of the countries, viz., Korea Republic, Belgium and Jordan. Among them Korea Republic has improved very significantly (30.48) over the period. The table also throws light to the fact that 8 countries have shown retardation over the same period. Except UK and USA, all are from Africa and belong to the low income group in the World Bank classification. These countries are Burundi, Ethiopia, Liberia, Mozambique, Niger and Sierra Leone. Most of these countries are suffering from economic and political turmoil. The table portrays that during the decades 1960-70 and 1970-80 most of the sample countries had improved in respect of human development: only eighteen countries (e.g. Algeria, Australia, Bangladesh, Burundi, Ethiopia, Gambia, Liberia, Malawi, Malaysia, Pakistan, Paraguay, Rwanda, Sweden, Trinidad and Tobago, Upper Volta, Uruguay, Zaire, Zimbabwe) evidenced retardation during the sixties and sixteen countries (Argentina, Denmark, Ethiopia, Gambia, India, Israel, Malawi, Mozambique, New Zealand, Niger, Sierra Leone, Sri Lanka, UK, Upper Volta, Uruguay and Zimbabwe) retarded during the seventies in human development. The table also depicts that only half of the countries have shown improvement during the eighties. In fact, the decade 1980 was a decade of disasters: the living standards of millions in Latin America even became lower than their standards of living in the early 1970s and in most of the Sub-Saharan Africa living standards had fallen to the levels last seen in 1960s. The period 1990-94 also has not shown any significant change in the scenario; forty-eight out of the ninety-two sample countries have shown decline in respect of human development.

It is of interest to compare the relative position of a country in respect of achievement indices and similar other composite indices measuring human development of a country. Table 2 presents rankings of the sample countries on the basis of the achievement index, weighted index formed with the same eight

TABLE 2

Rankings of the Countries: Different Indices

Country	*1960*					*1970*					*1980*				
	AI	*W8*	*PI*	*HI*	*PC*	*AI*	*W8*	*PI*	*HI*	*PC*	*AI*	*W8*	*PI*	*HI*	*PC*
1	*2*	*3*	*4*	*5*	*6*	*7*	*8*	*9*	*10*	*11*	*12*	*13*	*14*	*15*	*16*
Algeria	53	51	55	62	32	68	68	64	63	40	63	63	53	66	40
Argentina	15	15	26	21	20	16	16	26	26	22	21	21	31	26	26
Australia	4	4	7	5	4	6	6	6	8	4	4	4	6	9	8
Austria	9	10	22	14	16	14	14	19	17	14	12	12	9	14	10
Bangladesh	77	77	77	77	85	83	83	79	78	85	84	84	74	82	84
Barbados	29	27	25	20	29	27	27	31	18	26	29	28	32	21	29
Belgium	18	22	19	6	13	7	8	16	6	8	5	5	25	13	9
Benin	91	91	87	87	77	87	87	85	88	81	81	82	71	78	86
Bolivia	76	71	73	58	64	62	62	70	65	60	60	60	66	62	56
Brazil	39	41	37	42	47	42	42	50	44	45	39	39	48	44	38
Burundi	72	76	84	85	76	82	84	89	89	88	83	83	85	86	87
Caf. Rep.	80	85	90	90	74	81	81	87	85	78	80	80	91	83	81
Cameroon	74	78	80	80	72	78	78	83	86	65	71	71	78	74	63
Canada	5	5	9	10	3	5	5	8	12	3	10	10	10	10	2
Chile	30	31	36	32	25	32	32	38	30	29	31	31	38	32	33
Colombia	38	40	47	43	37	41	41	46	41	43	40	40	43	42	41

(Contd.)

TABLE 2 *(Contd.)*

1	*2*	*3*	*4*	*5*	*6*	*7*	*8*	*9*	*10*	*11*	*12*	*13*	*14*	*15*	*16*
Congo	67	64	53	44	66	61	61	49	56	54	62	62	58	59	58
Costa Rica	42	37	34	27	34	31	31	18	28	38	32	32	14	27	36
Cyprus	28	26	18	25	30	26	26	29	24	27	26	26	26	29	27
Denmark	7	9	5	6	5	1	1	10	4	5	1	1	11	4	6
Dom. Rep.	52	48	44	45	44	47	46	47	45	48	50	50	45	49	47
Ecuador	51	46	48	44	56	50	50	48	46	62	51	51	51	45	48
Egypt	48	54	67	59	73	56	56	63	61	69	54	54	55	64	55
El Salvador	55	50	43	49	57	51	51	41	49	57	55	55	44	50	65
Ethiopia	79	75	76	75	88	86	86	78	83	87	87	87	82	88	90
Finland	20	20	21	15	14	19	19	12	14	10	18	18	7	11	12
France	11	13	14	8	11	12	12	7	9	7	13	13	9	6	7
FRG	10	11	16	12	6	8	7	14	16	6	6	6	15	17	4
Gambia	73	86	89	92	71	90	91	92	92	73	91	91	92	92	66
Ghana	60	61	61	60	42	64	64	65	64	50	65	65	68	67	70
Greece	24	23	15	14	27	23	22	17	23	24	20	20	16	28	22
Guatemala	50	52	50	57	45	55	55	53	59	47	57	57	54	59	50
Guinea	89	90	81	88	61	91	90	90	87	72	88	89	89	89	71
Guyana	36	35	33	26	39	38	38	23	27	46	41	44	30	24	57
Haiti	78	73	62	72	84	74	74	71	72	86	75	74	60	76	83
Honduras	59	58	54	53	59	57	57	56	55	61	58	58	56	56	60
Hong Kong	23	24	28	28	46	25	25	15	29	31	25	25	8	19	20

Iceland	8	7	1	3	12	7	9	4	3	16	22	7	3	3	14
India	68	66	65	63	78	70	70	67	66	80	73	73	67	71	79
Iran	61	60	52	61	41	59	59	54	60	35	59	59	57	61	44
Iraq	58	59	63	65	31	52	54	60	68	37	44	47	49	60	30
Ireland	16	17.	13	13	22	20	20	11	15	23	22	22	20	18	23
Israel	12	8	20	23	21	10	10	22	21	19	14	14	22	23	19
Italy	14	14	10	17	18	13	13	27	19	18	3	3	18	16	16
Japan	21	19	17	16	24	18	18	5	7	13	19	19	2	1	11
Jordan	56	55	49	56	60	48	49	59	50	59	49	46	47	48	59
Kenya	71	72	69	73	82	69	69	62	67	82	69	70	70	63	82
Korea Rep.	46	43	39	37	68	39	37	42	34	49	36	36	34	33	41
Liberia	64	70	66	76	62	72	73	61	73	64	72	72	64	77	69
Madagascar	63	68	91	70	69	66	66	80	71	74	68	69	71	69	77
Malawi	86	84	83	74	92	85	85	84	79	92	86	86	84	85	89
Malaysia	40	42	41	47	50	45	45	40	48	45	46	45	40	51	34
Mauritius	37	39	35	39	48	40	40	36	36	63	37	38	46	41	51
Mexico	33	36	38	36	26	35	35	45	42	32	34	35	36	38	31
Morocco	65	63	58	66	70	63	63	55	70	56	64	64	61	68	54
Mozambique	88	87	79	85	55	84	82	74	80	52	85	85	81	79	72
Myanmar	69	62	60	50	90	60	60	66	52	89	56	56	65	58	88
Netherlands	13	12	3	4	9	15	15	3	5	9	15	15	4	5	13
New Zealand	3	3	11	7	7	3	4	13	10	15	11	11	13	8	17
Nicaragua	44	49	57	55	49	46	47	58	54	42	48	48	52	43	52

(Contd.)

TABLE 2 (*Contd.*)

1	*2*	*3*	*4*	*5*	*6*	*7*	*8*	*9*	*10*	*11*	*12*	*13*	*14*	*15*	*16*
Niger	87	88	84	89	83	88	88	82	90	79	78	88	86	90	76
Nigeria	83	83	72	81	52	77	77	75	75	58	90	78	76	75	53
Norway	17	16	4	2	10	17	17	2	1	11	9	9	5	7	5
Pakistan	76	67	71	71	79	71	71.	76	74	77	74	75	72	81	75
Panama	35	32	24	30	36	29	29	32	32	34	30	30	33	31	37 .
Papua NG	75	74	70	67	63	73	72	72	69	44	76	76	75	73	62
Paraguay	32	34	40	35	53	36	36	35	39	53	38	37	49	39	45
Peru	43	45	59	48	33	43	43	52	47	36	42	42	63	47	46
Philippines	45	44	45	40	67	44	44	43	40	67	49	49	41	46	61
Portugal	34	33	31	33	35	30	30	21	33	28	27	27	27	34	25
Rwanda	77	80	82	83	91	79	79	81	77	90	89	81	86	72	85
Sierra Leone	90	89	88	86	80	89	89	88	84	76	82	90	87	87	78
Singapore	25	25	27	34	38	22	23	28	35	30	24	24	24	31	21
Spain	22	21	12	19	23	21	21	20	20	20	17	17	12	20	18
Sri Lanka	41	38	30	30	43	37	39	33	38	68	45	44	37	36	68
Sudan	84	82	75	79	58	80	80	86	81	70	77	77	83	80	67
Suriname	31	29	32	29	28	33	33	34	31	33	33	33	29	35	32
Sweden	2	2	2	1	2	4	3	1	2	2	8	8	1	2	3
Syrian AR	57	56	64	54	54	53	52	51	57	51	43	43	42	52	35
Tanzania	85	74	74	82	86	67	69	69	58	84	70	69	69	54	80
Thailand	49	47	51	41	75	49	48	44	43	66	52	52	39	40	54

Togo	82	81	68	78	81	76	76.	68	76	75	79	79	80	84	73
Trin. & Tob.	27	28	29	22	19	34	34	30	25	21	35	34	21	24	42
Turkey	54	57	46	51	39	54	53	39	51	39	53	53	50	52	39
UK	6	6	6	9	8	11	11	9	11	12	16	16	23	15	15
Up Volta	92	92	92	91	89	92	92	91	91	91	92	92	90	91	92
Uruguay	19	18	33	18	17	24	24	25	22	25	23	23	28	22	28
USA	1	1	8	11	25	2	2	24	13	1	2	2	17	12	1
Venezuela	26	30	42	38	15	28	28	37	39	17	28	29	35	37	24
Zaire	62	65	78	68	87	75	75	77	82	83	66	67	73	65	91
Zambia	66	69	86	69	65	65	65	73	62	71	67	68	77	70	74
Zimbabwe	47	53	56	52	51	58	58	57	53	55	61	61	62	55	64

(Contd.)

TABLE 2 *(Contd.)*

Country	*1990*					*1994*				
	AI	*W8*	*PI*	*HI*	*PC*	*AI*	*W8*	*PI*	*HI*	*PC*
1	*17*	*18*	*19*	*20*	*21*	*22*	*23*	*24*	*25*	*26*
Algeria	57	59	51	59	45	47	48	48	56	43
Argentina	22	14	38	29	23	24	23	32	30	27
Australia	6	22	7	7	16	6	3	10	12	13
Austria	15	18	19	14	15	15	13	11	13	9
Bangladesh	83	84	75	82	68	80	80	76	78	71
Barbados	30	28	25	17	24	30	27	22	21	29
Belgium	3	1	27	10	9	2	9	9	5	5
Benin	81	81	76	87	77	76	78	82	84	69
Bolivia	66	66	55	71	64	59	57	58	55	59
Brazil	38	42	53	50	36	39	41	50	49	40
Burundi	82	82	81	86	89	85	84	83	85	85
Caf. Rep.	71	70	82	81	83	77	76	78	77	75
Cameroon	69	69	67	67	63	79	89	80	66	64
Canada	7	24	3	8	3	10	4	5	8	7
Chile	32	26	36	28	32	32	36	29	29	30
Colombia	36	35	33	38	43	37	40	35	38	41
Congo	70	71	68	65	57	68	69	71	69	66
Costa Rica	34	30	28	23	41	40	38	34	39	38
Cyprus	28	33	16	19	23	19	18	23	23	20
Denmark	9	6	13	18	4	8	12	19	19	26

Dom. Rep.	46	46	52	49	52	45	50	46	47	49
Ecuador	48	45	48	47	44	43	43	44	40	45
Egypt	59	61	65	69	61	56	54	64	68	49
El Salvador	54	53	59	56	60	54	53	53	52	58
Ethiopia	84	83	87	73	91	87	86	86	86	91
Finland	17	21	1	1	11	18	15	14	15	17
France	10	9	21	8	6	7	10	7	7	8
FRG	5	19	22	13	5	2	5	15	18	10
Gambia	86	88	90	89	76	83	83	87	88	77
Ghana	67	68	67	64	88	67	66	66	64	62
Greece	20	7	23	25	26	21	22	24	24	25
Guatemala	60	60	61	60	53	61	62	60	62	83
Guinea	92	92	91	92	81	89	89	89	81	61
Guyana	53	54	45	40	58	53	45	47	43	68
Haiti	75	78	71	77	79	71	72	72	75	79
Honduras	61	58	44	58	66	58	56	55	53	65
Hong Kong	24	8	9	24	12	29	33	20	22	4
Iceland	7	11	3	14	14	1	1	2	1	15
India	72	72	63	72	67	66	67	67	65	73
Iran	55	55	60	62	28	52	55	51	51	39
Iraq	43	39	46	44	40	57	60	61	61	54
Ireland	21	23	10	22	25	22	21	18	16	22
Israel	18	4	17	20	22	17	20	21	20	19

(Contd.)

TABLE 2 (*Contd.*)

1	*17*	*18*	*19*	*20*	*21*	*22*	*23*	*24*	*25*	*26*
Italy	4	3	15	15	19	3	7	8	6	12
Japan	19	19	2	2	10	20	19	1	2	3
Jordan	42	38	40	51	47	35	39	42	42	46
Kenya	68	67	66	63	79	64	64	59	60	72
Korea Rep.	29	13	32	30	37	25	29	26	27	28
Liberia	79	80	83	83	72	82	85	84	81	78
Madagascar	77	76	77	68	78	81	81	81	83	88
Malawi	87	87	88	84	85	88	87	85	82	87
Malaysia	39	43	34	45	35	36	34	36	44	32
Mauritius	41	47	42	43	51	41	35	39	46	23
Mexico	33	36	39	35	27	33	32	40	35	35
Morocco	62	62	64	70	59	60	63	65	70	52
Mozambique	88	86	84	85	75	91	91	88	87	81
Myanmar	58	56	57	54	78	62	61	62	59	84
Netherlands	12	12	12	6	13	13	14	6	4	11
New Zealand	11	29	18	12	18	12	8	17	14	18
Nicaragua	44	40	50	39	49	55	58	57	57	67
Niger	91	91	89	91	84	90	90	91	92	83
Nigeria	80	79	78	79	72	74	73	70	74	74
Norway	1	2	4	9	1	4	6	4	3	6
Pakistan	76	77	74	80	62	70	74	75	76	60

Panama	35	34	30	31	38	38	37	31	31	37
Papua NG	73	73	70	74	55	65	65	63	63	57
Paraguay	40	37	41	41	48	42	42	43	41	51
Peru	47	48	58	48	46	46	46	49	48	50
Philippines	51	51	54	46	56	49	52	45	45	56
Portugal	26	27	26	32	29	26	23	30	32	24
Rwanda	85	85	86	78	90	86	82	79	79	92
Sierra Leone	90	90	92	88	82	92	92	92	91	86
Singapore	25	20	29	33	8	28	30	25	28	2
Spain	14	5	6	21	21	14	17	12	11	21
Sri Lanka	45	44	31	34	54	51	49	33	33	55
Sudan	65	64	14	66	74	78	77	77	80	70
Suriname	37	41	43	37	31	34	31	37	36	48
Sweden	13	12	5	3	7	11	11	3	9	16
Syrian AR	50	49	47	57	39	48	51	54	54	42
Tanzania	64	72	72	53	87	75	71	69	72	89
Thailand	52	52	49	42	50	50	44	41	37	36
Togo	78	75	77	76	80	73	75	73	73	76
Trin. & Tob.	27	32	37	27	20	31	25	27	26	31
Turkey	49	50	56	40	43	44	47	52	50	44
UK	16	15	20	16	17	16	16	16	17	14
Up Volta	89	89	85	90	86	84	88	90	90	82
Uruguay	23	17	24	26	34	27	28	28	25	34

(Contd.)

TABLE 2 *(Contd.)*

1	*17*	*18*	*19*	*20*	*21*	*22*	*23*	*24*	*25*	*26*
USA	8	25	11	11	2	9	5	13	10	1
Venezuela	31	31	35	36	30	24	26	38	34	33
Zaire	67	74	73	75	92	72	70	68	67	90
Zambia	63	63	80	61	71	69	68	74	71	80
Zimbabwe	56	57	62	56	65	63	59	56	58	63

Notes: (1) AI : Achievement Indices
W8: Weighted Indices comprised of eight variables
PT: Physical Quality of Life Indices
HI: Human Development Indices
PC: Per Capita Real Gross Domestic Product

(2) In the tables some of the country names have been abridged as follows:
Caf. Rep. : Central African Republic
Dom. Rep. : Dominican Republic
FRG : Federal Republic of Germany
Korea Rep. : Korea Republic (South Korea)
Papua NG : Papua New Guinea
Syrian AR : Syrian Arab Republic
Trin. & Tob. : Trinidad and Tobago.

TABLE 3

Rank Correlations between Different Indices

(a) 1960

	AI	*W8*	*PI*	*HI*	*PC*
1	*2*	*3*	*4*	*5*	*6*
AI	1.00				
W8	0.99	1.00			
PI	0.96	0.96	1.00		
HI	0.97	0.97	0.97	1.00	
PC	0.89	0.89	0.87	0.87	1.00

(a) 1970

	AI	*W8*	*PI*	*HI*	*PC*
1	*2*	*3*	*4*	*5*	*6*
AI	1.00				
W8	1.00	1.00			
PI	0.96	0.96	1.00		
HI	0.98	0.98	0.97	1.00	
PC	0.91	0.91	0.89	0.88	1.00

(a) 1980

	AI	*W8*	*PI*	*HI*	*PC*
1	*2*	*3*	*4*	*5*	*6*
AI	1.00				
W8	0.99	1.00			
PI	0.95	0.96	1.00		
HI	0.97	0.97	0.97	1.00	
PC	0.93	0.93	0.91	0.89	1.00

(a) 1990

	AI	*W8*	*PI*	*HI*	*PC*
1	*2*	*3*	*4*	*5*	*6*
AI	1.00				
W8	0.98	1.00			
PI	0.94	0.93	1.00		
HI	0.97	0.95	0.94	1.00	
PC	0.94	0.92	0.90	0.91	1.00

(a) 1994

	AI	*W8*	*PI*	*HI*	*PC*
1	*2*	*3*	*4*	*5*	*6*
AI	1.00				
W8	0.98	1.00			
PI	0.94	0.93	1.00		
HI	0.97	0.95	0.94	1.00	
PC	0.94	0.92	0.90	0.91	1.00

indicators (Wtd8), Physical Quality of Life Index (PQLI) formed by Morris, Human Development Index (HDI) of UNDP and Per Capita Real Gross Domestic Product (PCRGDP). The rank correlation coefficients (Spearman) between the above mentioned indices and PCRGDP, presented in Table 3, depict that the overall achievement indices has very high rank correlation with the Wtd8, PQLI, HDI and PCRGDP. It has the lowest rank correlation with PCRGDP for all the years.

Table 4 presents Spearman rank correlation coefficients between the overall achievement indices of different years. There are very high correlation coefficients between the achievement indices of all the years indicating no significant changes in the ranking of the countries in respect of overall well-being over the last thirty-five years.

TABLE 4

Rank Correlations between Overall Achievement Indices of Different Years

	1960	*1970*	*1980*	*1990*	*1994*
1	*2*	*3*	*4*	*5*	*6*
1960	1.00				
1970	0.98	1.00			
1980	0.97	0.99	1.00		
1990	0.96	0.98	0.98	1.00	
1994	0.96	0.97	0.97	0.98	1.00

It has been expected that the initial achievement in an aspect plays significant role in determining the improvement of the country over the next decade or decades in that particular aspect. Table 5 presents relations between overall achievement indices (AI) at the initial point of time and the improvement indices (II) for the respective period, i.e., 1960 AI with 1960-94 II and 1960-70 II, 1970 AI with 1970-80 II, 1980 AI with 1980-90 II and 1990 AI with 1990-94 II. No significant relation has been observed between the initial achievement indices and the improvement indices in any one case which leads to the conclusion that improvement in well-being does not depend on achievement at the initial point of time.

TABLE 5

Correlation Coefficient between Achievement Indices and Improvement Indices

Indicators	*Years*				
Ach. Ind.	*1960*		*1970*	*1980*	*1990*
Imp. Ind.	*1960-94*	*1960-70*	*1970-80*	*1980-90*	*1990-94*
1	*2*	*3*	*4*	*5*	*6*
AI	0.04	0.15	0.04	0.01	0.00

Note: None of the correlation coefficients are significant.

8. CONCLUDING REMARKS

Human well-being is a complex concept and measurement of it is still more difficult. In this study human well-being has been defined as a social well-being function in terms of achievement and improvement indices and attempt has been made to measure human well-being of the sample countries in terms of the achievement index and the change of the same over a certain period of time in terms of the improvement index. The study focuses a tri-polar picture of the World—the countries from North America, Western Europe and Australia-New Zealand zone at the peak of human development, the South and Central America and the Caribbean countries and countries from the East Asia are at the middle level, while the countries from South Asia and Sub-Saharan Africa are lagging behind the rest of the world in respect of human well-being. The Rank correlation results show that there is no significant change in the scenario over the thirty-five years of the second half of this century.

REFERENCES

Atkinson, A.B. and F. Bourguignon (1982), "The Comparison of Multi-dimensional Distributions of Economic Studies", *Review of Economic Studies*, Vol. 12, pp. 183-201.

Atkinson, A.B. (1970), "On Measurement of Inequality", *Journal of Economic Theory*, Vol. 2, pp. 244-63.

Bairoch, P. (1975), The Economic Development of the Third World Since 1900, Methuen, London.

Bunge, Mario (1981), "Development Indicators", *Social Indicators Research*, Vol. 9, pp. 369-85.

Chakravarty, S.R. (1990), *Ethical Index Numbers*, Springer-Verlag, Berlin.

Chowdhury, O.M. (1991), "Human Development Index", *The Bangladesh Development Studies*, Vol. XIX, No. 3, pp. 125-27.

Cole, J.P. (1981), *The Development Gap*, John Wiley and Sons.

Das Gupta, Partha (1996), *An Inquiry into Well-Being and Destitution*, Clarendon Press, Oxford.

Das Gupta, Partha and Weale, Martin (1992), "On Measuring the Quality of Life", *World Development*, Vol. 20, No. 1, pp. 119-31.

Desai, Meghnad (1991), "Human Development : Concept and Measurement", *European Economic Review*, Vol. 35, pp. 350-57.

Drewnoski and Scott (1966), "The Level of Living Index", UNRISD, Geneva.

Dreze, Jean and Sen, A.K. (1989), *Hunger and Public Action*, Clarendon Press, Oxford.

——— (1990), *The Political Economy of Hunger*, 3 Volumes, Clarendon Press, Oxford.

——— (1995), *India: Economic Development and Social Opportunity*, Oxford University Press, Calcutta.

——— (1997), *Indian Development: Selected Regional Perspectives*, Oxford University Press, Calcutta.

Estes, Richard J. (1990), "Development under Different Political Systems", *Social Development Issues*, Vol. 13, No. 1, pp. 5-19.

——— (1993), "Toward Sustainable Development: From Theory to Praxis", *Social Development Issues*, Vol. 15, No. 3, pp. 1-29.

——— (1995), "Social Development Trends in Africa, 1970-94 : The Need for a New Paradigm", *Social Development Issues*, Vol. 17, No. 1, pp. 19-47.

——— (1996), "Social Development Trends in Asia, 1970-94: The Challenges of a New Century" , *Social Indicators Research*, Vol. 37, pp. 119-48.

——— (1996), "Social Development Trends in Latin America, 1970-94: In the Shadows of the 21st Century", *Social Development Issues*, Vol. 18, No. 1, pp. 25-52.

Estes, Richard J. (1997), "Social Development Trends in Europe, 1970-94: Development Prospects for the New Europe", *Social Indicators Research*, Vol. 42, No. 1, pp. 1-19.

Fishlow, Albert (1995), "Inequality, Poverty and Growth: Where Do We Stand?" Proceedings of the World Bank Annual Conference on Economic Development held in May 1995.

Gerson, E.M. (1976), "On Quality of Life", *American Sociological Review*, Vol. 41, pp. 793-806.

Haq, Mahbub ul (1996), *Reflections on Human Development*, Oxford University Press, Calcutta.

——— (1996), *Human Development Paradigm for South Asia*, Institute of Social Sciences, New Delhi.

——— (1997), *Human Development in South Asia*, Oxford University Press, Calcutta.

Hicks, N.L. (1982), "Sector Priorities in Meeting Basic Needs : Some Statistical Evidence", *World Development*, Vol. 7, pp. 567-80.

——— (1979), "Growth *vs.* Basic Needs: Is There a Trade Off?", *World Development*, Vol. 7, No. 11/12, pp. 985-94.

——— (1979), "Is There a Tradeoff between Growth and Basic Needs?", *Finance and Development*, June, Vol. 17, No. 2, pp. 17-20.

——— and Paul Streeten (1979), "Indicators of Development: The Search for a Basic Needs Yardstick", *World Development*, June, Vol. 7, No. 6, pp. 567-80.

Hirschberg, J.G., E. Maasoumi and D.J. Slottje (1991), "Cluster Analysis for Measuring Welfare and Quality of Life Across Countries", *Journal of Econometrics*, Vol. 50, pp. 1-13.

Kakwani, N.K. (1993), "Performance in Living Standards", *Journal of Development Economics*, Vol. 41, pp. 307-36.

Kelley, Allen C. (1991), "The Human Development Index: Handle with Care", *Population and Development Review*, Vol. 17, No. 2, pp. 315-24.

Kolm, S.C. (1969), "The Optimal Production of Social Justice", in Margolis, J. and Guittan, H. (eds.), *Public Economics*, Macmillan, London.

——— (1977), "Multi-dimensional Egalitarianism", *Journal of Econometrics*, Vol. 91, pp. 1-13.

Larsen, D.A. and Wilford, W.T. (1979), "The Physical Quality of Life Index: A Useful Social Indicator", *World Development*, Vol. 7, pp. 581-84.

Leipziger, D.M. and Lewis, M.A. (1980), "Social Indicators, Growth and Distribution", *World Development*, Vol. 8, pp. 299-302.

E. Maasoumi (1986), "The Measurement and Decomposition Analysis of Inequality in the World System", *American Sociological Review*, Vol. 53, pp. 838-52.

Majumder, Amita, Mazumdar, Krishna and Chakrabarti, Snigdha (1994), "Patterns of Inter- and Intra-regional Inequality: A Socio-Economic Approach", *Social Indicators Research*, Vol. 34, pp. 325-38.

Majumdar, Amita and Chakravarty, Satya R. (1996), "Achievement and Improvement in Living Standards", *Journal of Development Economics*, Vol. 50, pp. 189-95.

——— (1996), "Achievement and Improvement in Living Standards—An Empirical Analysis", *Social Indicators Research*, Vol. 37, pp. 269-80.

Mazumdar, Krishna (1995), "Classification of Countries: A Socio-Economic Approach", *Social Indicators Research*, Vol. 34, pp. 261-73.

——— (1996), "Level of Development of a Country: A Possible New Approach", *Social Indicators Research*, Vol. 38, No. 3, pp. 245-78.

——— (1996), "An Analysis of Causal Flow between Social Development and Economic Growth", *American Journal of Economics and Sociology*, Vol. 55, No. 3, pp. 361-83.

——— (1997), "Pair-wise Comparisons of Social Development of Selected Countries: 1960 to 1994: An Application of D^2-Statistics", *Social Indicators Research*, Vol. 44, pp. 155-94.

——— (1998), "Measuring Well-beings of the Developing Countries", *Social Indicators Research*, Forthcoming.

McNamara, R. (1971), "Address to the Board of Governors of the World Bank", Washington, DC : The World Bank, 1971, September 27.

Mehra, Y.P. (1977), "Money Wages, Prices and Causality", *Journal of Political Economy*, Vol. 85, pp. 1227-44.

Morawetz, D. (1977), *Twenty-five Years of Economic Development*, World Bank, Washington, D.C.

Morris, M.D. (1979), *Measuring the Condition of World's Poor: The Physical Quality of Life Index*, Pergamon Press, New York.

Nussabaum, Martha and Sen, A.K. (1993), *The Quality of Life*, Clarendon, Oxford.

Ram, Rati (1979), "International Income Inequality: 1970 and 1978", *Economics Letters*, Vol. 14, pp. 187-90.

——— (1980), "Physical Quality of Life Index and Inter-country Inequality", *Economics Letters*, Vol. 22, pp. 195-99.

——— (1982), "Composite Indices of Physical Quality of Life, Basic Needs Fulfilment and Income: A 'Principal Component' Representation", *Journal of Development Economics*, Vol. 11, pp. 227-47.

——— (1982), "International Inequalities in the Basic Needs Indicators", *Journal of Development Economics*, Vol. 11, pp. 113-17.

——— (1984), "Another Perspective on Changes in International Inequality from 1950 to 1980", *Economics Letters*, Vol. 16, pp. 191-96.

——— (1985), "The Role of Real Income Level and Income Distribution in Fulfilment of Basic Needs", *World Development*, Vol. 3, No. 5, pp. 589-94.

Ram, Rati (1986), "Causality between Income and Government Expenditure : a Broad International Perspective", *Public Finance*, Vol. XXXXI, No. 3, pp. 383-414.

——— (1986), "Government Size and Economic Growth: A New Framework and Some Evidence from Cross-Section and Time-Series Data", *The American Economic Review*, March, Vol. 76, No. 1, pp. 91-202.

——— (1987), "International Inequalities in Income and Index of Net Social

Progress", *Economics Letters*, Vol. 24, pp. 295-98.

——— (1989), "Level of Development and Income Inequality: An Extension of Kuznets-Hypothesis to the World Economy", *Kyklos*, Vol. 42, Fasc. 1, pp. 73-88.

——— (1992), "Inter-country Inequalities in Income and Basic Needs Indicators: A Recent Perspective", *World Development*, Vol. 20, pp. 899-905.

Rodgers, G.B. (1979), "Income and Inequality as Determinants of Mortality: An International Cross-sectional Analysis", *Population Studies*, Vol. 39, pp. 343-51.

Rostow, W.W. (1960), *The Stages of Economic Growth*, Cambridge University Press, Cambridge.

Sen, A.K. (1958), *Commodities and Capabilities*, North Holland, Amsterdam.

——— (1970), *Collective Choice and Social Welfare*, Holden Day, San Francisco.

——— (1973), *On Economic Inequality*, Oxford University Press, London.

——— (1981), *Poverty and Famines*, Oxford University Press, Oxford.

——— (1981), "Public Action and Quality of Life in Developing Countries", *Oxford Bulletin for Economics and Statistics*, Vol. 43, No. 4, pp. 287-319.

——— (1983), "Development Which Way Now?", *The Economic Journal*, Vol. 93, pp. 745-62.

——— (1987), *The Standard of Living*, Cambridge University Press, Cambridge.

——— (1992), *Inequality Re-examined*, Harvard University Press.

Shin, Doh C. (1980), "Does Rapid Economic Growth Improve the Human Lot?", *Social Indicators Research*, Vol. 8, pp. 199-221.

Shorrocks, A.F. (1978), "Income Inequality and Income Mobility", *Journal of Economic Theory*, Vol. 10, pp. 376-93.

Sims, C.A. (1972), "Money, Income and Causality", *The American Economic Review*, September, Vol. 62, pp. 540-52.

Slottje, D.J. (1991), "Measuring the Quality of Life Across Countries", *The Review of Economics and Statistics*, Vol. 73, pp. 684-93.

Spout, Ronald V.A. and Weaver, J.H. (1992), "International Distribution of Income: 1960-87", *Kyklos*, Fasc. 2, pp. 237-58.

Srinivasan, T.N. (1977), "Development Poverty and Basic Human Needs: Some Issues", *Food Research Institute Studies*, Vol. 16, No. 2, pp. 11-28.

Stewart, F. (1985), *Basic Needs in Developing Countries*, Johns Hopkins University Press, Baltimore, MD.

Streeten, P. (1977), "The Distinctive Features of a Basic Needs Approach to Development", *International Development Review*, Vol. 3, pp. 8-16.

——— (1981), *First Things First*, London, Oxford University Press and A.W. Heston (1984) "Improved International Comparison of Real Product and its Comparison: 1950-77", *Review of Income and Wealth*, Vol. 30, pp. 207-82.

——— (1984), "Basic Needs: Some Unsettled Questions", *World Development*, Vol. 12, No. 9, pp. 973-78.

Summers, R. and A.W. Heston (1984), "Improved International Comparison of Real Product and its Comparison: 1950-77", *Review of Income and Wealth*, Vol. 30, pp. 207-62.

——— (1984), "Improved International Comparisons of Real Product and its Comparisons: 1950-77", *Review of Income and Wealth*, Vol. 30, pp. 1-25.

——— (1988), "A New Set of International Comparisons of Real Product and Price Levels: Estimates for 130 Countries, 1950-85", *Review of Income and Wealth*, Vol. 34, pp. 1-25.

——— (1991), "The Penn World Table (Mark V): An Extended Set of International Comparisons, 1950-88", *Quarterly Journal of Economics*, pp. 327-68.

Theil, H. (1989), "The Development of International Inequality", *Journal of Econometrics*, Vol. 42, pp. 144-55.

Waldman, R.J. (1990), "Income Distribution and Infant Mortality", *Quarterly Journal of Economics*, pp. 1283-1302.

Ward, M. (1984), "Changing Patterns of Inequality in a Changing Global Order", *Kyklos*, Vol. 35, pp. 115-34.

Wheeler, D. (1980), "Basic Needs Fulfilment and Economic Growth: A Simultaneous Model", *Journal of Development Economics*, Vol. 17, pp. 435-51.

Wiedermann, Paul (1984), "Comparing the Process of Socio-economic Development in Non-market Economies: The EEC and CMEA", *Cambridge Journal of Economics*, Vol. 8, pp. 311-30.

Williams, D., C.A.E. Goodhart and D.H. Gowland (1976): "Money, Income and Causality: The U.K. Experience", *American Economic Review*, Vol. 66, pp. 417-23.

United Nations Development Program, *Human Development Reports*, different issues.

World Bank, *World Tables*, different issues.

World Bank, *World Development Reports*, different issues.

23

Human Development: Achievements in the Indian Economy

Bishwa Nath Singh and S.M. Humair Ahmad

I. THE CONCEPTUAL VIEWPOINTS

Human development is a process of enlarging people's choices and the three essential ones include to lead a long and healthy life, to acquire knowledge and to have access to the resources needed for a decent standard of living. But human development does not end there. Additional choices, highly valued by many people, range from political, economic and social freedom to opportunities for being creative and productive and enjoying personal self-respect and guaranteed human rights.

There are four major elements in the concept of human development—productivity, equity, sustainability and empowerment. The human development index (HDI) contains three indicators—life expectancy, educational attainment and real GDP, i.e. it indicates whether people lead a long and healthy life, are educated and knolwedgeable and enjoy a decent standard of living. It examines the average condition of all people in a country. HDI has become a measure of empowerment and is being increasingly used to monitor the progress of nations and of global society.

The HDI value for each country indicates how far that country has to go to attain certain defined goals; an average life of 85 years, access to education for all and a decent level of income. The closer a country's HDI is to 1, the less the remaining distance that a country has to travel.

II. HUMAN RESOURCE DEVELOPMENT *VIS-A-VIS* HUMAN DEVELOPMENT

Though the two concepts represent different approaches, but they are linked together by the fact that the broad-based concept of human development provides the necessary conditions that enable human resources to contribute to economic growth. The difference between what Streeten (1994) terms 'human resource developers' and the 'humanitarians' is that the former consider human being as 'means' to an end whereas the latter consider human beings as 'ends' in themselves. In fact, to the 'humanitarians' the human resource approach which acts towards people with a view to turning them into better human capital which in turn contributes to greater human prosperity is offensive. Here, education and health are the basic tools. Education includes training and health includes nutrition also through which life-expectancy may be raised. Whereas, the concept of human development is related to the fulfilment of basic needs, this approach emphasizes provision for all people the basic means of well-being which include among other things, food, health and education. Not only this, the UNDP's human development concept emphasising the enlargement of the range of people's choices goes much further than the concept of basic needs as it is based on functioning achievements rather than on commodity possession. The concept of human development encompasses empowerment, co-operation, equity in basic capabilities and opportunities, sustainability and security. Educational and health indicators are common to both the approaches, but the inclusion of per capita income is distinct to human development. The inclusion of incomes is justified on the ground that it enables the exercise of choice with respect to other two indicators. The difference also lies in the context of two basic indicators, i.e.

education and health. In the human development approach, education may be stressed more for its instrumental role and for its contribution to equity rather than merely as a means to raise productivity and incomes. Similar considerations in the health sector would imply according greater attention to basic health services than to curative care for the working population. Since several health problems in poverty ridden countries, particularly in South Asia, are due to poor living conditions, a more holistic approach towards health care which takes into account nutrition, water supply and sanitation and housing may be adopted in place of a narrow focus on only medical care. The entire gamut of social security also comes under its orbit.

Thus, the human development approach puts people at the centre stage and supports measures to promote education, health and nutrition even if the conventionally measured rates of return on these investments are zero. Since the advocates of human development attach a higher importance to the supply of social services, particularly public services, the use of the concept also implies a greater role and responsibility for public provisioning (Prabhu, 1996).

III. HUMAN DEVELOPMENT: INDIA AND ABROAD

India has been characterised as a country with a low level of human development with the country's rank in the Human Development Index (HDI) calculated by the UNDP being 135 among 174 countries in 1996. At this level, the position of the country is lower than not only that of China and Sri Lanka, the oft-quoted examples of success in human development at low levels of income, but also lower than that of Thailand and the Philippines which were similar to India in this respect till recently. Individual indicators such as literacy and infant mortality in the country in 1991 were lower than the levels attained by a country such as South Korea far back in 1960 (Prabhu, 1996). Of the 174 countries for which the HDI was calculated, 63 were in high human development category, 64 in the medium category and 47 in the low category. India, of course, belongs to this last category. The large gap in human development indicates that India has long way to go in the social domain compared to its competitor emerging markets. In 1992, nearly 30 per cent of world's people were living in the countries in the high human development category, 39 per cent were in the medium category and 31 per cent in countries in the low category where India is the major constituent. India's position is obvious from the figures below:

TABLE 1

Human Development Profile: India (1995)

HDI Rank (among 174 countries)	134	
HDI Value (on scale of 0 to 1)	0.439	
Human Development Group	Low	
Income Group	Low	
Human Development		
Life Expectancy (years)	1992	60.4
Adult Literacy (%)	1992	49.9
Real GDP per capita (PPP $)	1992	1,230
Daily calorie supply per capita	1992	2395
GNP per capita (US $)	1992	310
Human Deprivation		
Illiterate adults (15+) m.	1992	271.8
Illiterate females (15+) m.	1992	169.9
Malnourished children under 5 ('000)	1992	69,345
Children dying before age of 5 ('000)	1992	3,102
Rural people below Poverty Line (%)	1990	49
Urban people below Poverty Line (%)	1990	38

Sources: UNDP, *Human Development Report*, 1995.
Reproduced in brief in *Monthly Review*, PNB, Sept. 1995, pp. 472-73.

Not to talk of the developed countries of the west, even in company of Asian countries, our position is very poor. In the year 1994, the literacy ratio in South Korea was 97.9 per cent, in Thailand 93.5 per cent and in China 80.9 per cent, but in India only 52.2 per cent (*Economic Survey*, 1997-98). Likewise, life expectancy at birth stood at 77.1 years in Singapore, 72.5 years in Srilanka, 71.5 years in Republic of Korea, 68.9 years in China and 61.3 years in India (Table 2).

Further, we have inter-state disparity in our economy, Kerala followed by Tamil Nadu in recent years comes under the first category which has achieved high level of human development despite relatively modest level of income. In the second category are the states like Punjab and Haryana where substantial increase in income has taken place but the social opportunities have been lesser in availability in comparison to first category states. The third category is of the states such as Bihar, Madhya Pradesh, Orissa, Rajasthan and Uttar Pradesh where neither economic nor social opportunities have been realised and, therefore, position in the field of human development is very poor. The fourth category comprises of states like Maharashtra, Gujarat and Karnataka where the differences in their economic and social opportunities are not too large and their achievements from the point of view of human development are also somewhat moderate. However, the third category states account for more than 40 per cent of the country's

TABLE 2

Indicators of Human Development for Some Asian Countries—1994

Country	*Life Expectancy at birth (years)*	*Infant Mortality rate (per thousand birth)*	*Adult Literacy (per cent)*
China	68.9	43	80.9
Indonesia	63.5	53	83.2
India	61.3	72	52.2
Kerala State (India)	72.0	13	89.8
Malaysia	71.2	12	83.0
Philippines	67.0	36	94.4
Pakistan	62.3	80	37.1
Republic of Korea	71.5	10	97.9
Singaproe	77.1	5	91.0
Srilanka	72.2	16	90.1
Thailand	69.5	29	93.5

Source: UNDP, *Human Development Report*, 1997. Quoted in *Economic Survey*, Government of India, 1996-98, p. 140.

TABLE 3

Selected Indicators of Human Development for Major States* in India

Sl. No.	States	Life Expectancy at birth (years) (1989-93)	Literacy Rate, 1991 (%)			IMR	Deth rate	Birth rate
			Total	Male	Female		(Prov. estimates of the SSR—1996) (Per thousand)	
1.	Andhra Pradesh	60.6	44.09	55.13	32.72	66	8.3	22.7
2.	Assam	54.9	52.89	61.87	43.03	75	9.5	27.7
3.	Bihar	58.5	38.48	52.49	22.89	72	10.2	32.1
4.	Gujarat	60.1	61.29	73.13	48.48	62	7.6	25.5
5.	Haryana	62.9	55.85	69.10	40.47	68	8.1	28.8
6.	Karnataka	61.9	56.04	67.26	44.34	53	7.6	23.0
7.	Kerala	72.0	89.81	93.62	86.17	13	6.2	17.8
8.	Madhya Pradesh	54.0	44.20	58.42	28.85	97	11.1	32.4
9.	Maharashtra	64.2	64.87	76.56	52.32	48	7.4	23.2
10.	Orissa	55.5	49.09	63.09	34.68	95	10.7	26.8
11.	Punjab	66.4	58.51	65.66	50.41	52	7.5	23.5
12.	Rajasthan	58.0	38.55	54.99	20.44	86	9.1	32.3
13.	Tamil Nadu	62.4	62.66	73.75	51.53	54	7.9	19.2

14. Uttar Pradesh	55.9	41.60	55.73	25.31	85	10.2	34.0
15. West	61.5	57.70	67.81	46.56	55	7.8	22.8
All India	**59.4**	**52.21**	**64.13**	**39.29**	**72**	**8.9**	**27.4**

* Major states include states with population of 10 million and above as per 1991 census.

(a) Relate to population aged 7 years, and above for 1991 and excludes Jammu & Kashmir for All India.

Source: Government of India, *Economic Survey*, 1997-98, Table 10.5, p. 140.

population and their performance in the field of human development is far behind the national average (Table 3).

Not only this, despite the programmes of universal education and educational reforms carried out by the Governments (both Central and States), it is the rich and middle income groups that have benefited from the educational system the most. This is due to reason that the educational and social structure within which the educational system has to function is inegalitarian and perpetuates inequalities. The childhood of the poor children is characterised by poor nutrition and illiterate home environment which have negative mental effects. Even if they are able to complete their education, they find it difficult to procure jobs which are cornered by children belonging to the relatively rich classes on account of their better social contact and influence. Similar is the case of health facilities where majority of poor people have no access to reach them. 74.3 per cent of our population (*Census, 1991*) lives in rural areas but about 80 per cent of our modern medical facilities are located in urban areas and whatever medical and health facilities are available in rural areas, they are highly ill-equipped and ill-manned. The poor people will have to rely upon such poor facilities. The people living below the poverty line have also to suffer from the problems of undernutrition, poor calorie intake, unhygienic conditions and poor housing facilities. All such inequalities hamper their efficiency and productivity and compel them to have a non-dignified life. Their wants remain depressed and choices unfulfilled.

IV. FIVE YEAR PLANS AND HUMAN DEVELOPMENT IN INDIA: THE CASE OF LITERACY AND LIFE EXPECTANCY

India's Five Year Plans have made concerted efforts for the development of human resources as well as human development. Universalisation of education and expansion of health services have been the ambitious goals of our Five Year Plans. Literacy has been a priority on the national agenda as a tool of information and as an instrument of social change. Plan outlay on education increased from Rs. 153 crores in the First Five Year Plan to Rs. 19,600 crores in Eighth Five Year Plan (*India, 1998*). The expenditure on education as per cent of GDP also rose from 0.7 per cent in 1951-

52 to 3.3 per cent in 1995-96 (RE). Universalisation of elementary education has become our top priority. As a result, India has become the second largest country in the world with 151.5 million children in the age-group of 6-14 years enrolled in 1996-97, covering about 81 per cent of the children in this age-group. The number of primary schools have increased from 2.10 lakhs in 1950-51 to 5.98 lakhs in 1996-97 (*Economic Survey*, 1997-98, p. 143). During the same period the number of upper primary schools increased from 0.14 lakh to 1.71 lakhs. The gross enrolment ratio has gone up to 90.5 per cent in primary stage (Class I to V) and 62.3 per cent at upper primary stage (Class VI to VIII). Under the universalisation of elementary education programme in recent years, emphasis has been laid on enrolment and retention of girl child schooling and recruitment of rural women as teachers. Free education is provided to girls by various state governments/UTs while education is free for girls upto Class XII in Kendriya and Navodaya Vidyalayas. Vocational programmes with emphasis on entrepreneurship are being designed for girl dropouts. In order to empower rural population especially the poorest of the poor through the inputs of technical education, several schemes have been introduced. As a result of all such efforts, the ratio of literacy as well as acquisition of higher general and technical knowledge has gone up which can help us to lead our economy towards sustainable and equitable growth. The growth in literacy ratio is evident from Table 4.

TABLE 4

Literacy Rate in India (%)

Year	*Persons*	*Males*	*Females*
1951	18.3	27.2	8.9
1961	28.3	40.4	15.3
1971	34.5	46.0	22.0
1981	43.7	56.5	29.5
1991	52.2	64.2	39.2

Source: *Census of India*, 1991, Series 1, India, Paper 1 of 1991.

The growth rate of literacy during 1981-91 (8.5%) was

slightly higher than the growth rate of the previous decade (about 7 per cent). But, if the country moves at this rate in the current and coming decades, then it would not be possible to remove illiteracy before 2040 A.D. (even if some acceleration in the efforts of National Literacy Mission is granted). The situation regarding female literacy is still very discouraging and given the laggards like Rajasthan, Bihar, Uttar Pradesh, Madhya Pradesh and Orissa, it may not be possible to eradicate female illiteracy before 2060 A.D. (Ruddar Dutt, 1996). At the current rate of literacy growth, India will have the dubious distinction of having 500 million illiterates by the year 2000 A.D. This according to World Bank will constitute the 54 per cent of the world's illiterate population.

The situation in primary education as it obtains today is that the country has reached a gross enrolment level of 90.5 per cent in 1996-97 (*Economic Survey*, 1996-97, p. 144) at the primary level but despite this trend, the rate of literacy achieved in 1991 is only 52.2 per cent. In the case of rural females, the literacy rate was as low as 21 per cent. It is really shocking that in some states rural female literacy rate is below even 12% (Rajasthan 6.4%), Madhya Pradesh 10.5%, U.P. 11.6% and Bihar 11.8% (Datt, 1996, p. 97).

The paradox of rapid growth of population in the face of rising trend of enrolemnt can be explained in terms of high dropout rates—out of every 100 students enrolled in Class I, only 40 reach Class V and 23 reach Class VIII. All these dropouts add to the population of illiterates. Moreover, retention rates among the females are poor and only 16 to 18 per cent of those enrolled in Class I reach Class VIII.

Besides these facts, the features of our educational or universalisation of education programmes are as follows:

(i) Overall literacy rate in India is 52.2 per cent (1991) which is far below the cent per cent level of literacy achieved in Australia, Canada, United Kingdom and United State, etc.
(ii) The level of literacy in urban areas was 65 per cent as against 34 per cent in rural areas (1981).
(iii) The gap between male and female literacy ratio has narrowed down in urban areas, but is still very wide in rural areas.
(iv) In India, in 1992, the level of adult literacy was barely 49

per cent as against cent per cent in developed countries.

(v) Number of persons enrolled in higher education as percentage of population in the age group 20-24 was barely 9 per cent in 1992. This figure is quite large among low income countries, but in comparison to advanced countries, it is only one-fourth to one-third.

(vi) Further, the number of doctors and engineers per million of population works out to be 13 and 16 respectively which is much lower than the out-turn of engineers and doctors in advanced countries.

Life expectancy at birth has also been improving considerably during the plan period. During the decade 1961-71, it was 46.4 years and increased to 54 years in 1981 and stands at 60.8 years in 1992-93. One important factor depressing life expectancy has been the high level of infant mortality. During the last decades, infant mortality has shown a significant decline from 219 per thousand in 1961 to 72 in 1994. This is largely the result of an improvement of maternity services and better care of the children. Greater care of women due to change in our attitude towards women has also contributed to higher life expectancy of the female population in India. While poverty of the Indian people lies at the root of the phenomenon of short life span, the discovery of wonder medicines to control epidemics like plague, cholera, influenza or small pox, the general improvement in medical assistance—increase in the number of hospitals, doctors, nurses, midwives and better control of diseases have all helped to save life. In recent years, the public health measures taken under the various plans have further reduced death rates. Economic growth and relative improvement in the standard of living of the masses (though slightly) have also led to improvement in expectancy of life at birth. Even then, the present level of life expectancy in India does not compare favourably with the levels obtaining in other countries of the world (Table 2) and unless the level of earnings and standards of living of the masses are improved, highly appreciable results cannot be expected.

Thus, if the aim of human development is to enhance the capabilities of the bottom 40 per cent of the population, the two routes to such capability enhancement, viz. income generation and public provision of education, health and nutrition, cannot be divorced from each other. Further, sustained gains in human development can be made only if the poor have access to income and public policy facilitates their access to education, health and nutrition which in turn act to make the income distribution more egalitarian. In the absence of such a vision, the mutually reinforcing links between poverty, undernutrition, ill-health and inegalitarian nature of development could result in the phenomenon of social exclusion (Prabhu, 1996).

REFERENCES

Census of India, 1991, Series 1, Paper 2 of 1992, Final Population Total.

Datt, Ruddar, *Indian Economy*, S. Chand & Co. Ltd., New Delhi, 1997, p. 53.

Government of India, *Economic Survey*, 1997-98.

———, *India, 1998*, Publication Division, p. 69.

Prabhu, K. Seeta, 'Social Sectors in Economic Development: Some Issues', *The Indian Economic Association Conference*, Vol. 1996, Gwalior.

Streeten, Paul (1994), 'Human Development: Means and Ends', *AEA Papers and Proceedings*, Vol. 84(2), pp. 232-37.

24

Human Development in India: A Study of Inter-state Variation

NISAR AHMAD KHAN

The issues relating to human development have come to the fore in the last few decades because of the fact that the benefits of economic growth do not necessarily accrue to all sections of the community automatically. The ultimate objective of social and economic changes is human development, which has been defined as a process of enlarging human capabilities[1] and choices. Apart from the basic necessities such as food, clothing and shelter, other human choices include long life, good health, adequate education and participative decision-making. Thus, human development is multi-dimensional involving political, social and economic elements. It is not, therefore, surprising that countries do not rank identically on the income scale and human development scale.

Human development implies economic growth. Sustained improvement in human well-being is not possible without economic growth but at the same time, high economic growth need not necessarily translate into higher levels of human development. Economic growth requires effective policy management if it is to enrich human development. Conversely, if human development is to be durable, it must be continuously supported by economic growth. An imbalance between the creation of capabilities in people which is what human development aims to achieve and absorption of these capabilities in productive activities which is what economic growth can result in, can create social upheaval. Wastage of human resources can be most detrimental to any society. Human development has, therefore, to go hand in hand with economic growth.

India has done well on many dimensions of human development over the past four decades. Life expectancy was just 32 years in 1951 and in 1991 it increased to 59.4 years. Infant mortality rate which stood at 146 per thousand in 1951 came down to 80 in 1991. The literacy rate has gone up from 16.7 percent in 1951 to 52.2 percent in 1991. There is an apocryphal story about Lord Keynes, the economist. He was once asked, "How is your wife?" Keynes retorted, "compared to whose wife?" The benchmark for making comparisons is important. Our track record since independence pales into insignificance the moment we begin to make comparisons with other countries, be it in terms of standard economic indicators of physical quality of life indicators. Like, the Alice quote, we have done all the running to fall behind.

India during sixties and seventies remained in the group of 'weak link' countries characterized by slow progress of human development and constrained by low level of economic growth. The problem has been different during eighties onwards as the country has been suffering from lopsided development with rapid economic growth and slow human development. There has been widespread variation among the states in human development and economic growth. Surveying the human development in India, *Asia Development Report, 1996-97* observed:

> "Although there has been a significant improvement in social indicators, India still lags behind most Asian countries in these aspects. Poverty remains a serious problem, a large fraction of population has limited or no education and there are substantial disparities in social indicators across the states."[2]

The report has clearly pointed out that India is far behind in terms of human development and there is widespread inter-state variation in human development. The present study intends to measure this inter-state variation in human development by constructing Human Development indices for major states of India.

HUMAN DEVELOPMENT INDEX

The first *Human Development Index* was constructed by UNDP in 1990 and since then it has gone through a process of continuous modification. It is a composite index of achievements in the basic human capabilities in three areas—a long and healthy life, knowledge and a decent standard of living. Life expectancy, educational attainment and income are three variables which have been chosen to represent these three dimensions. The HDI value for a country indicates how far it has to go to attain certain defined long-term goals such as an average life span of 85 years, access to education to all and reasonably high per capita income for enjoying a decent standard of living. The index is used for inter-country comparison of human development and has been proved useful in boosting up the efforts of the governments of the countries, deficient in human development.

OBJECTIVES AND METHODOLOGY OF THE STUDY

The present study aims to construct Human Development Indices for 15 major states of India using a methodology similar to that of UNDP[3] so as to measure the inter-state variation in the human development in India. The year of the study is 1991. Though, it would have been better had we conducted the study for the year 1998, but we could not do so owing to non-availability of reliable data.

Since, the methodology used in the present study is similar to that of UNDP, it is pertinent to outline the UNDP methodology. It will also help in understanding the modifications made in it.

The HDI constructed by UNDP is based on three elements: longevity as measured by life expectancy at birth; educational attainment, as measured by a combination of adult literacy (two-third weight) and combined primary, secondary and tertiary enrolment ratios (one-third weight); and standard of living, as measured by real GDP per capita (PPP$).

For the construction of index, fixed minimum and maximum values have been established for each of these indicators:

(a) Life expectancy at birth: 25 years and 85 years.
(b) Adult literacy and combined enrolment ratios: 0 percent and 100 percent in both the cases.
(c) Real GDP per capita (PPP\$): PPP\$ 100 and PPP\$ 40,000.

For any component of HDI individual index can be computed according to general formula:

$$\text{Index} = \frac{\text{Actual } X_i \text{ Value} - \text{Minimum } X_i \text{ Value}}{\text{Maximum } X_i \text{ Value} - \text{Minimum } X_i \text{ Value}}$$

where, X_i value is the value of any indicator.

HDI is a simple average of the life expectancy index, educational attainment index and the adjusted real GDP per capita (PPP\$) index.

UNDP uses the above methodology for the construction of HDI with the objective of international comparison. For inter-state comparison, which is the aim of the present study, following modifications have been made in the above methodology.

In the UNDP methodology, the per capita real income of a country expressed in her currency is converted into dollars by taking into account the purchasing power of the currency of that country. This approach is for inter-country comparisons as the currency of different countries is different and its purchasing power also differs from country to country. But for inter-state comparison within a country there is no need to convert real per capita SDP into dollar. Further, state's real per capita domestic product may be used for the construction of HDI without making any adjustment in it for inter-state variation in the purchasing power in money. The justification for doing so is that most of the consumption goods are available at national prices. Some locally produced goods may be available at lower prices but this difference may be neutralized by higher prices in case of some other goods. However, ideally one should adjust the per capita SDP for inter-state variation in the purchasing power of money. But that will make our task difficult. So opting for simplicity the real per capita SDP may be taken as a sufficient indicator of the standard of living in the state. But instead of using the real per capita SDP, the present study following UNDP, has used logarithm of per capita SDP to reflect the conversion of income into good living.[4]

UNDP uses minimum and maximum values of per capita income which are the most extreme values observed or expected over a long period say 60 years. The minimum are those observed historically going back about 30 years, and the maximum are the limits of what can be envisioned in the next 30 years.

India's per capita income in 1950-51 at 1980-81 prices was Rs. 1126.9. It rose to Rs. 2215.8 in 1992-93. Thus, over a period of 42 years, it rose by 96.6 per cent implying 1.62 per cent annual increase. It is noteworthy that during the last 19 years the rate of increase in per capita income was 2.14 per cent as against 1.20 per cent during the first 23 years of economic planning. The per capita income of many states like Punjab, Haryana and Maharashtra has been much higher than the per capita income of the country. Hoping that the rate of growth of per capita income is likely to be more than 2.14 per cent in the coming decades owing to slow growth of population and liberalization and considering the high per capita income of some states, the maximum and minimum values of per capita income used in the present study at 1980-81 prices are Rs. 10,000 and Rs. 1,000 respectively.

Life expectancy in India was 32 years in 1950-51, it increased to 40 years in 1960-61 and 59.4 years in 1990-91. If this continues, the life expectancy is likely to be around 80 years in coming 25 to 30 years. Keeping in mind the above trend and life expectancy in developed countries as well as in underdeveloped countries, we have taken the maximum and minimum values of life expectancy as 80 years and 40 years respectively.

The maximum and minimum of the literacy rate as well as of the combined enrolment ratio, have been taken as 100 per cent and 15 per cent respectively. The minimum value has been decided on the basis of the literacy rate in India and in some of the backward states during fifties.

Unlike the UNDP, the Human Development Index constructed in the present study is based on four elements: life expectancy, educational attainment, real per capita SDP and urbanization. The maximum and minimum values of the level of urbanization are taken as 60 per cent and 5 per cent respectively, keeping in mind the level urbanization in India in 1951 and the present level urbanization in developed countries.

The HDI reduces all the four indicators to a common measuring rod by measuring achievement in each indicator as the relative distance from the desired goal. The maximum and the minimum values for each variable, which are fixed, are reduced to a scale between zero and one with each country (or state) at some point on the scale. In the present study due to non-availability of complete data for all the Indian states, only 15 major states have been selected for constructing HDI and for inter-state comparison.

LIFE EXPECTANCY INDEX

Life expectancy is a function of many variables. Prominent among those are health and nutrition. With expansion in the health facilities and increase in the availability of food, the life expectancy is likely to go up. Increase in life expectancy means the returns from human capital would go up as persons already trained and educated are likely to survive for more years.

Table 1 shows the life expectancy indices for 15 major states of India. A look at the table reveals that Kerala is on the top. The life expectancy in Kerala is very close to the life expectancy in developed countries. Madhya Pradesh is at the bottom with a life expectancy of 54 years. The gap in the life expectancy in two states Kerala, whose rank is one, and Punjab, whose rank is second, is quite large (5.6 years). In fact, there are only three states in the table whose life expectancy index is more than 0.60. There are 6 states in the table whose life expectancy index is less than 0.50. Thus, we observe large variation among the 15 states in life expectancy.

EDUCATIONAL ATTAINMENT INDEX

Educational Attainment Index was originally measured only through the adult literacy defined as "the percentage of persons aged 15 and over who can, with understanding, both read and write a short simple statement on everyday life".[5] HDR 1991 broadened this measure to incorporate mean years of schooling. As reliable data on mean years of schooling were not available, educational attainment now include adult literacy with the two-

TABLE 1

Life Expectancy Indices for Major States

Sl. No.	*States*	*Life Expectancy at Birth in Years (1989-93)**	*Life Expectancy Index*	*Rank*
1.	Andhra Pradesh	60.6	0.52	8
2.	Assam	54.9	0.37	14
3.	Bihar	58.5	0.46	10
4.	Gujarat	60.1	0.50	9
5.	Haryana	62.9	0.57	4
6.	Karnataka	61.9	0.55	6
7.	Kerala	72.0	0.80	1
8.	Madhya Pradesh	54.0	0.35	15
9.	Maharashtra	64.2	0.61	3
10.	Orissa	55.5	0.39	13
11.	Punjab	66.4	0.66	2
12.	Rajasthan	58.0	0.45	11
13.	Tamil Nadu	62.4	0.56	5
14.	Uttar Pradesh	55.9	0.40	12
15.	West Bengal	61.5	0.54	7

* Data relates to average over 1989-93 as estimated by SRS and centered at 1991.

Major states include states with population of 10 million and above as per 1991 census.

Source: Government of India, *Economic Survey*, 1997-98, p. 140.

third weight and gross combined primary, secondary and tertiary enrolment with one-third weight. In India up to now, the literacy rate data are available for population aged 7 years and above, therefore, the UNDP methodology has been slightly modified to include literacy rate in place of adult literacy.

The gross combined primary, secondary and tertiary enrolment termed as gross enrolment ratio has been defined by UNDP as "the number of students enrolled in a level of education, whether or not they belong in the relevant age group for that level, as the percentage of the population in the relevant age group for that level". The relevant age group in different levels of education has not been specified by UNDP. State-wise age-specific literacy rates data are not available in India as per 1991 census. For obtaining this information, following method has been used in the study:

State-wise data of population in various age groups are available for the year 1981. These figures of population of different states in the desired age groups have been inflated considering the population growth in period 1981-91 in the concerned state with the assumption that growth of population was evenly distributed in the various age groups. The break-up of age groups is as follows:

Primary level: 5 to 9 years, middle and higher secondary level: 10 to 19 years, higher education: 20 to 29 years. Projected population data in different age groups in different states are given in Table 2.

The combined enrolment figures for primary, middle, higher secondary and higher education pertaining to major states, for the academic year 1991-92 are given in the Table 2, combined enrolment expressed as percentage of the population in the age group 5 to 29 years is known as combined enrolment ratio. These ratios are given in Table 2.

Using the above information we have calculated the educational attainment indices for 15 states for the year 1991 by giving two-third weight to literacy rate and one-third weight to combined enrolment ratio. These indices are given in Table 2.

Table 2 shows that Kerala has the highest educational attainment. However, it does not reveal the whole story as the position of Kerala in terms of the two elements of educational attainment is not the same. While she enjoys the top position in terms of literacy rate, her position in terms of combined enrolment ratio is sixth. This is primarily because of poor enrolment percentage in higher education in which Kerala's rank is eleventh.

Kerala attained the highest literacy rate in the country inspite of the fact that State Government did not spend much on elementary and adult education.[6] This highlights the role of *non-governmental organizations* in expanding formal and non-formal education in the state.

Looking at the variation in the literacy rate and combined enrolment ratio among the states, we notice that there is widespread variation such that the difference in the literacy rates of the two states, Kerala, which is on the top, and Maharashtra, which

TABLE 2

Educational Attainment Indices for Major States

Sl. No.	States	Combined Population in the Age Group of 5-29 Years in 1991 (lakhs)	Combined Enrolment Primary to Higher Education in 1991-92 (lakhs)	Combined Enrolment Ratio 2 as % of 1	Literacy Rate in 1991 (%)	Combined Enrolment Ratio Index	Literacy Rate Index	Educational Attainment Index	Rank
1	*2*	*3*	*4*	*5*	*6*	*7*	*8*	*9*	*10*
1.	Andhra Pradesh	342.6	117.6	34.3	44.1	0.2270	0.340	0.3020	11
2.	Assam	119.9	55.2	46.0	52.9	0.3647	0.446	0.4187	6
3.	Bihar	447.6	125.2	27.9	38.5	0.1500	0.280	0.2400	15
4.	Gujarat	224.9	92.7	41.2	61.3	0.3100	0.540	0.4600	4
S.	Haryana	91.9	31.3	34.0	55.8	0.2230	0.480	0.3993	8
6.	Karnataka	268.2	90.1	33.6	56.0	0.2180	0.482	0.3942	9
7.	Kerala	158.8	61.6	38.8	89.8	0.2800	0.880	0.6800	1
8.	Madhya Pradesh	346.9	117.7	33.9	44.2	0.2220	0.340	0.3000	12
9.	Maharashtra	413.8	175.0	42.3	64.8	0.3211	0.586	0.4976	3

(Contd.)

TABLE 2 *(Contd.)*

1	*2*	*3*	*4*	*5*	*6*	*7*	*8*	*9*	*10*
10.	Orissa	168.1	57.6	34.2	49.1	0.2250	0.400	0.3400	10
11.	Punjab	108.8	37.7	34.6	58.5	0.2300	0.510	0.4200	7
12.	Rajasthan	169.6	71.3	42.0	38.5	0.3170	0.280	0.2900	13
13.	Tamil Nadu	274.7	131.0	47.6	62.7	0.3835	0.561	0.5019	2
14.	Uttar Pradesh	722.5	188.7	26.1	41.6	0.1300	0.310	0.2500	14
15.	West Bengal	376.8	139.4	37.0	57.7	0.2588	0.502	0.4211	5

Sources: 1. CME, *India's Social Sector*, Feb. 1996.

2. Govt. of India, *Economic Survey*, 1995-96, p. 171.

is at second place, is of 25 percentage points. The same difference between Kerala and Bihar, which is at bottom of the table, is of 51.3 percentage points. There are only two states, namely, Kerala and Tamil Nadu, whose educational attainment index is more than 0.50. However, the gap between the educational indices of above two states is quite significant. There are eight states in the table whose educational index is less than 0.40. We can have an idea of the variation in the educational attainments of the 15 states from the coefficient of variation of the educational attainment indices, which is 0.292356.

PER CAPITA INCOME INDEX

Per capita domestic products of 15 states for the year 1991-92 at 1980-81 prices is given in Table 3. The table shows large variation in per capita domestic products of the states. The highest per capita domestic product is of Punjab and the lowest is that of Bihar. An idea of the gap between the above two states can be had from the fact that per capita domestic product of Punjab is more than three times the per capita domestic product of Bihar. Madhya Pradesh, which is the largest state of India in terms of area, has a per capita domestic product which is less than half of the per capita domestic product of Punjab.

A look at the per capita SDP indices of the states in Table 3, reveal that there are only three states, namely, Punjab, Haryana and Maharashtra whose per capita SDP index is more than 0.50. Further, there are eight states in the table whose per capita SDP index is less than 0.30. The coefficient of variation in the per capita SDP index of 15 states is 0.468591.

URBANIZATION INDEX

Urbanization is a part of the development process. It may be taken as an indicator of human development on the assumption that compared to rural areas, life is better in cities. The basis of this assumption is that in cities, better facilities of schooling, health, transport, etc. are available. Further, cities offer relatively more lucrative employment opportunities. We therefore, have included urbanization in the construction of HDI, though the HDI constructed by UNDP does not include it.

TABLE 3

Per Capita Real SDP Indices for Major States

Sl. No.	*States*	*Per Capita SDP at 1980-81 Prices in 1991-92 (Rs.)*		*Per Capita SDP Index*	*Rank*
		Actual	*Log*		
1.	Andhra Pradesh	1,788	3.252	0.252	10
2.	Assam	1,887	3.280	0.280	8
3.	Bihar	1,122	3.050	0.050	15
4.	Gujarat	2,321	3.370	0.370	4
5.	Haryana	3,455	3.540	0.540	2
6.	Karnataka	2,255	3.350	0.350	6
7.	Kerala	1,826	3.260	0.260	9
8.	Madhya Pradesh	1,621	3.210	0.210	12
9.	Maharashtra	3,381	3.530	0.530	3
10.	Orissa	1,530	3.180	0.180	14
11.	Punjab	3,869	3.590	0.590	1
12.	Rajasthan	1,773	3.248	0.248	11
13.	Tamil Nadu	2,309	3.360	0.360	5
14.	Uttar Pradesh	1,589	3.200	0.200	13
15.	West Bengal	2,015	3.300	0.300	7

Source: *Indian Public Finance Statistics*, 1995, p. 82, Ministry of Finance, Govt. of India.

Table 4 gives urbanization indices for 15 states of India. The table shows that Maharashtra has the highest level of urbanization and Assam has the lowest level of urbanization. The difference between the above two states in the level of urbanization is such that the level of urbanization in Maharashtra is more than three times the urbanization level in Assam. A look at the urbanization index of states in the table reveals that there are only three states, namely, Maharashtra, Gujarat and Tamil Nadu, whose urbanization index is more than 0.50. The coefficient of variation in the urbanization index of states is 0.405132.

TABLE 4

Urbanization Indices for Major States

Sl. No.	*States*	*Urbanization in 1991 (%)*	*Urbanization Index*	*Rank*
1.	Andhra Pradesh	26.89	0.40	7
2.	Assam	11.10	0.11	15
3.	Bihar	13.14	0.15	14
4.	Gujarat	34.49	0.54	2
5.	Haryana	24.63	0.36	9
6.	Karnataka	30.92	0.47	4
7.	Kerala	26.39	0.39	8
8.	Madhya Pradesh	23.18	0.33	10
9.	Maharashtra	38.69	0.61	1
10.	Orissa	13.38	0.15	13
11.	Punjab	29.55	0.45	5
12.	Rajasthan	22.88	0.33	11
13.	Tamil Nadu	34.15	0.53	3
14.	Uttar Pradesh	19.84	0.27	12
15.	West Bengal	27.48	0.41	6

Source: CMIE, *India's Social Sector*, Feb. 1996, p. 2, Table 5.

HUMAN DEVELOPMENT INDEX

Human development index as per the methodology of UNDP, is the simple average of three indices: life expectancy index, educational attainment index, and real per capita income index.

We have constructed two human development indices, HDI* and HDI**, for 15 states of India pertaining to the year 1991. These two indices are given in Table 5. The HDI* in the table has been constructed, using the above definition of HDI. It is the simple average of three indices: life expectancy index, educational attainment index, and real per capita SDP index. HDI**, which is the other human development index in the table, is based on four indices. Among these four indices, three are the same as above and the fourth is urbanization index.

Table 5 shows that Kerala[7] is on the top of the table in HDI* but her rank is second in HDI** and Maharashtra, whose

TABLE 5

Human Development Indices for Major States

Sl. No.	*States*	*Life Expectancy Index*	*Educational Attain-ment Index*	*Per Capita SDP Index*	*Urbani-zation Index*	*HDI**	*Rank in HDI**	*HDI***	*Rank in HDI***	*Difference in rank (VI-VIII)*
	(I)	*(II)*	*(III)*	*(IV)*	*(V)*	*(VI)*	*(VII)*	*(VIII)*	*(IX)*	*(X)*
1.	Andhra Pradesh	0.52	0.30	0.25	0.40	0.3570	9	0.3680	9	0
2.	Assam	0.37	0.42	0.28	0.11	0.3566	10	0.2950	13	-3
3.	Bihar	0.46	0.24	0.05	0.15	0.2500	15	0.2250	15	0
4.	Gujarat	0.50	0.46	0.37	0.54	0.4430	6	0.4675	5	1
5.	Haryana	0.57	0.39	0.54	0.36	0.5014	4	0.4660	6	-2
6.	Karnataka	0.55	0.39	0.35	0.47	0.4314	7	0.4410	7	0
7.	Kerala	0.80	0.68	0.26	0.39	0.5800	1	0.5325	2	-1
8.	Madhya Pradesh	0.35	0.30	0.21	0.33	0.2866	13	0.2975	12	1
9.	Maharashtra	0.61	0.50	0.53	0.61	0.5458	3	0.5619	1	1
10.	Orissa	0.39	0.34	0.18	0.15	0.3033	11	0.2650	14	-3
11.	Punjab	0.66	0.42	0.59	0.45	0.5553	2	0.5290	3	-1
12.	Rajasthan	0.45	0.29	0.25	0.33	0.3300	12	0.3300	10	2

13. Tamil Nadu	0.56	0.50	0.36	0.53	0.4739	5	0.4879	4	1
14. Uttar Pradesh	0.40	0.25	0.20	0.27	0.2833	14	0.2800	11	3
15. West Bengal	0.54	0.42	0.30	0.41	0.4203	8	0.4177	8	0

* HDI—Human Development Index based on 1, 2 & 3.

** HDI—Human Development Index based on 1, 2, 3 & 4.

Source: Tables 1, 2, 3 and 4.

TABLE 6

Ranking of States by HDI and Per Capita SDP Index

Sl. No.	*States*	*Rank in HDI**	*Rank in HDI***	*Rank in Per capita SDP Index*	*Difference in Rank (II-IV)*	*Difference in Rank (III-IV)*
	(I)	*(II)*	*(III)*	*(IV)*	*(V)*	*(VI)*
1.	Andhra Pradesh	9	9	10	-1	-1
2.	Assam	10	13	8	2	5
3.	Bihar	15	15	15	0	0
4.	Gujarat	6	5	4	2	1
5.	Haryana	4	6	2	2	4
6.	Karnataka	7	7	6	1	1
7.	Kerala	1	2	9	-8	-7
8.	Madhya Pradesh	13	12	12	1	0
9.	Maharashtra	3	1	3	0	-2
10.	Orissa	11	14	14	-3	0
11.	Punjab	2	3	1	1	2
12.	Rajasthan	12	10	11	1	-1
13.	Tamil Nadu	5	4	5	0	-1
14.	Uttar Pradesh	14	11	13	1	-2
15.	West Bengal	8	8	7	1	1

Source: Table 5.

position is third in HDI* has the first position in HDI**. There are four states, West Bengal, Karnataka, Andhra Pradesh and Bihar whose rank is same in both the indices. Inclusion of urbanization in human development index has improved the HDI rank of 6 states in the table. The maximum gainer is Uttar Pradesh, whose rank has gone up by three points. The HDI rank of the remaining states in the table has gone down as a result of the inclusion of urbanization in the human development index. HDI** compared to HDI* shows more variation among the states in human development as measured by the coefficient of variation of the human development index.

Using HDI** for further analysis, we observe that Maharashtra has the highest HDI and Bihar has the lowest HDI and the difference between the two is such that the HDI of Bihar is less than half of the HDI of Maharashtra. There are only three states: Maharashtra, Kerala and Punjab whose HDI is more than 0.50. However, none of these states are near the level of human development in developed countries or the level of high human development (0.8 or more). They are at best in the category of medium human development (HDI of more than 0.5 and less than 0.8). All other states in the table have low level of human development. There are four states in the table: Bihar, Orissa, U.P. and Assam, whose HDI is less than 0.3, a very low level of human development. Thus, the analysis shows that the majority of the states in India have a low level of human development and there is large inter-state variation in it.

Table 6 gives ranking of 15 states by HDI and per capita SDP. The table shows that there are 6 states whose HDI rank (HDI**) is more than their per capita SDP rank. Prominent among them is Kerala[8], whose HDI rank is 7 points more than her per capita SDP rank. Madhya Pradesh, Orissa and Bihar are the three States in the table whose HDI and SDP ranks are same.

Comparing the HDI and per capita SDP ranks of the states, when HDI does not include urbanization, we find that there are only three states, viz. Kerala, Orissa and Andhra Pradesh, whose HDI rank is higher than their per capita SDP rank. Tamil Nadu, Maharashtra and Bihar are the three states whose HDI and per capita SDP ranks are same. On the basis of the above result we can say that inclusion of urbanization in the HDI has enabled many states to register high HDI rank as compared to their per capita SDP rank.

CONCLUSIONS

Though India is in the category of 'low human development' as per the human development report of UNDP, there are three states in India, viz. Kerala, Maharashtra and Punjab, which are in the category of medium human development. Kerala's achievements are exceptional in the sense that the level of human development has been achieved despite low per capita domestic product. However, the credit for this achievement goes more to *non-governmental organizations* rather than government. However, there are many states in India whose HDI is less than 0.30, which means very low level of human development.

The variation among the states in terms of life expectancy and literacy rate is quite alarming. The gap between the two states, Kerala and Bihar, in terms of life expectancy is of 13.5 years and that in terms of literacy rate is of 31.3 percentage points.

We can conclude by saying that the level of human development is quite low in many states of India and there is widespread inter-state variation in it. However, we cannot wait for substantial increase in income to improve the human development. An all out effort has to be made to improve it.

Notes and References

1. UNDP (1990), *Human Development Report, 1990*, Oxford University Press, New York. On the concept of capabilities, see Dreze, Jean and Sen, A.K. (1989), "Hunger and Public Action", Claredon Press, Oxford.
2. Asian Development Bank (1996), *Asian Development Outlook, 1996-97*, Oxford University Press, New York; p. 128.
3. UNDP (1996), *Human Development Report, 1996*, Oxford University Press, New York, p. 106.
4. "A further consideration is that the indicator should reflect the diminishing returns to transforming income into human capabilities. In other words, people do not need excessive financial resources to ensure a decent living. This aspect was taken into account by using logarithm of real GNP per capita for the income indicator". [UNDP, 1990, *op. cit.*, p. 12].
5. UNDP (1990), *op. cit.*, pp. 182-83.
6. "Association of Indian Universities" (1996), *University News*, March 25, pp. 22-23.
7. HDI rank of Kerala has gone down as a result of the inclusion of urbanization in the human development index. This is because of the peculiar definition of urban settlement in India. There are large number of rural settlements in Kerala, which satisfy all the conditions of urban settlements except the condition that 75 percent of the male work force in an area should be employed in non-agricultural occupations.
8. The real per capita income of Kerala is much higher than her real per capita domestic product due to the large amount of remittances sent by Keralites working abroad. So, the difference in her HDI rank and real per capita income rank is not as large.

PART C

POVERTY ALLEVIATION, EDUCATION AND HUMAN DEVELOPMENT

25

Human Development and Poverty: The Context of India

HEM CHANDRA LAL DAS

Recently the focus of policy prescription has shifted from structural adjustments and growth towards human development and poverty alleviation as indicated by the two major reports in 1990, the UNDP's *Human Development Report* (HDR) which was the first report in a planned annual series, and the World Bank's *World Development Report* (WDR) on poverty. These reports agree on two fundamental conclusions. Firstly, overall growth is essential for sustained human development and poverty alleviation, but it is insufficient for either of the two. It must be complemented by special programmes and policies such as redistributive measures, labour-intensive rural employment generating programmes and re-allocation of resources targeted to basic social and human expenditure. Secondly, the developing and donor countries have enough resources for such programmes, if only these resources are prudently and efficiently used in the priority areas of human development, instead of building arms, excessive policing and other areas of heavy expenditures including 'prestige projects'.

1. HUMAN DEVELOPMENT

It is important to distinguish between 'human development' and 'human resource development'. Traditionally, human resource is defined as the physical and mental capabilities of the people, as labour force, for production of goods, services and further knowledge, and human resource development is defined as the process of improving the quality and efficiency of the people as a factor of production. In economic terms, human resource development is equated with the accumulation of human capital and its productive employment, achieved through education and training, health and nutritional improvement, human power management and housing.

The UN agencies are now broadening the definition of human resource development to focus on options for fostering individual capacities to contribute to their own and others' well-being, mainly but not exclusively through employment in service or production; extend the concept beyond traditional labour force participation to include voluntarism and other forms of social contribution (e.g. informed and responsible parenthood); go beyond strict formal sector employment concepts to include works which are reflective of growing informal sector realities; and emphasize the inter-sectoral nature of effective human resource development policy and practice as inclusive of education or training, experience and work or other opportunities applying competencies in mutually useful and rewarding ways, as well as health, legislative and policy infrastructure for support.

Thus, human resource development is more than just investment in human factor of production. It is developing individual human resourcefulness and constitutes policies and programmes which will sustain equitable opportunities for continuing acquisition and application of knowledge/skills which promote individual autonomy and socio-economic progress and are mutually beneficial to individuals, the community and the larger environment of which they are a part.

Human development, on the other hand, is defined as the process of increasing people's choices and opportunities, in particular, those leading to a long and healthy life, to be knowledgeable; to find access to assets, employment and income needed for a decent standard of living; to participate fully in community decisions, and to enjoy human, economic and political freedom. Thus human development is the development by the people, of the people and for the people. People are not the inputs to some other ends, but are the active partners in and the objectives and beneficiaries of the development process.

The level of human development is measured by 'human development index' (HDI). The HDI is a composite index prepared by the United Nations Development Programme (UNDP) on a scale of 0 to 1, measured by three key components—longevity, knowledge and income, each measured by several parameters. Rankings are in descending order for 114 countries in 1970 and 130 countries in 1990.

The key components of HDI are longevity or life expectancy (proxy for health, nutrition and sanitation), knowledge and decent living standards. When adjusted for gender disparity using the relative shares of males and females in gross domestic product (GDP) and their life expectancy and educational attainment, HDI shows striking disparity between the two sexes, in most countries. The HDI is a relative measurement or ranking among countries and is still in the process of being further improved. One obvious short-coming is the equal weight given to the three key indicators of human development (Gurugharana, 1992).

The HDR gives formulae for assessing the relative focus of public expenditure on high priority areas for human development. The 'human expenditure ratio' (HER) as the percent of national income allotted to the social priority areas is the critical measure which indicates the actual commitment of a government to improve human lives through direct budgetary action.

Human Development Reports (1990-97)

The basic thesis of the HDRs (1990-97) is that it is people who matter—beyond the confusing maze of GNP numbers, beyond the curling smoke of industrial chimneys, beyond the endless fascination with budget deficits and balances of payment crises—it is people who matter. People must be at the centre of the development debate. What really counts is how they participate in economic growth and how they benefit from it. Production process is indispensible, but it cannot be allowed to obscure human lives. The focus of HDRs is on those human lives, how they change over time, how they share these opportunities, how the range of people's choices can be measured—whether economic or political, whether industrial or national. The study of people in national and global setting is the central pre-occupation and the central overwhelming mandate (Haq, 1994).

The '**concept and measurement of human development**' was the main theme of the HDR-1990. The HDR-1990 demonstrated that it is not only the income level of a society which matters, but how well that income has been translated into human lives. Costa Rica had a per capita income only one-third of Oman but its literacy rate was three times higher, its life expectancy ten years longer and its people enjoyed wide range of political freedom.

The '**financing of human development**' was the main theme of the HDR-1991. It argued that most of the developing countries can finance their essential human goals if they have the political will to lower their current military expenditures, privatise their inefficient public enterprises, correct their distorted development priorities, and improve their national governance.

The '**global dimension of human development**' was the main theme of the HDR-1992. This report concluded that income disparity between the richest one billion and the poorest one billion people had doubled over the last three decades and had reached a dangerously high level of 150 times. To put it in a perspective, the income disparity between the 20 percent of the people within nations is far smaller—5 times in Sweden, 6 times in Germany, 9 times in USA and 26 times (the highest) in Brazil. What might be considered politically and socially unacceptable within the nation is being quietly tolerated at the global level. What is more, trade and migration barriers have been denying developing countries—about $500 billion of global market opportunities compared to annual aid of $50 billion. For poor nations, it is better to enjoy equal access to global market opportunities than to be thrown a few small crumbs from the mighty table of the rich nations.

The HDR-1993 had the '**people's participation**' as its main theme, focussed on the irresistible urge of the people to participate in the events and processes which shape their lives. The report found that as many as 90 percent of the people on the globe have only a marginal participation in the real decision-making in their societies—particularly women, some ethnic groups, and certainly the poor. The society is still based on non-participation by the majority. The world is still a world of differences.

'New dimensions of human development' constituted the central theme of the HDR-1994 which focussed its attention on the security. Global security is not just security of territory, it is security of people. It is not security through arms. It is security through jobs, through human development, through environmental sustainability. It is not just security of nations, it is security of individuals in their homes and in the streets. It is not just safeguards against an unpredicted nuclear holocaust, it is a thoughtful response to the threatened travel of global poverty across international frontiers without a passport in the form of drugs, AIDS, pollution, illegal migration and terrorism. For human security, in the last analysis, is a child that did not die, a disease that did not spread, an ethnic violence that did not explode, a dissident who was not silenced. Human security is not a concern with weapons, it is a concern with dignity.

'Gender and human development' formed the basic subject of HDI-1995. The term 'gender' is generally used to indicate the differences between sexes. But more than physical differences, women are exposed to several prejudices and disabilities caused by social, political and economic barriers. Hence, the social scientists are now using the term 'gender' in a broader sense to indicate the social, political and economic handicaps which formed the basis of discrimination based on gender and they formed the subject-matter of several theories explaining gender-based discrimination. The elimination of gender-based discrimination was the main theme of the HDR-1995.

'Economic growth and human development' was the central focus of the HDR-1996. This report pointed out that the high economic growth is not necessarily linked with expansion of job opportunities. It lauded the East Asian Tigers which had emphasised employment generation with economic growth. The report suggested that the developing countries should invest in labour-intensive industries and strengthen the small scale and informal sectors since this would create employment opportunities.

The report called for a political commitment to employment by adopting it as a central policy objective. Defining employment as all ways of securing a livelihood, the report pointed out that people value their work for many reasons beyond only income. Employment empowers people not just economically but socially and politically. For women, earning an income is often critical in gaining more say in decision-making in the family and community.

According to the report, the countries like Indonesia, Malaysia, Singapore, South Korea, Hong Kong managed to achieve rapid growth in both per capita GNP and employment by investment in human capital with a focus on education, access to social services. This has paid big dividend and created a 'virtuous circle' in which worker's productivity had risen and triggered an increase in real wages which in turn attracted more investment in human capital.

'**Poverty alleviation and human development**' constituted the core subject of the HDR-1997. During the last 50 years various countries of the world have made laudable attempts for eradicating poverty. The developing countries have brought the infant mortality rate to half, malnutrition to one-third, 25 percent increase in admission of children to school since 1960, and the developing countries have made such an impressive progress during the last 30 years which the developed countries took 100 years. Still a large chunk of the world population is imprisoned in the condition of low income and suffocating life. About 1.3 billion people are compelled to lead their lives with less than US $ 1 per day. Developed nations also are suffering from poverty. Even in the developed countries of North America and Europe about 100 million people are living in poverty out of which 27 million are unemployed. In the world, there are at least 30 countries which have witnessed a decline in HDI in comparison to that in 1970.

The HDR-1997 has thrown light on the issue of universality, intensity and complexity of poverty and has suggested a six-point action plan for poverty alleviation. These points are: (a) initiative of people-oriented policies, (b) gender equality, (c) focussing on the plight of the poor, (d) better management of globalisation, (e) favourable political will, and (f) special action in special circumstances to avoid economic failures.

2. HUMAN DEVELOPMENT IN INDIA

Human Development Index (HDI) for India alongwith its rank and the number of countries has been presented in Table 1. The table reveals that the HDI value for India was 0.439, its rank was 95 among 130 countries in 1990. It means that 92 countries

TABLE 1

Human Development Index (HDI) and Relative Rank of India (1970 and 1990 to 1997)

Years	*Human Development Index (HDI)*	*India's Rank*	*Number of countries covered*
1970	0.254	82	114
1990	9.439	93	130
1991	0.308	123	160
1992	0.439	134	170
1993	0.309	134	173
1994	0.382	135	173
1995	0.439	134	173
1996	0.436	135	174
1997	0.446	138	175

Source: UNDP, *Human Development Reports* (1990 to 1997).

(70.77 percent) were above India and 37 countries (28.46 percent) were below India in the descending order list of HDI obtained by the various countries. In 1991 the HDI value for India was 0.308, its rank was 123 out of 160 countries, with the highest and the lowest indices of 0.993 and 0.048 obtained by Japan and Seirra Leone respectively.

In 1993 the HDI for India was 0.309 and its rank was 134 out of 173 countries. Thus, while in 1991 there were 133 (76.87 percent) countries above India and 39 (22.54 percent) countries below it in the context of human development index, in 1994 there were 133 (77.46 percent) countries with higher indices and 38 (21.96 percent) countries with lower indices of human development than that of India.

In 1995 the HDI for India was 0.439, its rank was 134 out of 173 countries. Similarly in 1996 and 1997, the HDIs for India were 0.436 and 0.446 with its ranks of 135th and 138th out of 174 and 175 countries respectively.

It may be noted with satisfaction that the average value of HDI has improved during 1990-97. However, such improvement is not unique for India and it is almost universal among more than 150 countries. Moreover, a look at relative ranking of India implicitly informs poor performance in fostering human development. In sum, although in absolute terms, there has been an improvement but in relation to other nations on the globe, effort in India towards human development has been sluggish during the period 1990-97 (Rao, 1997, p. 488).

Poverty

Poverty anywhere is a danger to peace and prosperity everywhere. Economic inequality and incidence of poverty portray the distributional consequences of the operation of the economic processes. They are generated and governed in a given distribution milieu by the interaction of economic and socio-political forces.

Poverty is a socio-economic phenomenon. Studies undertaken from time to time defined poverty in different ways. Nevertheless, the concept of poverty has, by and large, remained nebulous. It is difficult to define poverty in precise terms because its connotation not only differs from country to country, but also at different points of time in the same country. To be precise, the concept of poverty undergoes change with the economic development of the country.

Some economists have defined poverty in terms of 'basic' or 'minimum needs' which include, *inter alia,* food, clothes, education, housing and health. Generally, minimum physical quantities of different items of food or calorie or nutrition requirements to keep the body and soul together is determined. The money income needed to acquire the physical quantities is taken as the per capita expenditure of the consumer for a particular base year. Family whose income/expenditure is less than the 'critical level' (often termed as 'poverty line') are classified as poor. This is what is called generally 'absolute poverty'.

Thus, an individual or a family is called poor if its standard of living is below specified minimum, called the 'poverty line'. Traditionally, standard of living is measured by income or consumption. But the HDR has added 'human dimensions' to this concept, in particular educational attainment (proxy for knowledge) and life expectancy (proxy for health, nutrition, and sanitation). In the popular measure of poverty index, however, only the economic dimension is used, mainly because of the difficulty of assigning suitable weights to the social dimension. While using the poverty index it is important to remember that other aspects of welfare, such as health, life expectancy, education and access to public goods and resources are not adequately reflected by income/ consumption alone.

Another approach perceives poverty in terms of relative income. This approach envisages the estimation and comparison of income of bottom 5 or 10 percent of population with that of top 5 or 10 percent of population. It thus goes without saying that the concept of absolute poverty has more relevance for a developing economy like India than the relative one.

The commonly known measurement of poverty is in terms of the so-called Head-count ratio (HC). The Head-count index measures poverty incidence as the percent of population below poverty line. If Np is the number of individuals below the poverty lines, and N is the total population, then Np/N or its percent form is the head-count index of poverty. As a special case of the Foster-Greer-Thorbecke or FGT measure, the head-count index is also denoted by Po. It is the simplest and most widely used measure but ignores the 'depth' of poverty and the distribution of income among the poor. If income is transferred from a poor person to some one poorer or *vice versa*, this measure is not affected. Hence, this measure may not be suitable for devising and monitoring poverty alleviation programmes for the so-called hard core 'poor'. Thus, HC ratio is a crude and non-discriminatory measurement of poverty lacking the necessary refinements.

This takes one to Sen's P index of poverty measurement. According to Professor Sen, one should examine the income shortfall of each person from the poverty line. A weighted norm of the income shortfalls of the poor persons can be viewed as a measure of poverty. This is the basis of Sen's P index for poverty measurement. According to Sen, many systems of weighting are possible. But one important characteristic the weight may be required to satisfy is that a poorer person's income shortfall should receive a higher weight than the income shortfall of a person who is richer than the first person despite being below poverty line. One simple method of doing this is to take the rank values of the poor in the income ranking as the weights to be put on the income shortfalls of the different persons within the category of the poor.

Ginni Concentration Ratio

There is some amount of affinity between P coefficient and Ginni's Coefficient (or Ginni's Concentration Ratio). The Ginni coefficient is obtained by calculating the ratio of the area between the diagonal and Lorenz curve to the total area of the half square in which the curve lies.

Poverty in India

The problem of poverty in India is the problem of low national income and its unequal distribution, of slow pace of development and inequitable distribution of the small gains of development.

A comprehensive review of the literature on poverty and income distribution in India is available in *A Survey of Indian Econometric Literature* (eds. N.S. Iyengar and N. Bhattacharya: 1988). Since the publication of this survey, a large number of research papers, monographs and books have appeared, dealing with different aspects of poverty. Recently, there has been a growing interest in measuring the incidence of poverty than in measuring the inequality *per se*. These studies differ widely in respect of their definition, coverage, data-base and method of calculating the poverty line (Iyengar, 1989).

The Planning Commission used Rs. 20 at 1960-61 prices as the poverty line for all-India on a per capita monthly basis. Bardhan (1970) assumed a nutrition norm of 2,250 calories per head per day and used its expenditure equivalent of Rs. 180 per capita per annum at 1960-61 prices, based on National Sample Survey (NSS) data for rural India. Dandekar and Rath (1991), using the same source of data and calorie norm estimated the poverty cut-offs for rural and urban households as Rs. 180 and Rs. 270 at 1960-61 prices on a per capita and per annum basis. Ojha (1972) used a combination of NSS data and the official statistics of foodgrains availability. He assumed that 518 grammes of foodgrains per head per day could provide 80 percent of the calorie norm of 2,250 units in rural areas. Similarly, for the urban households, it was assumed that 432 grammes would provide 66 percent of the same norm. The corresponding monthly per capita expenditure limits were estimated to be Rs. 15 to Rs. 18 and Rs. 8 to Rs. 11 at 1960-61 prices for rural and urban sectors respectively. Ahluwalia (1978) used Rs. 180 per capita per annum at 1960-61 prices, used earlier by Dandekar and Rath (1971). Vaidyanathan (1974) assumed Rs. 240 per capita per month at 1960-61 prices as the rural poverty line, based on NSS data. Minhas (1970) using the national income statistics on consumption published by the Central Statistical Organisation (CSO) had estimated the poverty line for rural households as Rs. 200 at 1960-61 prices.

One needs to consider the state specific patterns of diet and price indices facing different fractile groups of income distribution and their variations to estimate the incidence and severity of poverty across different states—a fact long ignored by the Planning Commission and the Government in its bid to over-emphasise the success of poverty alleviation programmes. This was first suggested in a seminal paper by Ahluwalia (1978) who provided state specific poverty lines to estimate the percent of people in rural and urban areas in different states of India. Similar procedure was applied by Kakwani and Subbarao (1990), Chatterjee and Bhattacharya (1997), Mahendra Dev and Ranade (1997) among others, and also by Lakdawala Committee appointed by the Government of India.

While it is futile to use an all-India poverty line based on all-India dietary norm and all-India price indices to estimate the extent of poverty and inequality across the different states, it is clear from the discussion on poverty lines that the choice is arbitrary for all practical purposes so that various estimates of the incidence of poverty in India remain basically arbitrary in nature (Chatterjee, 1997). Tables 2 and 3 present the estimates of poverty and the severity of poverty based on two alternative all-India poverty lines, and Table 4 presents the state-wise, poverty percentage based on state specific poverty lines. It may be noted that the incidence of poverty is measured by the Head-count Ratio and the severity of poverty is measured by FGT Index.

Table 5 presents the state-wise distribution of population below the poverty line for 1993-94 based on Lakdawala criteria.

The policies of economic reforms and liberalisation initiated during the Eighth Five Year Plan under the pressure of the World Bank an the I.M.F. have not helped in solving the problems like poverty, unemployment, illiteracy, malnutrition, regional imbalances and ecological degradation. Rather these problems have been aggravated to some extent.

Growth with equity and social justice has been set as the

TABLE 2

Incidence of Poverty in India: Alternative Estimates

Years	*Rural*		*Urban*		*Ginni*	
	HC-I	*HC-II*	*HC-I*	*HC-II*	*Rural*	*Urban*
1	*2*	*3*	*4*	*5*	*6*	*7*
1970-71	57.33	45.29	45.89	37.06	0.288	0.346
1972-73	57.21	45.90	47.00	37.69	0.305	0.345
1973-74	56.17	44.50	49.20	39.33	0.282	0.317
1977-78	54.47	43.06	42.86	33.47	0.312	0.337
1983	49.02	37.54	38.33	28.77	0.301	0.334
1986-87	45.21	34.04	35.39	27.24	0.302	0.356
1987-88	44.88	32.44	36.52	27.23	0.302	0.356
1988-89	42.23	29.97	35.07	26.28	0.295	0.356
1989-90	36.69	24.84	34.76	26.28	0282	0.356
1990-91	37.48	25.97	35.04	26.00	0.277	0.340
1991	40.07	28.12	34.79	25.74	0.311	0.351
1992	46.12	33.95	36.37	27.56	0.298	0.356
1993	44.19	30.94	38.36	29.27	0.284	0.337
1993-94	39.65	27.65	30.94	22.63	0.285	0.345

Notes: 1. Poverty indicator marked with I refers to its being based on Planning Commission's all-India poverty line of monthly per capita total expenditure (MPCTE) of Rs. 49.09 for rural and Rs. 56.64 for urban at 1973-74 prices.

2. Poverty indicator marked with II refers to its being based on alternative all-India Poverty line of MPCTE of Rs. 15 for rural and Rs. 18 for urban at 1960-61 prices.

Source: S. Mahendra Dev and K. Ranade (1997), "Intensity of Poverty in India: State-wise analysis" in *Indian Development Report* (1997), Indira Gandhi Institute of Development Research, Bombay.

broad objective of the Ninth Five Year Plan. For this the Ninth Plan has the following objectives:

1. To create sufficient productive employment and to accord high priority to agricultural and rural development for eradicating rural poverty.

TABLE 3

Intensity of Poverty in India Based on Two Poverty Lines

Years	*Rural*		*Urban*	
	FGT-I	*FGT-II*	*FGT-I*	*FGT-II*
1970-71	0.0731	0.0481	0.0532	0.0353
1972-73	0.0754	0.0501	0.0532	0.0349
1973-74	0.0672	0.0430	0.0531	0.0342
1977-78	0.0685	0.0451	0.0481	0.0320
1983	0.0545	0.0345	0.0366	0.0231
1986-87	0.0460	0.0281	0.0354	0.0225
1987-88	0.0404	0.0238	0.0338	0.0211
1988-89	0.0354	0.0203	0.0319	0.0196
1989-90	0.0279	0.0154	0.0321	0.0199
1990-91	0.0316	0.0180	0.0327	0.0206
1991	0.0311	0.0171	0.0323	0.0203
1992	0.0423	0.0247	0.0338	0.0210
1993	0.0354	0.0197	0.0360	0.0223
1993-94	0.0314	0.0175	0.0264	0.0161

Source: S. Tendulkar and L.R. Jain (1997), "Economic Reforms and Poverty", *Economic and Political Weekly*, June.

2. To boost economic development with price stability.
3. Food and nutrition guarantee to all, especially the weaker sections of the society.
4. To provide basic minimum needs like safe drinking water, primary health care, universal primary education.
5. To check rapid growth in population.
6. To empower women and socially weaker sections like schedule castes, scheduled tribes, and other backward castes as agents of socio-economic transformation and development.
7. To ensure ecological and environmental potentiality of development process by social harmony and people's participation at all stages.
8. To encourage and develop people's participatory institutions like Panchayati Raj institutions,

TABLE 4

Incidence of Rural Poverty as per Expert Group and Official Estimates (1987-88)

Sl. No.	*States*	*Head-count Ratio for Rural Poor (as per Lakdawala Committee)*	*Official Estimates of Rural Poor*	*Difference between the two estimates (Col. 3-Col. 2)*
	1	*2*	*3*	*4*
1.	Andhra Pradesh	20.92	33.8	12.88
2.	Assam	39.35	24.5	-14.85
3.	Bihar	52.63	42.7	-9.93
4.	Gujarat	28.67	21.2	-7.47
5.	Haryana	16.22	25.0	-4.52
6.	Karnataka	32.82	35.9	3.08
7.	Kerala	29.10	16.4	-12.70
8.	Madhya Pradesh	41.92	41.5	-0.42
9.	Maharashtra	40.78	36.7	-4.08
10.	Orissa	57.64	48.3	-9.34
11.	Punjab	12.60	7.2	-5.60
12.	Rajasthan	33.21	26.0	-7.21
13.	Tamil Nadu	45.80	39.5	-6.30
14.	Uttar Pradesh	41.10	37.2	-3.90
15.	West Bengal	48.30	30.3	-18.00
	All-India	39.06	33.4	-5.66

Sources: 1. Lakdawala Committee and the Planning Commission.
2. Biswajit Chatterjee, "Poverty in India : What We Have Learnt?" *1st Amrit Jubilee (80th) Conference Volume*, Indian Economic Association, Hyderabad, December 29-31, 1997.

cooperatives, non-government and voluntary organisations.

9. To strengthen attempts for attaining self-reliance.

TABLE 5

State-wise Distribution of Population Below Poverty Line (1993-94)

States	*Population Below Poverty Line*					
	No. of people (Lakh)	*Percent*	*No. of People (Lakh)*	*Percent*	*No. of People (Lakh)*	*Percent*
	Rural		*Urban*		*Total*	
1. Andhra Pradesh	79.49	15.92	80.64	41.51	160.13	23.08
2. Arunachal Pradesh	3.62	45.01	0.19	13.15	3.81	40.18
3. Assam	94.33	45.01	3.45	13.15	97.78	41.46
4. Bihar	450.66	58.21	55.83	45.34	506.62	56.44
5. Goa	0.38	5.34	1.47	26.04	1.85	14.48
6. Gujarat	62.16	22.18	41.77	27.07	103.93	23.92
7. Haryana	36.56	28.02	5.85	13.09	42.41	24.21
8. Himachal Pradesh	15.40	30.34	0.43	5.56	15.83	28.39
9. J & K	19.05	30.34	1.74	8.58	20.79	25.03
10. Karnataka	95.99	29.88	60.58	40.21	156.57	33.18
11. Kerala	55.95	25.76	24.65	29.57	80.59	26.82
12. Madhya Pradesh	216.19	40.64	82.88	48.70	209.07	42.60
13. Maharashtra	193.33	37.93	138.33	34.03	301.65	38.43
14. Manipur	6.33	45.01	0.80	13.15	7.16	35.61
15. Meghalaya	7.09	45.01	0.49	13.15	7.58	38.95
16. Mizoram	1.64	45.01	0.52	13.15	2.16	28.47
17. Nagaland	4.85	45.01	0.33	13.15	5.18	38.95
18. Orissa	140.90	49.72	19.21	40.59	160.11	48.41
19. Punjab	17.76	11.95	5.87	9.08	23.63	11.08
20. Rajasthan	94.68	26.46	35.08	31.63	129.76	27.68
21. Sikkim	1.81	45.01	0.60	13.15	1.87	41.96
22. Tamil Nadu	121.70	32.48	89.65	44.34	211.35	36.63
23. Tripura	11.41	45.01	0.64	13.15	12.05	39.89
24. Uttar Pradesh	496.17	42.28	110.34	36.06	606.51	40.99
25. West Bengal	209.90	40.80	44.86	22.51	254.76	35.69
26. A. & N. Islands	0.73	32.48	0.37	44.34	1.10	35.71
27. Chandigarh	0.06	9.08	0.58	9.08	0.64	9.08
28. D. & N.H.	0.72	51.95	0.05	39.00	0.77	0.76
29. Daman & Diu	0.03	5.34	0.14	26.04	0.17	15.32
30. Delhi	0.19	1.90	14.64	15.31	14.83	14.04
31. Lakshadweep	0.06	25.76	0.10	29.57	0.16	28.03
32. Pondicherry	0.93	32.48	2.65	44.34	3.58	40.49
All-India	2440.19	39.23	794.17	35.66	3734.46	36.31

Source: Sunder Lal Kukreja, "घटते आंकड़े: बढ़ते गरीब", *Hindustan* (Sunday), New Delhi, 1996, p. 1.

The Government of India and the United Nations Development Programme (UNDP) have agreed to support community-based pro-poor initiatives. Called the Community Co-operation Frame, the overall objective of the project is to empower communities to work together for poverty alleviation. The executing agency of the programme support is the Ministry of Rural Areas and Employment, Government of India. The project will be implemented through government agencies, autonomous bodies, non-government organisations and the Panchayati Raj Institutions. The estimated date of completion of the project is March 2001. The overall objective is to support national efforts toward empowerment of communities for poverty alleviation through people-centered development. The key element of the programme is grass-root planning and self-reliance.

The world today is beset with many nagging problems, the major being poverty, hunger, ill-health and disease. A relentless struggle is on to overcome these problems, but human efforts have met with only partial success as the problems do keep growing.

We in India, too, have been waging a constant battle against these problems which have caused extreme misery to the entire world. Our measures to combat these problems especially since Independence are symbolic of our resolve to contribute our mite to the global efforts. Though we have succeeded on the food front to a great extent, our efforts for banishing poverty and containment of disease have yet to fully fructify. Let us work on the 6-point action plan: (a) food for all, (b) cloth for all, (c) house for all, (d) education for all, (e) health for all, and finally, (f) jobs for all.

References

Ahluwalia, M.S. (1978), "Rural Poverty and Agricultural Performance in India", *The Journal of Development Studies*, Vol. 20, No. 5.

Bardhan, P.K. (1970), *Poverty in India*, Statistical Publishing Society, Calcutta.

Chatterjee, Biswajeet and Swati Bhattacharya (1997), "Poverty in India—A Study of Inter-State Variations", Paper presented at DSA national conference on Fifty years of Indian Economic Development and Regional Imbalances, Department of Economics, Jadavpur University, March.

Dandekr, V.M. and Nilkanth Rath (1971), "Poverty in India : Dimensions and Trends", *Economic and Political Weakly*, Vol. 6, Nos. 1 and 2, January 2 and 9.

5. Dev, Mahendra S. and K. Ranade (1997), "Intensity of poverty in India : A State-wise Analysis", in Kirit Parikh (ed.), *India Development Report (1997)*, Indira Gandhi Institute of Development Research, Bombay.

Foster, J., J. Greer and Erick Thorbeck (1984), "A Case of Decomposable Poverty Measures", *Econometrica.*

Gurugharana, Kishor K. (1992), "Poverty Alleviation and Human Development: An Appraisal of the Nepalese Case", Paper presented at national economic conference on *The Future of Nepalese Economy*, organised by Nepal Foundation for Advanced Studies (NFFAS) and Friedrich Ebert Stiftung (FES), Kathmandu, Nepal, June 4-5.

Haq, Mahabub-ul (1994), "Human Development and Human Security", *Southern Economist*, Vol. 52, No. 18, January 15.

Iyengar, N.S. (1989), "Recent Studies on Poverty in India : A Survey", Presidential Address to the *26th Econometric Conference*, Indira Gandhi Institute of Development Research, Bombay, January 2-4.

Iyengar, N.S. and N. Bhattacharya (1988), *A Survey of Indian Econometric Literature*, Vol. 7, Allied Publishers, Bombay.

Kakwani, N. and K. Subbarao (1990), "Rural Poverty and its Alleviation in India", *Economic and Political Weekly*, March.

Kukreja, Sunder Lal (1996), "घटते आंकड़े: बढ़ते गरीब", *Hindustan* (Sunday), December 29, 1996, New Delhi.

Minhas, B.S. (1970), "Rural Poverty, Land Re-distribution and Development", *Indian Economic Review*, Vol. 5, No. 1.

Ojha, P.D. (1972), "Configuration of India's Poverty—Inequality and Levels of Living", in A.J. Tonesea (ed.) *Challenge of Poverty in India*, Vikas Publishing House, New Delhi.

Parikh, Kirit, (1997), *India Development Report (1997)*, Indira Gandhi Institute of Development Research, Bombay.

Rao, S. Kishan (1997), "Economic Reforms in India : How Robust or Bleak is the Performance of Human Development and Why?", *1st Amrit Jubilee (80th) Conference Volume*, The Indian Economic Association, Hyderabad, December 29-31, 1997.

Sen, Amartya K. (1974), "Poverty, Inequality and Unemployment", *Economic and Political Weekly*, Vol. 6, Nos. 31-33.

Srinivasan, T.N. and P.K. Bardhan (Eds.) (1974), *Poverty and Income Distribution in India*, Statistical Publishing Society, Calcutta.

Tonesea, A.J. (ed.) (1972), *Challenge of Poverty in India*, Vikas Publishing House, New Delhi.

Vaidyanathan, A. (1974), "Some Aspects of Inequality in Living Standard in Rural India", in T.N. Srinivasan and P.K. Bardhan (eds.), *Poverty and Income Distribution in India*, Statistical Publishing Society, Calcutta.

26

Poverty Alleviation Programme in India: A Critical Assessment

NASEEM A. ZAIDI

During the decades of 1950's and 1960's the development economists remained under a myth that the gains of economic growth automatically permeate to benefit the poor. Since early 1970's, it was realized that the process of trickle-down is not automatic and special poverty alleviation programmes are required to provide a 'safety net' for the poor to achieve the objective of development with social justice. Mahbub-ul-Haq aptly remarked, "We were taught to take care of our GNP as it will take care of poverty. Let us reverse this and take care of poverty as this will take care of GNP."[1]

While formulating the policies for the Fifth Five Year Plan in India, it was realized that larger resource allocation for better endowed regions, sectors and sections of society, neglecting the less privileged ones, was not an appropriate strategy for poverty alleviation. The new strategy adopted in the Plan was to initiate specific programmes to benefit the target groups in the areas of minimum needs, employment generation and asset formation, etc. But, inspite of plethora of programmes, the dream of poverty alleviation could not be translated into reality and it still remains a mirage. Under the New Economic Policy initiated in July 1991, the emphasis on 'Social Safety Nets' and adjustment being put through with a 'human face' seem to be hollow slogan than serious efforts to lift up the masses above poverty line.

POVERTY MEASUREMENT

In India, the divergence between the official claims about reduction in poverty ratios during the last decade as so, on one hand and the declining level of average wage goods particularly in rural areas has resulted in myths and misconceptions regarding the methodology of measurement of poverty levels. While statisticians might quibble with the definitions and methodologies, the fact remains that after half a century of freedom from colonial rule, half of the country still lives in a deprived condition.

The Task Force set-up by the Planning Commission on the basis of nutritional requirements recommended by the Expert Group of ICMR (1968) worked out the nutritional requirement as 2,400 and 2,100 calories per capita per day in rural and urban areas respectively. The criterion was followed for estimation of poverty during the Sixth Plan. The next step in the measurement of poverty is the identification of a group of food and non-food items that would ensure the required amount of calories. The Planning Commission converted the calories criterion into consumption expenditure that would ensure calorie intake. Consumption expenditure norms have been revised from time to time depending upon the real value of money affected by inflation. For 1993-94, the Planning Commission estimated poverty on the basis of Sub-Sample I of the data on household 'consumption' expenditure supplied by the National Sample Survey (NSS) Organization (50th Round, 1993-94) and used a 'poverty line' of Rs. 226.9 per capita per month for rural areas and Rs. 264.1 per capita per month for urban areas at 1993-94 prices.[2]

EXTENT OF ABSOLUTE POVERTY

There has been a considerable gap between the official and non-official estimates about the magnitude of poverty in India. As poverty alleviation indicates the success of economic policy, each

TABLE 1

Poverty Estimates in India

Years	*Percentage of persons below poverty line*							
	Planning Commission			*Expert Group*			*Tendulkar and Jain*	
	Rural	*Urban*	*Total*	*Rural*	*Urban*	*Total*	*Rural*	*Urban*
1987-88	33.4	20.1	29.9	39.1	40.1	39.3	44.8	38.5
1991-92							48.0	33.8
1993-94	21.7	11.8	18.9	40.2*	36.2*	39.0*		

* Estimated by Dr. S.P. Gupta.

Sources: 1. CMIE, *India's Social Sector*, February 1996, p. 261.

2. Tendulkar and Jain (1995), Economic Reforms and Poverty, *Economic and Political Weekly*, June 10, 1995.

successive government claims to reduce poverty level to a great extent. But, individual researchers expose the loopholes of the methodology adopted by the government in the estimation of poverty level. In India, poverty is measured in absolute terms which is defined as the number of people living below a specified minimum level of income/expenditure rather than in a relative term indicating relative income shares of various percentile groups within a given population.

It was claimed in the official estimates that the percentage of poor living below the poverty line had declined sharply from over 35 per cent in 1980's to under 20 per cent by the mid-90's. The Planning Commission constituted an Expert Group to look into the methodology of estimation of poverty at National and State levels. The group submitted its report in June 1993 and estimated poverty ratios in India for 1987-88. However, Dr. S.P. Gupta, Member, Planning Commission, using the methodology of Expert Group for poverty estimation estimated a poverty ratio of 39 per cent in 1993-94 against the Planning Commission Estimates of 18.9 per cent. In December 1998, the Planning Commission revised its own estimates on poverty and it was revealed that poverty ratio in India during 1994-95 was 39 per cent against the earlier underestimation at 18.9 per cent in 1993-94. The change was due to adoption of a modified version of methodology suggested by the expert group known as Lakdawala Committee and it was accepted that "the committee's method yields an estimate closer to ground reality."[3] The new estimates indicated that there was no decline in the proportion of poor since the mid-1980's and it stood at 39 per cent in the year 1987-88 as well as in 1994-95.

Earlier it was assumed by the Planning Commission that individuals under-state consumption expenditure and hence these estimates were 'adjusted' upwards. The Lakdawala Committee argued that since it was the rich, not the poor, who under-state their consumption expenditure, it was wrong to adjust expenditure upwards before arriving at a poverty measure.

UNDP in its annual report[4] advocated measuring poverty by direct indicators like health and education indicated by percentage of children under 5 who are underweight, percentage of births unattended by trained health personnel and percentage of women aged 15 years and above who are illiterate, and found these indicators to be superior to indirect monetary measure in terms of per capita expenditure as a large part of expenditure may be spent on non-essential goods and services. Emphasis was laid on female literacy in the report in the following words:

> "Educating women has a powerful multiplier effect on the well-being of families and on a society's general level of human development. As a woman becomes literate, fertility rate falls, infant and child health improves, children's educational level increases and household nutritional and sanitary conditions improve."[5]

UNDP called the measure as Capability Poverty Measure (CPM) and found that extent of deprived class in India was as high as 45-50 per cent.

The National Council of Applied Economic Research (NCAER), in a country-wide project[6] covering more than 33,000 households in rural India, adopting CPM concept of UNDP with slight modification, found the extent of poverty in rural India to be 45 per cent; by using 'wasting' concept (underweight children) and 52 per cent by using 'stunting concept' (short statured children). From all the above studies it may be concluded that 40-50 per cent of India's population is unprivileged and deprived of the basic necessities of life.[7]

OBSTACLES IN POVERTY ALLEVIATION

Special poverty alleviation programmes were launched in India about two decades back, but inspite of enormous financial resources diverted for achieving the goals the overall success has been dismal. The main causes of insufficient progress have been as follows:

1. Slow Progress of Agricultural Sector

As a large chunk of poor population depends upon agriculture, retarded growth of the sector has resulted in slow progress of poverty alleviation. Ahluwalia (1978)[8] demonstrated that the "proportion of rural poor fluctuates with agricultural performance and falls in period of good agricultural output". Apart from output, rising prices of wage-goods particularly foodgrains, have adversely affected poverty alleviation programmes. The number of rural people below the poverty line increased from 209 million in 1989-90 to 245 million in 1993-94. The real wages of unskilled workers fell in 1994-95 apparently due to steep rise in issue prices of foodgrains under the public distribution system. In general, the rapid increase in the prices of food articles in the period 1990-95 has adversely affected the real consumption of the poor. Per capita availability of cereals declined from 486.5 grams in 1990-91 to 434.2 in 1991-92 and further to 427.4 in 1992-93.[9] This was due to larger growth rate of population as compared to growth rate of cereal production. The growth rate of rice production declined in 1992-93 by 2.4 per cent as compared to previous year while a decline in 1995-96 was observed to be 1.4 per cent.

2. Slow Growth of Employment Opportunities

Higher dependency rate due to insufficient employment generation increases the level of human deprivation. Studies based on the NSS data for 1993-94 show that the rate of growth of non-agricultural employment particularly in rural areas, has slowed down.[10] The NSS data 1993-94 indicated that daily employment marginally declined in rural areas from 2.8 per cent during 1983-88 to 2.2 per cent during 1987-94. Economic reforms in India are mainly designed to benefit industrial sector, export sector and foreign investment. No reform has been suggested for agricultural sector, rural and urban unorganized sectors which provide a major chunk of employment opportunities.

3. Low Social Expenditure Ratio

Insufficient increase in public expenditure on social sector in general and poverty alleviation programmes in particular as a result of fiscal stabilization programme under the NEP has been one of the causes of slow progress of poverty alleviation programmes. "The massive increase in rural poverty by over 60 million people in the first 18 months of reforms was, to a very large extent, a direct result of the stabilization-*cum*-structural adjustment policies."[11] It has been found in various studies analysing the trends of social expenditure that while in case of the Union government, there has been some proportionate increases in public expenditure on social priority sector, in case of the states which account for 80 per cent of social expenditure, the declining trends have been decreased. S. Guhan[12] found that in case of the Union government during 1990-96, the outlay on rural development and social services as percentage of total expenditure increased from 22.1 per cent in 1990-91 to 31.3 per cent in 1995-96, in case of the states it remained static at 38 per cent during the period. S. Sudhakar[13] analysed the allocation pattern of government budgetary expenditure on social sector for the period 1986-96 and found that social expenditure in case of the state governments declined from an average of 43 per cent of the total expenditure during 1987-91 to 39.9 per cent for 1991-95. One of the reasons of lower social priority sector expenditure by the states was a declining trend of grants from the Union government to states which shrunk from the level of around 19 per cent of the total expenditure of the Union government during 1992-94 to 16 per cent in 1995-96 (B.E.).[14] The finances of the Union government are in disarray due to excessive burden of interest payment which takes 70 per cent of the tax revenue and 50 per cent of combined tax and non-tax revenue of the Union government.

4. Implemental Deficiencies

The strategies of successful implementation are crucial to poverty alleviation programmes. A. Aziz[15] (1994) reviewed the strategies of poverty alleviation programmes in India and pointed out the following deficiencies in the programmes:

(a) Inadequate project planning, particularly with regard to assessing project viability and sustainability.
(b) Inability to get cooperation at grass-root level.
(c) Leakage of benefits due to misidentification of beneficiaries and misutilisation of resources by the beneficiaries.
(d) Unproductive nature of assets acquired or created.
(e) Lack of political will and clout to implement the programmes successfully.

5. **Underutilisation of Financial Resources**

Poverty alleviation programmes in India suffer from a paradox. On one side there is a problem of financial resource crunch and on the other side underutilisation of the available resources, particularly due to above stated deficiencies, is a major problem. The utilization ratios under the various programmes have been summarized in Table 2.

TABLE 2

Utilization Ratios under Poverty Alleviation Programmes (All-India Level)

(Percentage of total allocation)

Programme	*Year of Reference*	*Utilization ratio*
1. Integrated Rural Development Programme	1995	38.2
2. Jawahar Rozgar Yojna	1994-95	45.5
3. Employment Assurance Scheme	1994-95	56.7

Source: CMIE, *India's Social Sector*, February 1996, Tables 279-82.

Due to poor implementation of IRDP, S. Guhan[16] found a good case for winding up the IRDP and for replacing it with alternative lending modalities such as project lending by NABARD for various economic activities which benefit groups of less privileged classes. Poverty alleviations in India has become a hollow slogan rather than a commitment on the part of the government or pressure groups in society. In the opinion of Kuldeep Mathur,

"The capitalist model of development has not provided adequate support for policies to remove poverty. In fact, the dominant class has supported the trickle down philosophy because that alone is a justification for pursuing the capitalist path of development".[17]

SUGGESTIONS FOR POVERTY ALLEVIATION

The following suggestions are worth consideration:

1. Poverty reduction in India is highly correlated with increase in agricultural output. Thus, there is strong case for diverting more resources to this sector.
2. Mostly poor get employment opportunities in unorganised sectors. Rapid growth of labour-intensive exports may provide a fillip in employment generation.
3. Special employment and poverty alleviation programmes comprising wage employment and credit linked self-employment play a crucial role in achieving the objectives. The implementation part of the programme should be modified in the light of various evaluation studies conducted by the government or private agencies and in the light of suggestions by individual researchers.
4. Higher allocation of public expenditure for social priority sector and to restructure the programme so that whatever amounts are spent are cost effective; and are necessary to get better results. This will require "an optimal mix of the different approaches to poverty alleviation such as employment generation, basic needs provision, welfare, asset creation, backward area development and social assistance."[18]
5. Creating durable assets to generate sustainable income rather than wage employment should be the ultimate goal of poverty alleviation programme. At present, nearly 60 per cent of the total outlay on poverty alleviation goes for employment generation. Guhan found that out of one rupee spent in the Jawahar Rozgar Yojna, only 14 paise reached the poor via effective net wage transfer.[19]

6. Any policy which controls inflation without adversely affecting employment opportunities may be helpful for poverty alleviation as it is the poor class which is hard hit by inflation.

Notes and References

1. Mahbub-ul-Haq (1971), Employment and Income Distribution in the 1970s: A New Perspective, *Development Digest*, October 1971, p. 7.
2. Centre for Monitoring Indian Economy (CMIE), (1996), *India's Social Sector*, Feb. 1998, p. 259.
3. Madhu Dandavate, *Times of India*, New Delhi, Dec. 8, 1996.
4. UNDP (1996), *Human Development Report*, New York, Technical Note 3.
5. *Ibid.*
6. NCAER (1998), *Human Development Profile of India—Selected Indicators*, New Delhi, November 1996.
7. *Ibid.*, p. S-1.
8. Ahluwalia, M.S. (1976), Rural Poverty and Agricultural Performance in India, *Journal of Development Studies*, Vol. 14, No. 3.
9. Government of India, Ministry of Finance, *Economic Survey, 1992-93*, Table 11.
10. A Shaky Balance Sheet (Editorial), *Economic and Political Weekly*, Special Number, September 1996, p. 2352.
11. Abhijit Sen (1996), Economic Reforms, Employment and Poverty, Trends and Options, *Economic and Political Weekly*, Special Number, September 1996, p. 2466.
12. S. Guhan (1995), Social Expenditure in the Union Budget, 1991-96, *Economic and Political Weekly*, May 6-13, 1995, p. 1095.
13. Sudhakar, S. (1998), Government Budgetary Expenditure on Social Sector in India, Indian Economic Association, *79th Conference Number*, December 1996, p. 221.
14. Government of India, *Economic Survey, 1995-96*, Figure 2.2.
15. Aziz, A. (1994), *Poverty Alleviation in India*, Ashish Publishing House, New Delhi, p. 21.
16. S. Guhan, *op. cit.*, p. 1101.
17. Kuldeep Mathur, Politics and Implementation of IRDP, *Economic and Political Weekly*, October 14-21, 1995, p. 2703.
18. S. Guhan, *op. cit.*, p. 1100.
19. S. Guhan (1994), Social Security Options for Developing Countries, *International Labour Review*, Vol. 133, No. 1.

27

Primary Education, Human Development and India's Disadvantaged Groups

ASOK BASU

Like many other countries, in India also the weaker sections of people, the disadvantaged groups, the poor, the females, and the scheduled castes (SC) and scheduled tribes (STs), lack access to basic social services like primary education and primary health care. This paper attempts to examine in brief the role of primary education in human development and intends to make an assessment of the magnitude of the gaps in primary education for the disadvantaged groups of people in India.

PRIMARY EDUCATION AND HUMAN DEVELOPMENT

Basically human development implies the capacity to expand the range of choices which will enable people to improve the quality of their lives. Among the various components determining the level of living or the quality of lives of people like education, health, nutrition, housing, social security, human freedom, etc.

effective expansion of primary education is the most important basic prerequisite which increases human capability in many ways. Educated citizens are assets of the nation. Being educated is a valuable achievement in itself even if it does nothing to increase production. Again, the proper use of the acquired capability through education for the pursuit of one's goal—economic, social, political and cultural—would be instrumental in enlarging people's income—earning and other opportunities and would enable to improve the quality of life.

Thus, on the one hand, acquisition of primary education helps workers to take advantage of technical change which directly increases their productivity and earning. They may also innovate new techniques and spread the benefits of such innovations among fellow workers thereby benefiting the entire process of production from positive externalities. A one year increase of average primary schooling can augment wages by more than 10%.[1] Labour being the principal asset of the poor, the earning capacity of the poor across the economy rises *pari passu* with improvement of their productivity. This will ultimately lead to reduction of poverty and better distribution of economic growth directing the economy towards development.

On the other hand, the large potential benefits released through the effective expansion of primary education contribute in many ways to increase people's capabilities and enable them to avail of a better living. It imparts health and nutrition information which improve family health and welfare. One year of mother's education has been associated with a 9% decrease in under 5 mortality.[2] Spread of primary education also reduces fertility. The annual rate of population growth in Kerala as per 1991 census was only 1.3% where male and female literacy were 94% and 86% respectively; whereas in U.P. it was 2.5% where male and female literacy were 56% and 25% respectively.[3]

The incidence of child labour—a curse to society—may largely be overcome through the arrangement of compulsory universal elementary education for the children in the age group of 6-14. Again, greater literacy enhances people's awareness and understanding of themselves, their surroundings, and of the world. All this facilitates, in general, the formation of public opinion that may lead to collective demand for the fulfilment of the basic needs of common people. In Kerala, near-universal literacy has been achieved by prolonged creative interaction between state committed to, and public demand for, the widespread provision of primary education.[4] Specifically, basic educational achievement of the weaker sections of people can make them conscious about their distressed position and can help them to organise collective movement to resist oppressions inflicted upon them. Various movements by the backward castes and classes of people in India in recent times are actually a trend in that direction. Another important quality of education is this that it reduces gender-based inequalities within the family.

Increasing expansion of primary education, and thereafter secondary education, have contributed significantly towards sustained high levels of economic growth and development in several East Asian economies—the Asian Tigers. Since 1960s these countries grew twice as fast as the rest of East Asia, three times as fast as Latin America, and faster than the industrial economies. And this high growth rate was accompanied by equitable distribution of benefits. Macro-economic models indicate that primary education was the largest contributor to such high economic growth in these countries.[5] *Thus, primary education has many facets of human development.*

PRIMARY EDUCATION AND INDIA'S DISADVANTAGED GROUPS

India's average educational attainment (excepting Kerala) is yet to reach the critical threshold where benefits are large enough to ensure a sustained high growth rate. Expansion of primary education has, of course, contributed an improved overall literacy which increased from 18% in 1951 to 52% in 1991. However, it is to be noted that in the field of elementary education India is still worse-off than the average of "low income countries other than India and China (as defined by the World Bank)."[6] Moreover, the overall returns on primary education are low—only about 60% of the enrolled complete primary education and at least half of them learn even less than 50% of the curriculum.[7]

Against this poor background, let us now turn our attention to the study of the gaps in educational attainment of the disadvantaged groups of people in India. Specifically we shall study the gaps between the poor children and the better-off—the poverty gap, between girls and boys—the gender gap, and between SC and ST children and others—the caste and tribal gap. The important indicators of such gaps in education outcomes are enrolment, attendance, retention and learning achievement.

POVERTY GAP

Among the three types of gaps mentioned above, *poverty gap is the most dominant phenomenon and often happens to be the main cause behind gender, caste and tribal gaps.* According to Economic Survey, 1995-96 of the Government of India, 19% of the population lived below the poverty line in 1993-94 although unofficial estimate is higher. Poverty affects all indicators of educational attainment—from enrolment to achievement. One-third of the rural children aged 6-11 in India are not in school, most of whom are from very poor families and rural girls; and one-half of non-enrolled urban children are from the poorest 20% of households.[8]

Table 1 indicates lower enrolment and higher dropout rates among the poor compared to the better-off in India in 1992-93 which were found by a survey conducted by National Council for Applied Economic Research (NCAER) in 15 major Indian states which contain more than 95% of the Indian population. In Tables 1, 2, 3, and 5, a negative value for a gap means that the indicator for the target group—the poor, girls or SC or ST students is lower compared to the other members of the group, i.e., the better-off, boys or non-SC or non-ST students, while a positive value means the opposite. Data in Table 1 show that the poorest households with less than Rs. 3,000 per capita annual incomes are on the average 25 percentage points lower in enrolment of their children than for children of the wealthiest households with per capita annual incomes of more than Rs. 10,000. In 5 out of 14 states (for which data are available) more than 20% of the poor children are not enrolled in school. On the other hand, the dropout rate for the poor children is much higher. *The average dropout rate of these children was four times higher than it was for children from more affluent households in 1992-93.*[9] The poverty gap for both enrolment and dropout is larger in rural than urban areas.

Again, children, with poor socio-economic status (SES) estimated on the basis of family income, parental education and

TABLE 1

Poverty Gap in Enrolment and Dropout Rates Among Children Ages 6-14 in 15 Major Indian States, 1992-93

(percentage points)

States	*Enrolment rate*[a]			*Dropout rate*[b]		
	All areas	*Rural areas*	*Urban areas*	*All areas*	*Rural areas*	*Urban areas*
Andhra Pradesh	-27	-32	-17	14	15	13
Assam	-15	-15	0	16	16	12
Bihar	-27	-25	-17	11	11	10
Gujarat	-5	-5	-5	7	8	5
Haryana	-1	0	-7	3	3	3
Karnataka	-22	-25	-14	11	9	7
Kerala	0	0	0	0	0	0
Madhya Pradesh	-27	-24	-13	6	5	4
Maharashtra	-9	-12	0	10	12	3
Orissa	-18	-18	-9	8	9	—
Punjab	-55	-5	-8	-12	0	-14
Rajasthan	-32	-33	-10	3	2	—
Tamil Nadu	-5	-6	0	8	9	7
Uttar Pradesh	—	—	—	—	—	—
West Bengal	-28	-23	-7	15	17	0
All India	-25	-17	-8	7	8	-4

—Not available.

Notes: Gap between children from households with per capita incomes of less than Rs. 3,000 and for children from households with per capita incomes of more than Rs. 10,000.

a. The enrolment rate is the number of children ever enrolled per hundred children in the age group 6-14.

b. The dropout rate is the average annual discontinuation rate of elementary-school-age children (percentage of ever enrolled children who discontinued at any time in the age bracket 6-14).

Sources: NCAER (1994): *Non-enrolment, Dropout, and Private Expenditure on Elementary Education: A Comparison Across States and Population Groups*, New Delhi,

Quoted from World Bank (1997): *Primary Education in India*, Table 5.2, p. 115.

occupation score lower in achievement tests in both arithmetic and language in low literacy districts of 8 Indian states as shown in Table 2. The gap in achievement between children from the highest and the lowest quartiles of socio-economic status on average is about one-third of a standard deviation.

TABLE 2

Poverty Gap in Achievement Among Grade 4 and 5 Students by Socio-Economic Status (SES) Quartile in Low-literacy Districts in Eight Indian States, 1993

(percentage of standard deviation)

States	*Arithmetic*			*Language*		
	SES 1-SES 4	*SES 2-SES 4*	*SES 3-SES 4*	*SES 1-SES 4*	*SES 2-SES 4*	*SES 3-SES 4*
Assam	-28	-46	-28	-23	-41	-12
Haryana	-24	-13	-12	-13	-16	-14
Karnataka	-49	-30	-26	-53	-34	-30
Kerala	-43	-38	-18	-59	-40	-15
Madhya Pradesh	-22	-21	-15	-17	-20	-14
Maharashtra	-32	-19	-13	-49	-31	-30
Orissa	-48	-43	-36	-54	-39	-40
Tamil Nadu	-22	-13	-08	-24	-22	-13
Average effect size	-34	-28	-20	-37	-30	-21

Note: SES 1 is the lowest quartile of socio-economic status, SES 2 is the second quartile, SES 3 is the third quartile, and SES 4 is the highest.

Sources: World Bank staff calculations based on data from NCERT (National Council of Educational Research and Training), NIEPA (National Institute of Educational Planning and Administration), and New Concept 1995—"Data from District Primary Education Programme Baseline Assessment Studies" in Eight Indian States, Diskettes, New Delhi.

Quoted from World Bank (1997): *Primary Education in India*, Table 5.4, p. 117.

GENDER GAP

In India gender gaps emerge in all education indicators—in enrolment (which is of course narrowing), retention—satisfactory attendance and staying at school, and also in learning achievement. *Among these the most significant gap for girls relate to retention.* "Some time-use studies of children in India suggest that girls have fewer hours available for schooling than do boys."[10] In general, the gender gap in education is larger in rural areas than in urban areas as shown in Table 3. According to 1991 census literacy rate for persons aged 7 and above was 52%— 64% for males and 39% for females indicating a gender gap of 25%.

Table 3 shows gender gaps in enrolment (1993-94), literacy for aged 7 and above (1991) and non-attendance rates (1992-93) in 15 major Indian states. Data in Table 3 indicate that gender gap in primary gross enrolment rate is 22 percentage points in 1993-94 (which was actually 32 percentage points in 1980-81).[11] For India as a whole the gender gap in attendance is 17 percentage points. Gender gap in both enrolment rate and attendance rate, of course, varies widely between states.

More girls than boys dropout of school at all levels. According to Education Statistics of India, Ministry of Human Resource Development, 1994, 45% of girls and 41% of boys drop-out between grades 1 and 5. Although gender gap in dropout rates is low and declining, in absolute term each year about 1 million more females than males dropout from schools without completing primary education.[12] So far as achievement status is concerned, girls are mostly slightly below than the boys. National Council of Education, Research and Training (NCERT) found in 1991 that average grade 4 achievement score was 47.1% correct for boys and 45.6% correct for girls.

CASTE AND TRIBAL GAP

Data from Census, National Sample Survey, and NCAER, all suggest that school participation—students enrolled and attending classes regularly—for both SC and ST children are lower than it is for general children. Literacy rates for the SCs and STs in 1991 were only 37% and 30% respectively compared to 52% for the population as a whole. Some disaggregated data point to *the*

TABLE 3

Gender Gap in Enrolment Rates (1993-94), in Literacy Rates for People Aged 7 and Above (1991), and Non-Attendance Rates (1992-93) in 15 Major Indian States

(percentage points)

States	*Enrolment rate, 1993-94*	*Literacy rate, Age 7 and above, 1991*	*Attendance rate 1992-93*[a]		
			All	*Rural*	*Urban*
Andhra Pradesh	-16	-22	-17	-20	-9
Assam	-9	-18	-7	-8	-7
Bihar	-42	-30	-35	-26	-17
Gujarat	-25	-24	-14	-17	-7
Haryana	-15	-27	-13	-16	-2
Karnataka	-9	-23	-12	-16	-5
Kerala	-3	-7	0	0	1
Madhya Pradesh	-26	-29	-14	-18	-3
Maharashtra	-9	-24	-10	-14	-3
Orissa	-39	-28	-15	-16	-10
Punjab	-5	-14	-6	-8	0
Rajasthan	-59	-34	-34	-39	-12
Tamil Nadu	-8	-23	-7	-11	-1
Uttar Pradesh	-31	-29	-25	-29	-7
West Bengal	-1	-20	-10	-9	-11
All IndIa	-22	-25	-17	-20	-6

a. The attendance rate is the percentage of population ages 6-14 in school.

Sources: For enrolment rates, India, Ministry of Human Resource Development, 1994. c. *Selected Educational Statistics*, 1993-94, New Delhi, Deptt. of Education.

For literacy rates, Nanda, A.R. (1992) : "Final Population Totals : Brief Analysis of Primary Census Abstract", Census of India, 1991, Series 1, Paper 2 of 1992, New Delhi : Controller of Publications. For attendance rates, International Institute for Population Sciences (IIPS, 1995): *National Family Health Survey*, 1992-93: *Various States and India*, Bombay.

Adopted from Table 5.5 and Table 5.6 of World Bank, 1997—*Primary Education in India*, pp. 120-21.

alarmingly low literacy rate among the female's belonging to SC and ST population. Thus, in India in 1981, the rural female literacy rate was as low as 8% among the SCs who represent 16% of the country's population, 7% among the STs representing 8% of the population. The most unfortunate was the literacy rate of the tribal women in rural Rajasthan being even less than 1%.[13]

Table 4 gives the enrolment rates for children age 5-9 computed from 1981 census which indicate a caste gap in enrolment of 10-20 percentage points and a tribal gap of 15-20 percentage points. Net enrolment rates for children age 6-14 estimated from a 1994 household survey by NCAER found similar gaps to exist nearly 15 years later—a 15 percentage point caste gap and a 17 percentage point tribal gap in enrolment.[14]

TABLE 4

Children Age 5-9 Enrolled in School by Caste Group in India, 1981

(percent)

Group	*Scheduled caste*	*Scheduled tribe*	*Others*
Rural males	32	29	43
Rural females	17	15	30
Urban males	49	49	70
Urban females	40	39	58

Source: Visaria, Pravin, Gumber, Aril, and Visaria, Leela (1992): "Literacy and Primary Education in India, 1980-81 to 1991", *Journal of Educational Planning and Administration*, 7(1).
Quoted from World Bank (1997): *Primary Education in India*, Table 5.12, p. 129.

According to the Department of Education statistics, dropout rates for the SC students came down to 50% in 1988-89 from 60% in 1980-81 for grades 1-5 which is rather insignificant compared to general students. The tribal gap in dropout rates, however, was much greater being about 17 percentage points in both 1980-81 and 1988-89 for grades 1-5.

Both SC and ST students' learning achievement is less than other students. The 1993 study presented in Table 5 shows caste

TABLE 5

Caste and Tribal Gap in Grade 4 or 5 Achievement in Low-Literacy Districts in Eight Indian States, 1993

(percentage of standard deviation)

States	*Caste gap*		*Tribal gap*	
	In arithmetic	*In language*	*In arithmetic*	*In language*
Assam	39	19	-34.	-27
Haryana	-28	-15	-21	-10
Karnataka	-26	-25	-33	-26
Kerala	-33	-41	0.1	-27
Madhya Pradesh	-18	-21	-15	-10
Maharashtra	-8	-2	9	19
Orissa	-9	-29	-46	-36
Tamil Nadu	-4	-17	-23	-10
Average effect size	-11	-16	-20	-16

Source: World Bank Staff Calculations based on data from NCERT, NIEPA, and New Concept 1995—"Data from District Primary Education Programme Baseline Assessment Studies" in Eight Indian States, Diskettes, New Delhi.

Abridged table from Table 5.16 of World Bank 1997—*Primacy Education in India*, p. 134.

and tribal gap in achievement in arithmetic and language in low-literacy districts in eight Indian states. The table reveals the SC and ST students' performance was lower in varying degrees mainly in 6 out of 8 states both in arithmetic and language. However, the SC students in Assam and the ST students in Maharashtra out-performed all students both in arithmetic and language.

Table 6 gives a summary account of the above discussion concerning gaps in primary education for different disadvantaged groups of people in India. However, it is to be followed with caution. Because data in this table belong to different years (1988-89 to 1994), have been drawn from different sources, relate to different population groups—all-India, major Indian states, and selected Indian states, and presented in different forms of measurement. Still we have forwarded them to have an overview of

TABLE 6

Summary Account of Average Poverty Gap, Gender Gap, and Caste and Tribal Gap in Enrolment, Literacy, Dropout Rate, and Achievement in India, 1988-89 to 1994

(percentage points[a]/percent[b]/percentage of standard deviation[c])

Category of gap	*Enrolment*	*Literacy*	*Dropout rate*	*Achievement**
Poverty	25[a]	—	300[b]	35.5[c]
Gender	22[a]	25[a]	4[b]	1.5[b]
Caste	15[a]	15[b]	insignificant[b]	13.5[c]
Tribal	17[a]	22[b]	17[a]	18[c]

—Not available.

* Percentage of standard deviation in achievement of the poor, SC and ST children is the average of achievement in arithmetic and language.

the existing situation. In a word, available data suggest that excepting the gap in achievement level of the girls, and the dropout rates of the girls and SC students all other indicators of gap for the disadvantaged groups are significantly high. Further, it has been noted earlier that the gender gap in attendance is considerably high being 17 percentage point.

CONCLUDING REMARKS

It is lamentable that India's primary education in general, and that of the disadvantaged groups in particular, is in a pathetic condition both in respect of coverage and achievement even after 50 years of independence, although it is the most powerful vehicle for human development. *The deep-rooted caste and class biases in our society are particularly responsible for so much neglect of primary education of the disadvantaged groups in India.* The poor are always the most neglected section of the society. Likewise, the upper caste attitude and vested interest in getting the advantage of cheap labour from SC and ST people stand in the way of spread of education among them. On the other hand, the root of gender gap in education lies in social values—the priority that society attaches to female education. When social role of rural women is confined to domestic work and child-bearing, female education is often deemed to be unnecessary. Parential attitude is also important. Parents are often reluctant to educate their daughter's since returns to investment in a daughter's education will flow to her husband's family. The primary need for fulfilling the objective of universal primary education of good quality in India is strong and lasting political will capable of overcoming the influence of power groups.

NOTES AND REFERENCES

1. World Bank (1991), *World Development Report*, p. 56, OUP, New York.
2. World Bank (1990), *WDR*, p. 81, OUP, New York.
3. Literacy is a major outcome of primary education although it can be attained through non-formal education. For the purpose of census, a person is deemed as literate in India if he or she can read and write any language with understanding.
4. Dreze, Jean and Saran, Mrinalini (1995), Primary Education and Economic Development in China and India: Overview and Two Case Studies. Basu, K. *et al.* (ed.) *Choice, Welfare, and Development*, p. 232, OUP, New York.
5. World Bank (1995), *Economic Development in India: Achievements and Challenges*, p. 100. The World Bank, Washington, D.C.
6. Sen, Amartya (1994), *Beyond Liberalisation Social Opportunity and Human Capability*, p. 19. Institute of Social Sciences, New Delhi.
7. *Economic Development in India* (1995), *op. cit.*, p. 120.
8. *Ibid.*, p. 113.
9. National Council of Applied Economic Research (NCAER, 1994)—Non-Enrolment, Dropout and Private Expenditure on Elementary Education: A Comparison Across State and Population Groups, New Delhi. Quoted from World Bank (1997), *Primary Education in India*, p. 114.
10. World Bank (1997), *Primary Education in India*, p. 121, The World Bank, Washington, D.C.
11. Gross enrolment rate is estimated as the percentage of total number of children in all primary grades entered on school registers to the number of children aged 6-10 as estimated from projections based on census data, *Ibid.*, pp. 81 and 120.
12. *Ibid.*, p. 123.
13. Dreze, Jean and Saran, Mrinalini (1995), *op. cit.*, p. 195 (Calculated from Verma, V.S. (1985), *A Handbook of Population Statistics*, Office of the Registrar General, New Delhi.
14. NCAER (1995), Elementary Enrolment Rates, Annual Discontinuation Rates and Non-Attendance Rates, New Delhi. Quoted in *Primary Education in India* (1997), *op. cit.*, p. 129.

28

Human Development Profile: A Study of Primary Educational Standards in Uttar Pradesh

K.N. Bhatt

THE BACKGROUND

The notion of human development can be visualized as the process of widening people's choices and the level of well-being they attain. It must ensure for the people three essential choices: to lead long and healthy life, to acquire knowledge and to have access to resources needed for a decent standard of living.[1] Thus, the central goal of human development can be taken as the expansion of human capabilities. It is with an explicit recognition of this basic end that debates on means and strategies can be adequately founded. In the existing social reality of India, the basic objectives of the development process should be directed towards removal of illiteracy, ill-health and social deprivation to expand individual freedom and elementary capabilities of human beings. Basic education, good health and other human attainments are not only directly valuable as constituent elements of our basic capabilities, these capabilities can also help in generating better economic success, which in turn can contribute to enhancing the quality of human life even more. The components of a good quality of life, including education, health and elementary freedom, have instrumental roles of immense value in making us more productive and helping us to generate more output and incomes. This will ensure participatory economic development and real social progress in the country.[2]

Recent work on economic growth theory has established that a 'residual' in development is impossible to be explained by physical capital alone. It has sharply brought out the contribution of education, experience and the human capital in the process of economic growth and development.[3] Our country can learn in this context from the experiences of the fast growing economies of the world, particularly of East Asia, where elementary education and labour skills have contributed enormously in the pace of development and economic expansion.

Thus, the role of elementary education in facilitating rapid and participatory process of development can hardly be overemphasized. It is the most crucial stage of learning and laying the foundation for personality, attitudes, habits, social confidence, learning skills and communicating capabilities among children. Several studies have shown that investment in primary education yields the highest rate of return to nation and that it has a significant impact on the productivity and general well-being of the masses. The crucial role of primary education in strengthening of inherent individual potential has been accepted from the very beginning of the Constitution of India in which the Directive Principles of State Policy under Article 45 enjoined upon the State to provide free and compulsory education to all children up to the age of 14 years by 1960. This was reiterated in the National Policy of Education in 1968 and 1986. In pursuance of our constitutional commitment, the country has made some progress in quantitative terms. However, we have utterly failed in respect of overall coverage, equitable distribution and most of all in the quality of education that is being given through the primary schools.[4]

PRIMARY EDUCATION SCENARIO IN U.P.

Comprising a large part of the country's population (138

million, 1991 census), the state of Uttar Pradesh is among one of the most backward states of India. In terms of Human Development Index, measuring life expectancy at birth, literacy levels and per capita income, the state is placed last among fourteen large states of India. It recorded a crude birth rate of 37 per thousand persons, infant mortality rate of 118 per 1,000 births, very high maternal mortality and very low gender ratio of 880 females per 1,000 males as per 1991 census. The State even today is far behind from the realization of the constitutional goal of free and compulsory education for all children up to 14 years of age which was envisaged to have been reached by 1960. The overall literacy rate remains at 41.6 per cent in the state against the national rate of 52.1 per cent. Male and female literacy rates are 55.4 per cent and 26 per cent compared to all India averages of 63.8 per cent and 39.4 per cent respectively.[5]

Further, literacy figures show sharp variations between different caste, gender and region specific population groups implying extremely low levels for disadvantaged groups. The figure for 7 + rural women literacy rate goes down to 19 per cent, it is at 8 per cent for SCs in rural areas and 8 per cent for whole rural population in the most educationally backward districts.[6] It is reported that over 80 lakh children in the age group of 6-14 years do not attend school; about 28 lakh do not have access to full basic educational cycle, out of which 13 Iakh are deprived of a primary school within their reach; and approximately 8,600 habitations do not have a primary school within walking distance.[7] At the root of these figures is an inefficient primary education system that usually enrols about 98 per cent of boys and 62 per cent girls, but loses approximately 40 per cent of the enrolled boys and 60 per cent of enrolled girls before they complete five years of education and acquire basic literacy skills. The learning achievements of those who complete the five years of schooling are also remain abysmally low.[8]

THE SCOPE OF THE PAPER

This paper is based on the findings of an empirical study conducted by the G.B. Pant Social Science Institute, Allahabad during the year 1995-96.[9] It highlights existing situation of primary school system in the State and suggests the desired areas of policy interventions for its improvement. The initial study was sponsored by the government of Uttar Pradesh under the 'Education For All' project with the funds received from the World Bank as a part of its multi-dimensional exercise to understand the real problems in the primary school system and initiate remedial measures. The data for the study was collected first hand through a sample survey of 135 randomly selected schools in Allahabad, Banda and Etawah districts of U.P. To assess the levels of learning, primary school students studying in Class-II and Class-V and dropout children, who withdrew from the school before completing primary schooling, were tested in language and mathematics. The test papers were developed by the NCERT for use in the country-wide survey on primary school attainments. Information was also collected about important environmental factors, which affect the teaching/learning process in primary schools. In addition to standardized papers, a number of schedules were convassed among sample students, head teachers, other teachers, dropouts, etc. to elicit information about the functioning of the school system in the sample districts. The learning achievements of the sample students were graded in a five-point achievement scale as depicted in the following table.

TABLE 1

Scale for Learning Achievement Levels

Sl. No.	*Grade*	*Percentage Score*
1.	Zero	0
2.	Below MLL	1-40
3.	MLL	41-59
4.	Near Mastery	60-79
5.	Mastery	80-100

Note: MLL= Minimum Levels of Learning.

LEARNING ACHIEVEMENTS

The sample of Class-V students who were administered tests in language and mathematics consisted of 1,805 children of whom

745 belonged to Allahabad, 380 to Banda and 680 to Etawah. In Class-II 1,633 students were tested of which 602 came from Allahabad, 448 from Banda and 583 from Etawah. Similarly, out of a total sample of 408 dropout cases, 151 were in Allahabad, 153 in Banda and 104 in Etawah.

The analysis of the test scores of Class-V students in language reveals that about 58 per cent of the examinees in Allahabad, 49 per cent in Banda and 61 per cent in Etawah district did not qualify for the MLL grade. 34 per cent in Allahabad, 35 per cent in Banda and 29 per cent in Etawah were placed in MLL grade. Only 7 per cent students in Allahabad, 14 per cent in Banda and 8 per cent in Etawah reached near mastery grade. In Mathematics test 79 per cent children in Allahabad, 60 per cent in Banda and 82 per cent in Etawah scored below MLL. The percentage of those reaching MLL remained only at 17 per cent, 30 per cent and 13 per cent for Allahabad, Banda and Etawah respectively. In Allahabad 3 per cent, in Banda 7 per cent and in Etawah 4 per cent attained near mastery grade (Table 2).

The achievement level of Class-II students in language test revealed that 7 per cent in Allahabad, 4 per cent in Banda and 10 per cent in Etawah got zero marks and 27 per cent, 26 per cent and 35 per cent children for the sample districts respectively remained below MLL level in the test. Similarly, the test results in mathematics show the poorest performance of these children as about 74 per cent in Allahabad, 75 per cent in Banda and 83 per cent in Etawah district scored either zero or remained below MLL. Only 26 per cent in Allahabad, 25 per cent in Banda and 17 per cent students in Etawah district could qualify for MLL. None of the children in all three districts could achieve near mastery or mastery in the test (Table 3).

The academic standards of the dropouts was also measured by their test scores in language and mathematics on five point MLL scale as adopted in the case of Class-V and Class-II students. The result showed that 48 per cent in Allahabad, 54 per cent in Banda and 76 per cent in Etawah scored zero marks in the language test. This shows that these children had reverted to complete illiteracy by the time the test was conducted. Similarly, in mathematics 52 per cent in Allahabad, 54 per cent in Banda and 63 per cent in Etawah secured zero marks and therefore reverted to complete ignorance in mathematical skills which they had acquired

TABLE 2

Achievement Levels of Class-V Students in Language and Mathematics

Levels	*Allahabad*		*Banda*		*Etawah*	
	Language	*Maths*	*Language*	*Maths*	*Language*	*Maths*
Zero	0	3	1	3	0	7
		(0.40)	(0.26)	(0.80)		(1.00)
Below MLL	431	587	186	229	417	558
	(57.85)	(78.80)	(48.95)	(60.30)	(61.32)	(82.10)
MLL	256	130	132	115	195	85
	(34.36)	(17.40)	(34.74)	(30.30)	(28.68)	(12.50)
Near Mastery	55	25	53	25	54	26
	(7.38)	(3.40)	(13.95)	(6.60)	(7.94)	(3.80)
Mastery	5	0	8	8	14	4
	(0.67)		(2.11)	(2.11)	(2.06)	(0.60)
Total	745	745	380	380	680	680
	(100.00)	(100.00)	(100.00)	(100.00)	(100.00)	(100.00)

Note: Figures in parenthesis denote column percentages.

Source: Data collected for the Baseline Study of Educational Standards in Primary Schools: A Study of Allahabad, Banda and Etawah Districts of Uttar Pradesh, G.B. Pant Social Science Institute, Allahabad, 1996.

by attending school (Table 4).

REASONS FOR SCHOOL DESERTION BY DROPOUTS

The dropout students enumerated several reasons for the desertion of their school. The most important among these reasons in Allahabad was urgency of household duties, which was the main cause of 33 per cent dropout cases. About 24 per cent of the dropouts left school either due to the compulsion of supplementing their family income or due to illness; and 14 per cent dropped out due to the inability of the parents to meet the cost of their education or their unwillingness to send children to school. Similarly, in Banda, the most important cause was the parental apathy, which accounts for 70 per cent of the total school

TABLE 3

Achievement Levels of Class-II Students in Language and Mathematics

Levels	*Allahabad*		*Banda*		*Etawah*	
	Language	*Maths*	*Language*	*Maths*	*Language*	*Maths*
Zero	42	207	17	190	58	433
	(7.00)	(34.40)	(3.80)	(42.40)	(9.90)	(74.30)
Below MLL	164	241	115	145	203	53
	(27.20)	(40.00)	(25.70)	(32.40)	(34.80)	(9.10)
MLL	95	154	77	113	129	97
	(15.80)	(25.60)	(17.20)	(25.20)	(22.10)	(16.60)
Near Mastery	118	0	85	0	62	0
	(19.60)		(19.00)		(10.60)	
Mastery	183	0	154	0	131	0
	(30.40)		(34.40)		(22.50)	
Total	602	602	448	448	583	583
	(100.00)	(100.00)	(100.00)	(100.00)	(100.00)	(100.00)

Note: Figures in parenthesis denote column percentages.

Source: Data collected for the Baseline Study of Educational Standards in Primary Schools: A Study of Allahabad, Banda and Etawah Districts of Uttar Pradesh, G.B. Pant Social Science Institute, Allahabad, 1996.

dropout cases. The next important urgencies were household duty and earn a living. In Etawah 36 per cent left school due to the urgency of household duties and 23 per cent deserted it due to their inability to afford expenses towards textbooks/notebooks (Table 5).

PERSONAL, FAMILY AND LEARNING BACKGROUND OF THE STUDENTS

All the Class-V students who were administered tests were interviewed to record their personal family and learning background to understand the process of teaching/learning in primary schools in detail. The results of data analysis in this context show that nearly all the students in the sample came from

TABLE 4

Achievement Levels of Dropout Students in Language and Mathematics

Levels	*Allahabad*		*Banda*		*Etawah*	
	Language	*Maths*	*Language*	*Maths*	*Language*	*Maths*
Zero	73	79	83	63	79	65
	(48.30)	(52.30)	(54.20)	(54.20)	(76.00)	(62.50)
Below MLL	45	43	27	27	12	27
	(29.80)	(28.50)	(18.00)	(17.60)	(11.50)	(26.00)
MLL	14	14	25	25	7	8
	(9.30)	(9.30)	(16.30)	(17.20)	(6.70)	(7.70)
Near Mastery	11	6	9	4	3	1
	(7.30)	(4.00)	(5.90)	(2.60)	(2.90)	(1.00)
Mastery	8	9	9	12	3	3
	(5.30)	(8.00)	(5.90)	(7.80)	(2.90)	(2.90)
Total	151	151	153	153	104	104
	(100.00)	(100.00)	(100.00)	(100.00)	(100.00)	(100.00)

Note: Figures in parenthesis denote column percentages.

Source: Data collected for the Baseline Study of Educational Standards in Primary Schools: A Study of Allahabad, Banda and Etawah Districts of Uttar Pradesh, G.B. Pant Social Science Institute, Allahabad, 1996.

very poor families. The male parent in majority of the cases worked as a wage earner in non-agricultural occupations. In most of the cases, the parents of the students were either illiterate or scantly educated. The proportion of educated parents with academic standards of more than primary level in three sample districts varied from 47 to 53 per cent in case of fathers and 9 to 23 per cent only in case of mothers (Table 6).

Very few students received assistance from the family in completing their home assignments. About 60 to 64 per cent students did not get help from the family members doing home work in all the three sample districts. 90 per cent students in Allahabad, 99 per cent in Banda and 99 per cent in Etawah reported that their teacher did not come to the class regularly. In the absence of the teacher, most of the time the students were

TABLE 5

Reasons for Discontinuance of Studies by Dropouts

Sl. No.	*Reasons*	*Allahabad*	*Banda*	*Etawah*
1.	Parents Do Not Want	12	107	5
		(7.90)	(69.90)	(4.80)
2.	To Assist in Household Work	49	12	37
		(32.50)	(7.80)	(35.60)
3.	To Earn A Living	18	12	9
		(11.90)	(7.80)	(8.70)
4.	To be Trained in Household Enterprise	3	0	1
		(2.00)		(1.00)
5.	Cannot Afford Textbooks/Notebooks	10	0	24
		(6.60)		(23.10)
6.	Illness/Not Keeping Well	18	1	13
		(11.90)	(0.70)	(12.50)
7.	To Get Married	11	1	8
		(7.30)	(0.70)	(7.70)
8.	Failure/Did Not Learn Anything	1	3	0
		(0.70)	(2.00)	
9.	Teachers Not Cooperative	3	1	3
		(2.00)	(0.70)	(2.90)
10.	School Too Far	5	0	0
		(13.30)		
11.	Others	15	1	4
		(19.90)	(0.70)	(3.80)
	Total	151	153	104
		(100.00)	(100.00)	(100.00)

Note: Figures in parenthesis denote column percentages.

Source: Data collected for the Baseline Study of Educational Standards in Primary Schools: A Study of Allahabad, Banda and Etawah Districts of Uttar Pradesh, G.B. Pant Social Science Institute, Allahabad, 1996.

TABLE 6

Distribution of Class-V Sample Students by Level of Parental Education Status

Sl. No.	*Category*	*Allahabad*		*Banda*		*Etawah*	
		Father	*Mother*	*Father*	*Mother*	*Father*	*Mother*
1.	Illiterate	193	565	111	217	162	375
		(25.90)	(75.80)	(29.20)	(71.30)	(23.80)	(55.10)
2.	Upto Primary	203	114	85	62	161	152
		(27.30)	(15.30)	(22.40)	(16.30)	(23.70)	(22.40)
3.	Above Primary	349	68	184	47	357	153
		(46.80)	(8.90)	(48.40)	(12.40)	(52.50)	(22.50)
	Total	745	745	380	380	680	680
		(100.00)	(100.00)	(100.00)	(100.00)	(100.00)	(100.00)

Note: Figures in parenthesis denote column percentages.

Source: Data collected for the Baseline Study of Educational Standards in Primary Schools: A Study of Allahabad, Banda and Etawah Districts of Uttar Pradesh, G.B. Pant Social Science Institute, Allahabad, 1996.

either left to their own or allowed to go out to play. The practice of giving homework was also reported to be quite infrequent as more than 55 per cent students complained that they were not given homework regularly. About 50 per cent respondents told that homework was seldom checked or corrected by their teachers. Similarly, about half of the students reported that monthly class tests are not held regularly and about 52 to 55 per cent said that the mistakes committed by them in the tests are never pointed out to them for correction in future (Table 7).

TEACHERS

The sample consisted of 426 teachers, out of which 132 came from Allahabad, 124 from Banda and 170 from Etawah. More than 15 per cent of the teachers in primary schools in Allahabad, 18 per cent in Banda and 13 per cent in Etawah were found untrained. The proportion of teachers who reported their educational qualification upto high school were 27 per cent in

TABLE 7

Responses of the Class-V Students on Other Important Factors Affecting their Studies

(In %)

Sl. No.	*Factors*	*Allahabad*	*Banda*	*Etawah*
1.	Proportion of Students Received Assistance from Family Members in Studies	41.07	36.32	37.65
2.	Proportion of Students Reporting their Teachers do not come Regularly to Class	89.80	99.20	99.30
3.	Proportion of Students Reporting Home Work Given by Teachers Regularly	43.76	43.16	37.71
4.	Proportion of Students Reporting Home Work corrected by Teachers Regularly	55.17	43.16	51.76
5.	Proportion of Students Reporting Monthly Class Tests Organized Regularly	44.60	50.80	49.00
6.	Proportion of Students Reporting Regular Feedback to Students on Class Tests by Teachers	46.40	47.70	45.00
	N=	745	380	680

Note: N = Total Number of Class-V Students in the Sample.

Source: Data collected for the Baseline Study of Educational Standards in Primary Schools: A Study of Allahabad, Banda and Etawah Districts of Uttar Pradesh, G.B. Pant Social Science Institute, Allahabad, 1996.

Allahabad, 31 per cent in Banda and 23 per cent in Etawah. 57 per cent teachers in Allahabad, 74 per cent in Banda and 69 per cent in Etawah had not taken advantage of the in-service training programmes organized by the department. This clearly indicates towards the lack of enthusiasm among them to improve their teaching skills.

Sub-Deputy Inspector (SDI) of schools is considered to be a friend, philosopher and guide to the primary teachers to help them not only in the academic matters but also in their routine service matters. The study results, however, suggest that 65 per cent of the sample teachers in Allahabad, 57 per cent in Banda and 80 per cent in Etawah were not happy with the role of SDIs. Similar dissatisfaction was expressed by the majority of teachers with the guidance and assistance they received from their Head Teacher. Another interesting finding of the study that came into light was about 58 per cent of teachers in Allahabad, 56 per cent in Banda and 32 per cent in Etawah were found engaged in teaching more than one class at a time (Table 8).

SCHOOLS

In all, 135 schools (45 schools in each sample district) were included in the sample as noted earlier. Most of these sample schools looked as a deserted and lone building, amidst dirt and squalor with stray animals freely roaming around in all the sample districts. Less than 1 per cent of the sample schools were found with enclosed compounds. About 98 per cent schools in Allahabad, 96 per cent in Banda and 93 per cent in Etawah needed additional classrooms ranging from 1 to 6 to be able to provide a roof over the heads of their students. Despite Operation Blackboard programme, sample schools did not have all the items supposed to have been provided to them in adequate quantity. About 91 per cent of the schools in Allahabad, 71 per cent in Banda and 64 per cent in Etawah district did not have mats for all students to sit on them. 36 per cent schools in Allahabad, 42 per cent in Banda and 22 per cent in Etawah did not have blackboards for all classes. Similarly, in Allahabad 76 per cent, in Banda 84 per cent and in Etawah 82 per cent schools did not provide chalk sticks and dusters to all their classes. More than half of the sample schools lacked safe drinking water facility and more than 90 per cent did not have electric connections and separate toilet facility for girls (Table 9).

AREAS FOR POLICY INTERVENTION

The foregoing analysis reveals that the level of academic achievements of students in primary schools of the sample districts in Uttar Pradesh is depressingly low, particularly in mathematics. Similarly, the lack of material facilities, dilapidated and isolated

TABLE 8

Information Pertaining to Sample Teachers

(In %)

Sl. No.	*Particulars*		*Allahabad*	*Banda*	*Etawah*
1.	Professional Training of Teachers	Trained	84.80	82.30	87.10
		Untrained	15.20	17.70	12.90
2.	Educational Qualification of Teachers	Up to High School	26.50	30.70	23.10
		Intermediate	39.40	37.90	45.90
		Graduates	34.10	31.40	31.00
3.	Teachers Having Undergone In-service Training	Yes	43.10	25.60	31.30
		No	56.90	74.40	68.70
4.	Level of Help Provided by SDIs to Teachers	Very Helpful	06.90	08.50	02.70
		Somewhat Helpful	28.40	34.20	17.30
		Not Helpful	64.70	57.30	80.00
5.	Level of Help Provided by Head Teachers to Fellow Teachers	Very Helpful	22.40	23.90	29.30
		Somewhat Helpful	17.20	20.50	19.30
		Not Helpful	60.40	55.60	51.40
6.	Teacher Engaged in Multi-grade Teaching	Engaged	57.80	56.40	32.00
		Not Engaged	42.20	43.60	68.00
	N =		132	124	170

Note: N = Total Number of Class-V Students in the Sample.

Source: Data collected for the Baseline Study of Educational Standards in Primary Schools: A Study of Allahabad, Banda and Etawah Districts of Uttar Pradesh, G.B. Pant Social Science Institute, Allahabad, 1996.

school buildings, unqualified and demotivated lot of teachers and unconcerned educational managers and planners appear to be responsible for making the general environment of teaching and learning processes in primary school system of the State an uninteresting and uninspiring activity. Though the existing situation is an outcome of several factors, the main areas in which purposeful policy interventions could be helpful in bringing about improvements are: inspection, supervision and support services;

TABLE 9

Some Important Data Pertaining to Schools

Sl. No.	*Particulars*	*Allahabad*	*Banda*	*Etawah*
1.	Schools Requiring Additional Classrooms (No. of Rooms Varying from 1-8)	97.80	95.60	93.30
2.	Schools having no Adequate Mats for All Students	91.10	71.10	64.40
3.	Schools having no Blackboards for All Classes	35.60	42.20	22.20
4.	Schools having no Chalk-sticks/Dusters for All classes	73.60	84.40	82.20
5.	Schools having no Safe Drinking Water Facility	65.40	49.90	53.30
6.	Schools without Separate Toilets Facility for Girls	91.10	91.10	88.90
7.	Schools without Playground	40.00	51.10	46.70
8.	Schools without Electric Connection	95.60	93.30	91.10
	N =	45	45	45

Note: N= Total Number of Class-V Students in the Sample.

Source: Data collected for the Baseline Study of Educational Standards in Primary Schools: A Study of Allahabad, Banda and Etawah Districts of Uttar Pradesh, G.B. Pant Social Science Institute, Allahabad, 1996.

academic and professional competence of teachers; and adequacy of material inputs.

Despite a large army of officials engaged for teacher supervision and support services, the primary schools are visited the least; classroom performance of the teachers is never inspected; they are hardly provided any academic guidance, even the head teachers rarely do so. The village community shows virtually no interest in the affairs of the school. The majority of the teachers have not undergone in-service training to improve their teaching performance which was observed to be of very low standard, particularly so in the teaching of mathematics and science. The inadequacy of basic facilities, teaching-learning materials and lack of motivation among teachers appears to be due to indifferent supervision system and lack of community's interest in school to a large extent. The primary school appeared deserted and forlorn because of the lack of enclosed compounds and absence of supervised sports and extra-curricular activities in the schools after school hours. This is so because teachers have neither been given residential facilities nor motivated to reside in the neighbourhood of the schools to organize these activities. The academic standards of the children and the teaching-learning environment of the primary schools could be substantially raised through purposeful policy interventions in these areas. The state government will have to immediately come forward to decide its educational and developmental priorities.

The persistent backwardness of elementary education system, not only limits the freedom and well-being of the people but also sustains high levels of mortality and fertility rates, brings in mass poverty and relative deprivation of weaker sections, particularly women. The low level of basic educational development also severely restricts the goal of economic development and deprives the people from taking advantage of the social and economic opportunities offered by the process of economic reforms and globalization. When the majority of population (as noticed in case of the state) who cannot read, write, count or follow written words and are unable to take advantage of the process of modernization, socio-economic disparities are bound to further widen and deprive people of even bare minimum necessities.[10] To save the nearly collapsing system of primary education in the State, radical corrective measures will have to be taken urgently. The State needs not only to make qualitative improvement in elementary education and enhance the learning achievements of the students in schools, but also ensure quantitative expansion of the system to make the facility available to those who are deprived of it. The system of basic education in the State should be used as an instrument of social change; ensure well-being and freedom of the people; and bring in a participatory process of economic and social development.

Notes and References

1. *Human Development Report (1997)*, UNDP, Oxford University Press, New York, p. 14.
2. Amartya Sen (1996), "Radical Needs and Moderate Reforms" in Jean Dreze and A.K. Sen (eds.): *Indian Development: Some Regional Perspectives*, Oxford University Press, New Delhi, pp. 2-7.
3. Gunnar Myrdal (1968), *Asian Drama: An Inquiry into the Poverty of Nations*, Vol. III, Kalyan Publishers, New Delhi, p. 1540.
4. G.C. Tewari and K.N. Bhatt (1996), Baseline Study of Educational Standards in Primary Schools: A Study of Allahabad, Banda and Etawah Districts of Uttar Pradesh, Project Report, G.B. Pant Social Science Institute, Allahabad, pp. 1-2.
5. U.P. Basic Education Project (1995), *Education for All*, State Project Office, Lucknow, p. 27.
6. Jean Drezes and Haris Gazdar (1996), "Uttar Pradesh the Burden of Inertia in Jean Dreze and A.K. Sen (eds.), *Indian Development: Some Regional Perspectives*, Oxford University Press, New Delhi, p. 42.
7. U.P. Basic Education Project (1995), p. 28.
8. G.C. Tewari and K.N. Bhatt (1996), p. 2.
9. This paper heavily draws information from the study conducted by G.C. Tewari and K.N. Bhatt (1996), *Ibid.*
10. Amartya Sen (1996), pp. 21-22.

PART D

HUMAN DEVELOPMENT: CASE STUDIES

29

Human Development and Deprivation in South Asia

M.A. Razzaque

Without basic literacy and numeracy, people's ability to adopt to changing production methods and technologies is severely constrained. A programme of action for the LDCs was adopted in the Second United Nations Conference on the LDCs in 1993. The key commitments were to generate accelerated and sustained economic growth for LDCs, to speed up efforts to improve education, training, health and sanitation, to allocate more donor GNP to aid, to enhance for export from LDCs and to significantly reduce their debt burden. Among many other mid-term review in 1995 shows that: (1) During 1990-93 the average annual growth of the LDCs in real GDP was 1.6% whereas during 1980-90 it was 2.2%. (2) The real GDP per capita in the LDCs fell by 1.2% annually in 1990-93, compared to 0.3% in 1980-90. (3) Since the average income per capita is declining at an accelerated pace in the LDCs, this suggests grim prospects for future development. (4) As regard human resource development, the adult literacy rate increased from 42% in 1985 to 47% in 1993, and the life expectancy at birth from 50 years in 1990 to 52 years in 1993. But the pace of such improvements has been slowing, and their sustainability has come into question due to the very weak performance in economic growth.

Among the LDCs the South Asian countries are the most illiterate region in the world; its adult literacy rate is 48% compared to 77% in the rest of the developing world and with a GNP per capita of $309, it is the poorest region of the world. Its GNP per capita is only one-third of the average for the developing world. The total population of fifty of the smaller UN member countries is less than the population of South Asia. This population could have become the real wealth of these nations, had sufficient investment been made in human development. But South Asia spends less than 5% of its combined GNP on the human resource variables education and health. South Asia's share of global real GDP (in ppp dollars) has gone down from 6.9% in 1960 to 5.3% in 1993, showing that the rate of economic advancement in this region has not kept pace with the rest of the world. According to World Bank, as a result of this slowdown in growth, over 500 million people of this region were living in absolute poverty in 1993. The illiterate adult population rose by 14% from 32% to 46% during 1960-93, so adult literacy in this region increased at a much slower pace than in other region. South Asia contains one-half of the world's illiterate people.

Human Development and of Deprivation in South Asia

The human development index measures the average achievements in a country in three basic dimensions of human development—longevity, knowledge and decent standard of living. A composite index, the human development index (HDI) thus contains three variables: life expectancy, educational attainment (adult literacy and combined primary, secondary and tertiary enrolment) and real GDP per capita (in ppp $). On the other hand, human poverty index measures deprivation in basic human development in the same dimensions as the HDI. The variables used are the percentage of people expected to die before age 40, the percentage of adults who are illiterate, and overall economic provisioning in terms of the percentage of people without access to health services and safe water and the percentage of underweight children under five. Table 1 gives the basic human indicators for SAARC countries.

TABLE 1

Basic Human Development Indicators of SAARC Countries

	India	*Pakistan*	*Bangladesh*	*Nepal*	*Sri Lanka*	*Bhutan*	*Maldives*
Estimated Population (mill), 1993	902	133	115	21	18	1.6	0.2
Annual Pop. Growth rate (%), 1960-93	2.2	3.0	2.5	2.4	1.8	1.9	2.7
Life expectancy at birth (years), 1994	61.3	62.3	56.4	55.3	72.2	51.5	62.8
Adult literacy rate (%), 1994	51.2	37.1	37.3	27	90.1	41.1	93
Adult female literacy rate, 1994	36	23	25	13	86	25	93
Combined gross enrolment ratio (%), 1994	56	38	39	55	66	31	71
Infant mortality rate, 1994 (per 1,000 live births)	79	95	91	84	15	125	56
GNP per capita (US$)	300	430	220	190	600	170	820
GNP Annual growth rate (%), 1980-93	5.0	6.1	4.5	4.6	4.6	7.6	6.6
Real GDP per Capita (ppp$), 1994	1,348	3,154	1,331	1,137	3,277	1,289	2,200
Human Dev. Index, 1994	.446	:446	.368	.347	.711	.338	.611
Gender-related Dev. Index, 1994	.419	.392	.339	.321	.694	—	.600

Source: *Human Development in South Asia,* 1997.

The HDI value for each country indicates how far the country has to go to attain certain defined goal: an average life span of 85 years, access to education for all and a decent standard of living. The HDI shows the distance a country has to travel to reach the maximum possible value 1. The ranking of the SAARC countries by their HDI shows that except Sri Lanka and Maldives, all other countries of SAARC region have not achieved even the median value of the HDI.

The Human Deprivation Measure (HDM) in a way is the reverse the Human Development Index (HDI). The HDM like the HDI is based on three variables: health deprivation (measured by access to safe drinking water and underweight children under five), education deprivation (measured by adult illiteracy and children out of school), and income deprivation (measured by the lack of a minimum income needed for the basic necessities of life). Just as the HDI extends the GNP measure to include other aspects of human capabilities not captured by income estimates, the HDM extends the measure of income poverty to include broader characteristics of poverty and deprivation of human capabilities and opportunities. The HDM for some of the South Asian countries are given in Table 2.

Bangladesh has the highest percentage (48%) of income poor people in SAARC region and it has the highest percentage of capability poor people (61%). A remarkable point is she is having

TABLE 2

Human Deprivation Measure (HDM) for some SAARC Countries

Country	*Population (%) in South Asia*	*Health Deprivation Measure*	*Education Deprivation Measure (%)*	*Income Deprivation Measure (%)*	*HDM value (%)*
Bangladesh	10	31	73	48	61
India	77	32	53	25	40
Pakistan	11	58	65	34	57
Sri Lanka	2	54	17	22	31
South Asia	100	35	56	28	44

Source: *Human Development in South Asia*, 1997.

highest value in income deprivation measure, the health deprivation measure is lowest for Bangladesh in the SAARC region. Small territory and better performance in family planning motivation have contributed a lot in reducing deprivation in health in Bangladesh. It is to be noted that human deprivation measure is far greater than income deprivation measure for all the countries. The highest difference between income deprivation measure and human deprivation measure is for Pakistan. Deprivation in education and health is more pronounced in Pakistan than income deprivation. The human deprivation is least for Sri Lanka in the region and its major contribution is from health deprivation. Geographical location and conflict between racial groups may be the key reasons for such a value of the health deprivation in Sri Lanka.

The data shows that human deprivation is far more widespread than is reflected by the measure of income poverty alone. It shows that 44% people in South Asia are capability poor but only 28% are income poor. Thus, human poverty far exceeds income poverty. Naturally, the solution to human poverty lies not in huge income transfers or in an unsustainable network of public charity. Thus, the emphasis must be on building human capabilities and enabling people to stand on their own feet so that they are able to compete in the market. Estimates of additional investment needed in human priority areas—universal primary education, basic health care for all, safe drinking water for all, nutrition for all malnourished children, family planning services for 80% married couple in the SAARC nations by 2010 are given in Table 3. The estimated investment costs are calculated with the assumptions that per unit cost of: (i) providing basic education to a child is $30, (ii) health care and clinical services is $12 person, (iii) for providing safe drinking water is $5.3 per person, (iv) nourishing a child is assumed to be $10, (v) providing family planning services is assumed at $18 per couple.

These estimates are based on the estimated population for in 2010.

The SAARC nations should set their objectives on building human capabilities and enabling people to stand on their own feet. The nations must invest additional amount in the priority areas—universal primary education, basic health care for all, safe drinking water for all, nutrition for all malnourished children, family

TABLE 3

Estimates of Additional Investment in some Human Priority Areas

(in Million $)

Priority Areas Country	*India*	*Paki-stan*	*Bangla-desh*	*Nepal*	*Sri Lanka*	*Bhutan*
Universal Primary education	23,050	7,919	4,582	1,014	401	68
Basic Health Care for all	19,028	6,115	5,774	—	243	67
Nutrition for all malnourished children	24,444	6,557	3,485	1,059	568	
Family planning services for 80% of married couple	626	91	134	17	7.3	—
Total estimated cost	17,324	3,590	2,402	508	178	—
Population in 2010 (million)	1,220	202	181	22.8	34	

Source: *Human Development in South Asia*, 1997.

planning services for at least 80% of married couple. The additional investments needed for the above sectors can be fruitfully met with international co-operation. Recent developments in the nuclear weapon sector clearly indicate that the SAARC nations have the potential to accumulate investments. The honest desire and transparency of the governments of SAARC countries are essential for meeting the additional investments by the year 2010 for the upliftment of our human capabilities.

REFERENCES

Human Development Report, 1997.

Human Development in South Asia, 1997.

30

Human Development in SAARC Countries

R. PUSHPAVATHI

Economists from developing countries have struggled for a long time with the concept and practice of development relevant for their economies. Many of them, emerging from the western citadels of learning in the 50's and 60's, were armed with the neo-classical conviction that the real purpose of development was to increase national income and all it required was an increase in saving and investment and accumulation. Yet there has been a considerable evolution of economic thinking in the last three decades leading to a widespread consensus that the purpose of development is not just to enlarge incomes, but enlarge people's choices extending to basic education, good health, minimum sanitary conditions, political freedom, cultural identity, personal security, community participation, environmental security, ecological balance and many other areas of human well-being. Development must deal with not just the economy but the entire society and people must be put at the centre stage. Economic growth does not automatically translate into human development. A link between growth and human lives must be created through conscious state policies. When the benefits of growth are hijacked by powerful pressure groups, which is often the case in developing economies, it leads to human deprivation.

Prof. Mahbub-ul-Haq, a distinguished economist, former finance minister of Pakistan, president of the Human Development Centre at Islamabad and Special Advisor to the UNDP administration, who recently passed away in July, 1998 was the chief architect of the Global Human Development Reports published by the UNDP since 1990.[1] He was of the firm view that quality of life was more important than mere GDP. Human Development Reports have analysed strategies for translating economic growth into human development on the one hand and translating human development into sustainable growth on the other.

Human Development Reports have gained prominence in the discourse of development primarily because they captured a place of special importance for developing a new index of progress—Human Development Index (HDI). In fact, when the first HDR was published in 1990, it very much upset the then U.S. President George Bush by giving the U.S.A 17th rank in terms of HDI in the world—a rank lower than Eastern Europe, Japan and others. The HDR's have had enormous influence on public policies in several countries including India.

The concept of human development is of special importance to South Asian economists for two reasons. Firstly, this was South Asia's contribution to economic analysis because the chief architect of the concept was Dr. Mahbub-ul-Haq, who was helped in its shaping by several other distinguished economists from South Asia like, Amartya Sen, Megnad Desai from India, Dr. Ponna Wignaraja, Sushil Sirivandana from Srilanka and Dr. S. Maqsood Ali from Bangladesh and A.A.Waqif from Pakistan. Secondly, the real challenge of human development lies in the South Asian economies. It is a matter of deep concern that South Asia is slipping behind the rest of the world in terms of its human development indicators and is emerging as the most deprived region in the world. This reality is still not adequately recognised by National Planners and international policy-makers. As per the HDR in South Asia, 1997, the region is characterised as the poorest, the most illiterate, the most malnourished, the least gender-sensitive, the most militarised with highest human deprivation.[2]

South Asia contains over one-fifth of humanity and this population of 1.2 billion is growing rapidly. This rapidly multiplying population has become a liability rather than an asset because sufficient investment has not been made in human development during the past 40 years. This contrasts sharply with East Asia in Human Resource Development. Though both the regions started with the same level of per capita income, the per capita income in East Asian countries has increased by about four times as fast as in South Asia. China with the largest population in the world has reached a HDI rank of 106, with life expectancy at 69.2, adult literary 82% and IMR at 38 per 1,000 in 1995.

In view of the dismal picture of human development in South Asian countries, an organisation like SAARC can play a very important and vital role very much like the OECD and UNCTAD, in reducing the military tensions and extending regional cooperation in the task of alleviation of poverty and human deprivation through a well-formulated, coordinated, mutually cooperative and concentrated plan of action in the next ten to fifteen years.

In this paper an attempt has been made to study the progress of Human Development in SAARC countries, the real challenges facing these countries in the 21st century and how Regional cooperation among these countries can go a long way in achieving the human development goals. This will enable the SAARC to emerge as one of the strong organisations whose voice can no longer be ignored by the world.

Human Development in SAARC Countries

Table 1 presents the country profiles of the SAARC nations in terms of human development indicators. All the countries in South Asia, with the exception of Sri Lanka and Maldives have HDI ranks ranging between 138 and 155. Even after four decades, these countries—whose HDI values in 60's were between 0.130 to 0.206—have not been able to increase it to above 0.5; whereas other East Asian countries like, Malaysia, Thailand, Philippines and Korea were able to more than double the HDI values in the same period, China has come out with an excellent performance from 0.248 in 1960 to 0.650 in 1995, improving its HDI rank to 106 and qualifying as a medium Human Development country. Among the SAARC countries with low HDI values, Bhutan and

TABLE 1

Country Profiles in Human Development (SAARC Countries)

	Population (in Millions)	*Land area (1,000 Sq Kms)*	*Real GDP per capita (PPP $) 1995*	*HDI Rank*	*HDI Value*	*GDI Rank*	*GDI Value*	*HPI % 1995*	*GEM Rank*	*GEM Value*
India	902	3,288	1,422	139	0.451	128	0.424	35.9	95	0.228
Pakistan	133	796	2,209	138	0.453	131	0.399	46.0	100	0.179
Bangladesh	115	144	1,382	147	0.371	140	0.342	46.5	80	0.305
Sri Lanka	18	66	3,408	90	0.716	70	0.700	20.6	84	0.286
Nepal	21	141	1,145	152	0.351	148	0.327	—	—	—
Bhutan	1.6	47	1,382	155	0.347	147	0.330	44.9	—	—
Maldives	0.2	0.30	3,540	95	0.683	17	0.668	—	76	0.341

Source: UNDP: Human Development Report, 1998.

Nepal have lowest values of 0.341 and 0.357 respectively. India and Pakistan stand on the same footing with HDI values at 0.451 and 0.453. Bangladesh has lower value than India and Pakistan at 0.371.

Human Development Profile (Table 2) shows that except Sri Lanka and Maldives, all the SAARC countries show a below-average performance. India, Pakistan, Sri Lanka and Maldives have fared well in life expectancy at birth being above 60 while that of Bangladesh, Bhutan and Nepal is less than 60 years. Adult literacy is at 52% in India, while Pakistan (37.8%) and Bangladesh (38.1%) show a dismal picture with more than half the population being illiterate.

TABLE 2

Human Development Profile (SAARC Countries)

	Life Expectancy at Birth 1995	*Adult Literacy rate (%) 1995*	*Combined first, second and third level Gross Enrolment Ratio (%) 1995*
India	61.6	52.0	55
Pakistan	62.8	37.8	41
Bangladesh	56.9	38.1	37
Sri Lanka	72.5	90.2	67
Nepal	55.9	27.5	56
Bhutan	52.0	42.2	31
Maldives	63.3	93.2	71

Source: *Human Development Report*, 1998, p. 128.

With reference to GDI the countries show a value of less than 0.5 (except Sri Lanka and Maldives) reiterating the fact that women bear the greatest burden of human deprivation in South Asia. The deprivation of South Asian women becomes more obvious when we look at the GEM values which stand at 0.23 for all SAARC countries, the lowest among all regions of the world including sub-Saharan Africa. Among the SAARC countries, the lowest GEM rank is that of Pakistan at 100. Pakistani women are the most downtrodden and worst sufferers having a GEM value of 0.179. India's GEM value is at a low of 0.228, while Bangladesh seems to fare better having a GEM value of 0.305. It is a matter of surprise that while Sri Lanka has high values of HDI (0.716) and GDI (0.700), its GEM value is only 0.286 lower than that of Bangladesh.

GDI profile (Table 3) confirms the low status of women in South Asian countries particularly with reference to literacy, enrolment ratio and share of earned income.

Human Poverty Index in the SAARC countries reveals the fact that more than 35% of the population live in poverty except Sri Lanka at 20.6%. Human Poverty Profile (Table 4) show that the performance of these countries is the poorest as far as sanitation is concerned. More than half of the population does not have access to sanitation in India, Bangladesh, Nepal and Bhutan. In the case of Sri Lanka and Maldives, the percentage is around 30.

In the sphere of human development, South Asia can learn a lot from the experience of East Asian economies. The SAARC countries have to shift the focus of government policies to human priority areas, viz. primary education, basic health facilities and the basic human needs of safe drinking water and sanitation facilities to the poorer sections of the population. A determined and conscious effort by the state is essential to improve the HDI values.

According to the *Human Development Report in South Asia*, 1997, a comprehensive human priority package can be financed by earmarking 1.6% of South Asia's GDP, to overcome human deprivation in the next fifteen years. In summary, it requires primary schooling for 126 million children, basic health care for 6% million people, safe drinking water for 770 million people, adequate nutrition for 87 million children and provision of family planning devices to 287 million married couples. On various assumptions derived from international experience, the total cost of this package will amount to $129 billion during the next fifteen years i.e. $8.6 million a year. Assuming that the GDP grows by an average of 5% p.a. over the next fifteen years, South Asian countries can finance this package by earmarking 1.6% of their GDP on average.[3] While this is a significant cost, it can be managed primarily through recasting and restructuring budget priorities.

TABLE 3

Gender-Related Development Profile (SAARC Countries)

	Life Expectancy at Birth (years) 1995		*Adult Literacy rate (%) 1995*		*Combined first, second and third level Gross Enrolment Ratio (%) 1995*		*Share of Earned Income (%) 1995*	
	Female	*Male*	*Female*	*Male*	*Female*	*Male*	*Female*	*Male*
India	61.8	61.4	37.7	65.5	46.5	60.1	25.4	74.6
Pakistan	63.9	61.8	24.4	50.0	27.0	53.1	20.6	79.4
Bangladesh	57.0	56.9	26.1	49.4	30.9	39.6	23.1	76.9
Sri Lanka	74.8	70.3	87.2	93.4	67.9	64.7	35.5	64.5
Nepal	55.6	56.3	14.0	40.9	42.6	66.6	33.4	66.6
Bhutan	53.7	50.4	28.1	56.2	31.0	31.0	32.3	67.7
Maldives	62.0	64.6	93.0	93.3	71.0	71.0	35.3	64.7

Source: *Human Development Report*, 1998, p. 132.

TABLE 4

Human Poverty Profile (SAARC Countries)

	People not expected to survive to age 40 (as % of total population) 1995	Adult Literacy Rate (%) 1995	Population without access to			Under Weight Childern under age five (%) 90-97	Children not reaching grade 5 (%) 1995	Real GDP per capita (PPP$)	
			% Safe Water 1990-96	% Health Services 1990-95	% Sani-tation 1990-96			Poorest 20% 1980-94	Richest 20% 1980-94
India	16	48.0	19	15	71	53	38	527	2,641
Pakistan	15	62.2	26	45	53	38	—	907	4,288
Bangladesh	21	61.9	3	55	52	56	—	606	2,445
Sri Lanka	6	9.8	43	7	37	38	2	516	9,897
Nepal	22	72.5	37	—	82	47	48	455	1,975
Bhutan	28	57.8	42	35	30	38	18	—	—
Maldives	13	6.8	4	—	34	38	7	—	—

Source: Human Development Report, 1998, p. 146.

TABLE 5

Trends in Human Development in Selected Asian Countries

HDI Value

	1960	*1970*	*1980*	*1992*	*1995*
India	0.206	0.254	0.296	0.382	0.451
Pakistan	0.183	0.244	0.287	0.393	0.453
Bangladesh	0.166	0.199	0.234	0.309	0.371
Sri Lanka	0.475	0.506	0.552	0.665	0.716
Nepal	0.128	0.162	0.209	0.289	0.351
Bhutan	—	—	—	—	0.347
Maldives	—	—	—	—	0.683
Korea	0.398	0.523	0.666	0.859	0.894
Thailand	0.373	0.465	0.551	0.798	0.838
Philippines	0.419	0.489	0.557	0.621	0.677
China	0.248	0.372	0.475	0.644	0.650
Malaysia	0.330	0.471	0.687	0.794	0.834

A STRATEGY OF DEVELOPMENT AT THE MICRO TERRAIN

The South Asian economies have enormous development potential in terms of human power and natural resources. If these countries encourage civil society initiatives and tap their potential fully at the micro-level, cost-effective measures for the delivery of social services and community development can be achieved. In fact, several grass-root experiments undertaken in several parts of these countries demonstrate the capacity of the poor to use their own creativity, local resources and knowledge for capital accumulation. A few such successful experiments are listed below.

Bangladesh

1. Grameen Bank, 1976—credit to the poor, covering 35,783 villages.
2. Bangladesh Rural Advancement Committee (BRAC), 1972—Community Development for the poorest of the poor, covering four districts of Bangladesh.

TABLE 6

Trends in Human Development (Regional Aggregates)

	Sub-Saharan Africa	*Arab States*	*South Asia*	*East Asia*	*South-East Asia and Pacific*	*Latin America and the Caribbean*	*Least developing countries*	*All developing countries*	*Eastern Europe and CIS*	*Industrial Countries*	*World*
Life Expectancy (Yrs.)											
1960	39.9	45.5	43.9	47.5	45.3	55.3	39.1	46.0	66.6	68.6	50.2
1995	50.6	63.5	61.8	69.3	64.7	69.2	51.2	62.2	68.1	74.2	63.6
Infant Mortality Rate											
1960	166	166	163	146	127	107	170	149	55	39	129
1995	104	55	74	37	48	35	109[b]	65	26	13	60
Access to Safe Water (%)											
1975-80	—	—	—	—	—	60	—	—	—	—	—
1990-96	—	—	—	—	—	77	57	71	—	—	—
Under Weight Children under age five (%)											
1975	31	20	68	26	46	18	—	40	—	—	—
1990-97	30	17	50	16	34	10	39[b]	30	—	—	30[b]
Adult Literacy Rate (%)											
1970	31	31	32	53	66	74	30	48	—	—	—
1995	57	56	51	82	87	87	49	70	99	99	78

Gross Enrolment Ratio for All Levels (%age 6-23)											
1980	39	47	37	51	51	59	32	46	—	—	—
1995	42	58	52	65	61	69	36	57	75	83	62
Real GDP Per Capita (PPP $)											
1960	996	—	698	729	732	2137	562	915	—	—	—
1995	1,707	4,454	1,724	3,359	3,852	5,982	1,008	3,068	4,109	1,6337	5,990

3. Proshika, 1976—Skills for the poor, covering 22 districts of Bangladesh.
4. Rangpur-Dinajpur Rural Service (RDRS), 1990—Social Literacy Centres, North Bengal.

India

1. Working Women's Forum (WWF), 1970—Empowering women in urban slums, Tamil Nadu.
2. SEWA (Self-employed Women Association), 1972—Trade union for poor women, Ahmedabad.
3. Jawahar Rozgar Yojana (JRY), 1980—Employment for the poor—creating employment—750 to 850 million mandays per year, throughout the country.
4. Employment Guarantee Scheme, 1972—Productive Employment opportunity to the rural areas, Maharashtra.
5. Janma Bhoomi Programme, 1997—People's movement for reconstruction and development of the society—a comprehensive programme of social mobilisation of the people, particularly the poor, organising the community around specific interests such as thrift and credit groups, youth groups, Vạna Samrakhnana Samithis, water user's association, education committees and health committees with appropriate support structures, covering the entire state of Andhra Pradesh.

Pakistan

1. Edhi Trust, 1957—The poor man's messiah, covering 320 centres all over Pakistan.
2. Orangi Pilot Project, 1955—Cost effective Social Services particularly sanitation—benefitting 28,000 families by 1992.
3. Baanhn Bell, 1987—For forgotten people in remote villages—Benefitting 200,000 persons in about two hundred settlements.
4. Buniyad, 1993—Accelerating female literacy, covering 500 centres in Punjab Province.

Sri Lanka

1. Sarvodaya Shramadana Movement (SSM), 1990—Integration of low caste families, providing relief and rehabilitation programmes for the victims of ethnic conflicts and the disabled.
2. SANASA, 1979—Credit for the rural poor, a national movement.
3. Sarvodaya Women's Movement (SWM), 1987—a movement for the empowerment of women, covering 64 villages in Sri Lanka.

Nepal

1. Small Farmer Development Programme (S.F.D.P.), 1975—Provision of credit services to subsistence farmers, covering 140,000 households in 575 villages by 1992.

All these successful experiments point out the need for a mobilisation strategy at micro-terrain which can successfully tap the development potential of the people on the one hand and the natural resources of the region on the other. Most of schemes are also cost-effective, requiring less capital. It has been amply demonstrated that when the poor are organised and actively participate in development programmes, they are able to move away from a condition of dehumanisation and bare survival to a position of systematic economic strength. Such activities, in course of time, increase income generating and saving capacity of the poor. A strategy of development, systematically undertaking such schemes to the doorstep of the poor countrywide, can lead to a new capital accumulation process—a process very different from the conventional macro-development strategies. Adoption of such innovative approaches with a material basis on the ground, can alleviate poverty and human deprivation in a reasonable time-frame.

The agenda for the next SAARC meeting should be to formulate such a strategy of development by using the expertise available in the region to reach the goal of human development.

Arthur Lewis is correct in observing the following:

> The LDCs (less developed countries) have within themselves all that is required for growth. Their development does not in the long-run depend on the existence of the developed countries and their potential for growth would be unaffected even if all the developed countries were to sink under the sea."[4]

This statement is very true as far as human development in South Asia is concerned.

S.P. Gupta, former World Bank Economist has warned that a social time bomb is ready to explode unless our blind faith in the benefits of market economy is contained and unless social safety nets are positioned to take care of the poor. The ticking of the poverty bomb is more dangerous to the SAARC region than the nuclear bomb. Without eradicating the worst forms of poverty and human deprivation in the region, SAARC will not have any credibility in the world.

Notes and References

1. M.D. Morris first introduced the concept of the Physical Quality of Life Index (PQLI) which combines infant mortality, life expectancy at age one and literacy into a single composite index.
2. UNDP, *Human Development in South Asia*, 1997, p. 2.
3. *Ibid.*, pp. 106-9.
4. Lewis, W.A., *The Evolution of International Economic Order*, 1978.

References

Bhattacharya, Debesh (1993), *The Political Economy of Development*, Academic Publishers, Calcutta.

Dreze, Jean and Sen, Amartya (1998), *India—Economic Development and Social Opportunity*, OUP, New Delhi.

Dreze, Jean and Sen, Amartya (1998), *Indian Development Regional Perspectives*, OUP, New Delhi.

Hanumanth Rao, C.H. and Linneman, Hans (Ed.) (1996), *Economic Reforms and Poverty Alleviation in India*, Sage Publications.

Morris, M.D. (1979), *Measuring the Condition of World's Poor: The Physical Quality of Life Index*, Pergamon Press, Oxford.

Waqif, A.A. (1994), *Employment Generation and Poverty Alleviation in South Asia: Some Perspectives and Scenarios*, New Delhi.

Wignaraja, Ponna and Srivardana, Susil (1998), *Pro-Poor Planning Through Social Mobilization in South Asia.*

The World Bank (1997), *World Development Report.*

Asian Development Bank, *Asian Development Outlook* (1996 and 1997).

Mahbub-ul-Haq (1997), *Human Development in South Asia,* 1997, The Human Development Centre, Oxford.

UNDP, *Human Development Report,* 1998.

31

Measures of Human Development and Related Concepts: A Case Study of Tamil Nadu

C.B. PADMANABHAN AND KANAKASABAI NAGARAJAN

The neo-classical view point is reflected in the concept of Human Resource Development, the theories of human capital and the more recent theories of endogenous growth. These are called human resource developers by Streeten (1994). In this approach the HRD is a means to an end of economic growth and it is regarded as human capital. The formation of human capital or its accumulation has to be carefully encouraged and monitored.

LIMITATIONS OF HUMAN CAPITAL APPROACH

Of course, critics are not wanting for this approach on various grounds which are not merely semantic but of substantive implications for government policy and theoretical clarification e.g. the traditional human capital neo-classical approach is narrow and views educational process as organised on an assembly line basis and concepts from main stream economics are applied to education, resulting in that branch of study called economics of education. Tapas Majumdar has been pleading for quite some time now for a new economics of education to rectify the drawbacks in the traditional economics of education. In particular, he referred to a category mistake which is an application of 3 ideas generally used in what Majumdar calls main-line economics which are applied to economics of Indian education and inappropriate conclusions are drawn. They are: (1) the marginal rate of return on capital as defined by Solow; (2) based on that definition the marginal social rate of return defined to include the externalities of an investment decision; and (3) the definition and characterisation of optimisation exercise. Corresponding to the above 3 are: (1) marginal rate of return on capital invested on education, (2) the marginal social rate of return on capital invested in education, and (3) the implied optimisation process of the private or social decision-makers in investment in education.

The more recent theories of human capital focussing attention on endogenous growth, the origins of which are attributed to Paul Romer and Robert Lucas among others. Romer is of the view that technological progress is not an exogenous factor influencing development but the result of deliberate action taken in response to market incentives or as sociologists would hold that innovative approaches are adopted as a sequence to the process of education. One can note in this strand of thinking an approach to inter-disciplinarity with concern for change and innovation and its relationship with education. Lucas on the other hand would emphasise that education enables external economies or externalities to be obtained as benefits of education. Both the approaches point to the need for imparting more dynamism in the approach to economic growth by education or HRD.

EMERGENCE OF HUMAN DEVELOPMENT APPROACH

Another approach is human development which UNDP has been advocating since 1990 and it has a great deal of policy orientation. These humanitarians as Streeten would call them, defined human development as a process of enlarging peoples' choices and in the development literature it came into lime-light with the appearance of World Development Report, 1980 which felt dissatisfied with the performance of economic growth in seventies and reducing economic poverty at a satisfactory pace.

Therefore, it pleaded for different but interrelated strategies viz., increasing employment, meeting basic needs, reducing inequalities of income and wealth and raising productivity of the poor and it related them with Human Resources Development which WDR called human development to emphasise that it is both an end and a means for economic growth. On this basis human development encompassed education and training, better health and nutrition and fertility reduction. It is of some significance to note that WDR 1980 report did not sharply distinguish between HRD and HD and there is considerable growth of literature on human development and construction of HD indices, etc. C.H. Hunumantha Rao has quite significantly called social development at the local or grass-root human development and its integration with the strategy for economic growth on the one hand and the strategies for target-oriented programmes at the grass-root level like alleviation of poverty programmes. The major hypothesis of this paper is that there should be better clarity about the various concepts and indices of human development which have grown vastly so that their use for sound human development at the policy level can be appreciated and what is more it should be better integrated with HRD which ought to be a more powerful tool in the strategy for economic growth. It is high time that sectoral approach is adopted for identifying the areas of HRD that can be helpful in reducing capital-output ratio and those sectors where human development can make human capital more effective in promoting economic growth. The plan of this paper is as follows: first of all a review of different HD indices are given; secondly, there is a discussion of their use; and third and last section draws conclusion about how human resource development can contribute to growth with the help of better and more human development.

A REVIEW OF DIFFERENT KINDS OF HDIs

This part of the paper reviews the different HDIs which have been put forward by agencies like UNDP and as worked out by research scholars. The focus of attention is developing countries like India and Indian states like Tamil Nadu or districts, where the removal of poverty is a major problem and where apart from overall macro-planning for economic growth, there are specific target-oriented programmes for poverty removal. The central hypothesis here is that such plans and programmes can be made more effective by promoting more and better human development particularly at the village, district or taluka level in rural sector. For making the existing physical and human capital more effective, and reduce capital-output ratios, human development is essential. But for undertaking such human development programmes there is need for compiling HDI year after year as Tamil Nadu has been doing and monitor the progress. Chronologically, 1990 UNDP report was the first one to calculate HDI by combining indicators of life expectancy, educational attainment and income into HDI, acknowledging its limitations like the inability of any single index to capture such a complex concept like HD, possibility of improvement, etc. Various improvements have been effected like improved desegregation by region within a country by different groups like social class or income or other items of disparities. Year after year, UNDP reports have been improving methodologies and coverage of HDIs and it has evoked different kinds of comment as for example 1997 report making a researcher question the very need for it.

1993 UNDP DEFINITION OF HDI

HDI is a process of enlarging peoples' choices. In principle, these choices can be infinite and change over time. But at all levels of development, three essential ones are for people to lead a long and healthy life, to acquire knowledge, and to have access to resources for a decent standard of living. If these choices are not available, many other opportunities will remain inaccessible.

1994 report has been described by P.R. Brahmananda as a major exercise to evolve a new composite well-being indicator approximating to Sen's capability notion. It defined the core of development activity, as enhancement of the capacity to function. In the words of Brahmananda: "Development, in the HDR, is described as the build-up of capability to enjoy the components of well-being assumed to be normally sought by human beings. Longivity, ability to read and write and thus of enjoyment of opportunities to be knowledgeable and to consciously participate in transactions with other human beings in society, ability to have access to higher education, learning of crafts and skills, and to be endowed with capacity to earn and command goods and services, are all supposed to be the components of well-being. The international index of human development is made out of: (a) average life expectancy at birth in different countries in terms of years, (b) the proportion of literate adult population above 15, (c) The mean years of schooling of children (below 15), and (d) adjusted (specially at higher levels) per capita income in terms of the Kravis-Heston (Pennsylvania University)—measures of purchasing power parities of different countries' currencies in U.S. dollars. Together (b) and (c) refer to the educational status of population. (a) is the resultant of general availability of, and access to, subsistence, nutritional food, medical and health facilities, and of immunity from internal disorders, wars, environmental, natural and other hazards to life. (d) Refers to capacity to purchase consumption goods and services".

Tamil Nadu Government has been every year preparing HDI for inclusion in the economic appraisal document and the following Tables 1 and 2 give the ranking of the states on the basis of per capita income and physical quality of life index. Even though on the basis of per capita income Tamil Nadu is 7th, in term of PQLI, it is 3rd among states which clearly shows the advantage of having PQLI.

The 1995-96 economic appraisal document has prepared an inter-state development index with a view to measuring the gains made in the social welfare front and the improvement achieved in the standard of living of people and quality of life due to economic development. It has used the following variables for construction of index: (1) per capita income, (2) infant mortality rate, (3) literacy rate, (4) life expectancy at birth, (5) per cent of agricultural workers to that population, (6) per capita food production, (7) per cent of population below poverty line, (8) unemployment rate (usual status), (9) road length per sq. km., (10) per capita value-added by manufacturing sector, and (11) registration of Motor Vehicle per 1,000 persons.

Keeping the All India average as 100, index for different variables for each state has been arrived at by using this method. In respect of three negative variables, viz. percentage of agricultural workers to total population, percentage of population below poverty line and unemployment rate, the reciprocal of original data has been used to construct the index. Thus, by adding the index obtained for each variable, the composite index has been arrived at. The overall index is given below:

Inter-State Development

Sl. No.	*States*	*Index*
1.	Punjab	2,268
2.	Kerala	1,978
3.	Haryana	1,597
4.	Maharashtra	1,440
5.	Tamil Nadu	1,288
6.	Gujarat	1,276
7.	Karnataka	1,163
8.	Himachal Pradesh	1,086
9.	Assam	1,058
10.	Uttar Pradesh	1,053
11.	West Bengal	1,049
12.	Madhya Pradesh	1,043
13.	Orissa	1,037
14.	Bihar	907
15.	Rajasthan	907
	All India	**1,100**

Tamil Nadu is 5th and above All India average.

A.K. Sivakumar (1991) attempted to develop a Human Development Index on the lines suggested by the Human Development Report of UNDP 1990 for 17 states for which data on all the three indicators, state domestic product, life expectancy at birth and literacy rate, were available. The life expectancy at birth projected by the expert committee on population for 1981-86 have been weighted by the 1981 sex ratio to arrive at combined life expectancy. The annual growth rate in adult literacy rates between 1971 and 1981 have been used to project adult literacy rate in 1987. For each state the ratio of the per capita state domestic product to national per capita income 1987 prices have been computed. Using these three indicators, the HDI for each state are constructed. The 17 states based on HDI has been classified into medium and low HDI states. While Haryana, Maharashtra, Punjab and Kerala fall into the former category, all

TABLE 1

Physical Quality of Life Index (PQLI) : By Major States (as of 1991)

States	Life Expectancy at birth	Rank	IMR	Rank	Literacy Rate	Rank	Composite Index	Rank	Life Expectancy at Birth (81-91)	Basic Data IMR (91)
1. Andhra Pradesh	52	7	70	9	45	11	56	8	58	73
2. Assam	36	13	67	12	53	9	52	9	52	81
3. Bihar	38	12	72	6	39	14	50	10	53	69
4. Gujarat	50	7	72	6	61	4	61	6	58	69
5. Haryana	57	5	73	5	55	8	62	5	60	68
6. Karnataka	58	3	68	10	56	7	61	6	61	77
7. Kerala	78	1	95	1	91	1	88	1	68	78
8. Madhya Pradesh	35	14	48	14	43	12	42	15	52	122
9. Maharashtra	58	3	76	4	63	2	66	3	61	60
10. Orissa	39	11	46	15	49	10	45	13	53	126
11. Punjab	64	2	79	2	57	6	67	2	63	53
12. Rajasthan	40	10	68	10	39	14	49	11	54	77
13. Tamil Nadu	49	9	77	3	63	3	63	4	57	57

14. Uttar Pradesh	31	15	61	13	42	13	45	13	50	93
15. West Bengal	50	7	71	8	58	5	60	13	57	70
All-India	45		67		52		55		55	80

CMIE, *Basic Statistics relating to the Indian Economy*, Volume II, States, September 1993, Bombay.

Notes: (i) The basić data on these three dimensions lacked a uniform reference year. In every case, however, the latest available information was depended upon. In as much as the reference years are not wide apart from one another, the readings made may be taken to reflect the correct position.

(ii) The method adopted by Morris David Morris in 'Measuring Time Conditions of India's Poor' in 1982 forms the basis for working out the PQLI of different States in this exercise.

TABLE 2

Ranking of States by Per Capita Income

States	*Per Capita Income at constant prices 1990-91 (Rupees)*	*Rank*
1. Andhra Pradesh	1,831	10
2. Assam	1,799	11
3. Bihar	1,189	15
4. Gujarat	2,,613	4
5. Haryana	3,499	3
6. Karnataka	2,055	5
7. Kerala	1,886	9
8. Madhya Pradesh	1,729	12
9. Maharashtra	3,522	2
10. Orissa	1,615	14
11. Punjab	3,744	1
12. Rajasthan	1,894	8
13. Tamil Nadu	1,965	7
14. Uttar Pradesh	1,628	13
15. West Bengal	1,979	6
All-India	2,239	

other fall into the latter category.

HDI BY DISTRICTS IN TAMIL NADU

A study by Arumugam, has been done with the following objectives: (a) to measure the levels of deprivation in the key indicators, (b) the reasons for deprivation among the districts in the State, (c) whether the governmental economic and social activities spread through uniformly among the districts or not, and (d) the need for sustained economic and social improvement for the development of the districts. For the measurement of HDI for the districts in the State as per the UNDP approach, the variables employed are real DDP per capita, life expectancy and the female literacy. The DDP per capita is meant to register the command over the resources to enjoy a decent standard of living. The longevity (life expectancy) is clearly a valuable aspect of good life. As the data on adult literacy by districts are not available, female literacy is considered as better indicator on education. As women become literate, fertility rate falls, infant and child health improves, children's educational level increases and household nutritional and sanitary conditions improve.

The foregoing paragraphs have given different kinds of human development indices with special reference to their use for promoting economic growth and poverty removal. The Eighth Plan had the major objective of human development and the mid-term appraisal of that Plan had given social indicators for India from 1951-52 onwards.

The ranking of the HDIs for the Districts in Tamil Nadu are given on next page.

Hanumantha Rao has indicated though not explicitly the following as important social indicators at the local level. Provision of minimum needs, such as elementary education, adult education, primary health centres, potable drinking water, public distribution of foodgrains, housing, etc. Social development raises the skills and awareness of the rural poor, enables them to bargain for better terms in rural market for wage, credit, etc. and eventually results in slowing down population growth. In this manner, human development can reduce poverty and prepare the rural poor for effective participation in the development process. For achieving all these, removal of human poverty rather than income poverty should be the objective.

A look at the Table 1 which presents the State-wise PQLI for 1991 and Table 2 for the State-wise per capita Income for 1990-91 would give the following high points:

(i) By the composite PQLI, Tamil Nadu was positioned fourth among the major States. It is pertinent to note that the State was in the seventh place with reference to per capita income;

(ii) By the three component indices, the State held the following relative positions: (a) the ninth highest Life Expectancy; (b) the third lowest Infant Mortality Rate, and (c) the second highest Literacy Rate. The achievement of Tamil Nadu in these spheres are

	Districts	*HDI*
I.	**Medium Human Development (Between 0.50 and 0.80)**	
1.	Tuticorin	0.7889
2.	Chennai	0.6401
3.	The Nilgiris	0.5897
4.	Coimbatore ·	0.5495
5.	Thirunelveli	0.5454
6.	Kanyakumari	0.5328
7.	Thiruvellore	0.5135
8.	Kanchipuram	0.5135
II.	**Low Human Development (Below 0.50)**	
9.	Cuddalore	0.4840
10.	Sivagangai	0.4763
11.	Thanjavur	0.4658
12.	Thiruvarur	0.4658
13.	Virudhunagar	0.4465
14.	Perambalur	0.3943
15.	Karur	0.3943
16.	Thiruchi	0.3943
17.	Nagappatinam	0.3850
18.	Vellore	0.3460
19.	Ramanathapuram	0.3354
20.	Theni	0.3280
21.	Madurai	0.3280
22.	Pudukkottai	0.3075
23.	Dindigul	0.2919
24.	Erode	0.2587
25.	Villupuram	0.2495
26.	Namakkal	0.2136
27.	Salem	0.2136
28.	Thiruvannamalai	0.1977
29.	Dharmapuri	0.1674

* It can be seen that no district in the state has high human development index and two-thirds of the districts have low human development index. Low ranking districts are low in everything.

commendable when viewed against the relative size of its population (6.60% of all-India), which was much higher than in respect of Kerala (3.44%), Punjab (2.40%) and Haryana (1.95%) as of 1991.

32

The Concept of Human Development and its Implications— Understanding in Terms of the System Approach

(A Case Study of West Bengal Economy)

BASABI BHATTACHARYA

I. INTRODUCTION

The concept of human development, as recently introduced by the UNDP in its *Human Development Report*, 1990, has, of late, come to the focus in the field of development economics. As distinguished from economic development, human development encompasses a broader spectrum of factors, in addition to income, working upon the overall human well-being. Transmission of the benefits of development for the human welfare is the crux of the concept. As a natural corollary, the concept of human deprivation emerges at the surface because if benefits of development are not spread adequately over an economy, some regions may remain deprived of the benefits. Thus, within an economy there may exist relative deprivations of human well-being among its sub-regions. Till date, the research on human development has proceeded along the lines of establishing the logical validity of the concept itself. technical formulations of the Human Development Index as also the various modifications of the index, and the empirical estimations of these at the national, state and district levels. It has not been hitherto explored what the varying levels of human development of different regions do virtually imply.

The present paper intends to analyse the concept of human development in terms of the system approach. The application of this approach in economic analysis has hardly any precedence. But analysis on human development, which is measured from the relative human deprivation of one region to the other, necessitates an adoption of a holistic approach which originates from the General System Theory. The intention here is to bring out explicitly what the varying levels of human development of different sub-regions within an economic system exactly indicate in terms of the forward and the backward linkages. Stated more clearly, if human development is understood as a process built up over time, then the differing values of the Human Development Index of the various regions in an economy reflect, as a backward linkage, how this process has worked upon these regions. Further, if the pattern of variation in the human development levels of the different sub-regions of an economy is extensive and persistent over time, then it is important to examine its impact, as a forward linkage, on the entire economy. For an economy, understanding of these linkages is important because any outcome apprehended to have adverse effects on the economy may be counteracted beforehand through suitable policy implementations. The entire analysis is based on the crucial concept of balance in an economic system embedded in the system approach.

While introducing the system approach, only the basic postulates, as being applied in natural and social sciences in the contemporary world, are theoretically discussed here. For the purpose of establishing the logical arguments in the paper, some empirical work done by the author earlier is cited in the appendix.

In Section 2, direction of research on human development is briefly surveyed. Section 3 provides an introduction to the system approach in contrast with the traditional functionalist approach. Section 4 attempts to justify the conceptual relevance of the system approach in human development analysis. Section 5 discusses how the various economic events are explained simultaneously by the adoption of the system approach to the human development analysis. It also refers to some supporting empirical evidence of the West Bengal economy. Finally, in the concluding section, the paper is summarized and some policy prescriptions are suggested.

2. DIRECTION OF RESEARCH ON HUMAN DEVELOPMENT

Until recently, research on human development has followed broadly two lines. First, beginning from the formulation of the original HDI, there have been series of technical modifications over the successive years, and, secondly, the empirical estimations of the index. The original concept of human development stems from the realization that GNP is only a measure of income and not a satisfactory measure of welfare since the ultimate well-being of the society depends on the uses to which income is put, not on the level of income itself. Several attempts have been made to represent human well-being in the form of an index (Morris and McAlpin, 1982, Mukherjee *et al.*, 1981). The most recent endeavour in this line of approach is the Human Development Index formulated by the United Nations Development Programme (UNDP). The index measures relative deprivation in overall perspective which includes health and education along with income. The components originally taken are life expectancy at birth, adult literacy rate and logarithm of income. The HDI is obtained as the following:

The deprivation index I_{ij} for the jth country with respect to the ith component is defined as:

$$I_{ij} = \frac{\left({}_{max}X_{ij} - X_{ij}\right)}{\left({}_{max}X_{ij} - {}_{min}X_{ij}\right)}$$

The average deprivation indicator I_j is given by:

$$I_j = \frac{1}{3}\sum_{i=1}^{3} I_{ij}$$

Finally, the HDI for the jth country is measured by $HDI_j = (1 - I_j)$. Regarding the formulation of the index, several points are raised and attempts are being made with respect to the choice of dimensions, the choice of indicators, the choice of minimum and maximum values, the weights attached to the components, etc. Subsequent improvements in the basic index have been made by including mean years of schooling with the adult literacy rate in the education component, using a modified way of allowing for diminishing marginal utility in the income component and so on. Consideration of freedom dimension has also been thought of. But, Human Freedom Index (HFI) has been kept separate from the HDI. The recent HDR, 1997, has presented the Human Poverty Index (HPI), since human poverty is considered more than income poverty only. The three types of deprivation taken in this index are survival deprivation, deprivation in education and knowledge, and deprivation in economic provisioning. Although HPI has a broader coverage than the HDI, it basically conveys more or less the same message as the HDI regarding the overall deprivation. However, the empirical evidence of West Bengal economy cited in the paper, is based on the estimation of the original HDI.

Regarding the empirical research on this field, the UNDP itself is providing estimations of HDI of different countries in the world in its Annual Reports along with the details of the deprivations with regard to the individual components of the index. Recently, Human Development Centre, Pakistan is also estimating various aspects of human development in South Asia which are published in Human Development in South Asia, Annual Report, 1997. Apart from these, there are some empirical estimations by the individual researchers.[1]

The brief survey reveals that human development has not so far been considered in the light of its implications. It is therefore felt necessary to examine the forward and backward linkages of the varying levels of human development within an economic region.

3. THE SYSTEM APPROACH

The system approach is based on the visualization of things as a whole. Systems are recognized as integrated wholes of their subsidiary components 'but never as the mechanistic of parts in isolable causal relations' (Laszlo, 1972, p. 15). The entities or subsidiaries interact among each other and exhibit some regularity of relationships. Thus, instead of concentrating on the basic building blocks, or basic substances, the system approach emphasizes the basic principles of organization (Capra, 1982, p. 286), or the nature in which the components or parts transact among themselves. The main focus of the system approach is on the recognition of complexes of elements standing in interaction (Bertalanffy, 1971, p. 32), as contrasted to the functionalist approach which considers entities in isolation. Therefore, a system appears not just as a set but as a connected set of elements possessing the characteristics of wholeness owing to its consequence (Blauberg, *et al.*, 1977, p. 126). It is for these qualifications that the system approach can explain the interacting happenings of the world order.

Contemporary sciences are discovering the existence of entities within the organized wholes in many realms of investigations. System sciences are correspondingly springing up everywhere. The concept is general in character with multi-disciplinary applicability. Thus, whatever be the system—physical, biological, social, economic or informational, the stress is on the examination of the nature of interlinkage among the parts. The origin of system theory can be traced to Bertalanffy's paper on 'An Outline Of General Systems Theory' (Bertalanffy, 1950). Since then, wide applications of this approach are being found in various fields of study.[2] However, in economic science limited use of this approach is found.[3]

The conceptual framework of the system approach needs to be clarified first. The most important concept in the system approach is the design of a system. The pattern of system organization is hierarchical in nature. Any system may be conceived of being composed of several sub-systems and every sub-system is a self-organizing whole consisting of still smaller entities. In other words, every system acts as a part of a larger whole. Next, the nature of relationship within any system reflects whether the interaction among the entities are smooth enough to be indicated as a balanced system. In a human body system, for example, balance requires, among other things, a smooth flow of blood all over the body. If for any reason, this smooth flow is disrupted, some parts are deprived of their requirement and continued deprivation might degenerate and cripple these parts, ultimately affecting the body itself. This systemic interdependence is true of all conceivable systems.

In economic systems, it is the nature of the flow of resources, physical or financial, that indicates its balance. Smoothness of the flow of resources in an economic system refers to its adequacy and efficiency so that all the entities, including the nodal entity, mutually interact to nourish each other and operate in a full swing. In an unbalanced system, sub-systems continue to vary widely in strength and reciprocity of exchange relations and the relatively deprived regions in an economy become gradually weak. It is important to distinguish between the causes and symptoms of an imbalance in a system. The irregularity of relationships which may throw a system off-balance is taken as its cause and when such irregularities lead to the occurrence of some events or mishaps, symptoms of imbalance are exhibited. For the lack of a system overview, there arises a tendency to identify wrongly the symptoms as causes or diseases. Symptomatic functional policies, therefore, fail, quite often, particularly when the problems originate from system imbalance. In the presence of a high degree of inter-relatedness in the contemporary world, isolated study of different parts originating from the functionalist approach leads only to such symptomatic treatment.

4. RELEVANCE OF THE SYSTEM APPROACH TO HUMAN DEVELOPMENT STUDIES

In recent studies, some attempts are being made to understand the linkages in the process of economic development. Experiences of development over the last few decades reveal disparate rates of growth between and within regions of an economy which create much the same range of problems as disparate rates of growth between the developed and the underdeveloped countries. The major lines of analysis that have emerged in this direction are the mobility field theory, central place theory and the growth pole strategy, all of which fall within the restricted scope of spatial or regional economics. However, while the notion of interdependence is taken into consideration in these theories, still the theories lack a comprehensive system overview of the economy at large. Further, manifestations of system disorder are not clearly and explicitly understood in these studies. In development economics, some scattered observations are found which appreciate the idea of looking an economy in its entirety and suggest achievement of balance within this entirety.[4] The importance of the system approach in development economics lies in the fact that economic development essentially implies transition of economic systems from one state to another brought about by an interplay of various economic and non-economic factors.

The methodological approach adopted in this study is to visualize an economy as a system with its components as its sub-systems which may be defined as per the requirements of the study—it may be regions, activity sectors or administratively classified growth centers at the state, district or block levels. Here the levels of human development, measured by the UNDP's formulation of the Human Development Index (HDI) (HDR, 1990), is taken to indicate the system balance. Since HDI is derived from the deprivation index which reflects the relative deprivation of one region to the other in an economy, application of the system approach for an examination of system balance appears particularly relevant for understanding the implication of the concept of human development. This study postulates that extensive relative deprivation of a particular pattern persisting over a period of time indicates system imbalance with some basic irregularities in the interrelationships among its sub-systems. The irregularity may be in the form of some directional bias or disruption in physical and financial flow relations and extensive dominance of some sub-systems leading to setting in of an alarming degree of relative deprivation.

The first basic question that arises when there is a system imbalance is that how these different values of the HDI are arrived at ? Some regions must have been relatively deprived than the others in an extensive manner of health, educational and income earning facilities in the process of development. As a natural corollary, one may understand that the flow of physical and financial resources have been in favour of some particular regions keeping the other regions highly deprived overtime. In developing economies, the most common evidence of this problem is exhibited in the urban directional flow of physical and financial resources creating a wide rural-urban gap in various aspects of human life.

The second question is if the system design is such that the resources are in favour of flowing in a particular direction in an economy, then what may be apprehended as a natural outcome, occurring as a forward linkage or system response? The deprivation thus created would make some regions poor than the others in the broader sense of the term which includes deprivation of health and educational facilities along with income deprivation. Existence of continued deprivation of this sort may encourage migration from lower human development regions to higher human development regions. Provided that the considerations of distance, cost and adaptability factors in migration are not strong enough to attach people with the place of origin, then, if facilities do not move towards people, people move towards facilities (HDR, 1991, p. 80). If the process continues to quite a noticeable extent, then the higher human development regions would be facing problems of over-crowding and unemployment which would eventually threaten its own human development level. Any attempt to implement anti-migration policies at the surface would only be a symptomatic treatment. System approach provides us the insight to look into the cause of the problem arising from the economic system design and treat the cause accordingly.

Another natural outcome of the process of excessive migration to the higher human development region would be the growth of informal sector in the in-migration region. A major feature of the developing economies is the urban directional flow of physical and financial resources, and the exodus to the urban regions is not usually matched by the corresponding growth of urban employment opportunities. For this reason, urban sub-regions of the contemporary developing economic systems are experiencing massive growth of the urban informal sector. This is again another symptom or manifestation of system imbalance which would not be solved by a symptomatic treatment of providing employment opportunities in the formal sector.

The above discussion brings to the surface some glaring facts of serious concern for developing economic systems. System imbalance revealed through human development levels results in economic mishaps in the form of poverty, excessive rural-urban migration and growth of urban informal sector—all of which are linked up in a system chain.

5. EVIDENCE FROM WEST BENGAL ECONOMY

As an evidence of the theoretical discussion in the preceding sections, economy of West Bengal is cited here. In West Bengal, for about a couple of centuries, Calcutta had been the center of colonial rule and the major port for external trade. This may have some contribution towards framing of the typical design of its economic system. It may even be contended that there is a high degree of centralization in the system around Calcutta. In some studies (Maikap, 1972), mention is made of the uni-nodal character of the West Bengal economy.

For citing the case of West Bengal economy, only the main results of the empirical estimations are mentioned in the paper.[5] Tables A1 and A2 in the Appendix, where HDIs of West Bengal districts are estimated for 1981 and 1991, reveal that there exists substantial variation in relative deprivation among the different districts of West Bengal. The districts West Dinajpur, Coochbehar and Maldah are the most deprived ones in terms of human development facilities, while Calcutta, Howrah, Hooghly and Burdwan are the privileged districts. Between 1981 and 1991, the HDI ranks of the districts have slightly altered and the extent of relative deprivation has slightly decreased. But the general pattern has remained almost the same indicating that there exists an imbalance in the economic system design of West Bengal.

In order to examine the nature of this imbalance, correlation coefficients of the HDI with the levels of urbanization and the shares of primary, secondary and tertiary sectors in the total state domestic product are estimated in Table A3. The results reveal that the districts with higher shares of the primary sector, that is, those which are predominantly rural, have low human development levels and HDI has highest positive association with the level of urbanization for both 1981 and 1991. This indicates an urban orientation in human development in West Bengal with a strong urban directional flow of physical and financial resources thus keeping the rural regions poor with overall deprivation.

For analysing the impact of system imbalance of this nature in West Bengal district in-migration data (1981) are regressed upon the district HDIs (1981) in Table A4. The results indicate that in-migration to district total areas and particularly to district urban areas are significantly determined by the human development levels of the districts. Moreover, migration from rural to urban areas of different districts is found to be strongly influenced by the HDI. A study by Sarkar (1988) also reveals that literacy rate, which is one of the components in HDI, operates as a major explanatory variable for migration in West Bengal and stands stronger than the Harris-Todaro rural-urban income differential argument. The migration profile within West Bengal reveals that there is a general tendency to flow towards the urban regions of Calcutta and its agglomeration. While it is true that the major part of migration is of the nature of rural-urban migration, the reverse process, i.e. urban-rural is also there, which the conventional theories fail to explain. People are often found to prefer to be even in the rural areas near the central place as a second best alternative rather than to be in the remote urban areas. In West Bengal, a sizeable migration takes place from the remote urban areas of other districts to the rural areas near Calcutta and other developed districts like Burdwan.[6]

Along with this migration towards the Calcutta centric region in West Bengal, several studies (Romatet, 1983, Bose, 1978, Bannerjee, 1982) reveal the magnum and growing size of the informal sector in Calcutta and the tremendous exploitative conditions under which this group of urban labour force operates. Growing urban labour force in Calcutta does get into different sorts of informal activities that meet various types of growing urban demand although these workers lie much below the poverty level (Mukherjee, S.). A micro-level study on the Socio-Economic Problems of the Unorganized Sector in Calcutta (Bhattacharya, *et al.*, 1976) reveals that most of the unorganized sector workers in Calcutta are migrants.

The existence of a high degree of relative human deprivation within West Bengal is, therefore, seen to give rise to overall poverty in the deprived region leading to migration to the higher human development regions which, ultimately, is resulting in congestion and massive growth of informal sector in these regions. The final consequence of this system imbalance is that the high human development regions, instead of generating spread effects over the economy, are themselves getting degenerated with a downward pull on the entire economy.

6. CONCLUSION AND POLICY IMPLICATIONS

The system theoretic analysis on human development provides a new dimension to its research. The research on human development has so far progressed along some technical modifications of the human development index and empirical estimations of the HDI. This paper highlights a very important aspect of understanding the implications of varying levels of human development of different regions through forward and backward linkages. The system approach adopted in this study locates the existence of disorder or imbalance in any economic system in the substantially varying human development levels of its sub-systems. The system imbalance in an economy is explained by the disrupted or some directional flow of physical and financial resources within the economy. In the case of West Bengal, cited as an example in this paper, the basically rural regions have higher relative human deprivation indicating an urban directional resource flow persisting over time. Due to this imbalance, several economic phenomena take place as symptoms of economic disorder. Therefore, overall poverty of the rural regions, excessive migration towards the urban and Calcutta centric regions and immense growth of urban informal sector are taking place in a system chain. Further, persistent happening of these phenomena is ultimately weakening the nodal growth centre with the result that the entire economy is caught in a system trap syndrome.

A way out from this impasse, which is evident in many of the developing economies of the world, is to go for establishing a balance in the economic system. This will be attained through smoothening the flow of physical and financial resources including the basic facilities for living all over the economy. A comprehensive policy for redirecting social investments is needed. Investments in public infrastructure and services need to be directed away from the centre to encourage the growth of local markets and small industries with rural links so that a number of efficiently operative growth centres in the rural exchange network may be established. Provision of public infrastructure to the less developed areas includes redirection of medical, educational, water supply, electricity, sanitation and transport facilities so that employment opportunities are created, rural unemployment is reduced, rural poor cross the poverty line and in general human development level of hitherto deprived people is lifted up. All these would bring about a long-term balanced interdependence among the sub-systems or sub-regions in an economy. The system overview of the conceptualization of human development has brought these issues into light.

Notes and References

1. For India Human Development Index for the major states have been estimated by Shiva Kumar, A.K. (1991) and Bhattacharya, B. (1996).
2. Brauers, W.K. (1976), Gouger, J.D. and Knapp, R.W. (1974), Degreen, K.B. (1970), Watt, K.E. (1966), Milsum, J.H. (1966), Shelly, G. and Cashman, T.J. (1975) etc.
3. Gaude, J. and Peek, P. (1976) mention that to analyze the economic effects of migration, it is necessary to investigate the relation between migration and the rest of the economy through a model of the whole economic system.
4. Levis, A.H. and Quance, C.Y. (1978), Lakshmanan, T.R. (1981).
5. Some of the empirical estimations are published earlier in Bhattacharya, B. (1996) and Bhattacharya, B. (1998). Therefore, the relevant tables are given in the appendix of the paper.
6. For details see Bhattacharya, B. (1996).

References

Bannerjee, N. (1982), "Survival of the Poor" in H.I Safa (ed.), *Towards a Political Economy of Urbanisation in Third World*, Delhi: Oxford University Press, pp. 175-87.

Bertalanffy, Von L. (1950), "An Outline of General System Theory", *British Journal for Philosophy of Science*, Vol. 1, No. 2, pp. 134-65.

———, (1971), *General Systems Theory: Foundations, Development, Applications*, London: Allen Lane.

Bhattacharya, B. (1996), "Inter-District Migration in Response to Disparities in Human Development—A Case Study of West Bengal in Roy Chowdhury, A. and Sarkar, D. (eds.), *Economy of West Bengal: Problems and Prospects*, Calcutta : Allied Publishers.

Bhattacharya, B. (1998), "Urbanisation and Human Development in West Bengal—A District Level Study with Inter-State Comparisons" in *Economic and Political Weekly* (forthcoming).

Bhattacharya, S., Ganguly, P. and Dutta, P. (1976), *A Micro-Level Study on the Socio-Economic Problems of the Unorganised Sector in Calcutta*, Report of the research project, Jadavpur University.

Blauberg, I.V., Sadovsky, V.N and Yudin, E.G. (1977), *Systems Theory: Philosophical and Methodological Problems*, Moscow: Progress Publishers.

Bose, A.N. (1974), "The Informal Sector in Calcutta Metropolitan Economy", WEP Urbanisation and Employment Research, *Working Paper No. 5*, Geneva: ILO.

Brauers,W.K. (1976), *System Analysis and Decision Models*, Amsterdam, North-Holland: Elsivier.

Capra, F. (1982), *The Turning Point*, London: Flamingo: Fontana Paperbacks.

Couger, J.D. and Knapp, R.W. (1974), *System Analysis Techniques*, New York: Wiley.

Degreen, K.B. (1970), *System Psychology*, New York: McGraw Hill.

Gaude, J. and Peek, P. (1976), "The Economics Effects of Rural-Urban Migration", *International Labour Review*, Vol. 14, No. 3.

Human Development Centre (1977), *Human Development in South Asia*, Karachi, Oxford University Press.

Lakshmanan, T.R. (1981), *A Systems Model for Rural Development*, Magoya: UNCRD, Mimeo.

Laszlo, E. (1972), *The Systems View of the World*, New York: Braziller.

Levis, A.H. and Quance, C.Y. (eds.) (1978), *Systems Theory Applications to Agricultural Modelling*, Washington, D.C., US Deptt. of Agricultural and National Science Foundation.

Maikap, A.K. (1972), "Correcting Regional Imbalance in West Bengal and the Role of Market Towns and Centres" in Bhattacharya, D. (ed.), *Focus on West Bengal Problems and Prospects*, Samatat Prakashani.

Milsum, J.H. (1960), *Biological Control Systems*, New York: McGraw Hill.

Morris, D.M. and Mcalpin, M.B. (1982), *Measuring the Condition of India's Poor: The Physical Quality of Life Index*, New Delhi: Promilla & Co.

Mukherjee, M., Gayen, G. and Roy, I. (1981), "A Quantitative Study of Inter-State Variation in Social Development", *Journal of Income and Wealth*, Vol. 5, No. I, January.

Mukherjee, S., "Informal Sector—Only Hope of the Urban Poor in Metropolis", Mimeo.

Romatet, E. (1983), "Calcutta's Informal Sector : Theory and Reality", *Economic and Political Weekly*, Vol. XVIII, No. 50, December, pp. 2115-28.

Sarkar, P. (1988), "Determinants of Rural-Urban Migration in West Bengal", Dasgupta, B. (ed.), *Urbanization, Migration and Rural Change: A Study of West Bengal*, Calcutta: A. Mukherjee & Co. Pvt. Ltd., pp. 261-27.

Shelly, G. and Cashman, T.J. (1975), *Business Systems Analysis and Design*, California: Anahein Publishing.

Shiva Kumar, A.K. (1991), "UNDP's HDI: A Computation for the Indian States", *Economic and Political Weekly*, Oct. 12,

United Nations Development Programme (1990, 1991, 1992, 1993, 1994, 1995, 1996 and 1997), *The Human Development Report*, Oxford: Oxford University Press.

Watt, K.E. (1966), *Systems Analysis in Ecology*, New York: Academic Press.

APPENDIX TABLE 1

Human Development of West Bengal Districts, 1981

Districts	*Human Development Index (HDI)*	*HDI rank*	*DDP rank*
Calcutta	1.0000	1	1
Howrah	0.7374	2	2
Hooghly	0.6767	3	3
Burdwan	0.5990	4	4
Darjeeling	0.5581	5	5
24-parganas	0.5367	6	6
Bankura	0.4373	7	7
Purulia	0.3631	8	8
Birbhum	0.3057	9	9
Nadia	0.2966	10	10
Midnapore	0.2832	11	11
Jalpaiguri	0.2528	12	12
Murshidabad	0.1707	13	13
West Dinajpur	0.1107	14	14
Coochbehar	0.0766	15	15
Maldah	0.0000	16	16

Note: Components of the HDI taken here are infant survival rate, literacy rate above 7 years and per capita district domestic product.

Source: *Census of India, 1981, Social and Cultural Tables, Series,* 23, Part IVA and Child Mortality Estimates of India, Occasional Paper No. 5 of 1989; Govt. of West Bengal State Statistical Abstract, 1978-89, Bureau of Applied Economics and Statistics.

APPENDIX TABLE 2

Human Development Index of West Bengal Districts, 1991

Districts	*Human Development Index (HDI)*	*HDI rank*	*DDP rank*
Calcutta	1.0000	1	1
Howrah	0.7671	2	2
Hooghly	0.6956	3	3
Burdwan	0.6521	4	5
24-parganas	0.6409	5	4
Midnapore	0.5398	6	12
Birbhum	0.4866	7	7
Bankura	0.4344	8	8
Darjeeling	0.3979	9	6
Nadia	0.3891	10	10
Purulia	0.3351	11	9
Jalpaiguri	0.3026	12	11
Malda	0.1980	13	16
Murshidabad	0.1852	14	13
Coochbehar	0.1034	15	15
West Dinajpur	0.0524	16	14

Note: Components of the HDI taken here are infant survival rate, literacy rate above 7 years and per capita district domestic product.

Source: *Census of India, 1991, Primary Census Abstract, Paper 2 of 1992* and Final Population Totals; Paper I and Paper II, Sample Registration System (for unpublished data on infant mortality rate). Central Statistical Organisation, 1991. *Estimates of State Domestic Product and Gross Fixed Capital Formation,* 1992, and *Statistical Pocket Book.*

APPENDIX TABLE 3

Correlates of HDI with Structural Indicators of Development at West Bengal District Levels

Structural indicators of development	*Human development index*	
	1981	*1991*
UR	0.85	0.81
	(6.04)	(5.17)
DPP	-0.86	-0.74
	(-5.65)	(-4.12)
DPS	0.61	0.54
	(2.88)	(2.40)
DPT	0.71	0.61
	(3.77)	(2.88)

Notes: (1) URi-Share of urban population in total population in the ith district.

DPPi = Share of the primary sector in the total domestic product of the ith district.

DPSi = Share of the secondary sector in the total domestic product of the ith district.

DPTi = Share of the tertiary sector in the total domestic product of the ith district.

(2) Figures in the parenthesis indicate the t-values.

(3) Values of the structural indicators are taken as the averages over period 1970-71 to 1980-81 and 1980-81 to 1990-91 for estimating correlates of HDI (1981) and HDI (1991) respectively.

Sources: *State Statistical Abstract, 1978-89*, Bureau of Applied Economics and Statistics, Govt. of West Bengal; *Census of India, 1971, General Population Tables Series 22*, Part IIA (I), *Census of India, General Population Tables Series 22*, and *General Economic Tables Series 23*, Part IIIA & B (I). Other Sources are same as Tables A1 & A2.

APPENDIX TABLE 4

Estimated Regression of Migration to Districts in West Bengal, 1981

Eqn. No.	*Development Variable*	*Intercept*	*Independent Variable*	
	Set I: Migration to Total Areas of Districts			
1.	TT=	21.0244+	58.7000 HDI	R^2 = 0.6093
		(6.0046)	(12.5618)	Adj. R^2 = 0.5814
		(3.5014)	(4.6729)	F (1/14) = 21.8360
			29.0757 HDI	
2.	TR=	17.7764	(10.6133)	R^2 = 0.3486
		(5.0732)	(2.7372)	Adj. R^2 = 0.3021
		(3.5039)		F(1/14) = 7.4923
			27.5633 HDI	
3.	TU=	3.1698+	(7.4060)	R^2 = 0.4973
		(3.5401)	(3.7218)	Adj. R^2 = 0.4614
		(0.8954)		F(1/14)= 13.8516
	Set II: Migration to Total Areas of Districts			
4.	UT=	-4.6393+	62.2879 HDI	R^2 = 0.8004
		(3.9727)	(8.3110)	Adj.R^2 = 0.7860
		(-1.1678)	(7.4946)	F(1/14)= 56.0000
			34.3101	
5.	UR=	-4.5014+	HDI	R^2 = 0.7503
		(2.5284)	(5.2894)	Adj. R^2 = 0.7325
		(-1.7804)	(6.4866)	F(1/14) = 42.0750
			26.8513 HDI	
6.	UU =	0.0980+	(6.4220)	R^2 = 0.5553
		(3.0698)	(4.18 12)	Adj. R^2 = 0.5235
		(0.0319)		F(1/14)= 17.4820
	Set III: Migration to Total Areas of Districts			
7.	RT=	20.2495+	14.1173	R^2 = 0.0769
		(5.7093)	HDI	Adj. R^2 = 0.0058
		(3.5468)	(13.5682)	F(1/13) = 1.0826
			(1.0405)	

8. RR =	18.0435+	9.0787 HDI	R^2 = 0.0395
	(5.2225)	(12.4113)	Adj. R^2 = 0.0343
	(3.4550)	(0.7315)	F(1/13)= 0.5351
		5.0324 HDI	
9. RU =	2.205+	(1.8787)	R^2 = 0.3557
	(0.7605)	(2.6788)	Adj. R^2 = 0.3061
	(2.7950)		F(1/13) = 7.1757

Notes: 1. Figures in the parentheses in the first and second rows are s.e. t-values respectively.

2. The dependent variables which are regressed upon the HDI are the following: UT, TU & TR are the total migration from total, urban and rural areas of other districts respectively; UT, UU & UR are the urban migration from total, urban and rural areas of other districts; RT, RU & RR stand for the rural migration from the similar areas mentioned above. For further details, see Bhattacharya, B. (1996).

Source: *Census of India, 1981, Migration Tables, Series 23, Part VA and B.* For HDI sources are same as in Table A1.

33

Human Resource Development and Human Development Index in Western India

ANJU KOHLI AND SADHNA KOTHARI

Human resource is an extremely important source of energy and a versatile source. The resource is fairly stable in the short-run and is quite dependable. Human beings are not only instruments of production but also ends in themselves, that is, why human resource is a key factor in the process of growth and development. However, due to socio-cultural reasons, it is not always possible to dispose-off, utilise or regulate this resource in any manner one may like to do. So it becomes necessary to know in quantitative terms the number of people living in a country at a particular time, the rate at which they are growing and the composition and distribution of population.

The study of human resource is vital from the point of view of economic welfare. The concept of human resource development has two dimensions—first dealing with their development, and, second with regard to their utilisation. These two are interlinked and feed upon each other to respond the desired socio-economic objectives.[1] The focus of the present paper is analysis of characteristics of human resources in Gujarat, Haryana, Madhya Pradesh, Punjab, Rajasthan and Uttar Pradesh of Western India individually and comparatively, to identify the backward states on the basis of human development index and to emphasise the factors on which human development depends. The data for the study are collected from Census of India (1991),[2] Economic Survey (1996-97, 1997-98).[3] With the help of various quantitative techniques, the data collected on different human development indicators are analysed. An attempt is also made to highlight the results through cartographic techniques.

Table 1 shows some of important human resource characteristics—decadal population growth rate, sex ratio, percentage of urban population, percentage of working population, number of persons per household, density of population—of selected six states of India.

The rate of population growth depends on rate of fertility, mortality and migration. Migration in India is a small proportion

TABLE 1

Human Resource Characteristics

States	*Population growth rate (1981-91)*	*Sex ratio*	*% of urban population*	*% of total workers*	*Density of population per sq. km.*	*Number of persons per household*
Gujarat	21.19	934	34.49	40.23	211	5.51
Haryana	27.41	805	21.63	31.00	372	6.30
Madhya Pradesh	26.84	931	23.18	42.82	149	5.65
Punjab	20.81	882	29.55	30.88	403	5.92
Rajasthan	28.44	910	22.88	38.87	129	6.04
Uttar Pradesh	25.48	879	19.84	32.20	473	6.23
Region	25.02	890	25.26	36.00	290	5.94
India	23.85	927	26.13	37.50	273	5.51

Source: Census of India (1991).

of its population and reduction in the population growth rate can occur if the mortality rate increases or the fertility rate decreases. Population growth rate has serious impact on the socio-economic structure, quality of life and environment of the state. Table 1 shows lowest decadal population growth rate is in Punjab (20.81) and highest in Rajasthan (28.49). The average decadal growth rate of the region is 25.02, higher than the national average 23.85. The states having the decadal population growth rate above the average are Haryana, Madhya Pradesh, Rajasthan and Uttar Pradesh and below the average growth rates are Punjab and Gujarat. Migration figures of the census show migration in these states is low, so natural increase in population has taken place.

In any study of the population analysis the *sex composition* plays a vital role. It is affected by the differentials in the mortality conditions of males and females, sex selective migration and the sex ratio at birth. Table 1 shows highest sex ratio is in Gujarat and lowest in Haryana. The average sex ratio of the western region is 890 while that of nation is 927. Punjab, Uttar Pradesh and Haryana are having below average sex ratio while Gujarat, Madhya Pradesh and Rajasthan are having above average. The level of sex ratio shows the status of females in the states which is almost half of the population.

Percentage of urban population reflects the urbanization in the state which is associated with development and change. Highest percentage of urban population is in Gujarat (34.49) and lowest in Uttar Pradesh (19.84). The average percentage of the urban population in the region is 25.26, which is less than the national average 26.13. The states having the percentage of urban population above average are Gujarat and Punjab, while below average are Madhya Pradesh, Rajasthan, Haryana and Uttar Pradesh.

The ratio of productive and the unproductive population depends on *percentage of working population* in the state. This also shows the dependency ratio in the state. Highest percentage of working population is in Madhya Pradesh (42.82) and lowest in Punjab (30.88). The migration figures of the census show inter-state migration in Punjab and Haryana is higher than other states which has reduced the percentage of working population in these states. The average percentage of the working population in the region is 36.0 which is less than the national average 37.5. The states having the percentage of working population above average are Madhya Pradesh, Gujarat and Rajasthan, while below average are Uttar Pradesh, Haryana and Punjab.

Density of Population shows the concentration and congestion of population in the state. Highest density of population is in Uttar Pradesh (423) and lowest in Rajasthan (129). The average density of population in the region is 290 which is higher than the national average 273. States having density of population above average are Uttar Pradesh, Punjab, Haryana while below average are Gujarat, Madhya Pradesh and Rajasthan.

The *household size* of the population has also socio-economic implications. Larger the size of the family, larger will be socio-economic burden on the family. Table 1 shows developed states like Punjab and Gujarat have less number of persons per household than less developed states like Rajasthan, Uttar Pradesh and Madhya Pradesh, only exception is Haryana. The average size of per household in the western region is 5.94 higher than the national average 5.51. Larger number of persons per household is in Haryana (6.30) while Gujarat is having least number (5.51). The states having above average number of persons per household are Haryana, Uttar Pradesh, Rajasthan while Punjab, Madhya Pradesh and Gujarat are having less than the average.

The six states of western region are classified in to areas of less backward, medium backward and highly backward[4] on the basis of human development index which is composite of following human development indicators:

(a) Life expectancy (LE)
(b) Infant mortality rate (IMR)
(c) Death rate (DR)
(d) Birth rate (BR)
(e) Literacy rate (LR)
(f) Per capita state domestic product (PSP)

In these indicators, life expectancy, infant mortality rate, death rate, birth rate are the measures of longevity and capture several aspects of welfare because of their close correlation with nutrition, health and other important biological and social achievements. Literacy is essential and significant factor in human resource development and per capita state domestic product reflects good standard of living.

Human Development Index (HDI) is constructed according to the methodology used in the human development index in the UNDP's human development report.[5] The maximum deprivation is set to one and no deprivation equal to one.

The deprivation indicator I_{ij} for the jth state with respect to ith variable is:

$$I_{ij} = \frac{\left(\text{Max } X_{ij} - X_{ij}\right)}{\left(\text{Max}_j\, X_{ij} - \text{Min}_j\, X_{ij}\right)}$$

$$I_{ij} = \frac{\sum I_{ij}}{n}$$

$$\text{HDI}_j = (1 - I_j)$$

Following Table 2 shows the deprivation indicators and human development index of the study area.

Table 2 shows human development index of the region (0.417) is very low in comparison to India (0.447). India itself is in the block of countries of low human development index. Average index of the world is 0.764 and highest index is 0.960 of Canada.[6] It is apparent from the table, human development is low in all the six states of the region. On the basis of human development index these states can be grouped into three categories:

Areas of High Backwardness

Rajasthan, Madhya Pradesh and Uttar Pradesh have human development index very low between 0 to 0.30. Rajasthan is having below average life expectancy, above average infant mortality rate, above average birth rate, below average literacy rate and below average state domestic product. Madhya Pradesh and Uttar Pradesh along with these indicators have even above average death rate. Rajasthan is having lowest literacy rate, Madhya Pradesh is lowest in life expectancy, highest in infant mortality rate, highest in infant mortality rate, highest in death rate and Uttar Pradesh is having highest birth rate and lowest per capita state domestic product.

MAP

Western India : Backwardness in Human Resource Development (1991)

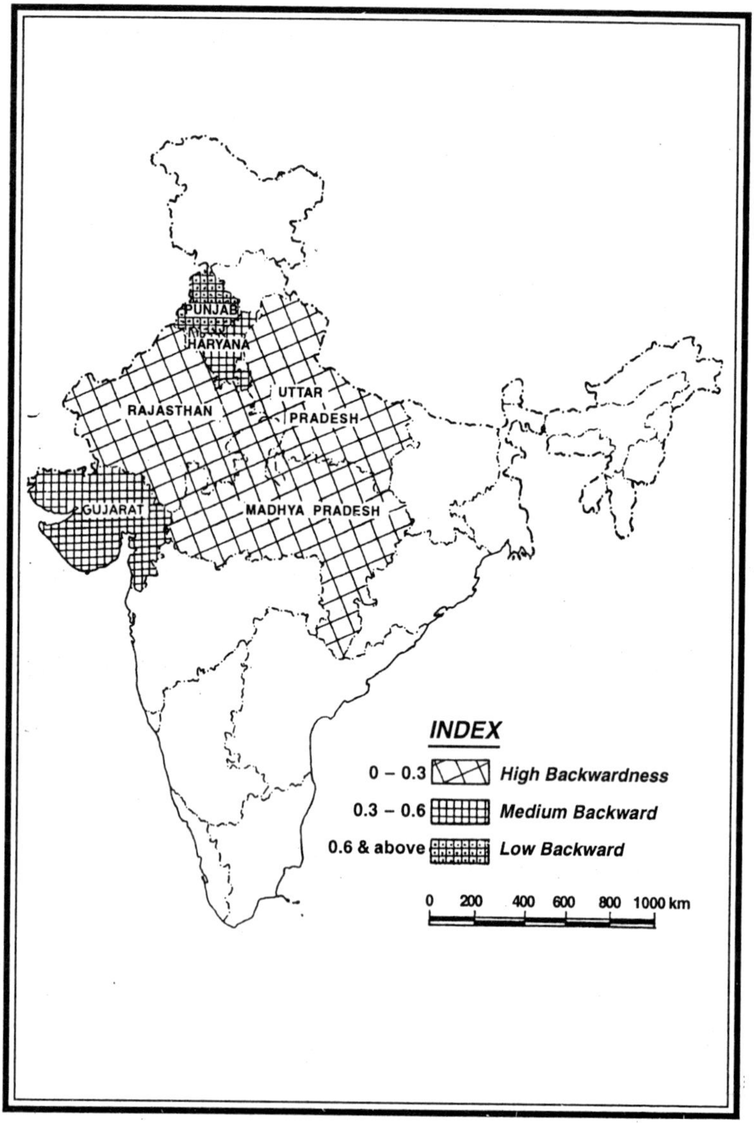

TABLE 2

Deprivation Indicators and Human Development Index

States	*LE*	*IMR*	*DR*	*BR*	*LR*	*PSP*	*AV*	*HDI*	*Rank*
Gujarat	0.66	0.48	0.02	0.59	0.63	0.49	0.478	0.532	3
Haryana	0.50	0.56	0.01	0.70	0.71	0.28	0.460	0.534	2
Madhya Pradesh	0.95	0.99	0.07	0.99	0.82	0.76	0.763	0.237	6
Punjab	0.33	0.44	0.01	0.47	0.68	0.21	0.357	0.643	1
Rajasthan	0.77	0.76	0.03	0.97	0.99	0.72	0.707	0.293	4
Uttar Pradesh	0.89	0.90	0.04	0.98	0.93	0.78	0.753	0.247	5
Region	0.67	0.69	0.03	0.78	0.79	0.54	0.583	0.417	—

Source: Computed.

Areas of Medium Backwardness

Gujarat and Haryana have human development index between 0.30 to 0.60. The life expectancy in Gujarat is average, infant mortality rate, death rate and birth rate are below average while literacy rate and per capita state domestic product is above average. Haryana is also having above average life expectancy, below average death rate, above average literacy rate and per capita state domestic product.

Areas of Low Backwardness

Among the selected six states only Punjab is having above 0.60 human development index. Punjab is having highest life expectancy, lowest infant mortality rate, birth rate and death rate, highest per capita state domestic product and relatively high level of literacy.

Table 3 shows that out of six states of the study area, three states are in the high backwardness category, two states in medium backwardness and only one in low backwardness. These categories are also depicted in the enclosed figure. Madhya Pradesh state is highest backward in human resource development. The value of χ^2 (0.42) and of variance ratio (0.56) also shows non-homogenity in human development index.

An achievement of the target of human resource development depends largely on the availability and functioning of accessible education and health institutions. Education develops basic skills and abilities and thereby boots productivity. Whereas level of health is equally important input for development, it is hypothesised in the present study that there is positive and close association between human resource development and educational and health amenities. The estimated correlation coefficients of human development index with education and health are as follows:

TABLE 3

Estimated Correlation Coefficient (HDI, Education and Health)

Var.	*Education*	*Health*
HDI N=6	+ 0.27	+ 0.83

Critical value (1-Tail, .05) = + or - .73.
Critical value (2-Tail, .05) = +/– .81.

The estimated correlation coefficients are in accordance with the hypothesised signs. The relationship of human development index with health amenities is significantly higher than educational facilities. But the whole western region like the national trend is having less health institutions than educational institutions.

A simple linear regression model is also built to highlight the causal relationship of human development index with explanatory variables, education and health. Following Table 4 shows the regression results:

TABLE 4

Regression Results

Explanatory Variables	*Regression Coefficients*	*Dependent Variable*
Education	0.2217 (1.619)*	HDI
Health	7.5960 (3.706)**	
Constant = 2.0561 R^2 = 0.83 R^2 = 0.72	F ratio = 7.5752	

't' values are in parentheses.

* significant at 5% level.

** significant at 10% level.

The regression results also support the hypothesised relationship. The 't' value of education is significant at 5% and health at 1% level of significance. The values of R^2 and F-ratio also confirm the formulated hypothesis.

POLICY IMPLICATIONS

The study of human resource development in western India, i.e., of Rajasthan and its adjoining states reveals the western region as a whole and its constituent states have high population growth rate, low sex ratio, less urban population, high dependency ratio, high average size of the household and high concentration of population in comparison to the national average. A comparative study of six states of western India show Punjab, Haryana and Gujarat are relatively more developed in human resources. Human development index is also constructed on the basis of life expectancy, infant mortality rate, birth rate, death rate, literacy rate and per capita state domestic product to identify the areas of less, medium and more backward. On this basis Punjab is less backward and Madhya Pradesh is most backward with a small difference of Uttar Pradesh. Human development depends on many factors. Among these, in the present study the relationship of human development index is observed with education and health. The results show health amenities have greater influence on human development than educational facilities, whereas in India as well as in the region the number of former is less than the later.

On the basis of this study, it is suggested that there is need to develop human resources. Recently, the government has taken various steps to develop human resources like programme of education for all by 2000 A.D. For the effective implementation of these programmes, it is necessary to integrate human resource development and the development planning. Along with the development of human resource there should also be proper utilisation of human resources because of the close linkages between two.

Notes and References

1. P. Brahm (1997): 'Human Resources and Manpower Development', *Manpower Journal.*
2. *Census of India* (1991).
3. *Economic Survey* (1996-97, 1997-98).
4. Tripathi, B.S. and R.P. Tiwari (1997), 'Changing Pattern in Human Resource Development of Madhya Pradesh', *Geographical Review of India*, No. 4, Vol. 37.
5. United Nations Development Programme (1990), *Human Development Report, 1990*, Oxford University Press, New York.
6. *World Development Report*, 1996.

34

Human Resource Development and Management in Small Scale Industry—Coimbatore District: A Case Study

K.S. Sivaprakash

The study has been undertaken in Human Resource Development and Management problem *vis-a-vis* practices in selected small-scale industrial units in and around Coimbatore District. Human Resource Development is gaining widespread currency in India as well as in many other countries around the globe. Some pursue it like zealots. Some others see it as the current fad in management circles which must be pursued to keep up with Joneses and there are some who see it with outright cynicism. But since the idea is still evolving and taking shape it is not easy to delineate its scope and limits.

The ever present need to humanise organisations and the social imperative of accelerating the process of industrialisation, a third set of factors have come into existence to draw fresh attention to the human resource development in organisations, the factors are:

(i) **Increasing Competition**

Due to the recent changes in national policies, business organisations faced increasing competition in market place. It requires better human resource to compete.

(ii) **Pressures for Growth**

One of the best antidotes to organisational decline and death is continuous growth and expansion. Managers of these larger organisations need a higher level of managerial skills.

(iii) **Rapid Technological Change**

The fast pace of changes in technology are major pressure on organisations these days. Change in technology demands frequent changes in organisational structure and systems as well as change in the required skills.

(iv) **Dearth of Suitable Human Power**

Due to a lack of sufficient industrialisation, increasing competition and changing technologies, many organisations face the problem of getting suitably trained and skilled persons at various levels.

(v) **Changing Needs of People**

Due to various sociological changes, the needs and aspirations of employees charge from time to time. These needs are related to work benefits, career growth, etc.

The broad scope of the major disciplines which are making significant contribution towards human resource management and development is as follows:

(a) Psychology

The focus is on studying an individual, his needs, aptitudes, motivations, aspirations, behaviour, etc., and the consequences of all these for the individual. The attempt is to understand differences amongst individuals.

(b) Sociology

The focus shifts from individuals to aggregates of human beings. Sociologists study groups, communities, societies as well as crowds, mobs, and social movements, etc.

(c) Socio-Psychology

This is a compound of sociology and psychology. The focus is on interpersonal relations, group and inter-group dynamics, group effectiveness, social roles and the impact of all these on the individual involved.

(d) Anthropology

This discipline focuses on culture, the norms, the values, symbols, myths and legends, rituals and ceremonies.

(e) Political Science

This discipline focuses on the aspects of social power and in it, the alternative for social governance are studied.

(f) Economics

Emphasis here has been mainly on the material aspects of human societies and behaviour of industrial firms under the assumption that human beings are rational.

(g) Organisational Behaviour

This is the latest and most significant discipline in the context of human resource development in organisations. It encompasses the study of behaviour of individuals and groups in organisations as well as behaviour of organisations as social, political and cultural entities.

Human Resource Development is an applied area which utilises the knowledge and technology from all these disciplines and particularly from organisational behaviour, design and development.

Human Resource Management on the other hand includes the traditional functions of personnel and administration such as employee data files, job evaluation, compensation, benefits, security, safety, health, etc. It also has an important focus on development encompassing, recruitment, staffing, performance and potential appraisal, succession planning, training and education, etc.

In the present study I had taken certain Small Scale Industries at random for analysing the aspects of Human Resource Development and Management Practices. They are:

The industries/units belonging to Rubber, Plastic, Petroleum and Coal products, Metal products, Machinery and Machine tools, Transport Equipment and Parts and other industries. The year for which the analysis is taken for study is 1994-95 (one year), the data collected for the group of industries are secondary data. And regarding the sample used in the present study is inferred from the respondents which are selected at random from each industry. The paper highlights the fact that personnel problems and other management problems can also arise even in SSI (Small Scale Industries), and therefore, importance is given to the need for implementing Human Resource Development and Management Practices in these units.

It is proposed to examine the validity of the following two hypothesis:

(a) The industry/firm is small to have personnel problems. We think that through daily contacts with their employees, we can easily solve personnel problems. We feel their informal, open-door policy will alert them to any serious personnel problems or we think we have the insights needed to hire the kind of people who never create personnel problems; and
(b) in view of the small size, limited scale of operations and paucity of funds, the small scale units, when compared with large scale units, have very limited scope for applying the personnel functions in a scientific manner.

In the present study which consists of 442 small scale units belonging to Rubber, Plastic, Petroleum and Coal products, Metal products, Machinery and Machine tools, Transport Equipment and parts and other industries group located in Coimbatore district (Tamil Nadu State) are taken, during the year 1994-95 registered under *District Industries Centre* in Coimbatore, which is shown in the Table 1, a few industries have been selected for the present study which satisfy the following criteria:

- Employment of 100 and above persons,
- Location of the unit within Coimbatore urban agglomeration limits, and
- Existence of the unit for 10 years above.

TABLE 1

Profile of Sample Units: Location and Employment Size (1994-95)

Industry Groups	*City and Industrial Estate*	
	Units	*Employment*
1. Rubber, Plastic, Petroleum and Coal products	77	354
2. Metal products	56	299
3. Machinery & Machine tools	221	1,003
4. Transport Equipment and parts	16	74
5. Other Industries	72	180
Total	442	1,910

Source: DIC, Coimbatore District.

Care has been taken while selecting the units, to give due importance to the location factor also to find out the difference in HRD and HRM practices among these units. It is believed that most of the units are located in the city premises and industrial estate and started by educated unemployed, assisted by liberal grants from government they would be adopting some of the important HRD practices to improve performance and productivity. Interestingly, the size of employment in both city units and industrial units is satisfactory with 1,910 (persons employed).

It explains the significant differences in skill composition among firms.

The skill of labour force content is highest in machinery and machine tools followed by Metal products, Transport Equipment and parts, other industries and Rubber, Plastic, Petroleum and Coal products, of industry is in the order mentioned. The unskilled workers in the total work force is more in Rubber, Plastic industries moreover followed by other industries. The Transport Equipment and parts, Metal products, machinery and machine tools follow the other way mentioned above.

Employees of an organisation should be able to perform those duties and functions that will increase business and profitability and the entrepreneur should provide a healthy atmosphere encouraging employees to use their capacities fully. Unfortunately, most entrepreneurs in the study do not assign high priority to personnel function, leading to the adoption of defective, and subjective recruitment and selection policies. That is according to the skill, efficiency in the job work, etc.

In the present study I had taken HRM attitudes and practices in various units. The Human Resource Management plays a vital role in the industries.

TABLE 2

HRM Attitudes and Practices in Sample Unit

HRM Attitudes	*No, of Entrepreneurs*	*Function*	*Daily time devoted to various functions*			*Total*
			0 to 1 hrs.	*1 to 3 hrs.*	*3 to 6 hrs.*	
1. HRM Most Important	Nil	a. Production	126	188	128	442
2. HRM Equally Important	178	b. Finance	—	287	155	442
3. HRM Least Important	194	c. Marketing	168	—	274	442
4. No need for HRM	70	d. Personnel	191	251	—	442
		e. Others	169	273	—	442

From the Table 2 we can infer that HRM practices is Nil for certain entrepreneurs, and that 40 per cent of the entrepreneurs inform least importance about HRM practices. 30 per cent take equally important status about HRM practices and 20 per cent suggest that there is no need for HRM practice.

It would be interesting to find that 50 per cent units have accorded high priority to training.

Nearly 60 per cent of the entrepreneurs who have agreed that training is necessary to improve employees performance did not offer any training to improve employee performance and also did not offer any training facilities to employees. Apart from the training for 3 or 6 months (Skilled and Unskilled), acquired

TABLE 3

Training Programme in Small Units

Attitudes	*Yes*	*No*	*Neutral*
1. Training needs of SSI will be less when compared to a large scale organisation	328	66	48
2. Training is needed to improve employee performance and to reach higher positions	378	64	—

Practices	Yes	No
1. Do you train your employee?	326	116
2. Any problem in providing training?	248	194

through government institutes, the entrepreneurs imparted on-the-job training to employees in their respective industry as apprenticeship.

TABLE 4

Training Programmes in Sample Units

Category Nature of Training	*Duration of the Training Programme*			*Training Cost (Rs.)*	*Training Cost borne by*	*Training Problem*
	0 to 2 Months	*2 to 4 Months*	*4 to 6 Months*			
Skilled on the job	14	36	12	400-500	Employer	Financial (17)
Unskilled on the job	11	48	13	300-350	-do-	Absence of Trainer (12) Employee disinterestedness (8) Production dislocation (16)

Note: Apprenticeship Training for 6 months in Textile unit in Coimbatore (Skilled).

Table 6 infers that employers have shown great reluctance to continue that training programme beyond 3 months, because the workers will be gaining extra knowledge in their respective fields, an example is illustrated for reference. It pictures the training cost (salary), training cost borne by and training problem such as financial crisis, absence of trainers, employee disinterestedness and production dislocation. Where training facilities are provided, all the employees have agreed that training has helped in improving performance, and make them more versatile. Training, contrary to expectations, did not bring in monetary benefits. But they can find jobs anywhere, after receiving on-the-job training, in the specified field such as Machinery, Transport Equipment, Metal products, etc.

In the present study where I had included HRD Practices, to find out the effectiveness of the programmes in the sample units, two measures have been adopted.

Table 5 reveals employee response towards HRD practices in the units studied. Despite having a proper Human Resource Management practices and attitudes, 194 units, 67 employees have expressed dissatisfaction over their placement. In respect of training efforts, out of 312 units, 53 employees have expressed dissatisfaction regarding their emolument after receiving training and 108 have remained neutral because their position has improved marginally after training. When confronted with the question: "Given a chance, would you join this concern again?" They have ranked or provided answers in the under laid Table 6, would you join this organisation?

Most employees (203) have agreed that adopting HRD practices would enhance their personnel worth to the concern and over the years they have developed an attachment with the company because of good policies, good pay and good boss. Not surprisingly, most employees have come out with negative answers regarding pay and job security which were not satisfactory even in units where HRD practices have been adopted. And on the other hand, employees have come out with neutral answers regarding job security and good boss which were not satisfactory in certain units where HRD practices are implemented/adopted.

TABLE 5

How Satisfactory are the Employees in Units Adopting HRD Practices? Employee Responses

HRD practices	*Adopted Units*	*Rubber, Plastic Petroleum and Coal products*	*Metal products*	*Machinery and Machine tools*	*Transport Equipment and parts*	*Other Industries*	*Sy.*	*Unsy.*	*Neut.*
1. HRM Attitude and Practices	194	78	32	27	18	37	89	67	38
2. Training Activities	321	128	89	49	22	24	138	53	108

Notes: Sy.—Satisfactory.
Unsy.—Unsatisfactory.
Neut.—Neutral.

TABLE 6

Maximum No. of units wherein HRD practices have found some expression	*Employees who gave*		
	Positive answers	*Negative answers*	*Neutral answers*
1. Personal attachment with the company	203	167	53
2. Job Security	189	126	127
3. Good Pay	278	138	—
4. Good Boss	126	263	72

CONCLUSION

The present study reveals three important things:

1. Personnel problems can also arise in SSI despite employer's closeness to and personal contact with employees and it is a serious problem that must be solved satisfactorily in order to improve performance of employees.
2. HRD and HRM can be adopted in small scale organisation, and that too, quite successfully. In the units where HRD practices found meaningful expression, the organisational health of the units is far better than those where HRD has not been implemented.
3. Human Resource Development is not a mere theoretical concept. It is a professional innovation necessitated by the exigencies of the situation, fuelled by human idealism, supported by a growing knowledge about human systems, and chiselled by pioneering practitioners.

REFERENCES

Pareek, U. (1981), *Beyond Management*, Oxford and IBH Publishing Co. Pvt. Ltd., New Delhi.

Gupta, R.K. and Pareek, U. (1982), Training of OD Facilitators, In:

Chattopadhyay, S. and Pareek, U. (eds.), *Managing Organisational Change*, Oxford and IBH Publishing Co. Pvt. Ltd., pp. 183-96, New Delhi.

Nadler, L. (1979), *Developing Human Resources*, 2nd Education, Austin: Learning Concepts.

Rao, M.G. (1993), *Management of Human Assets*, Discovery Publishing House, New Delhi.

Rao, U.S.P. (1991), *Human Resource Management in Small Industry*, Discovery Publishing House, New Delhi.

Anil K. Khandelwal (1988), *Human Resource Development in Banks*, Oxford and IBH Publishing Co. Pvt. Ltd., New Delhi.

John Bratton and Jeffrey Gold (1994), *Human Resource Management (Theory and Practice)*, Macmillan Press Ltd., London.

Index

A

Achievement Indices and Improvement Indices, 261
Construction, 261
Agricultural Sector, 342
Slow Progress, 342
Ahmad, S.M. Humair, 289
A.K. Sen's Contribution to Human Development, 89
Ali, S. Maqsood, 384
Alternative Measures of Well-being, 149
Birth, 149
Annapoorani, R., 159
Areas of High Backwardness, 433

B

Bagehot, Walter, 102
Banerji, Pritosh, 232
Baptiste, Jean, 102
Baster, Nancy, 170
Basu, Asok, 347
Bhattacharya, Basabi, 410
Bhattacharya, N., 330
Bhatt, K.N., 359
Bhowmick, Swagata Das, 148
Brahmananda, P.R., 401

C

Caste and Tribal GAP, 353
Challenges in the 21st Century, 69
Changing Needs of People, 440
Psychology, 440
Sociology, 440
Socio-Psychology, 441
Anthropology, 441
Political Science, 441
Economics, 441
Organisational Behaviour, 441
Choice of Indicators, 255
Clark, C., 230
Concept and Measurement of Human Development, 324
Concept of Human Capital in the History of Economic Thought, 102
Concept of Human Development, 71
Concept of Human Development and its Implications, 410
Constraints in Investment on Education within a Backward Community, 136

D

Das, Hem Chandra Lal, 321
Deprivation in Health, 117
Desai, Megnad, 384
Developing Countries, 59
Issues, 59
Development of Developing Countries, 3
Human Capabilities Approach, 3
Dev, Mahenda, 331

Dhanasekaran, Kasturi Bai, 123
Dhillon, S.S., 241
Distinction between Human Resource Development and Human Development, 171
Drewnowski, Jan, 170
Duraisamy, P., 101

E

Economic Development and HRD, 34
Economic Development and Human Development, 91
Economic Growth and Human Development, 172, 325
Relationship, 172
Economic Growth and its Impact on Human Development, 167
Economic Value of Education, 37
Simple Correlation Approach, 37
Residual Approach, 38
Rate of Return Approach, 38
Forecasting Manpower Needs Approach, 38
Educational Attainment Index, 306
Education and Economic Growth, 39
Employment Assurance Schemes, 131
Employment Opportunities, 342
Slow Growth, 342
Engel, Ernst, 102
Environmental Deterioration, 118
Essential Qualitative Components, 32
Evaluating Poverty Alleviation Programmes, 129
Evidence from West Bengal Economy, 418
Expenditure on HRD, 126
Experience of Field Research Operation Network, 144
Extent of Absolute Poverty, 339

F

Fidzani, N.H., 3
Fifth Five Year Plan, 338
Financing of Human Development, 324
Fisher, Irving, 102
From Growth to Human Development, 15
Equity, 15
Priority Social Spending, 16
Increasing Opportunities, 16
From Human Development to Growth, 16

G

Gandhi, M.K., 39
Gandhi, P. Jegadish, 57
Gender and Human Development, 325
Gender Empowerment Measures, 51
Gender Gap, 353
Gender-Related Development Index, 50, 114
Gender-Related Health Index, 33
Ghosh, Arabinda, 95
Global Dimension of Human Development, 324
Gounden, Nalla, 38
Guha, Biswajit, 211
Gupta, S.P., 340, 396

H

Haq, Mahbub-ul, 211
Harbison, F.H., 4
HDI, 31, 44, 401
Computation, 31
Cross Countries Comparison, 46
1993 UNDP Definition, 401
Computation, 44
Heller, W., 230
High HDI Countries, 83
Housing Deprivation, 117

HRD, 27, 61
  Agenda, 61
  Indicators, 61
  Environment, 27
  Current Status, 27
  Programmes and Processes, 28
HRD in India, 62
HRD in India and Developing Countries, 125
Human Capabilities Development Programmes, 8
Human Capital Approach, 6, 398
  Limitations, 398
Human Capital, 37, 58
  Importance, 58
  and Economic Growth, 103
  Development, 134
Human Capital on Human Development, 186
  Role of Investment, 186
Human Development Approach, 399
  Emergence, 399
Human Development Expenditure, 119
  Generation of Resources, 119
Human Development Index, 159
  Concept and Estimation, 159
Human Development, 1, 53-54, 73, 82, 168, 230, 322, 412
  Profile, 53, 359
  Trends, 54
  Components, 73
  and Human Resource Development, 75
  and Poverty Eradication, 72
  Level, 17
  Change, 17
  and Economic Growth, 12
  Paradigm, 151
  Need for the Study, 168
  in India, 78, 211
  A Modified Measure, 230
  India and Abroad, 291
  Direction of Research, 412
  Concepts and International Standards, 42
  Approach, 74
  and Human Security, 59
  Determinants, 82
  Index, 113, 303, 313
  Achievements in the Indian Economy, 289
  Conceptual Issues and Realities, 57
  and Poverty, 112, 321
  through Poverty Alleviation, 123
  Reports, 323
  Economic Growth Nexus, 13
Human Development Studies, 415
  Relevance of the System Approach, 415
Human Development undertaken by International Organisations, 169
  Studies, 169
Human Poverty Index, 33, 115
Human Poverty, 74, 117
  Indicators, 117
  Profile, 390
Human Resource Characteristics, 430
Human Resource Development, 60
  and Management in Small Scale Industry, 439
  in the Global Context, 124
  vis-a-vis Human Development, 290
Human Resources and Economic Development, 26
Hussain, Ishrat Z., 38

I

Incidence of Poverty in India, 126
Indexes of Welfare and Poverty, 90
India, 19, 20, 78, 95, 164, 173, 197, 292, 296, 297, 301, 326, 340
  Human Development and Government Policies, 173
  Human Development, 79
  Indices of Gender Inequalities, 78

HDI and GDI for Major States, 164
Interstate Comparison and Human Development, 197
Links for Human Development to Economic Growth, 20
Links from Economic Growth to Human Development, 19
Development Planning and Grassroot Level Democracy, 95
Human Development Profile, 292
Human Development, 326
Poverty Estimates, 340
Literacy Rate, 297
Poverty Alleviation Programme, 338
Human Development, 301
Five Year Plans and Human Development, 296·
Investment in Human Beings, 37
Economic Analysis, 37
Iyengar, N.S., 330

J

Jawahar Rojgar Yojana, 131
Jhargram, 142
Experience of Psychological Research Centre, 142

K

Kaur, Jasmeet, 241
Khan, Nisar Ahmad, 301
Kohli, Anju, 429
Kothari, Sadhna, 429
Kothari, V.N., 38-39
Kuzners, Simon, 5
Kuznets, S., 230

L

Lack of Personal Security, 118
Lakdawala Committee, 341
Learning Achievements, 362
Life Expectancy Index, 306
Low HDI Countries, 85
Low Social Expenditure Ratio, 343

M

Mahbub-ul-Haq, 62, 384
Mahore, R.Y., 26
Majumdar, Tapas, 399
Mandal, Debabrata, 197
Manna, Mausumi, 134
Marshal, Alfred, 9, 89
Mathur, Kuldeep, 344
Mazumdar, Krishna, 254
McCulloch, 102
Measures of Human Development Related Concepts, 398
Measuring Human Resource Development, 241
Measuring Human Well-being of the Countries, 254
Medium HDI Countries, 84
Mehta, Ashir, 12
Mid-day Meal Programme, 174
Minimum and Maximum Values of Indicators, 31
Mishra, R.S., 71
Morris, Morris D., 150

N

Nagarajan, Kanakasabai, 398
Nair, N.K, 232
Nair, P.R. Gopinathan, 36
Nanjundappa, D.M., 68
Nettimi, N., 3
New Dimensions of Human Development, 325
Non-Market Benefits of Human Capital, 109
Nurkse, R., 230

O

Obstacles in Poverty Alleviation, 342

P

Padmanabhan, C.B., 398

Pandit, H.N., 38
Parnes, Bos, 38
Petty, William, 102
Pillai, G. Karunakaran, 112
Post-Reform Trends, 66
Poverty, 328
Poverty Alleviation and Human Development, 326
Poverty Alleviation, 345
  Suggestions, 345
Poverty Gap, 350
Poverty in India, 330
Poverty Measurement, 339
Prakash, M.K., 232
Pressures for Growth, 440
Primary Education and Human Development, 347
Primary Education and India's Disadvantaged Groups, 349
Primary Education, Human Development and India's Disadvantaged Groups, 347
Primary Health Service Facilities, 174
Provision of Housing Facilities, 174
Public Distribution System, 129
Pushpavathi, R., 383

R

Rajasekhar, A., 89
Rao, A. Suba, 233
Rao, H. Venkateswara, 38
Rationale Behind Choice of Each Indicator, 256
  LIFE, 256
  INFS, 257
  ADLI, 257
  CALO, 258
  UPOP, 258
  PHYS, 258
  TPRP, 259
  PCAR, 259
  PCRGDP, 259
Razzaque, M.A., 377
Reddy, P. Kodandarami, 89
Reddy, S. Narapa, 89
Returns to Education and Health, 103
  Methodology, 103
Return to:
  Education: Global Estimates, 104
  Gender Differences, 106
  Indian Estimates, 105
  in Farm Production, 108
  Health, 107
  Investment in Human Capital, 101
Roscher, William, 102
Rural Works Programmes, 131

S

Safe Drinking Water, 173
SAARC Countries, 383, 385
  Human Development, 383, 385
School Desertion by Dropouts, 364
  Reasons, 364
Schultz, Theodore W., 39, 58, 102
Sen, A.K., 89, 91
Sen, Amartya, 151, 384
Sen, Arindam K., 134
Sengupta, Keya, 167
Shah, K.R., 233
Shiva Kumar, A.K., 232
Sidywick, Henry, 102
Significance of Human Resources, 4
Simon, Herbert, 36
Singh, H., 190
Singh, Inderjeet, 230
Singh, R.D., 189
Singh, Reena, 230
Sirivandana, Sushil, 384
Sivakumar, A.K., 403
Sivaprakash, K.S., 439
Six-Point Action Plan, 118
Smith, Adam, 102
Social Choice and Individual Values, 90
South Asia, 377
  Human Development and Deprivation, 377
Srivastava, Kaushal, 186
Srivastava, Tanuja, 186
Streeten, Paul, 5
Students, 365
  Personal, Family and Learning Background, 365

Subramanian, M.S., 82

T

Tamil Nadu, 406
  HDI by Dsitricts, 406
Thunen, Johann H. Von, 102
Tilak, B.G., 38

U

United Nations Development Programme, 242
Universalisation of Primary Education, 174
U.P., 360
  Primary Education Scenario, 360
Urbanization Index, 311

V

Verma, N.M.P., 42
Vivekanand, Swami, 36

W

Walras, Leon,102
Waqif, A.A., 384
Western India, 429
  Human Resource Development and Human Development Index, 429
Wignaraja, Ponna, 384

Z

Zaidi, Naseem A., 338